NIGHT'S DomiNioN

VOLUME 1

AN ONI PRESS PUBLICATION

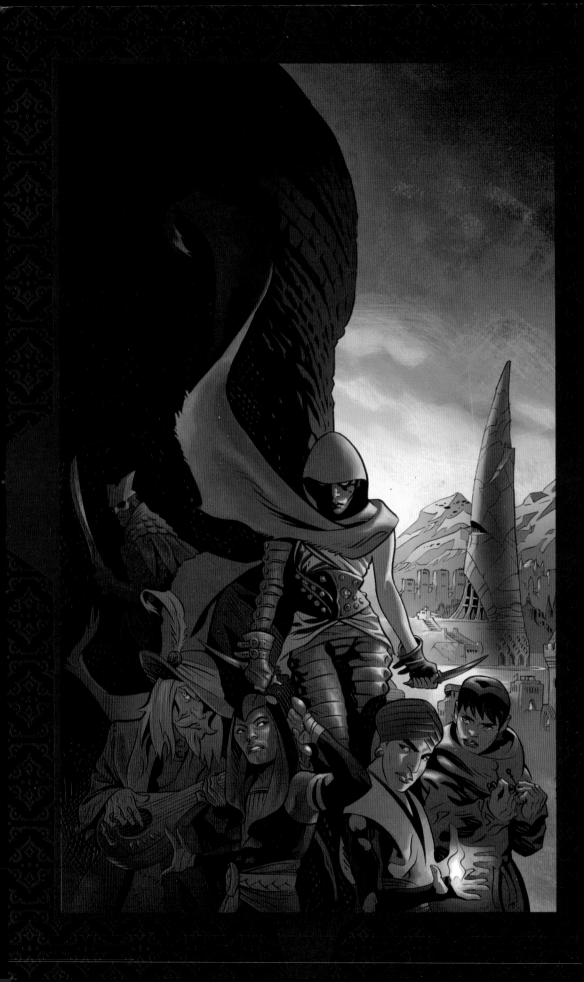

NIGHT'S DOMINION

VOLUME 1

WRITTEN & ILLUSTRATED BY
TED NAIFEH

LETTERED BY
ADITYA BIDIKAR

EDITED BY
ROBIN HERRERA

DESIGNED BY
KEITH WOOD

PUBLISHED BY ONI PRESS, INC.

JOE NOZEMACK publisher

JAMES LUCAS JONES editor in chief

ANDREW MCINTIRE v.p. of marketing & sales

DAVID DISSANAYAKE sales manager

RACHEL REED publicity coordinator

TROY LOOK director of design & production

HILARY THOMPSON graphic designer

ANGIE DOBSON digital prepress technician

ARI YARWOOD managing editor

CHARLIE CHU senior editor

ROBIN HERRERA editor

ALISSA SALLAH administrative assistant

BRAD ROOKS director of logistics

JUNG LEE logistics associate

Oni Press, Inc.
1305 SE Martin Luther King Jr. Blvd.
Suite A
Portland, OR 97214
USA

First edition: June 2017

onipress.com
facebook.com/onipress • twitter.com/onipress
onipress.tumblr.com • instagram.com/onipress

@tednaifeh • tednaifeh.com

Originally published as issues 1-6 of the Oni Press comic
series *Night's Dominion.*

ISBN 978-1-62010-410-1 • eISBN 978-1-62010-411-8

Library of Congress Control Number: 2016960957

10 9 8 7 6 5 4 3 2 1

PRINTED IN SINGAPORE.

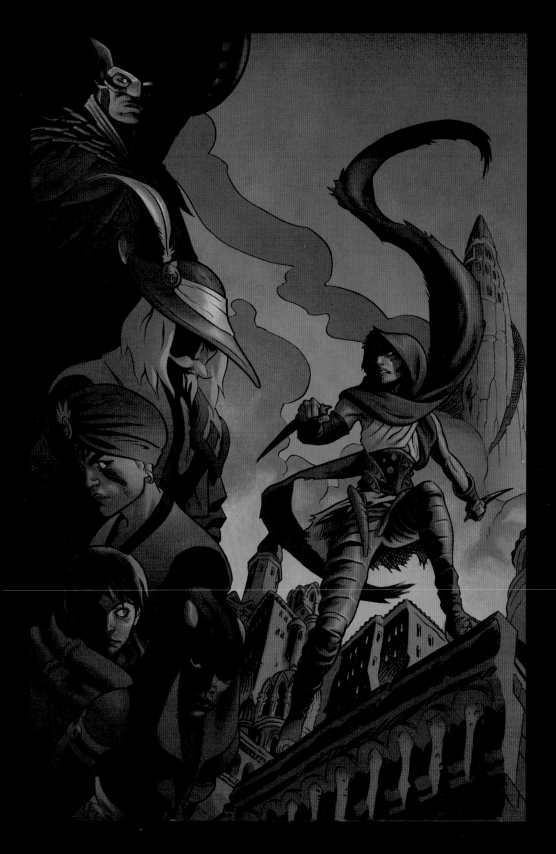

CHAPTER 1

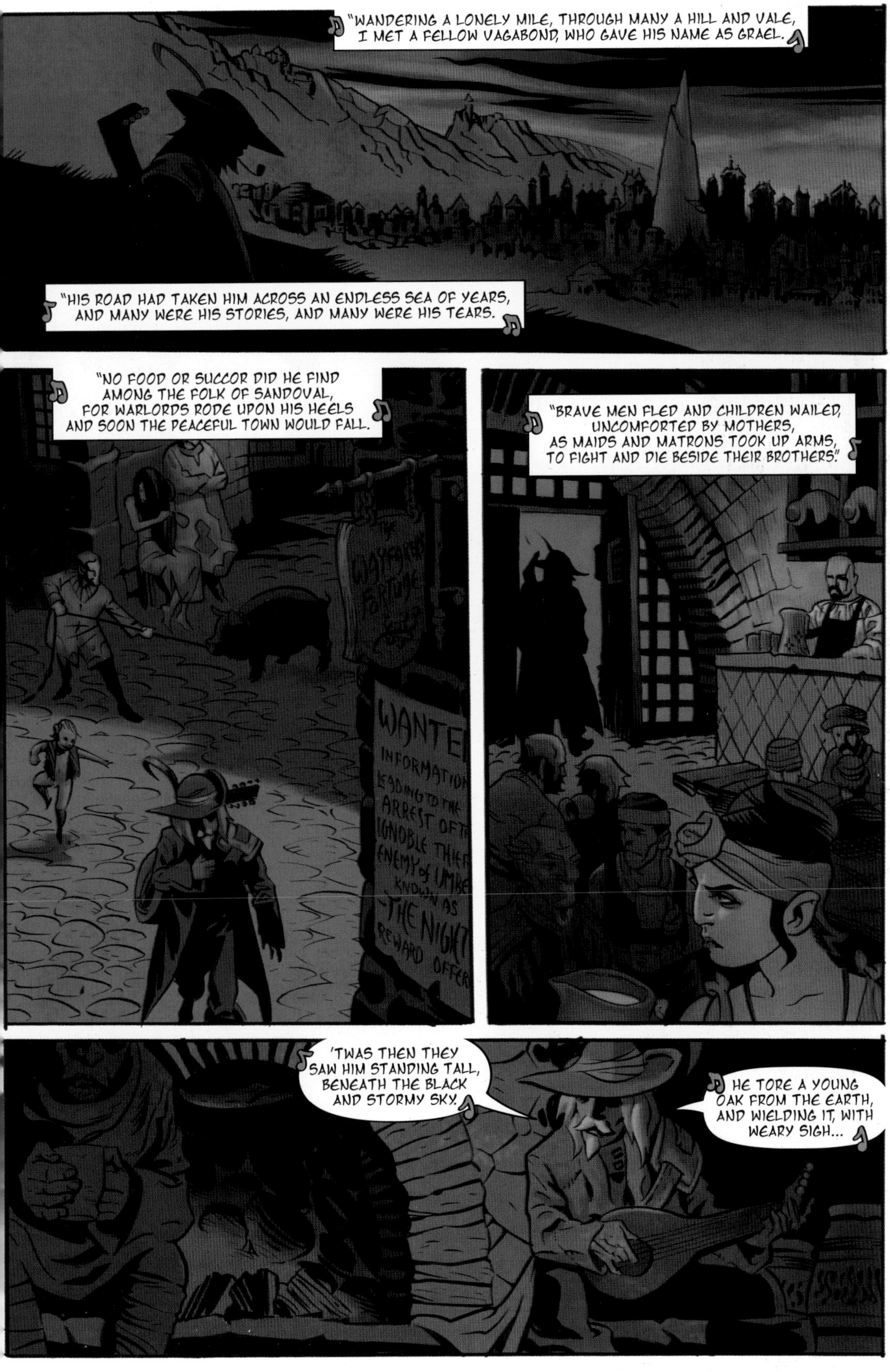
"WANDERING A LONELY MILE, THROUGH MANY A HILL AND VALE, I MET A FELLOW VAGABOND, WHO GAVE HIS NAME AS GRAEL.
"HIS ROAD HAD TAKEN HIM ACROSS AN ENDLESS SEA OF YEARS, AND MANY WERE HIS STORIES, AND MANY WERE HIS TEARS.
"NO FOOD OR SUCCOR DID HE FIND AMONG THE FOLK OF SANDOVAL, FOR WARLORDS RODE UPON HIS HEELS AND SOON THE PEACEFUL TOWN WOULD FALL.
"BRAVE MEN FLED AND CHILDREN WAILED, UNCOMFORTED BY MOTHERS, AS MAIDS AND MATRONS TOOK UP ARMS, TO FIGHT AND DIE BESIDE THEIR BROTHERS."
'TWAS THEN THEY SAW HIM STANDING TALL, BENEATH THE BLACK AND STORMY SKY.
HE TORE A YOUNG OAK FROM THE EARTH, AND WIELDING IT, WITH WEARY SIGH...

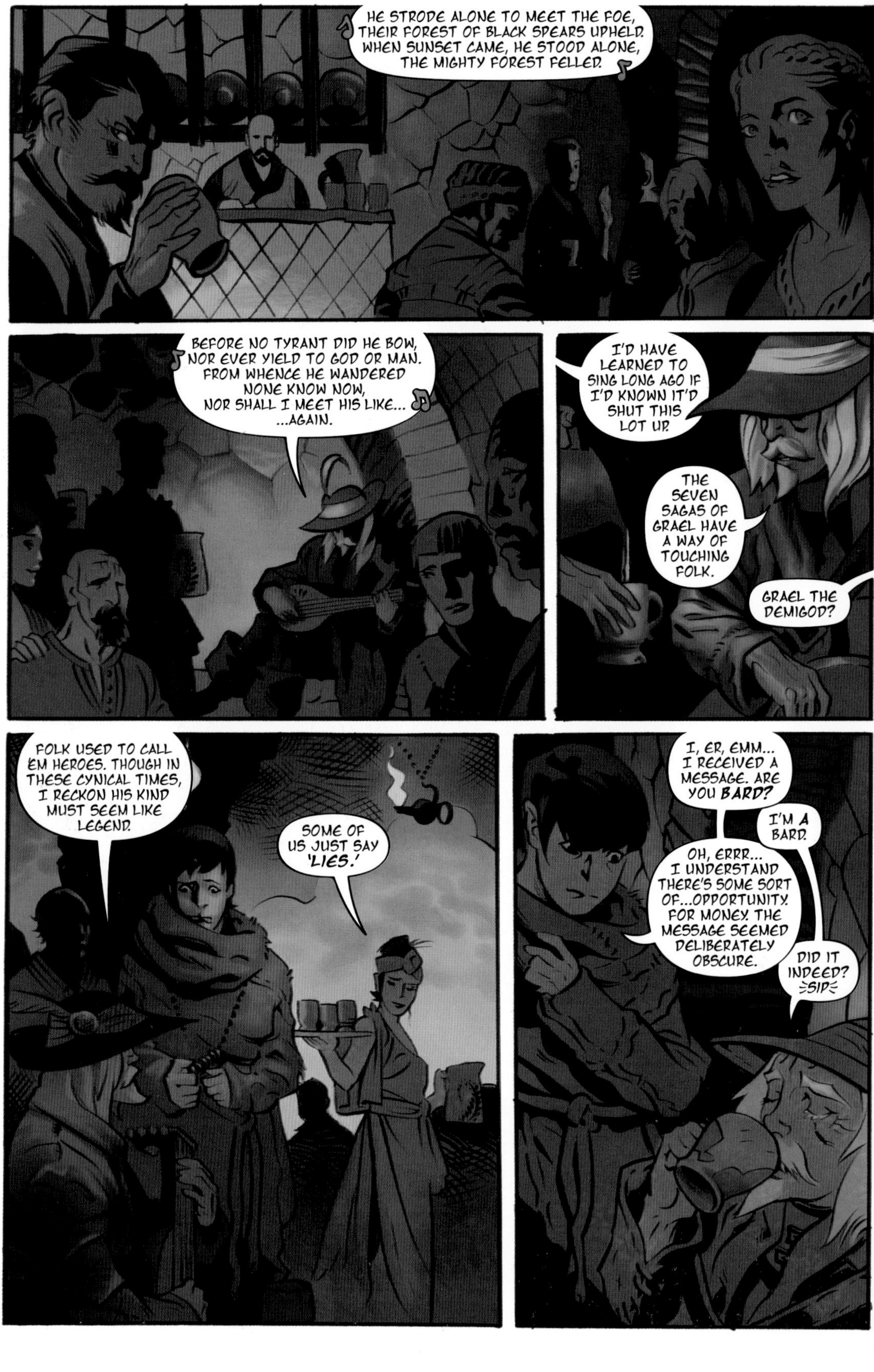
HE STRODE ALONE TO MEET THE FOE, THEIR FOREST OF BLACK SPEARS UPHELD. WHEN SUNSET CAME, HE STOOD ALONE, THE MIGHTY FOREST FELLED.
BEFORE NO TYRANT DID HE BOW, NOR EVER YIELD TO GOD OR MAN. FROM WHENCE HE WANDERED NONE KNOW NOW, NOR SHALL I MEET HIS LIKE... ...AGAIN.
I'D HAVE LEARNED TO SING LONG AGO IF I'D KNOWN IT'D SHUT THIS LOT UP.
THE SEVEN SAGAS OF GRAEL HAVE A WAY OF TOUCHING FOLK.
GRAEL THE DEMIGOD?
FOLK USED TO CALL 'EM HEROES. THOUGH IN THESE CYNICAL TIMES, I RECKON HIS KIND MUST SEEM LIKE LEGEND.
SOME OF US JUST SAY *'LIES.'*
I, ER, EMM... I RECEIVED A MESSAGE. ARE YOU ***BARD?***
I'M A BARD.
OH, ERRR... I UNDERSTAND THERE'S SOME SORT OF...OPPORTUNITY. FOR MONEY. THE MESSAGE SEEMED DELIBERATELY OBSCURE.
DID IT INDEED? SIP

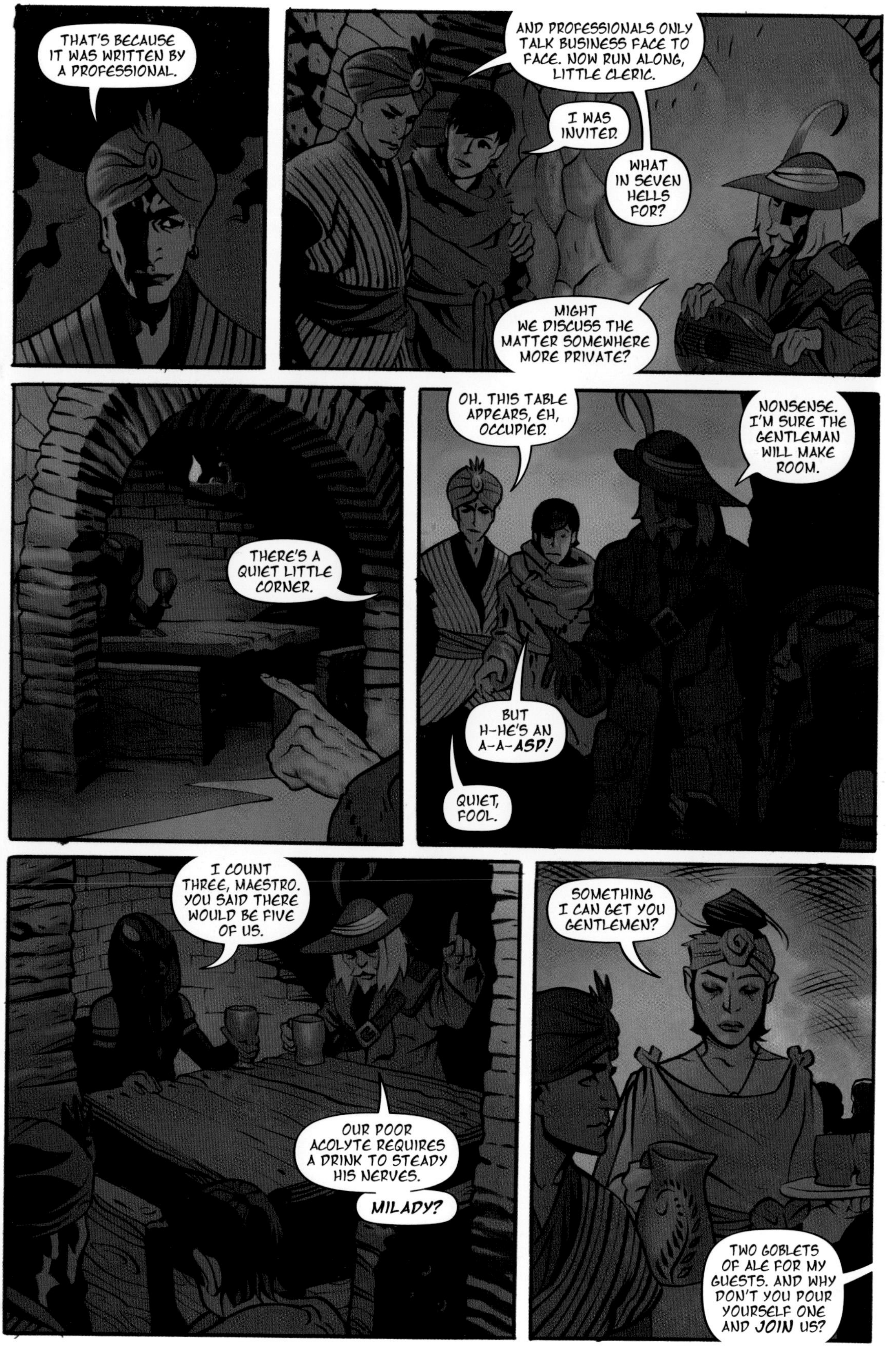

THAT'S BECAUSE IT WAS WRITTEN BY A PROFESSIONAL.
AND PROFESSIONALS ONLY TALK BUSINESS FACE TO FACE. NOW RUN ALONG, LITTLE CLERIC.
I WAS INVITED.
WHAT IN SEVEN HELLS FOR?
MIGHT WE DISCUSS THE MATTER SOMEWHERE MORE PRIVATE?
THERE'S A QUIET LITTLE CORNER.
OH. THIS TABLE APPEARS, EH, OCCUPIED.
NONSENSE. I'M SURE THE GENTLEMAN WILL MAKE ROOM.
BUT H-HE'S AN A-A-ASP!
QUIET, FOOL.
I COUNT THREE, MAESTRO. YOU SAID THERE WOULD BE FIVE OF US.
OUR POOR ACOLYTE REQUIRES A DRINK TO STEADY HIS NERVES.
MILADY?
SOMETHING I CAN GET YOU GENTLEMEN?
TWO GOBLETS OF ALE FOR MY GUESTS. AND WHY DON'T YOU POUR YOURSELF ONE AND JOIN US?

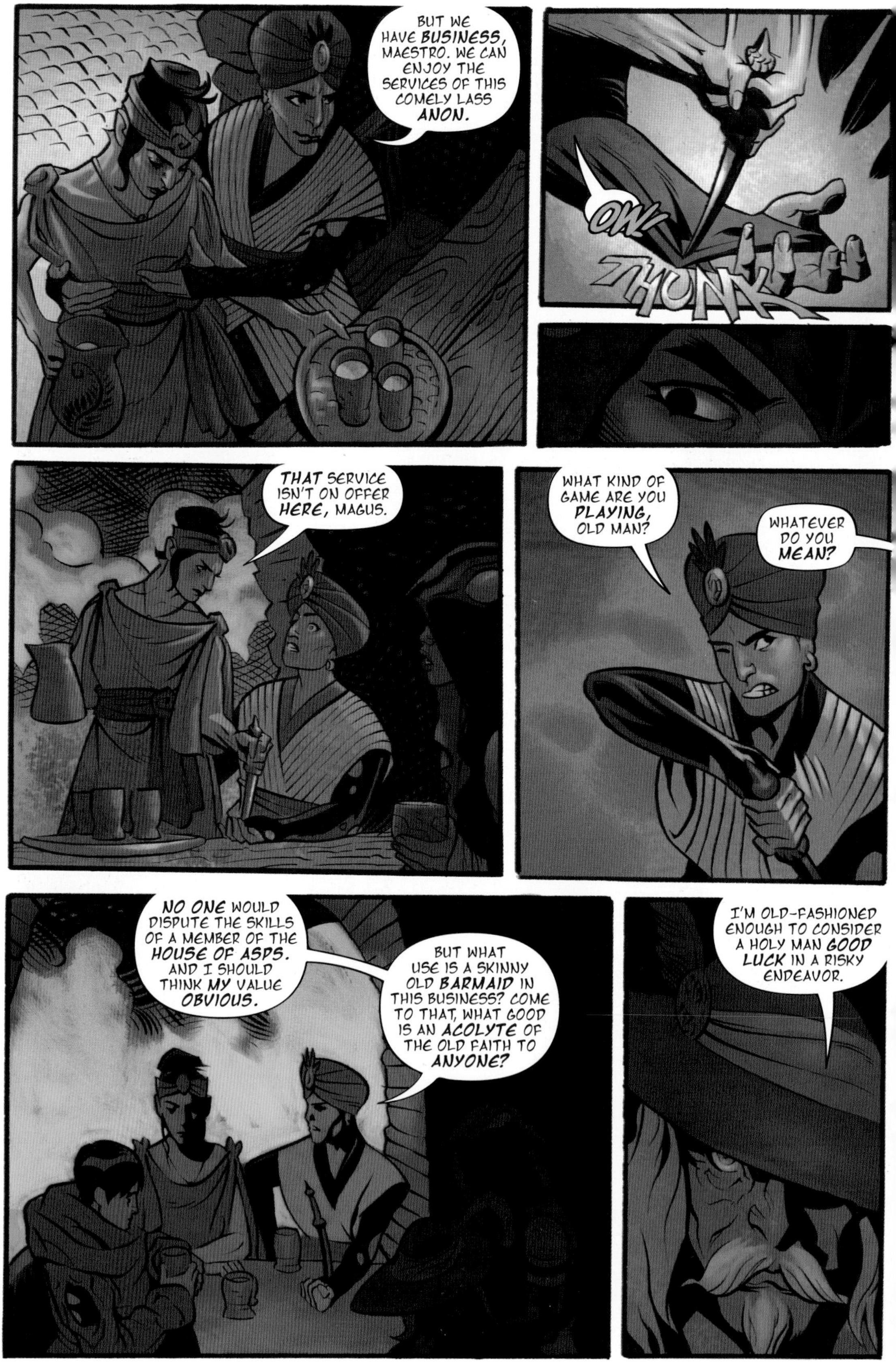

BUT WE HAVE BUSINESS, MAESTRO. WE CAN ENJOY THE SERVICES OF THIS COMELY LASS ANON.
OW!
THUNK
THAT SERVICE ISN'T ON OFFER HERE, MAGUS.
WHAT KIND OF GAME ARE YOU PLAYING, OLD MAN?
WHATEVER DO YOU MEAN?
NO ONE WOULD DISPUTE THE SKILLS OF A MEMBER OF THE HOUSE OF ASPS. AND I SHOULD THINK MY VALUE OBVIOUS.
BUT WHAT USE IS A SKINNY OLD BARMAID IN THIS BUSINESS? COME TO THAT, WHAT GOOD IS AN ACOLYTE OF THE OLD FAITH TO ANYONE?
I'M OLD-FASHIONED ENOUGH TO CONSIDER A HOLY MAN GOOD LUCK IN A RISKY ENDEAVOR.

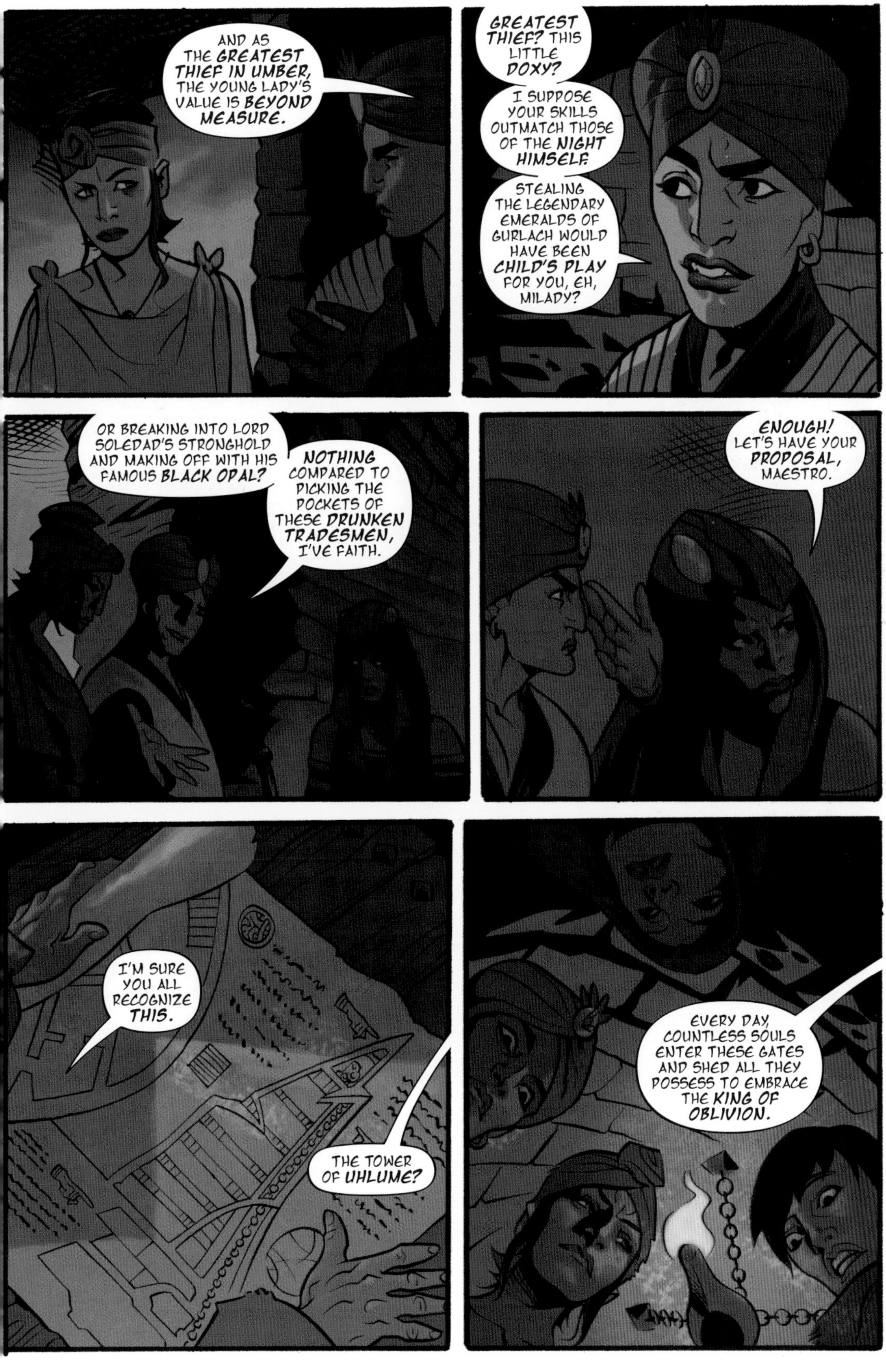
AND AS THE GREATEST THIEF IN UMBER, THE YOUNG LADY'S VALUE IS BEYOND MEASURE.
GREATEST THIEF? THIS LITTLE DOXY?
I SUPPOSE YOUR SKILLS OUTMATCH THOSE OF THE NIGHT HIMSELF.
STEALING THE LEGENDARY EMERALDS OF GURLACH WOULD HAVE BEEN CHILD'S PLAY FOR YOU, EH, MILADY?
OR BREAKING INTO LORD SOLEDAD'S STRONGHOLD AND MAKING OFF WITH HIS FAMOUS BLACK OPAL?
NOTHING COMPARED TO PICKING THE POCKETS OF THESE DRUNKEN TRADESMEN, I'VE FAITH.
ENOUGH! LET'S HAVE YOUR PROPOSAL, MAESTRO.
I'M SURE YOU ALL RECOGNIZE THIS.
THE TOWER OF UHLUME?
EVERY DAY, COUNTLESS SOULS ENTER THESE GATES AND SHED ALL THEY POSSESS TO EMBRACE THE KING OF OBLIVION.

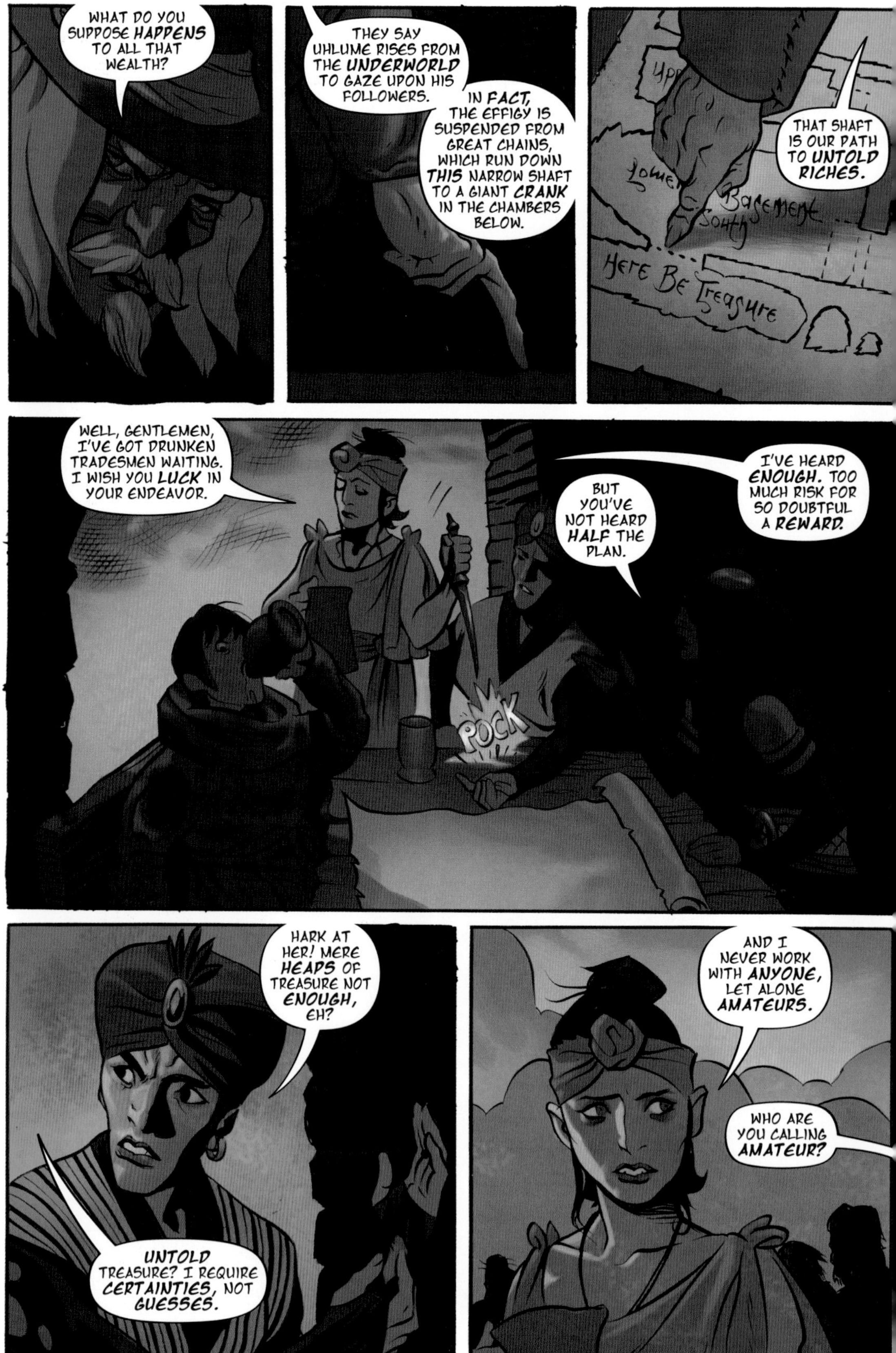
WHAT DO YOU SUPPOSE HAPPENS TO ALL THAT WEALTH?
THEY SAY UHLUME RISES FROM THE UNDERWORLD TO GAZE UPON HIS FOLLOWERS.
IN FACT, THE EFFIGY IS SUSPENDED FROM GREAT CHAINS, WHICH RUN DOWN THIS NARROW SHAFT TO A GIANT CRANK IN THE CHAMBERS BELOW.
Lower
Basement
South
Here Be Treasure
THAT SHAFT IS OUR PATH TO UNTOLD RICHES.
WELL, GENTLEMEN, I'VE GOT DRUNKEN TRADESMEN WAITING. I WISH YOU LUCK IN YOUR ENDEAVOR.
I'VE HEARD ENOUGH. TOO MUCH RISK FOR SO DOUBTFUL A REWARD.
BUT YOU'VE NOT HEARD HALF THE PLAN.
POCK
HARK AT HER! MERE HEAPS OF TREASURE NOT ENOUGH, EH?
UNTOLD TREASURE? I REQUIRE CERTAINTIES, NOT GUESSES.
AND I NEVER WORK WITH ANYONE, LET ALONE AMATEURS.
WHO ARE YOU CALLING AMATEUR?

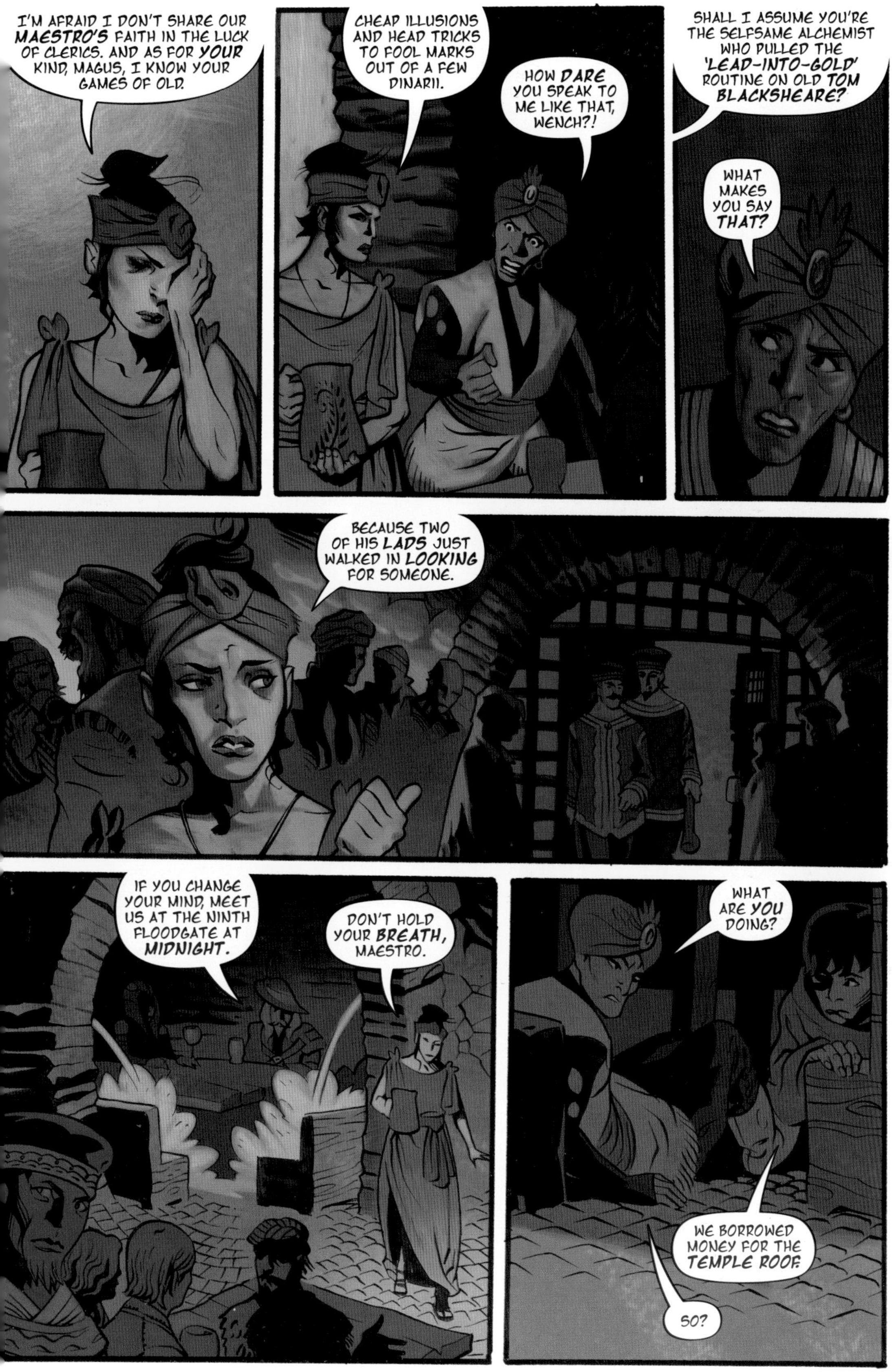
I'M AFRAID I DON'T SHARE OUR MAESTRO'S FAITH IN THE LUCK OF CLERICS. AND AS FOR YOUR KIND, MAGUS, I KNOW YOUR GAMES OF OLD.
CHEAP ILLUSIONS AND HEAD TRICKS TO FOOL MARKS OUT OF A FEW DINARII.
HOW DARE YOU SPEAK TO ME LIKE THAT, WENCH?!
SHALL I ASSUME YOU'RE THE SELFSAME ALCHEMIST WHO PULLED THE 'LEAD-INTO-GOLD' ROUTINE ON OLD TOM BLACKSHEARE?
WHAT MAKES YOU SAY THAT?
BECAUSE TWO OF HIS LADS JUST WALKED IN LOOKING FOR SOMEONE.
IF YOU CHANGE YOUR MIND, MEET US AT THE NINTH FLOODGATE AT MIDNIGHT.
DON'T HOLD YOUR BREATH, MAESTRO.
WHAT ARE YOU DOING?
WE BORROWED MONEY FOR THE TEMPLE ROOF.
SO?

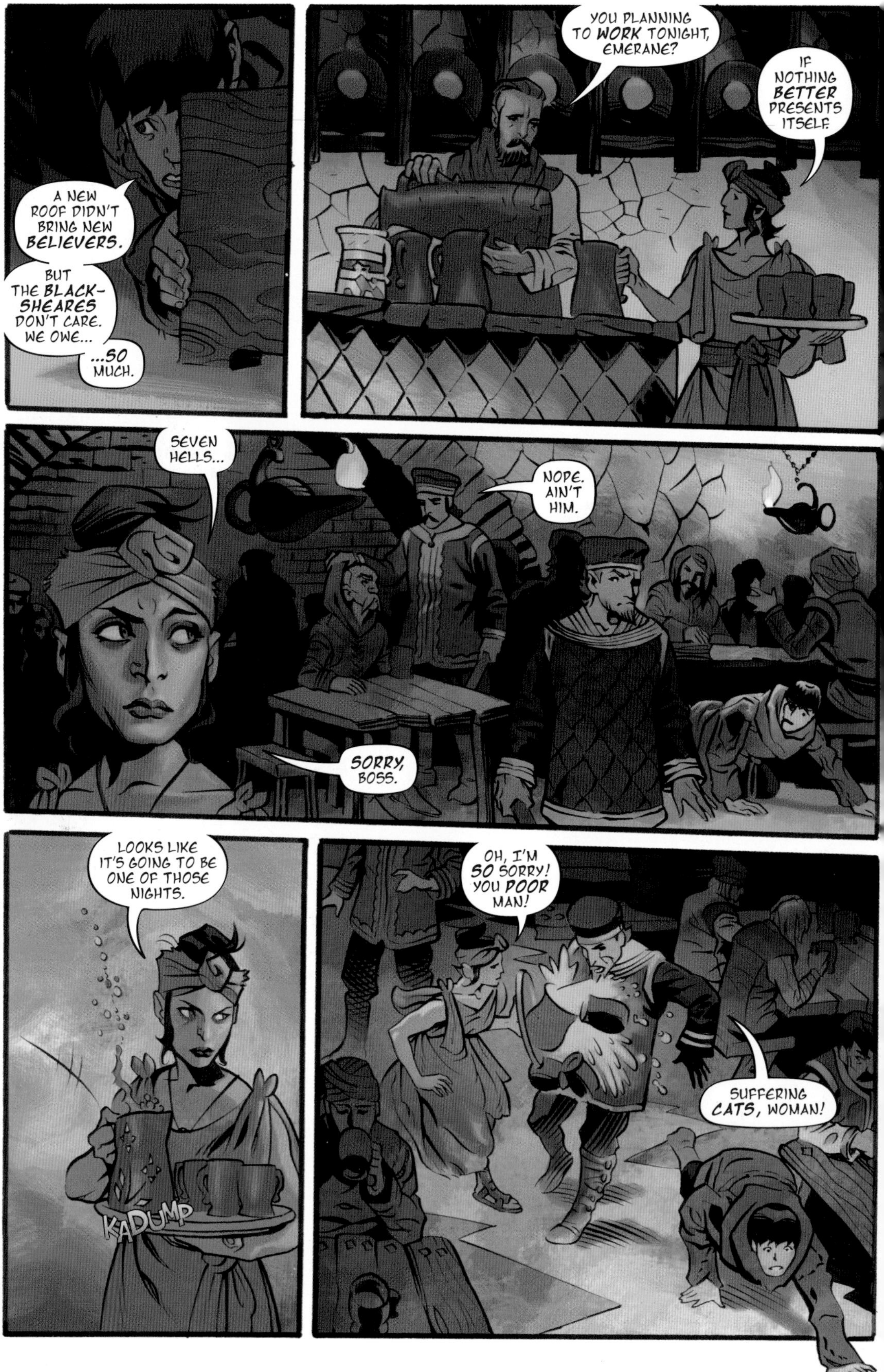
A NEW ROOF DIDN'T BRING NEW BELIEVERS.
BUT THE BLACK-SHEARES DON'T CARE. WE OWE...
...SO MUCH.
YOU PLANNING TO WORK TONIGHT, EMERANE?
IF NOTHING BETTER PRESENTS ITSELF.
SEVEN HELLS...
NOPE. AIN'T HIM.
SORRY, BOSS.
LOOKS LIKE IT'S GOING TO BE ONE OF THOSE NIGHTS.
KADUMP
OH, I'M SO SORRY! YOU POOR MAN!
SUFFERING CATS, WOMAN!

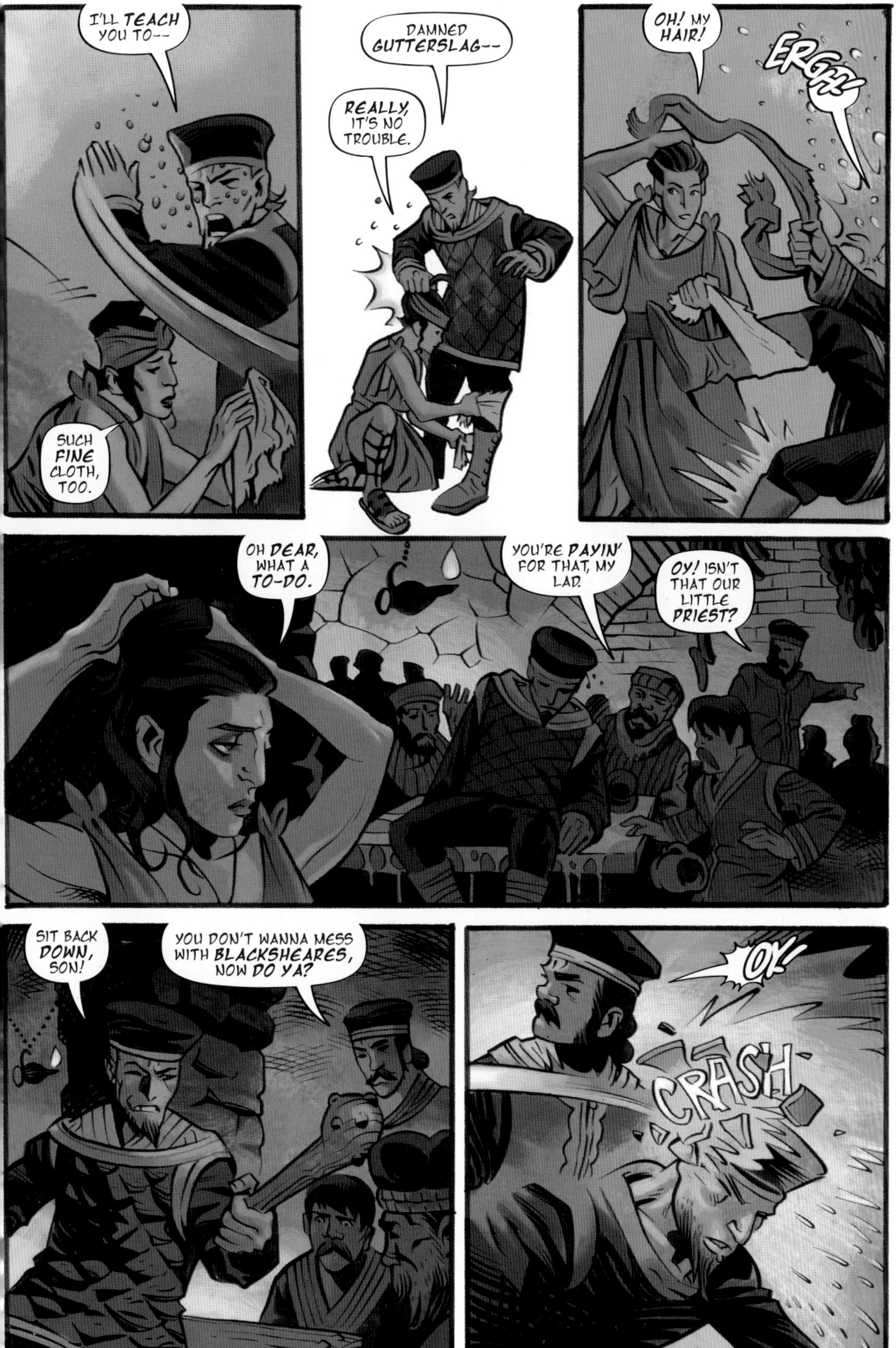
I'LL TEACH YOU TO--
SUCH FINE CLOTH, TOO.
DAMNED GUTTERSLAG--
REALLY, IT'S NO TROUBLE.
OH! MY HAIR!
ERGH!
OH DEAR, WHAT A TO-DO.
YOU'RE PAYIN' FOR THAT, MY LAD.
OY! ISN'T THAT OUR LITTLE PRIEST?
SIT BACK DOWN, SON!
YOU DON'T WANNA MESS WITH BLACKSHEARES, NOW DO YA?
OK!
CRASH

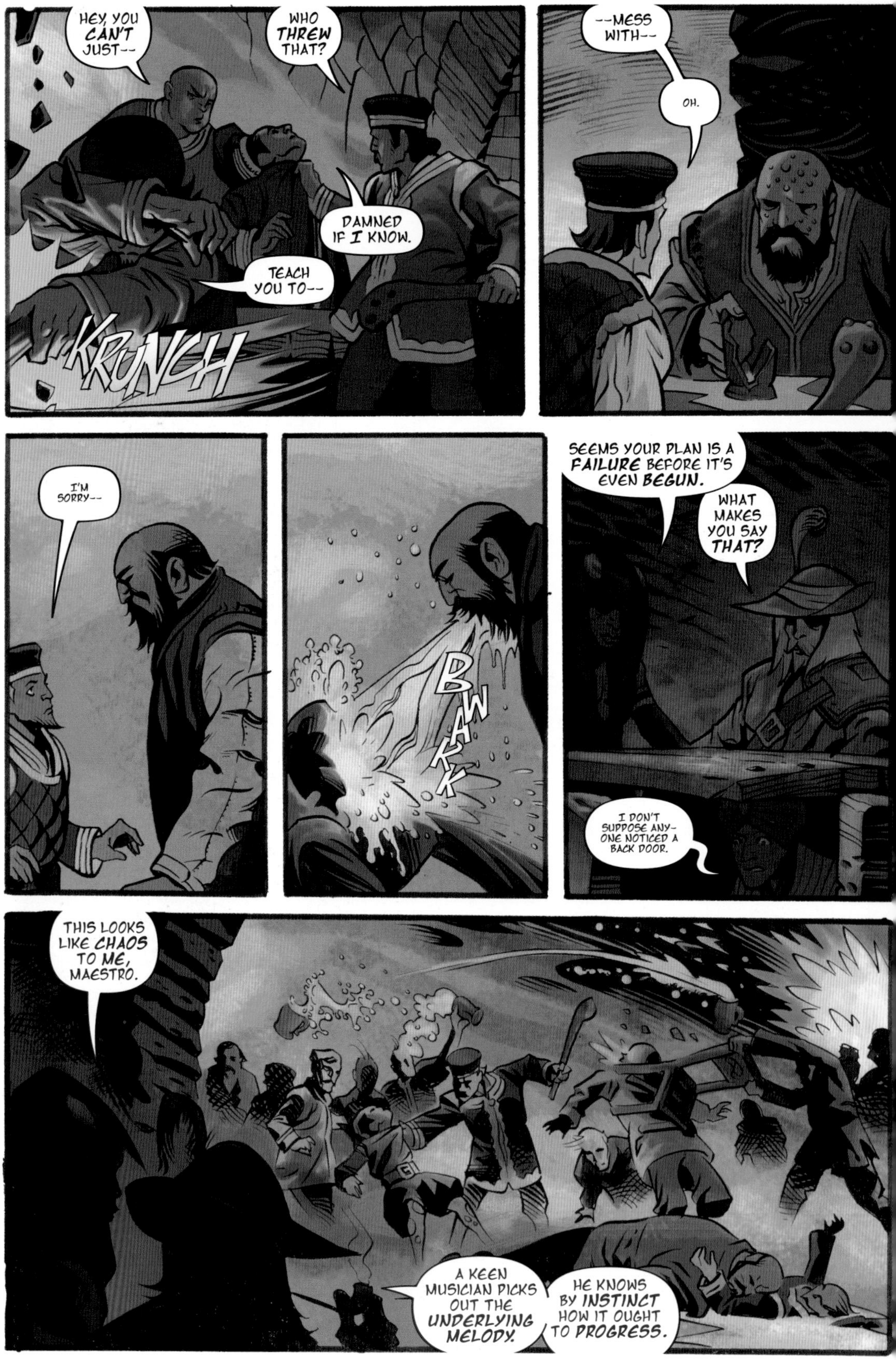
HEY, YOU CAN'T JUST--
WHO THREW THAT?
DAMNED IF I KNOW.
TEACH YOU TO--
KRUNCH
--MESS WITH--
OH.
I'M SORRY--
BWAKK
SEEMS YOUR PLAN IS A FAILURE BEFORE IT'S EVEN BEGUN.
WHAT MAKES YOU SAY THAT?
I DON'T SUPPOSE ANY-ONE NOTICED A BACK DOOR.
THIS LOOKS LIKE CHAOS TO ME, MAESTRO.
A KEEN MUSICIAN PICKS OUT THE UNDERLYING MELODY.
HE KNOWS BY INSTINCT HOW IT OUGHT TO PROGRESS.

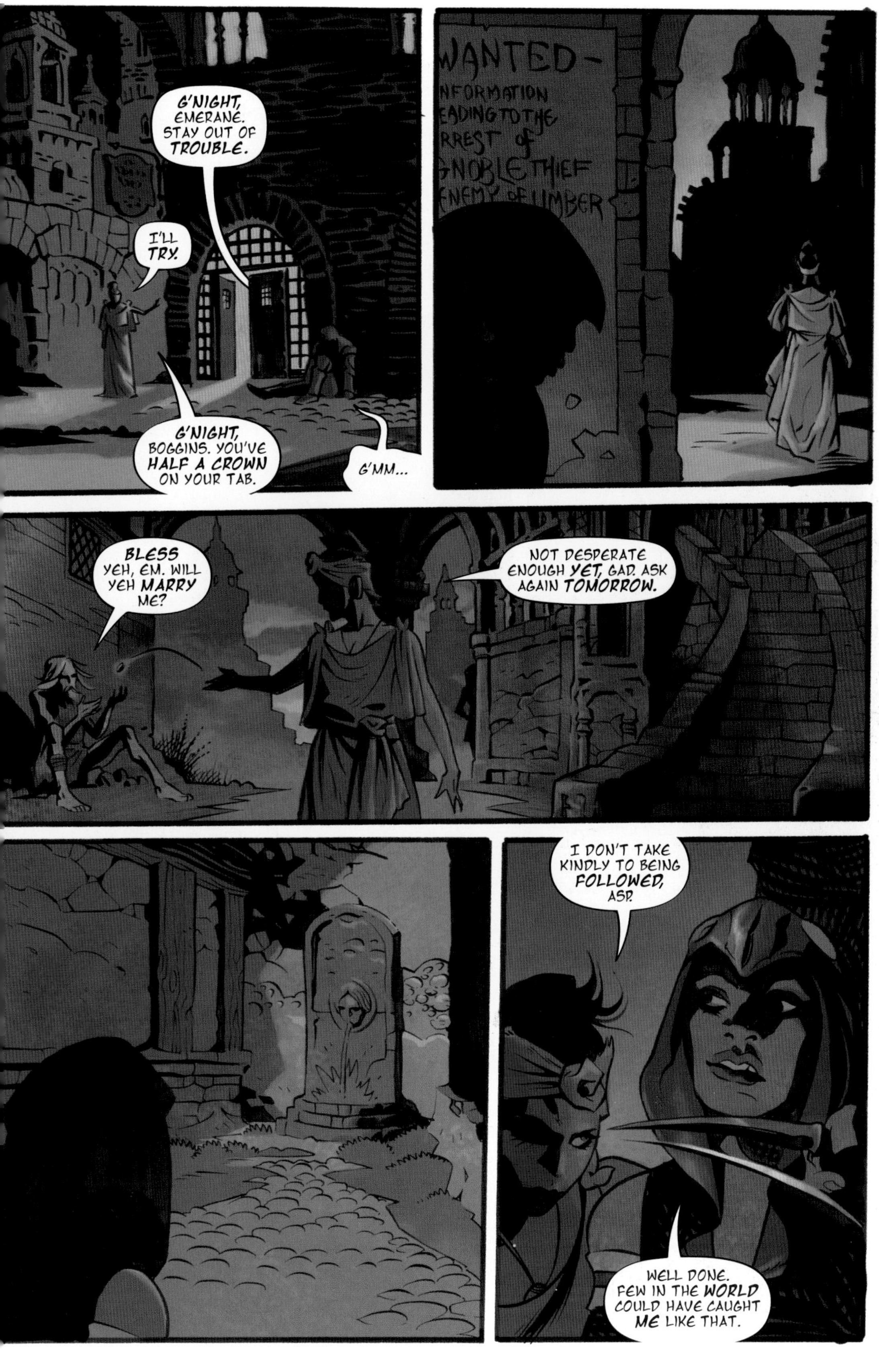
G'NIGHT, EMERANE. STAY OUT OF TROUBLE.
I'LL TRY.
G'NIGHT, BOGGINS. YOU'VE HALF A CROWN ON YOUR TAB.
G'MM...
WANTED-
NFORMATION
EADING TO THE
RREST of
GNOBLE THIEF
ENEMY of UMBER
BLESS YEH, EM. WILL YEH MARRY ME?
NOT DESPERATE ENOUGH YET, GAD. ASK AGAIN TOMORROW.
I DON'T TAKE KINDLY TO BEING FOLLOWED, ASP.
WELL DONE. FEW IN THE WORLD COULD HAVE CAUGHT ME LIKE THAT.

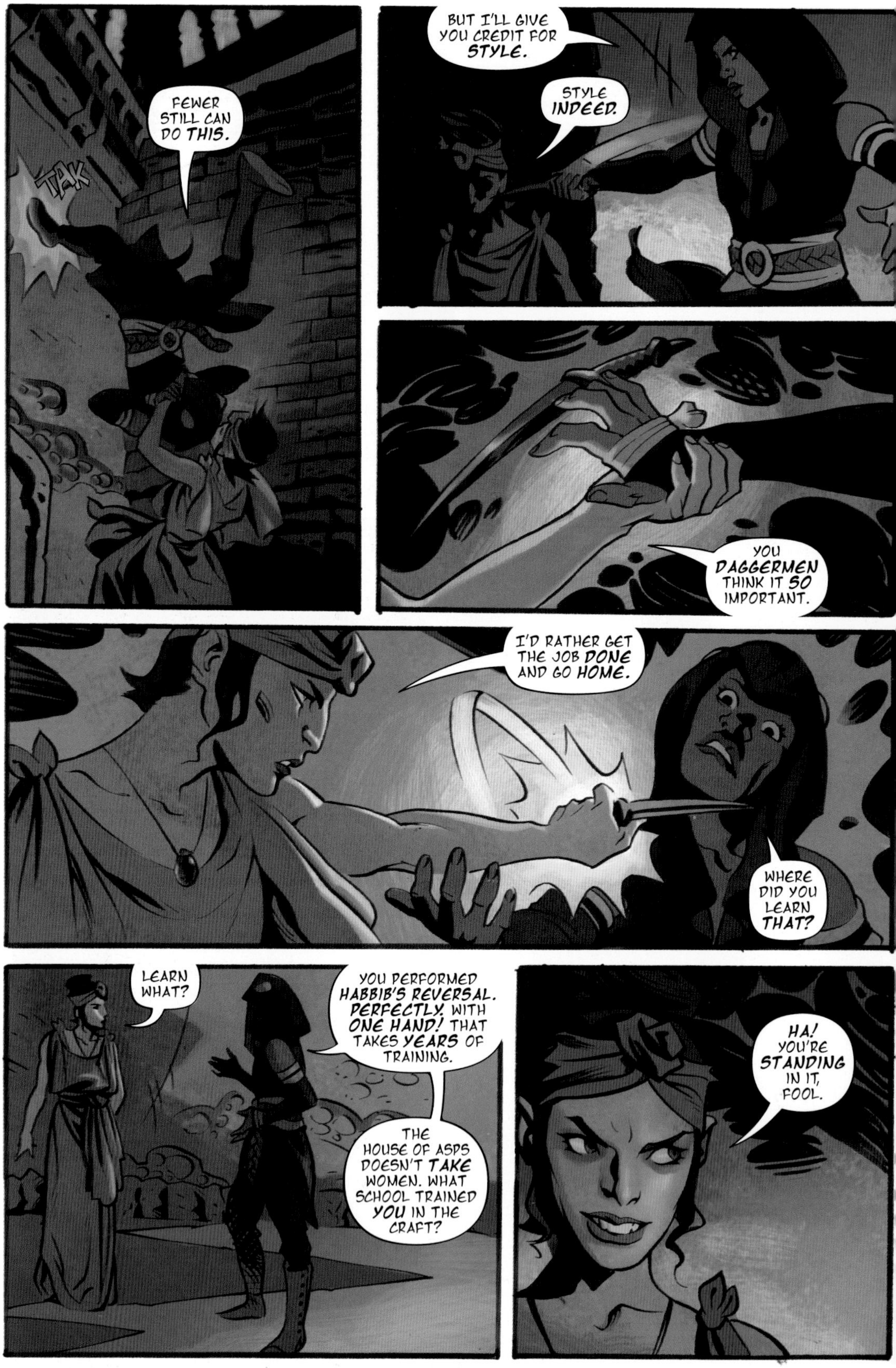
FEWER STILL CAN DO THIS.
TAK
BUT I'LL GIVE YOU CREDIT FOR STYLE.
STYLE INDEED.
YOU DAGGERMEN THINK IT SO IMPORTANT.
I'D RATHER GET THE JOB DONE AND GO HOME.
WHERE DID YOU LEARN THAT?
LEARN WHAT?
YOU PERFORMED HABBIB'S REVERSAL. PERFECTLY. WITH ONE HAND! THAT TAKES YEARS OF TRAINING.
THE HOUSE OF ASPS DOESN'T TAKE WOMEN. WHAT SCHOOL TRAINED YOU IN THE CRAFT?
HA! YOU'RE STANDING IN IT, FOOL.

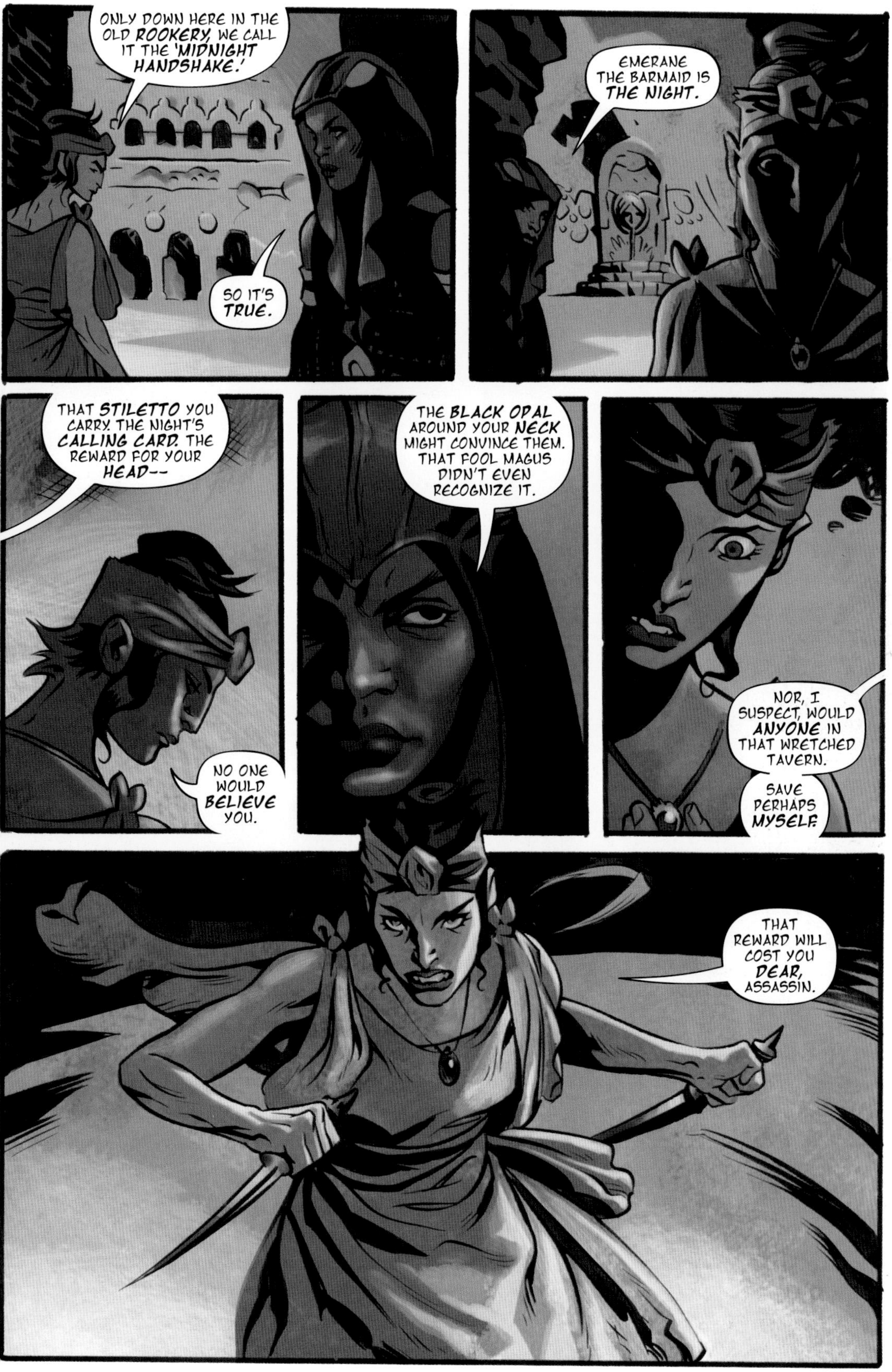
ONLY DOWN HERE IN THE OLD ROOKERY, WE CALL IT THE 'MIDNIGHT HANDSHAKE.'
SO IT'S TRUE.
EMERANE THE BARMAID IS THE NIGHT.
THAT STILETTO YOU CARRY. THE NIGHT'S CALLING CARD. THE REWARD FOR YOUR HEAD--
NO ONE WOULD BELIEVE YOU.
THE BLACK OPAL AROUND YOUR NECK MIGHT CONVINCE THEM. THAT FOOL MAGUS DIDN'T EVEN RECOGNIZE IT.
NOR, I SUSPECT, WOULD ANYONE IN THAT WRETCHED TAVERN.
SAVE PERHAPS MYSELF.
THAT REWARD WILL COST YOU DEAR, ASSASSIN.

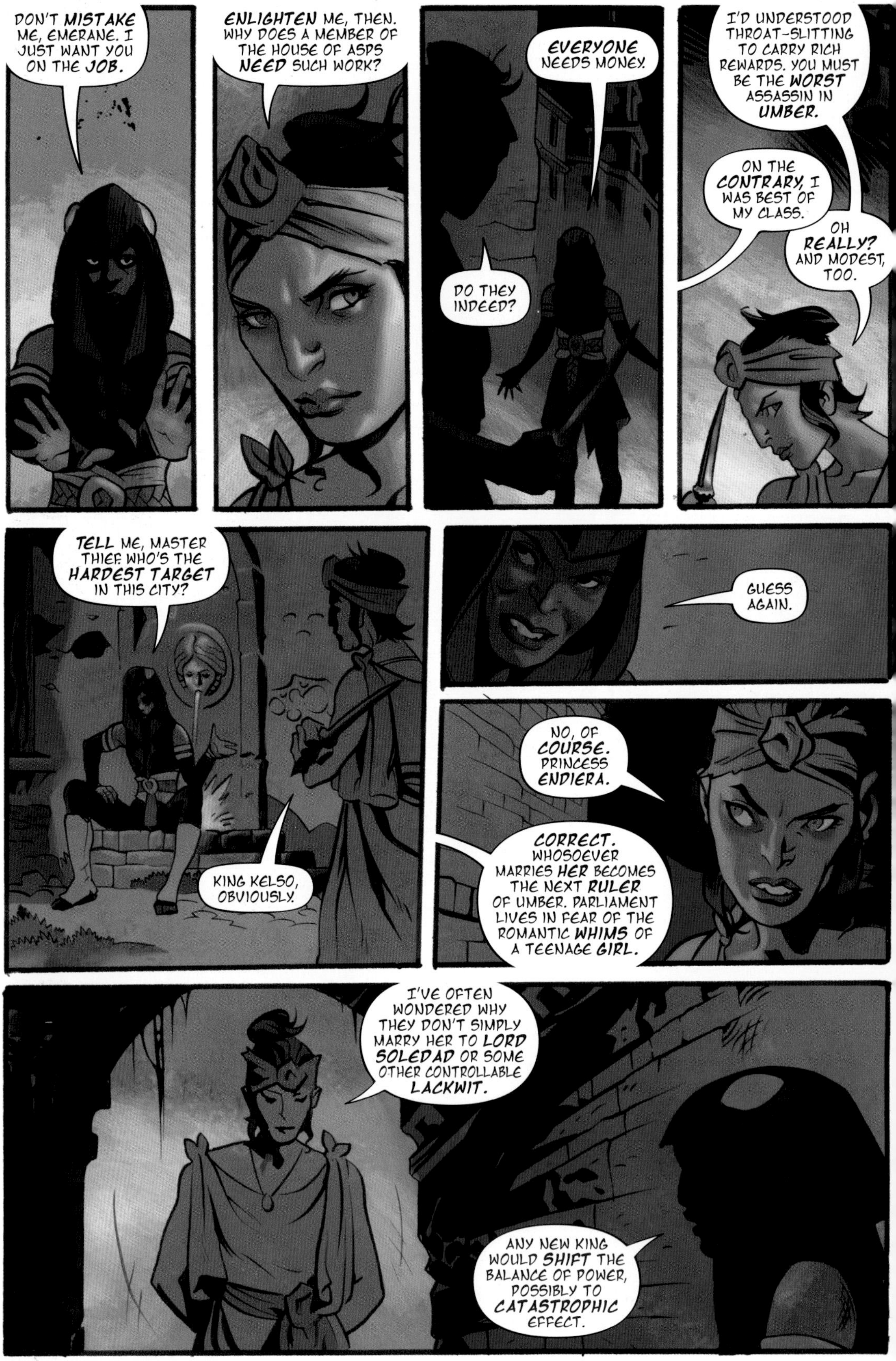
DON'T MISTAKE ME, EMERANE. I JUST WANT YOU ON THE JOB.
ENLIGHTEN ME, THEN. WHY DOES A MEMBER OF THE HOUSE OF ASPS NEED SUCH WORK?
EVERYONE NEEDS MONEY.
DO THEY INDEED?
I'D UNDERSTOOD THROAT-SLITTING TO CARRY RICH REWARDS. YOU MUST BE THE WORST ASSASSIN IN UMBER.
ON THE CONTRARY, I WAS BEST OF MY CLASS.
OH REALLY? AND MODEST, TOO.
TELL ME, MASTER THIEF. WHO'S THE HARDEST TARGET IN THIS CITY?
KING KELSO, OBVIOUSLY.
GUESS AGAIN.
NO, OF COURSE. PRINCESS ENDIERA.
CORRECT. WHOSOEVER MARRIES HER BECOMES THE NEXT RULER OF UMBER. PARLIAMENT LIVES IN FEAR OF THE ROMANTIC WHIMS OF A TEENAGE GIRL.
I'VE OFTEN WONDERED WHY THEY DON'T SIMPLY MARRY HER TO LORD SOLEDAD OR SOME OTHER CONTROLLABLE LACKWIT.
ANY NEW KING WOULD SHIFT THE BALANCE OF POWER, POSSIBLY TO CATASTROPHIC EFFECT.

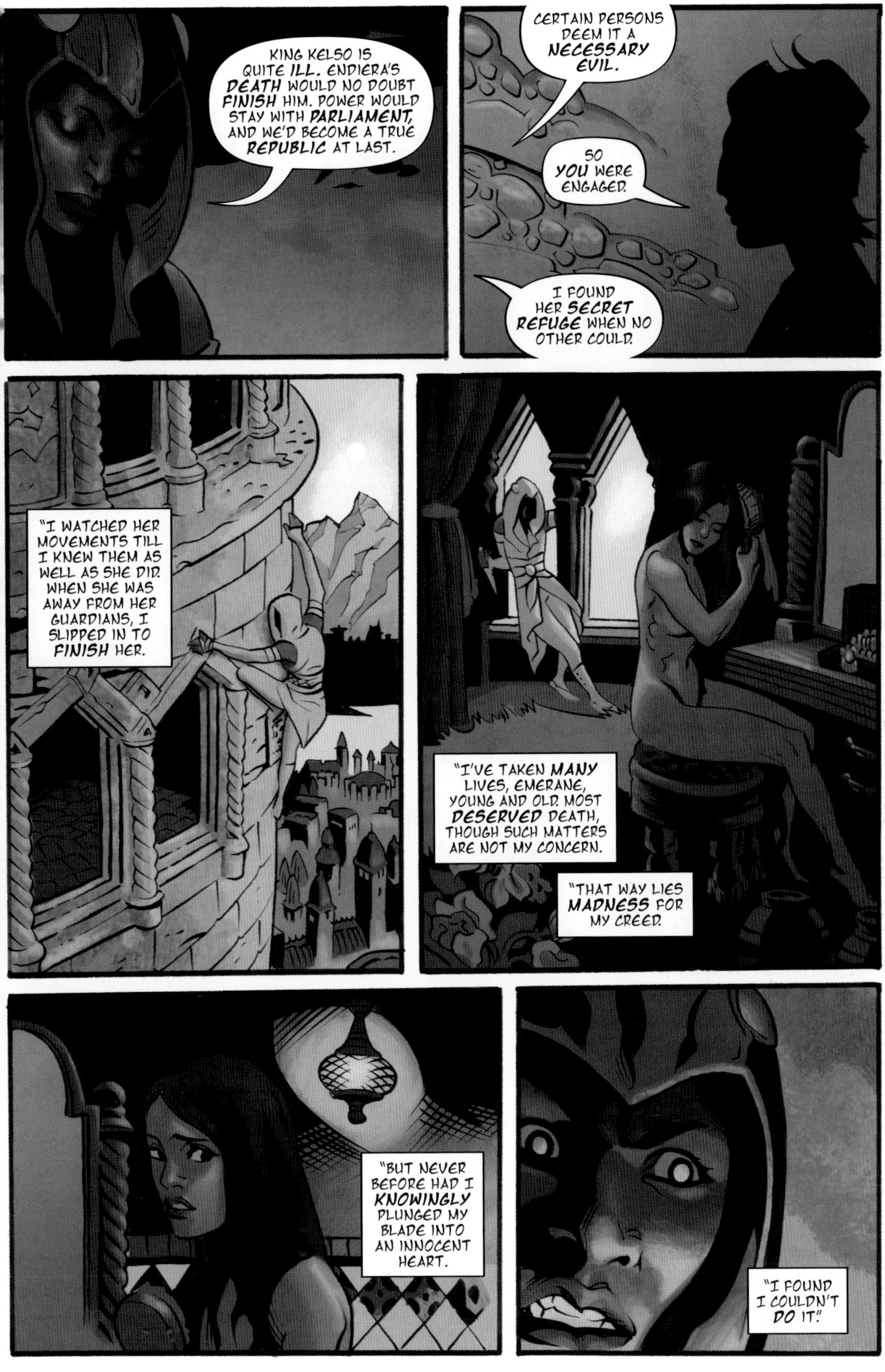
KING KELSO IS QUITE ILL. ENDIERA'S DEATH WOULD NO DOUBT FINISH HIM. POWER WOULD STAY WITH PARLIAMENT, AND WE'D BECOME A TRUE REPUBLIC AT LAST.
CERTAIN PERSONS DEEM IT A NECESSARY EVIL.
SO YOU WERE ENGAGED.
I FOUND HER SECRET REFUGE WHEN NO OTHER COULD.
"I WATCHED HER MOVEMENTS TILL I KNEW THEM AS WELL AS SHE DID. WHEN SHE WAS AWAY FROM HER GUARDIANS, I SLIPPED IN TO FINISH HER.
"I'VE TAKEN MANY LIVES, EMERANE, YOUNG AND OLD. MOST DESERVED DEATH, THOUGH SUCH MATTERS ARE NOT MY CONCERN.
"THAT WAY LIES MADNESS FOR MY CREED.
"BUT NEVER BEFORE HAD I KNOWINGLY PLUNGED MY BLADE INTO AN INNOCENT HEART.
"I FOUND I COULDN'T DO IT."

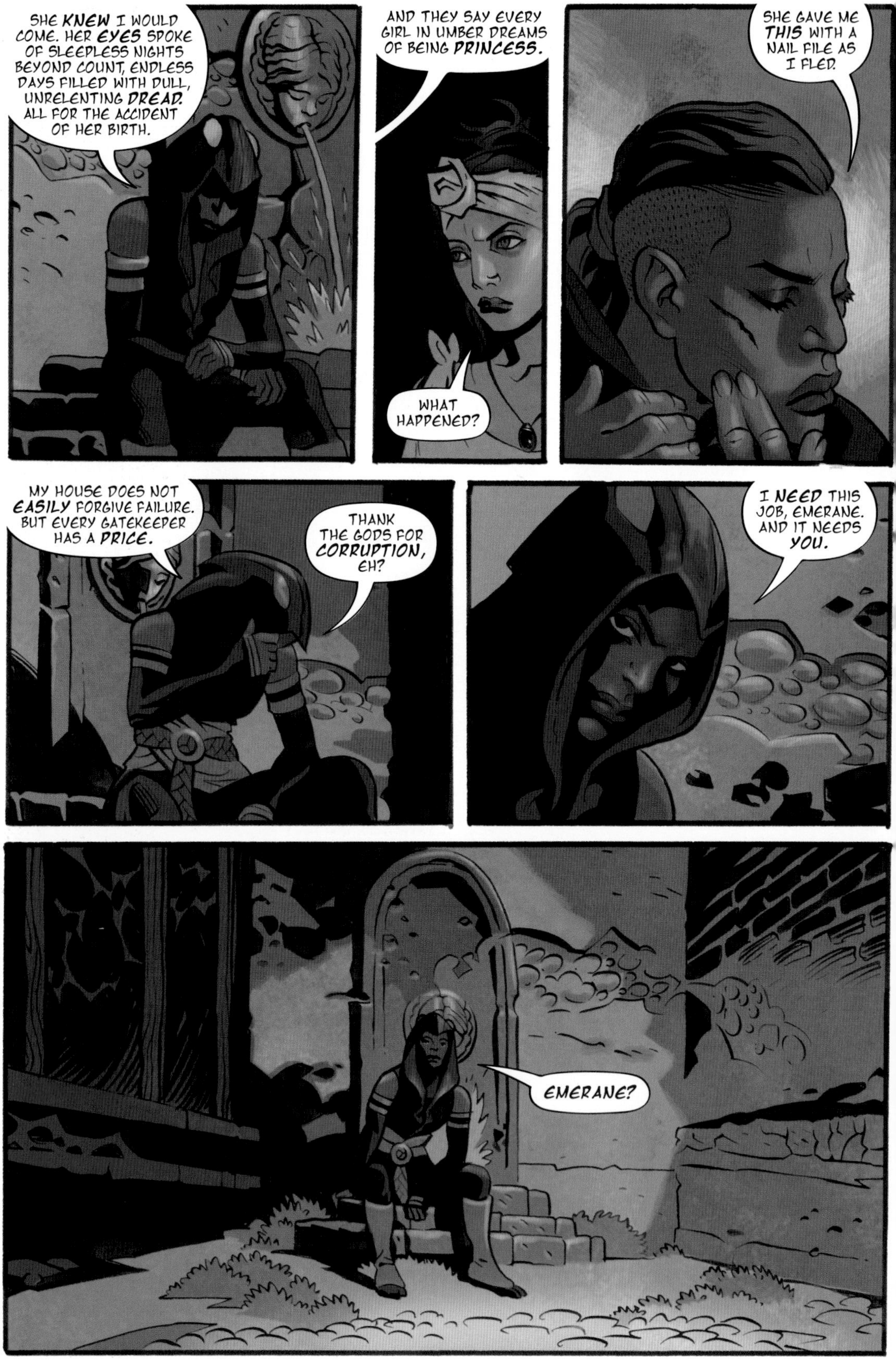
SHE KNEW I WOULD COME. HER EYES SPOKE OF SLEEPLESS NIGHTS BEYOND COUNT, ENDLESS DAYS FILLED WITH DULL, UNRELENTING DREAD. ALL FOR THE ACCIDENT OF HER BIRTH.
AND THEY SAY EVERY GIRL IN UMBER DREAMS OF BEING PRINCESS.
WHAT HAPPENED?
SHE GAVE ME THIS WITH A NAIL FILE AS I FLED.
MY HOUSE DOES NOT EASILY FORGIVE FAILURE. BUT EVERY GATEKEEPER HAS A PRICE.
THANK THE GODS FOR CORRUPTION, EH?
I NEED THIS JOB, EMERANE. AND IT NEEDS YOU.
EMERANE?

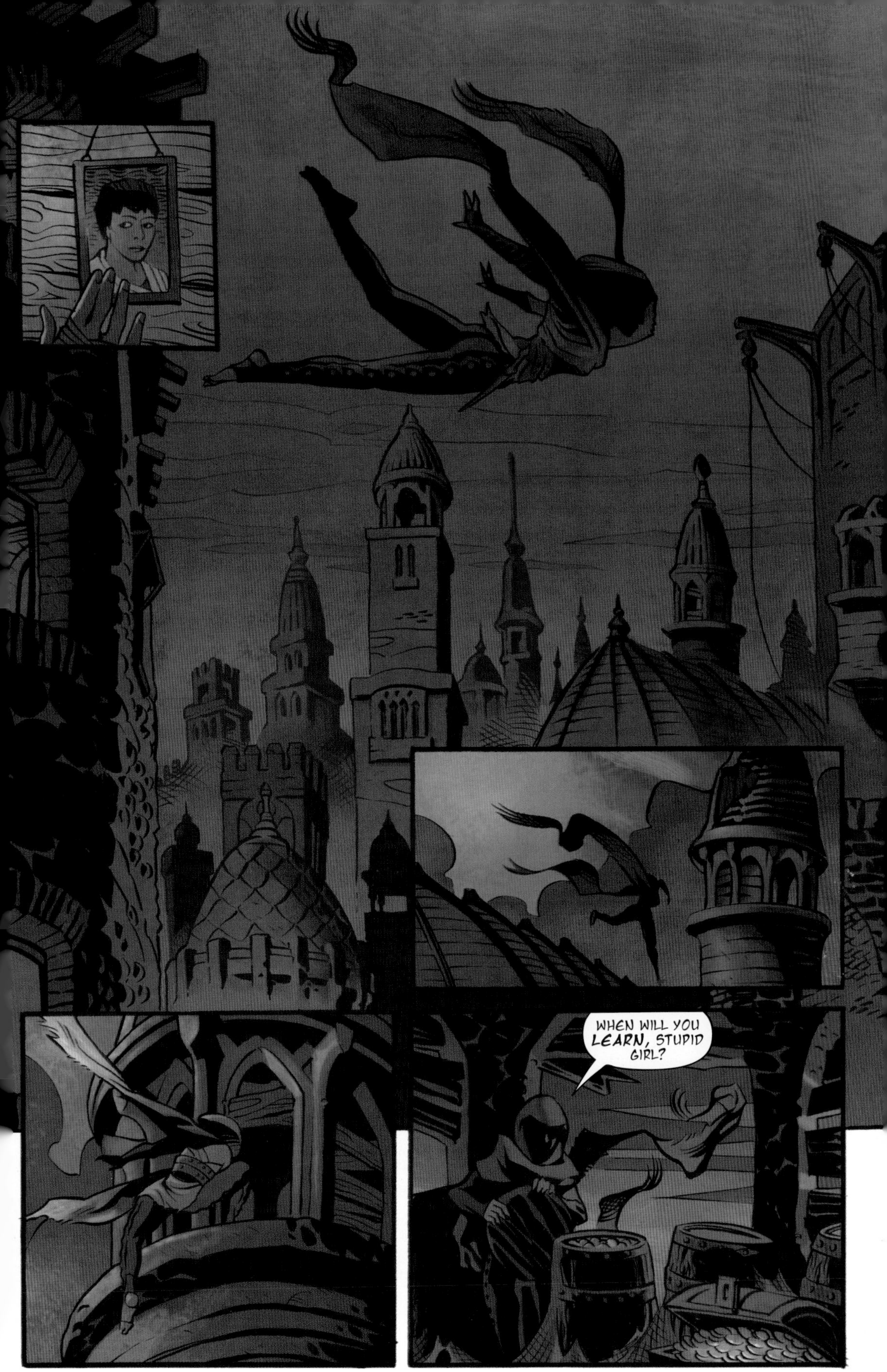
WHEN WILL YOU LEARN, STUPID GIRL?

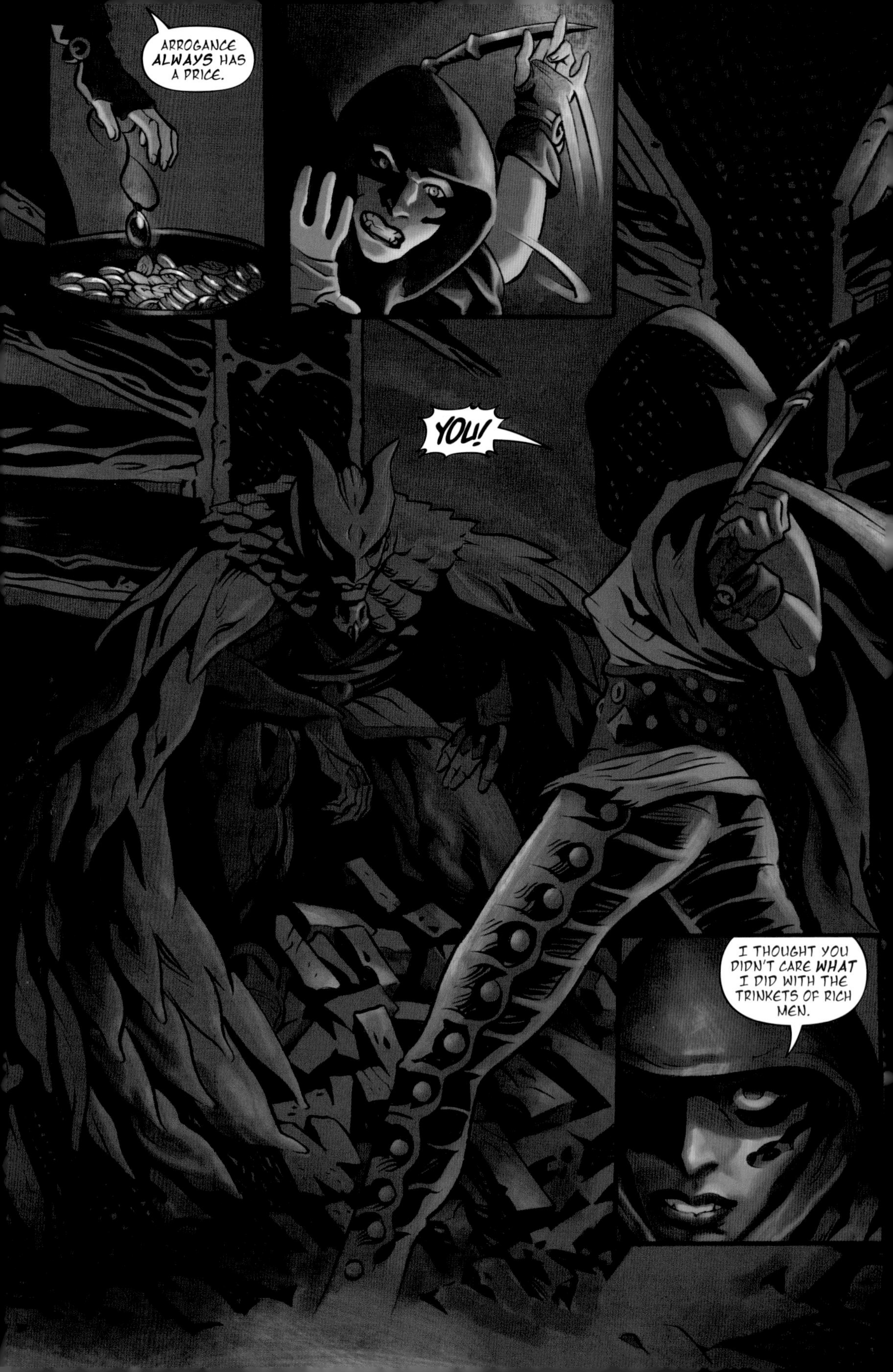
ARROGANCE ALWAYS HAS A PRICE.
YOU!
I THOUGHT YOU DIDN'T CARE WHAT I DID WITH THE TRINKETS OF RICH MEN.

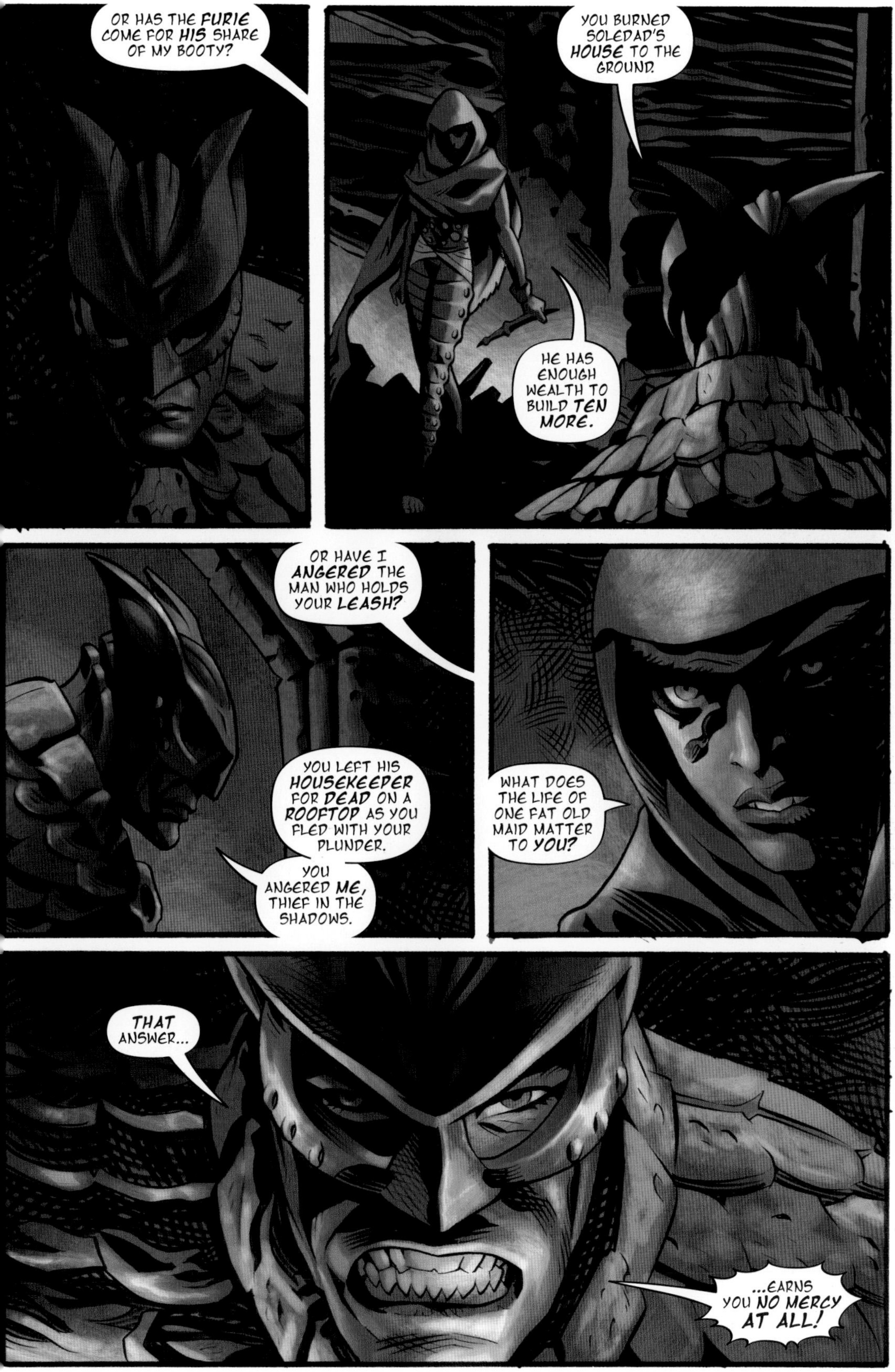
OR HAS THE FURIE COME FOR HIS SHARE OF MY BOOTY?
YOU BURNED SOLEDAD'S HOUSE TO THE GROUND.
HE HAS ENOUGH WEALTH TO BUILD TEN MORE.
OR HAVE I ANGERED THE MAN WHO HOLDS YOUR LEASH?
YOU LEFT HIS HOUSEKEEPER FOR DEAD ON A ROOFTOP AS YOU FLED WITH YOUR PLUNDER.
YOU ANGERED ME, THIEF IN THE SHADOWS.
WHAT DOES THE LIFE OF ONE FAT OLD MAID MATTER TO YOU?
THAT ANSWER...
...EARNS YOU NO MERCY AT ALL!

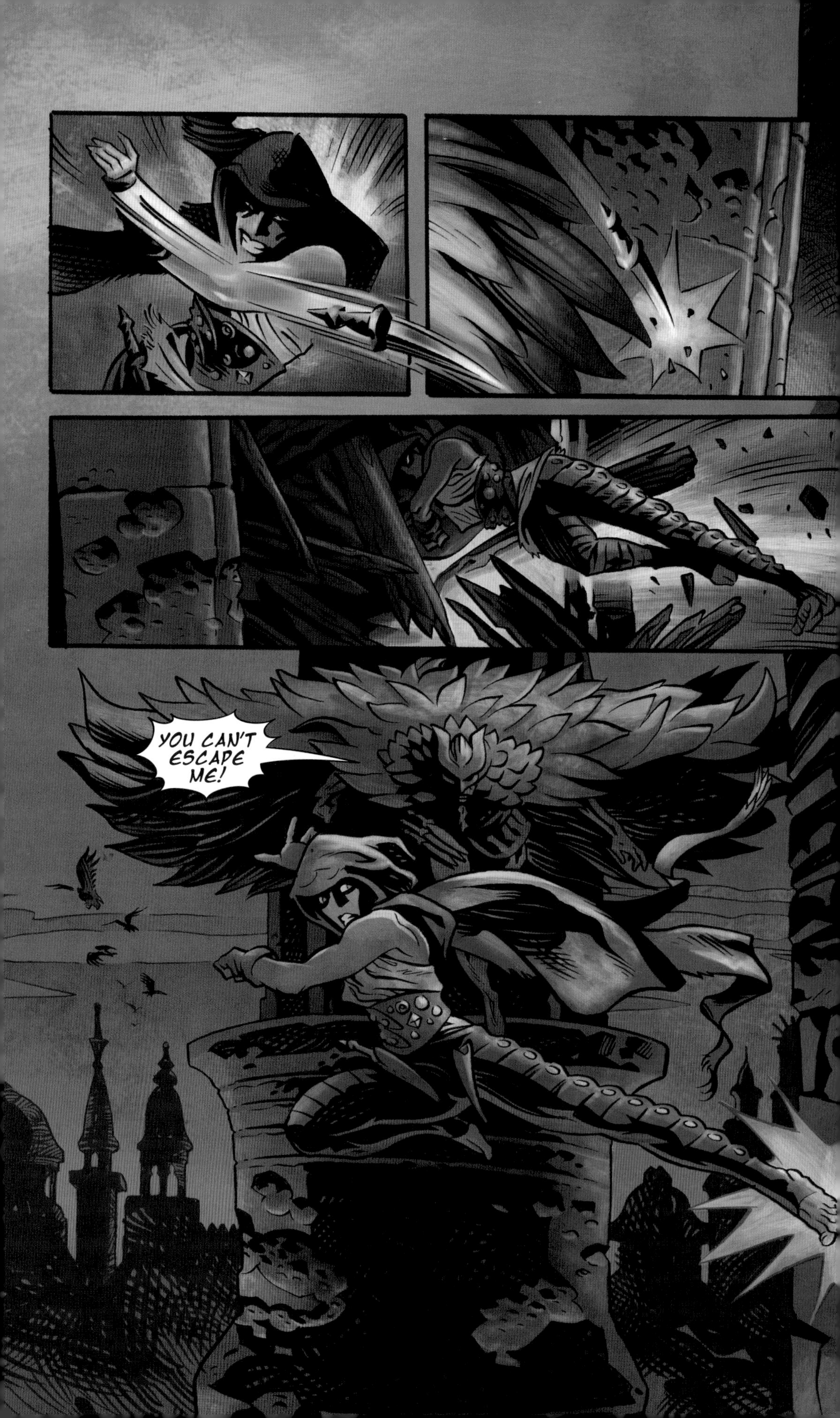
YOU CAN'T ESCAPE ME!

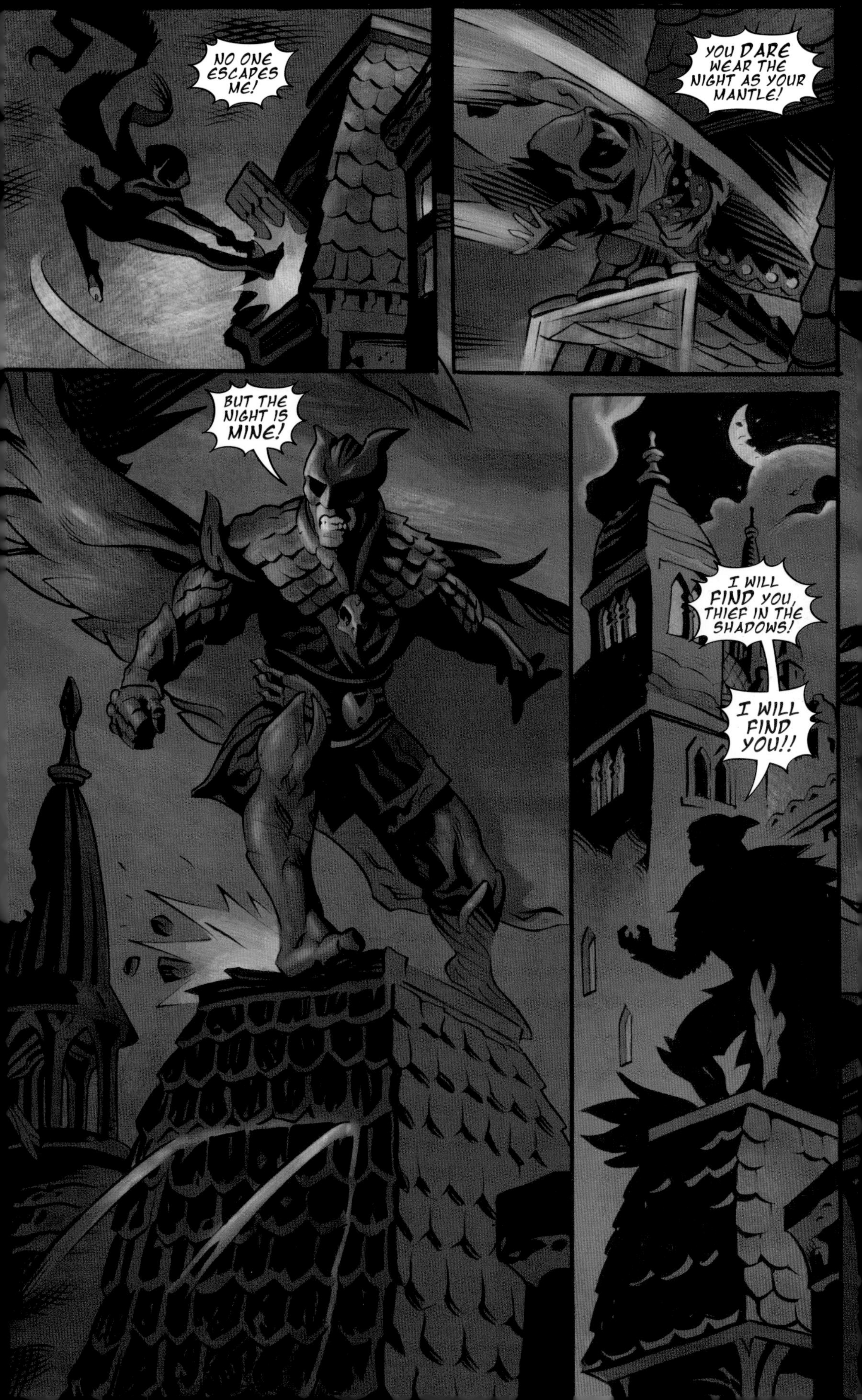
NO ONE ESCAPES ME!
YOU DARE WEAR THE NIGHT AS YOUR MANTLE!
BUT THE NIGHT IS MINE!
I WILL FIND YOU, THIEF IN THE SHADOWS!
I WILL FIND YOU!!

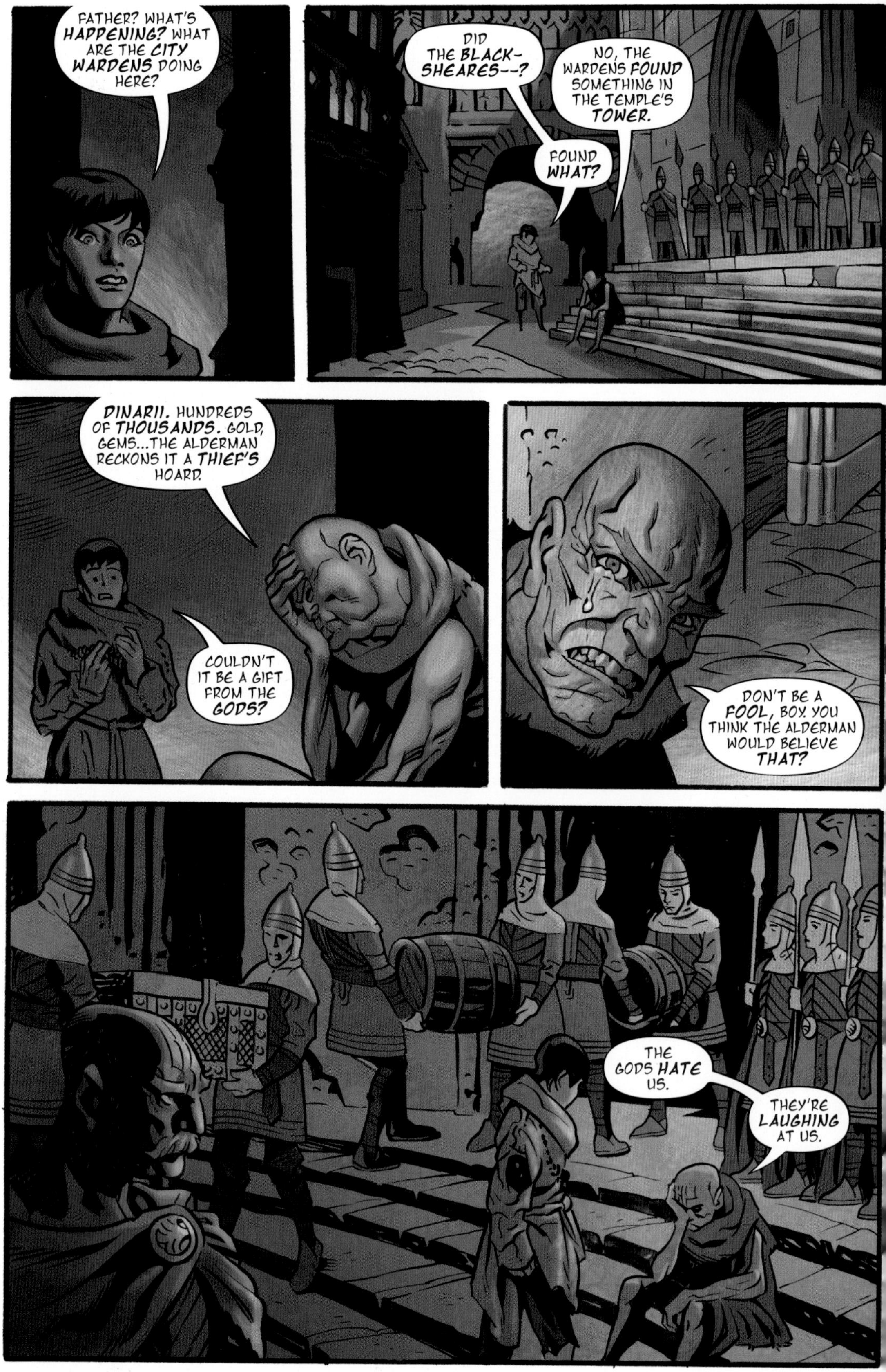
FATHER? WHAT'S HAPPENING? WHAT ARE THE CITY WARDENS DOING HERE?
DID THE BLACK-SHEARES--?
NO, THE WARDENS FOUND SOMETHING IN THE TEMPLE'S TOWER.
FOUND WHAT?
DINARII. HUNDREDS OF THOUSANDS. GOLD, GEMS...THE ALDERMAN RECKONS IT A THIEF'S HOARD.
COULDN'T IT BE A GIFT FROM THE GODS?
DON'T BE A FOOL, BOY. YOU THINK THE ALDERMAN WOULD BELIEVE THAT?
THE GODS HATE US.
THEY'RE LAUGHING AT US.

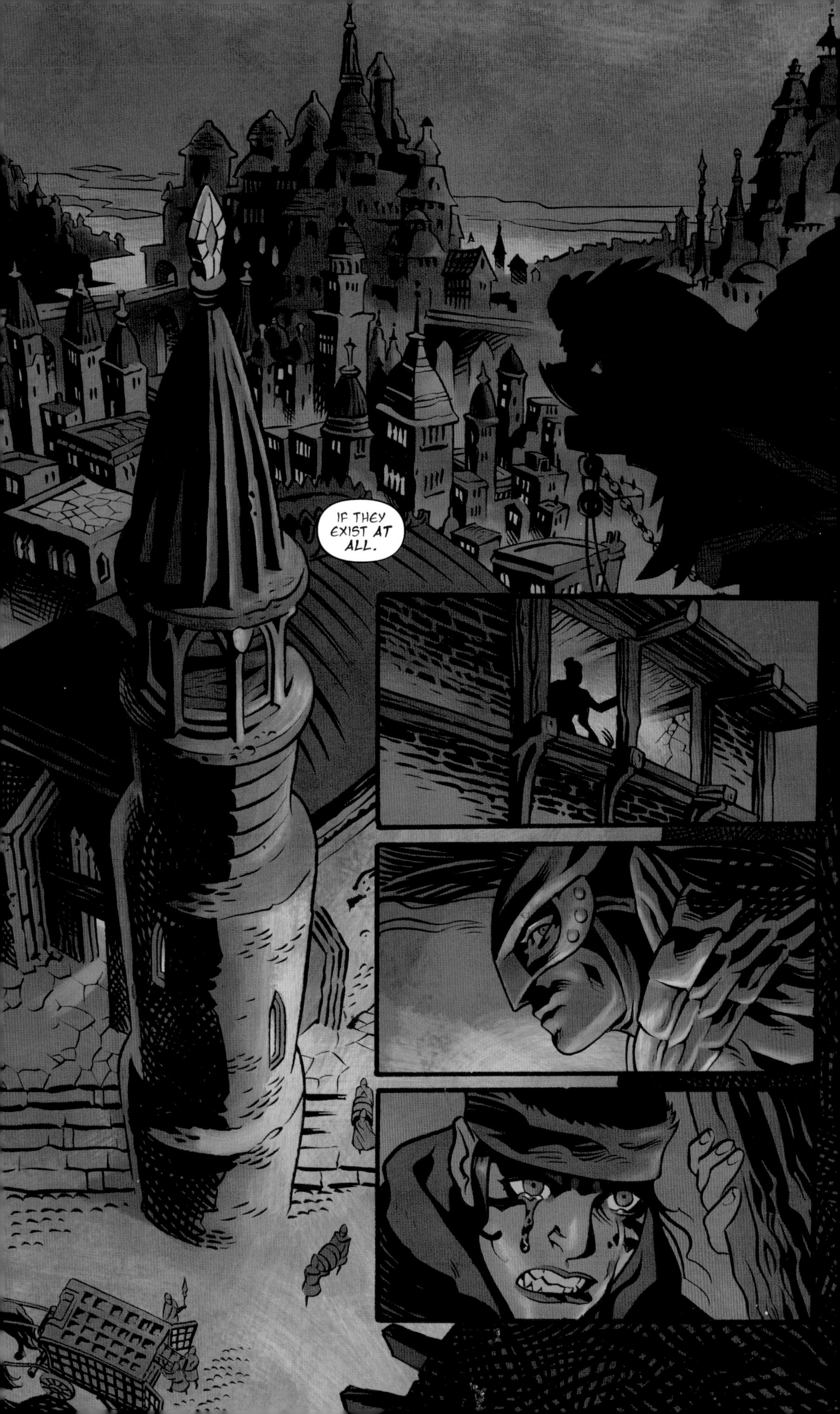
IF THEY EXIST AT ALL.

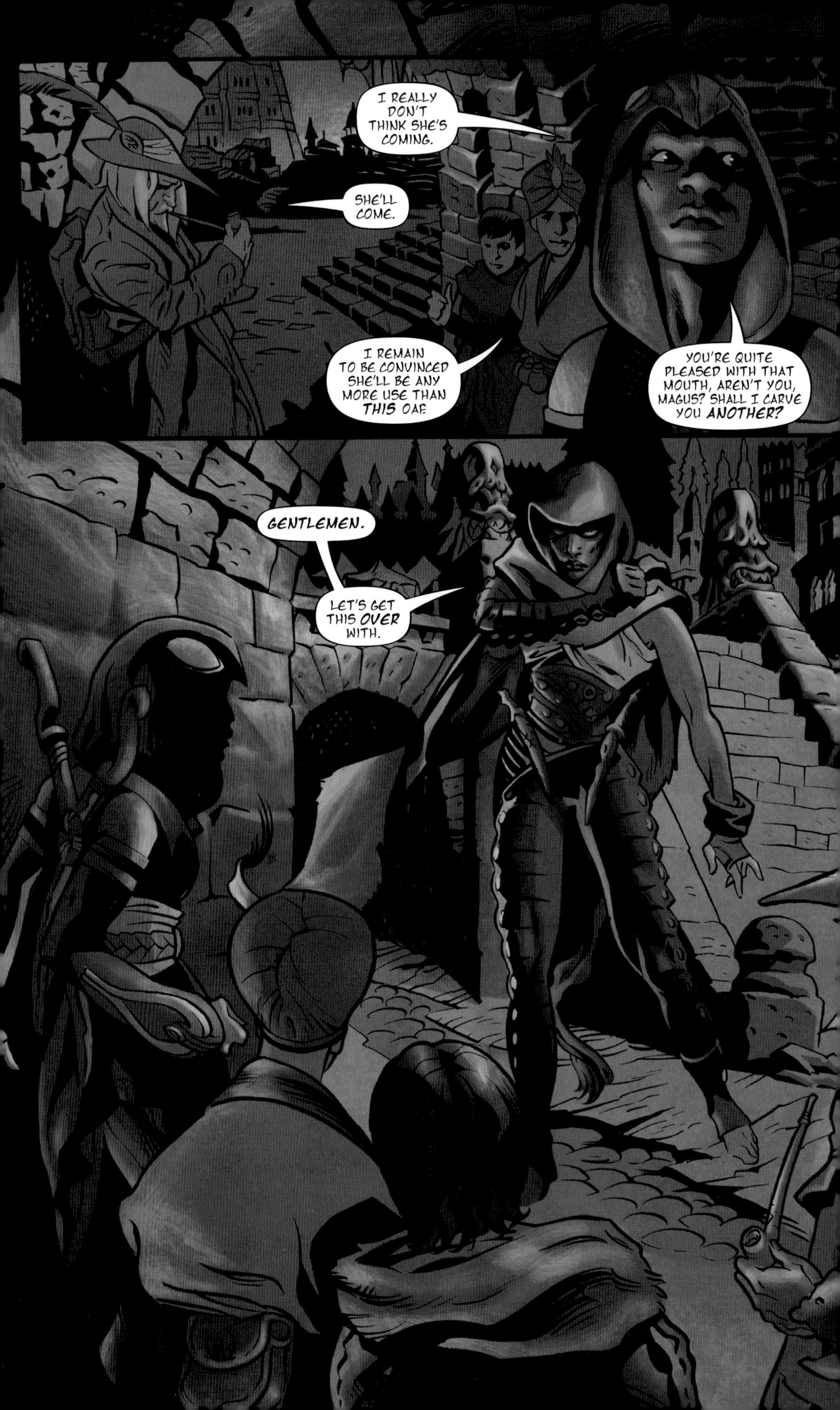
I REALLY DON'T THINK SHE'S COMING.
SHE'LL COME.
I REMAIN TO BE CONVINCED SHE'LL BE ANY MORE USE THAN THIS OAF.
YOU'RE QUITE PLEASED WITH THAT MOUTH, AREN'T YOU, MAGUS? SHALL I CARVE YOU ANOTHER?
GENTLEMEN.
LET'S GET THIS OVER WITH.

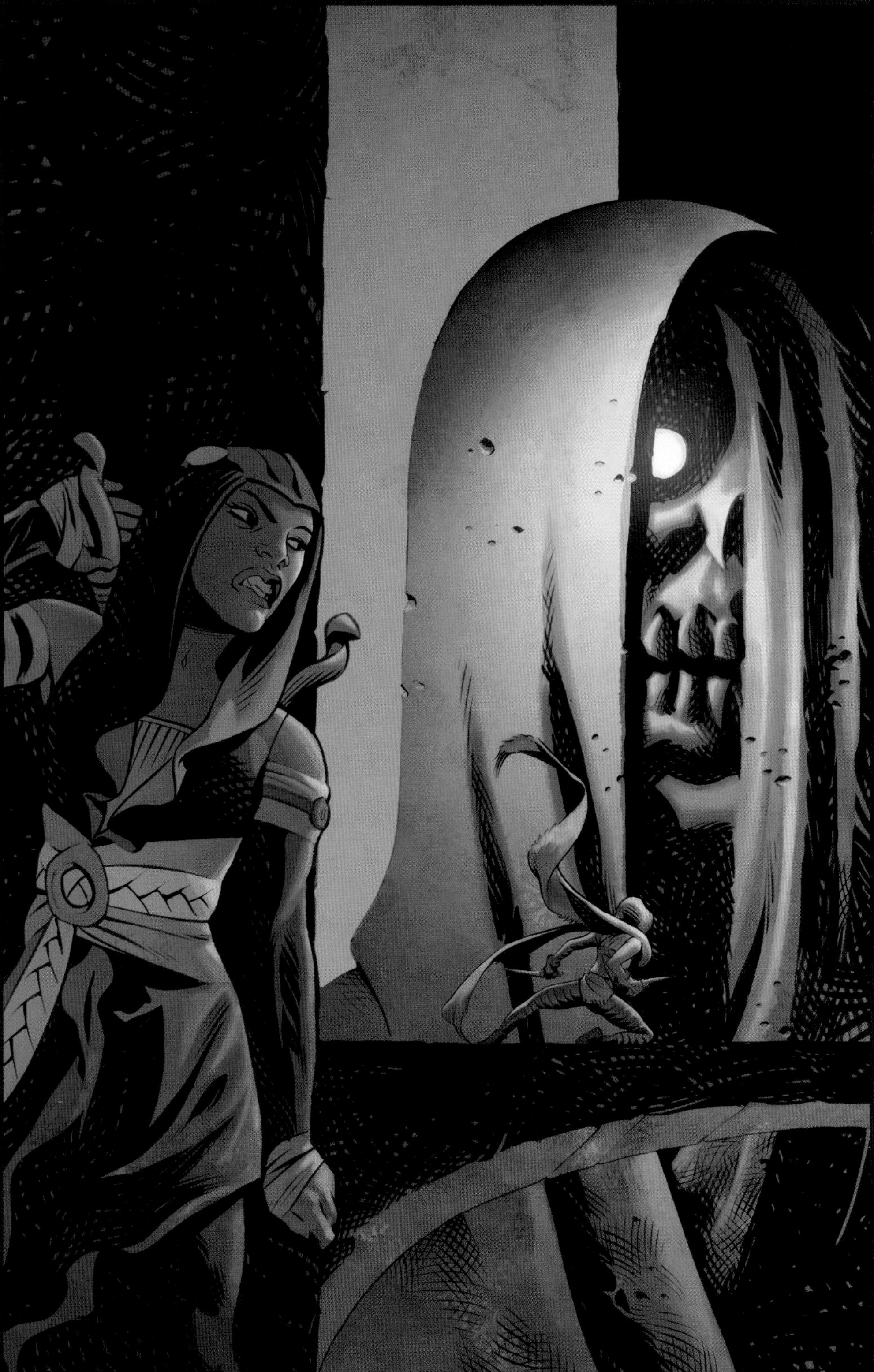

Chapter 2

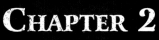

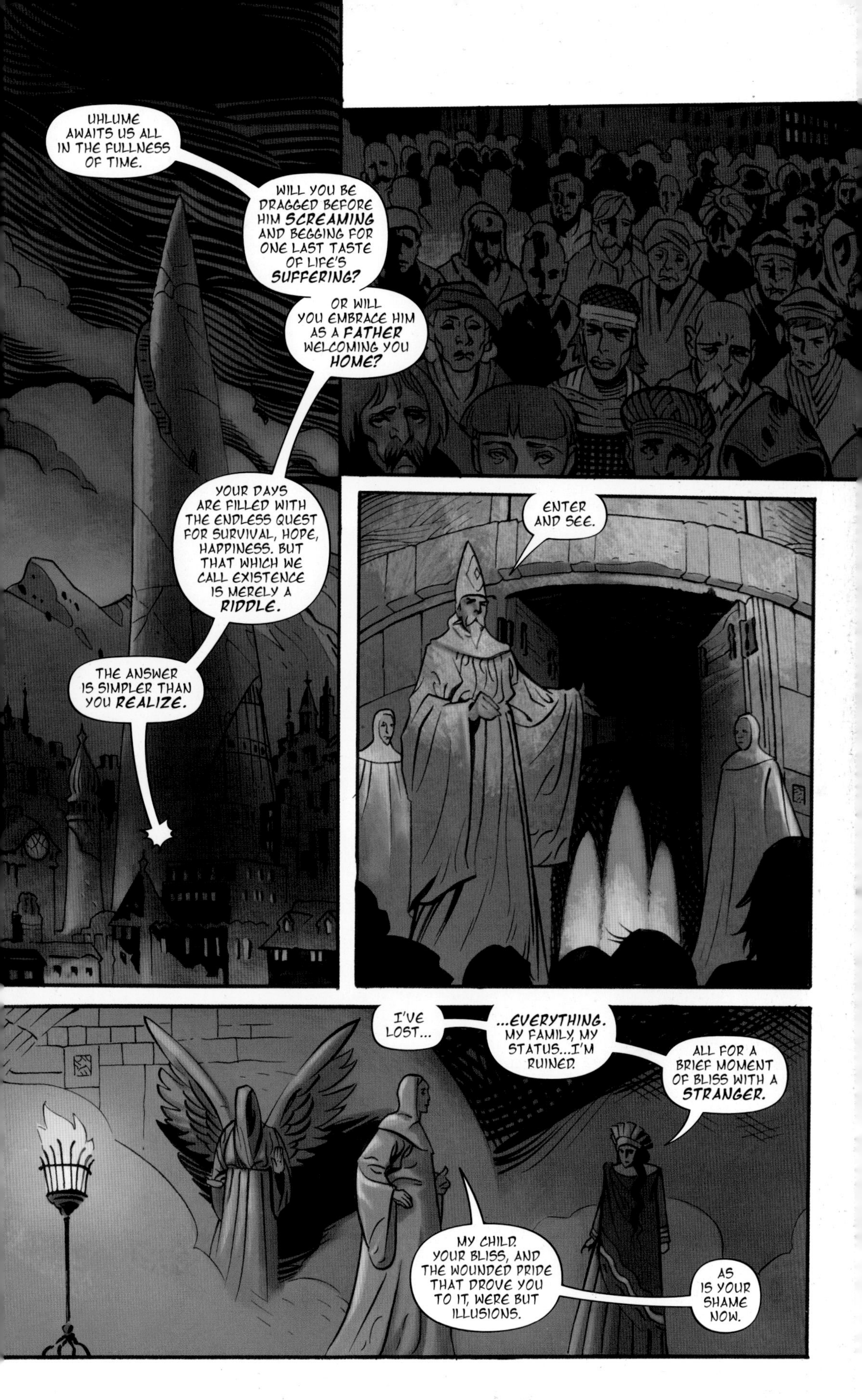
UHLUME AWAITS US ALL IN THE FULLNESS OF TIME.
WILL YOU BE DRAGGED BEFORE HIM SCREAMING AND BEGGING FOR ONE LAST TASTE OF LIFE'S SUFFERING?
OR WILL YOU EMBRACE HIM AS A FATHER WELCOMING YOU HOME?
YOUR DAYS ARE FILLED WITH THE ENDLESS QUEST FOR SURVIVAL, HOPE, HAPPINESS. BUT THAT WHICH WE CALL EXISTENCE IS MERELY A RIDDLE.
THE ANSWER IS SIMPLER THAN YOU REALIZE.
ENTER AND SEE.
I'VE LOST...
...EVERYTHING. MY FAMILY, MY STATUS...I'M RUINED.
ALL FOR A BRIEF MOMENT OF BLISS WITH A STRANGER.
MY CHILD. YOUR BLISS, AND THE WOUNDED PRIDE THAT DROVE YOU TO IT, WERE BUT ILLUSIONS.
AS IS YOUR SHAME NOW.

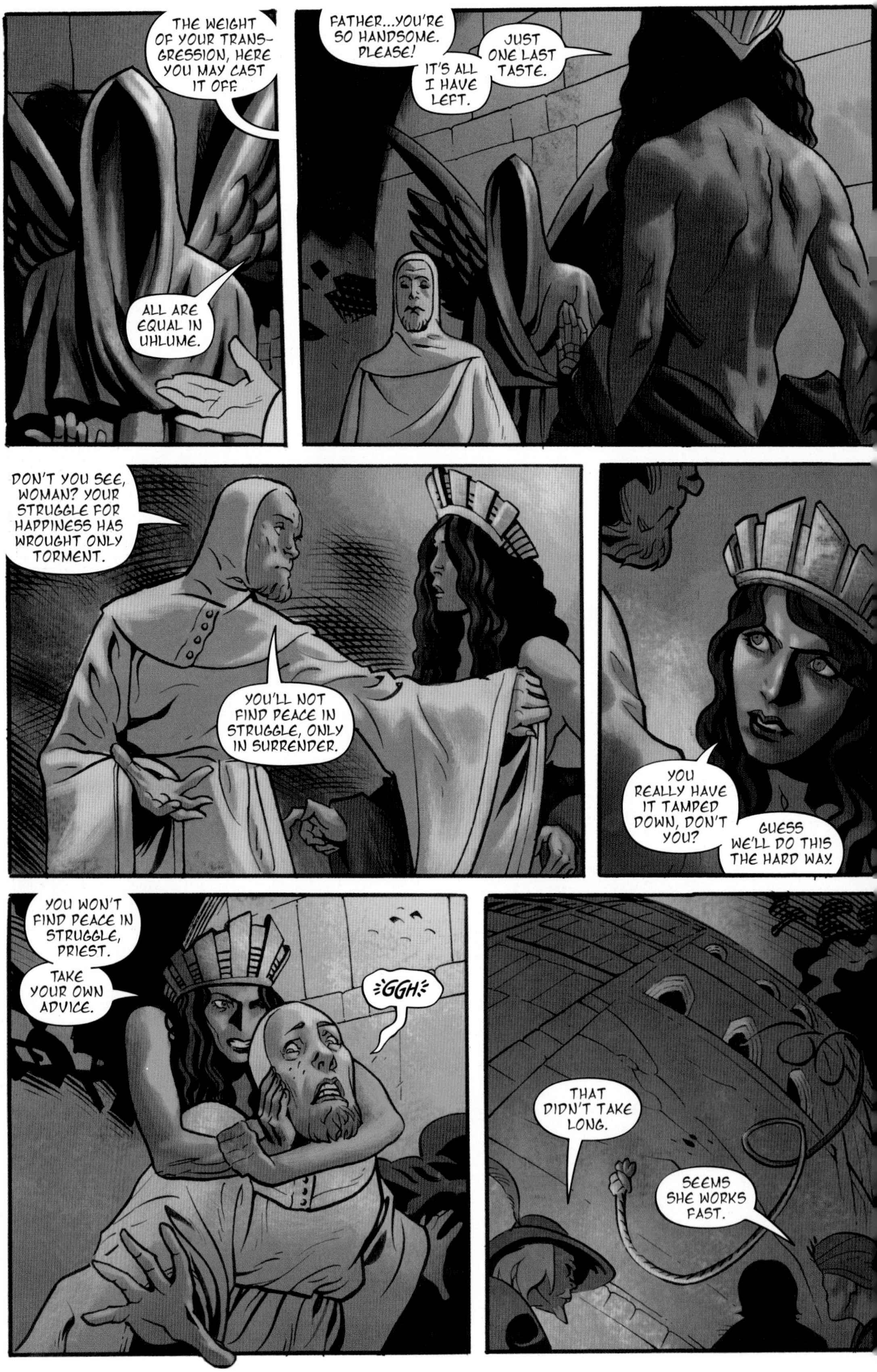
THE WEIGHT OF YOUR TRANSGRESSION, HERE YOU MAY CAST IT OFF.
ALL ARE EQUAL IN UHLUME.
FATHER...YOU'RE SO HANDSOME. PLEASE!
IT'S ALL I HAVE LEFT.
JUST ONE LAST TASTE.
DON'T YOU SEE, WOMAN? YOUR STRUGGLE FOR HAPPINESS HAS WROUGHT ONLY TORMENT.
YOU'LL NOT FIND PEACE IN STRUGGLE, ONLY IN SURRENDER.
YOU REALLY HAVE IT TAMPED DOWN, DON'T YOU?
GUESS WE'LL DO THIS THE HARD WAY.
YOU WON'T FIND PEACE IN STRUGGLE, PRIEST.
TAKE YOUR OWN ADVICE.
GGH
THAT DIDN'T TAKE LONG.
SEEMS SHE WORKS FAST.

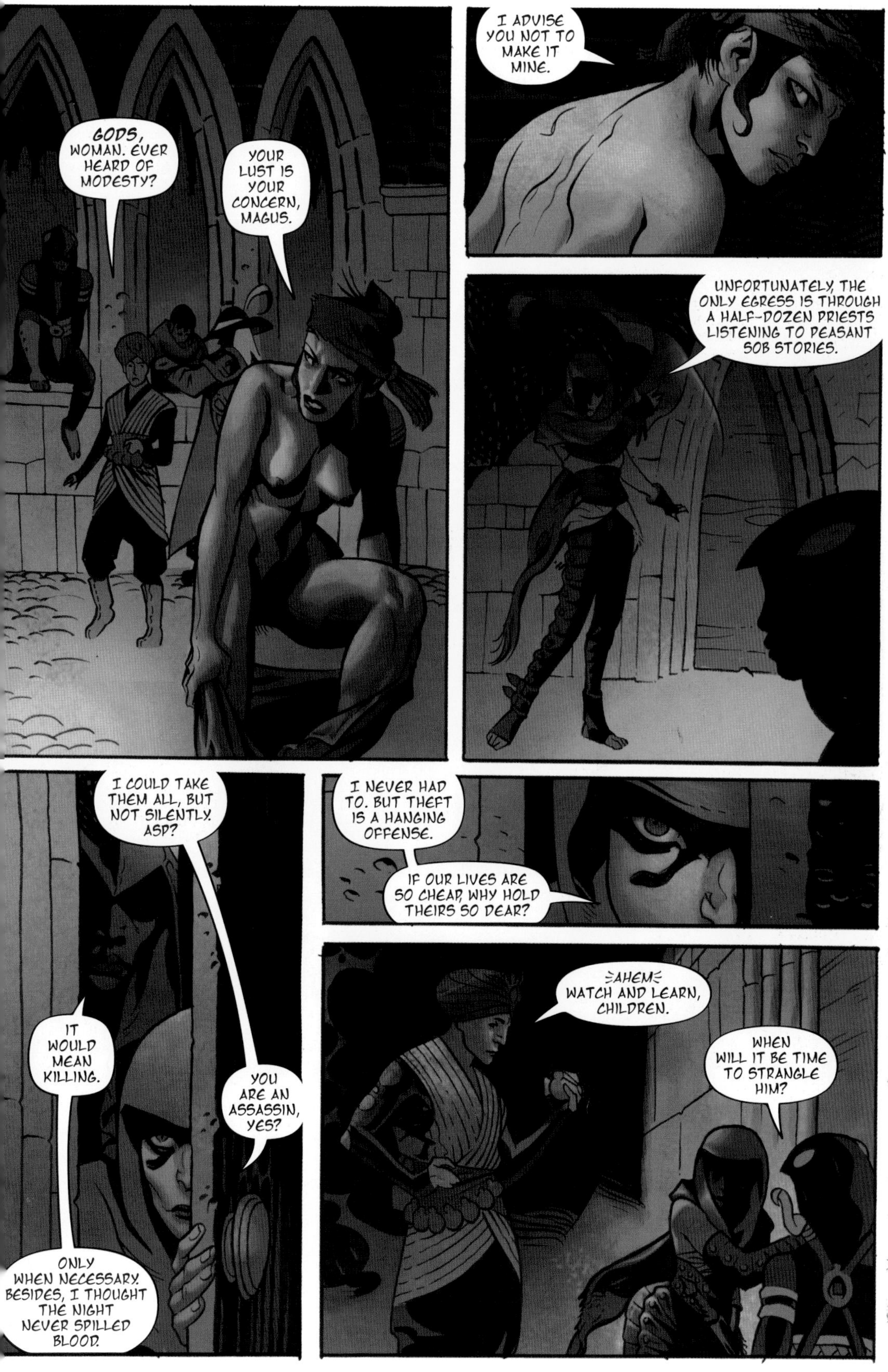
GODS, WOMAN. EVER HEARD OF MODESTY?
YOUR LUST IS YOUR CONCERN, MAGUS.
I ADVISE YOU NOT TO MAKE IT MINE.
UNFORTUNATELY, THE ONLY EGRESS IS THROUGH A HALF-DOZEN PRIESTS LISTENING TO PEASANT SOB STORIES.
I COULD TAKE THEM ALL, BUT NOT SILENTLY. ASP?
IT WOULD MEAN KILLING.
YOU ARE AN ASSASSIN, YES?
ONLY WHEN NECESSARY. BESIDES, I THOUGHT THE NIGHT NEVER SPILLED BLOOD.
I NEVER HAD TO. BUT THEFT IS A HANGING OFFENSE.
IF OUR LIVES ARE SO CHEAP, WHY HOLD THEIRS SO DEAR?
AHEM
WATCH AND LEARN, CHILDREN.
WHEN WILL IT BE TIME TO STRANGLE HIM?

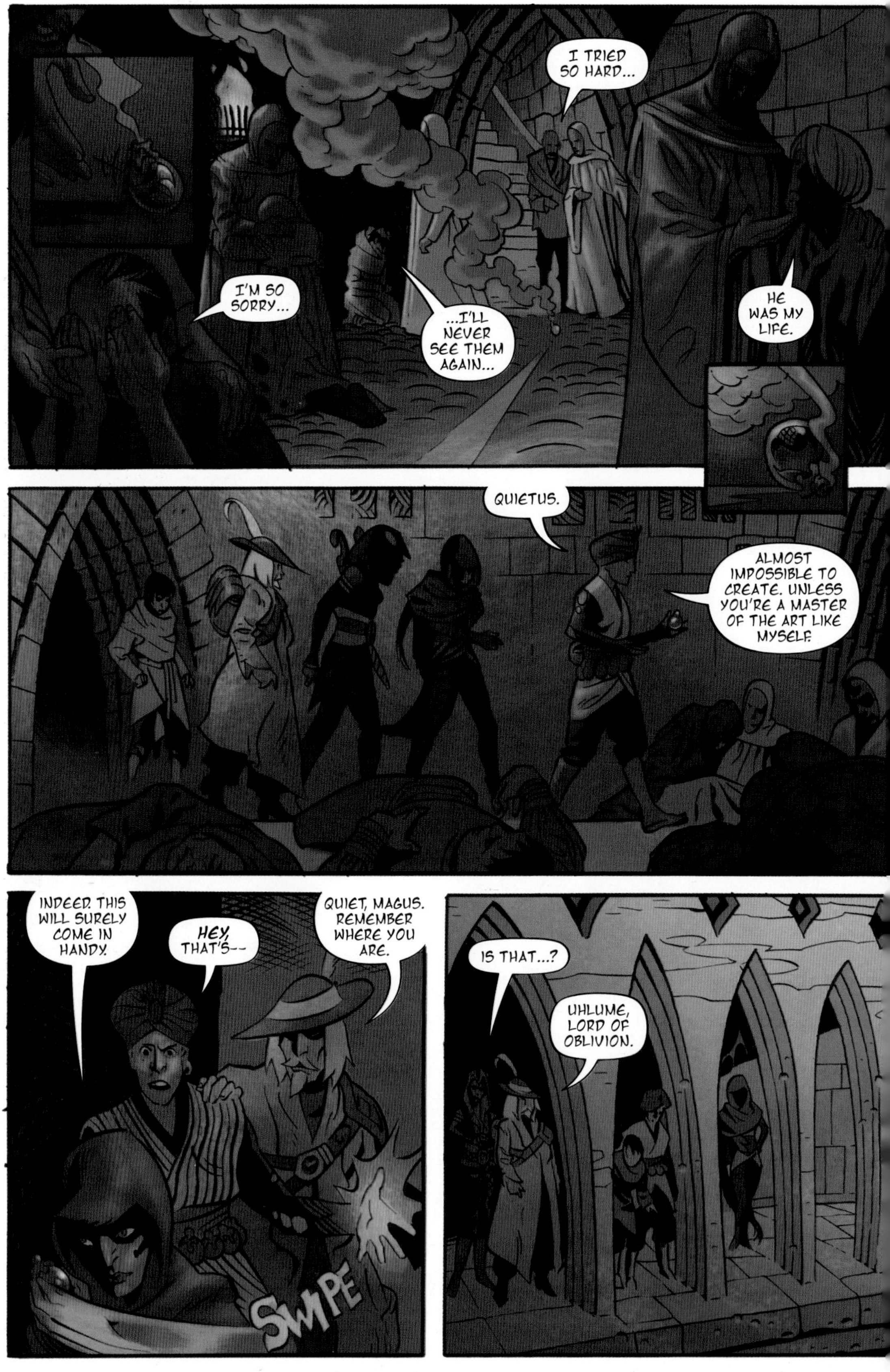
I TRIED SO HARD...
I'M SO SORRY...
...I'LL NEVER SEE THEM AGAIN...
HE WAS MY LIFE.
QUIETUS.
ALMOST IMPOSSIBLE TO CREATE. UNLESS YOU'RE A MASTER OF THE ART LIKE MYSELF.
INDEED. THIS WILL SURELY COME IN HANDY.
HEY, THAT'S--
QUIET, MAGUS. REMEMBER WHERE YOU ARE.
SWIPE
IS THAT...?
UHLUME, LORD OF OBLIVION.

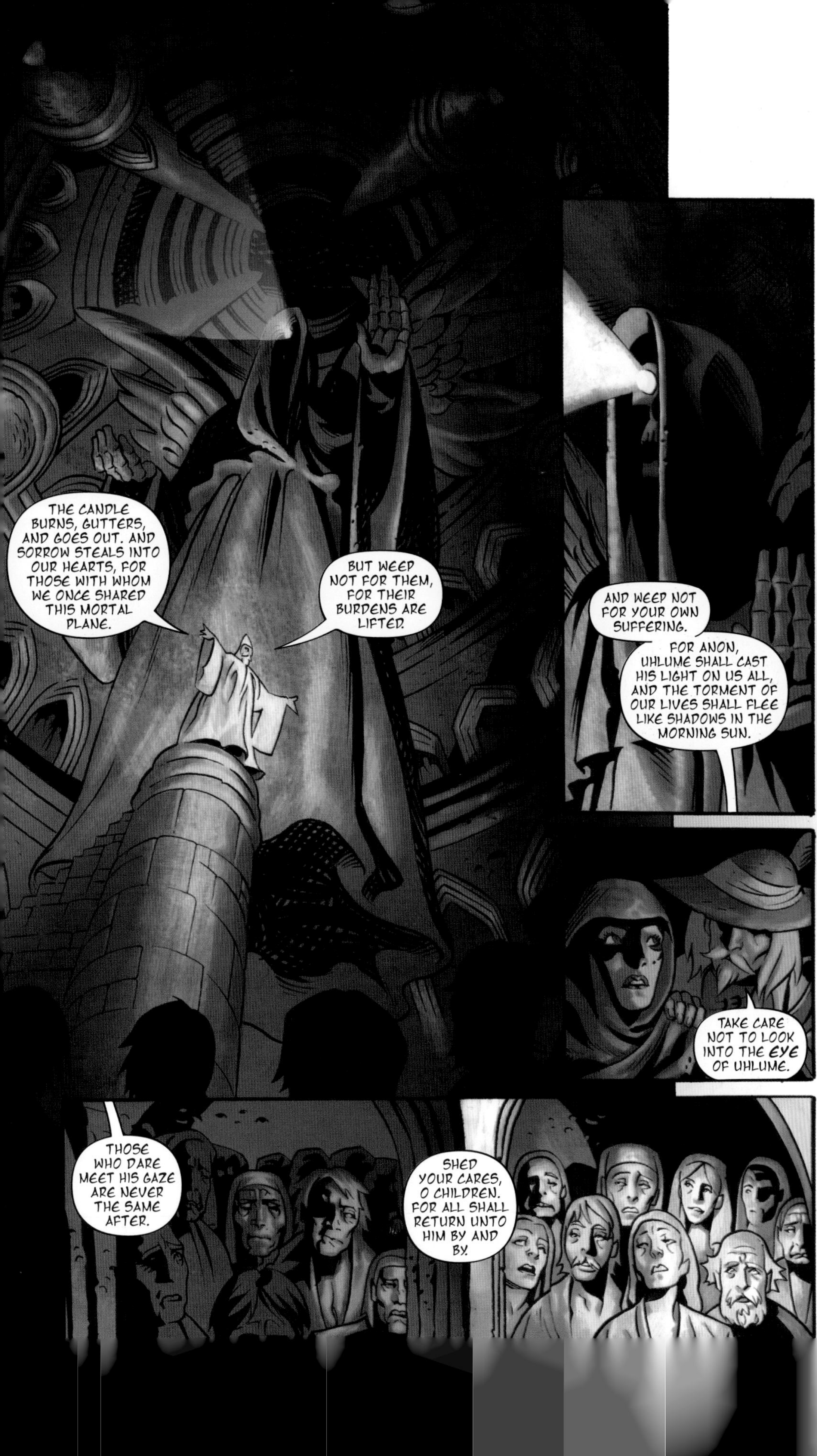
THE CANDLE BURNS, GUTTERS, AND GOES OUT. AND SORROW STEALS INTO OUR HEARTS, FOR THOSE WITH WHOM WE ONCE SHARED THIS MORTAL PLANE.
BUT WEEP NOT FOR THEM, FOR THEIR BURDENS ARE LIFTED.
AND WEEP NOT FOR YOUR OWN SUFFERING.
FOR ANON, UHLUME SHALL CAST HIS LIGHT ON US ALL, AND THE TORMENT OF OUR LIVES SHALL FLEE LIKE SHADOWS IN THE MORNING SUN.
TAKE CARE NOT TO LOOK INTO THE *EYE* OF UHLUME.
THOSE WHO DARE MEET HIS GAZE ARE NEVER THE SAME AFTER.
SHED YOUR CARES, O CHILDREN. FOR ALL SHALL RETURN UNTO HIM BY AND BY.

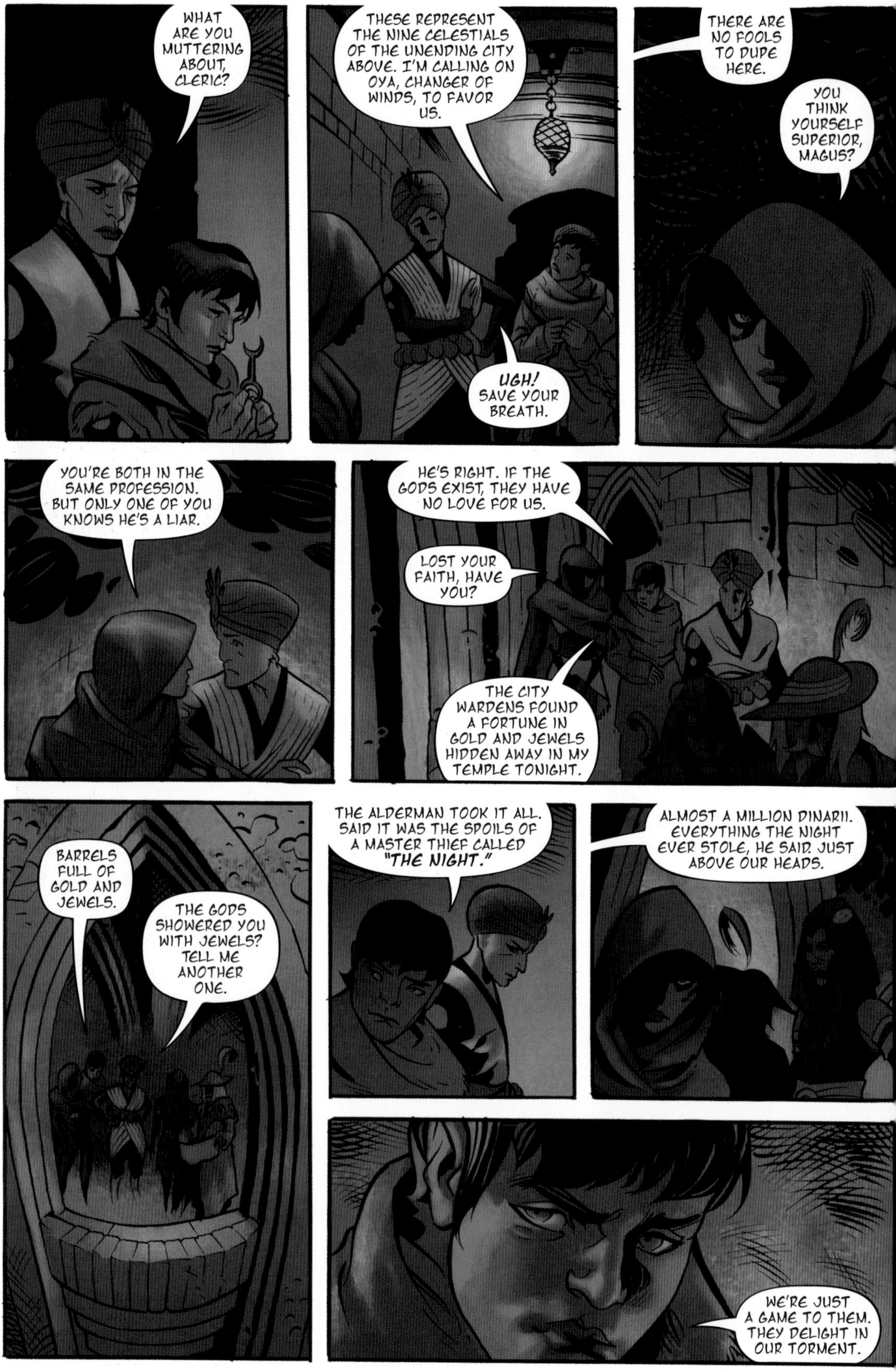
WHAT ARE YOU MUTTERING ABOUT, CLERIC?
THESE REPRESENT THE NINE CELESTIALS OF THE UNENDING CITY ABOVE. I'M CALLING ON OYA, CHANGER OF WINDS, TO FAVOR US.
UGH! SAVE YOUR BREATH.
THERE ARE NO FOOLS TO DUPE HERE.
YOU THINK YOURSELF SUPERIOR, MAGUS?
YOU'RE BOTH IN THE SAME PROFESSION. BUT ONLY ONE OF YOU KNOWS HE'S A LIAR.
HE'S RIGHT. IF THE GODS EXIST, THEY HAVE NO LOVE FOR US.
LOST YOUR FAITH, HAVE YOU?
THE CITY WARDENS FOUND A FORTUNE IN GOLD AND JEWELS HIDDEN AWAY IN MY TEMPLE TONIGHT.
BARRELS FULL OF GOLD AND JEWELS.
THE GODS SHOWERED YOU WITH JEWELS? TELL ME ANOTHER ONE.
THE ALDERMAN TOOK IT ALL. SAID IT WAS THE SPOILS OF A MASTER THIEF CALLED "THE NIGHT."
ALMOST A MILLION DINARII. EVERYTHING THE NIGHT EVER STOLE, HE SAID. JUST ABOVE OUR HEADS.
WE'RE JUST A GAME TO THEM. THEY DELIGHT IN OUR TORMENT.

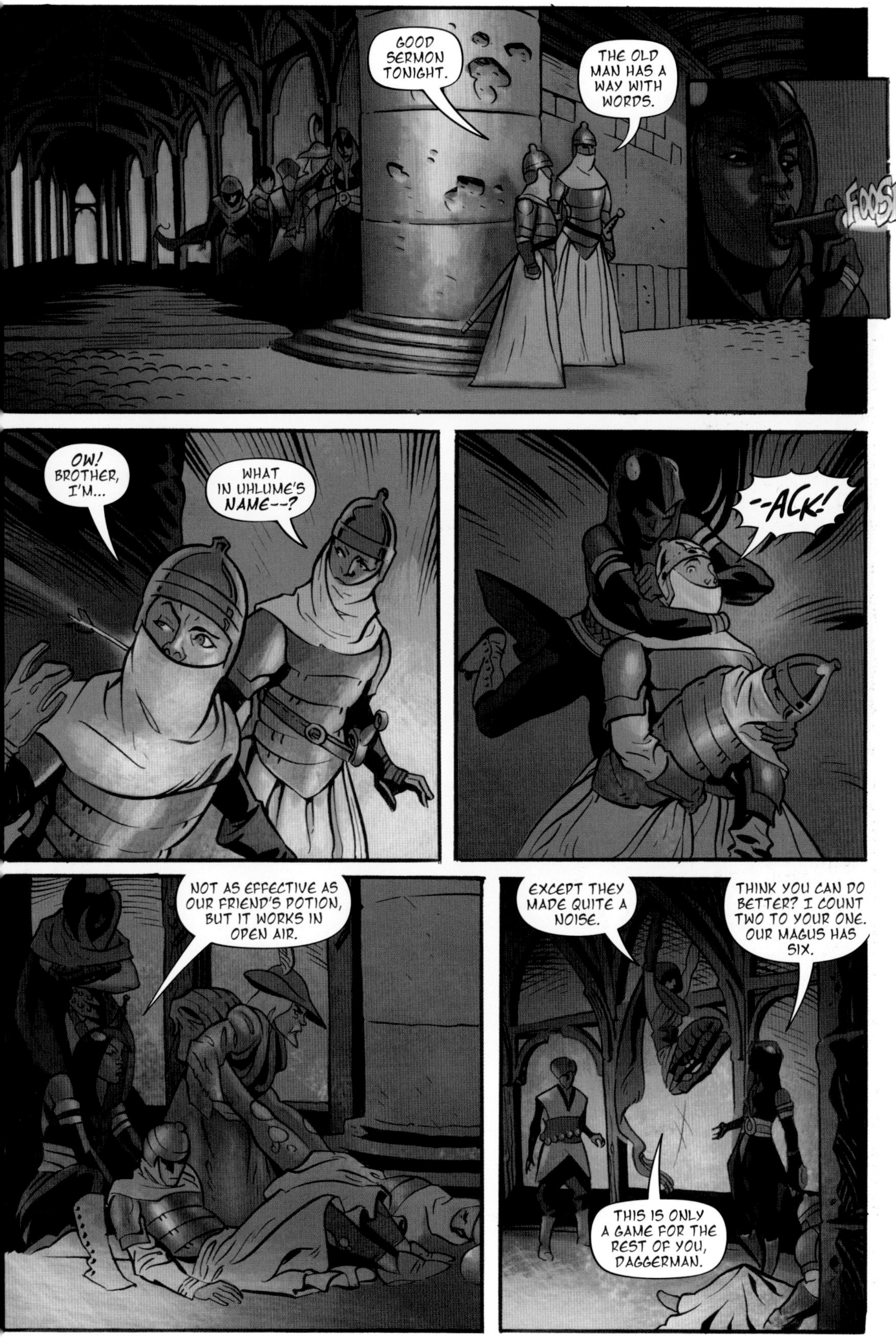
GOOD SERMON TONIGHT.
THE OLD MAN HAS A WAY WITH WORDS.
FOOSH
OW! BROTHER, I'M...
WHAT IN UHLUME'S NAME--?
--ACK!
NOT AS EFFECTIVE AS OUR FRIEND'S POTION, BUT IT WORKS IN OPEN AIR.
EXCEPT THEY MADE QUITE A NOISE.
THINK YOU CAN DO BETTER? I COUNT TWO TO YOUR ONE. OUR MAGUS HAS SIX.
THIS IS ONLY A GAME FOR THE REST OF YOU, DAGGERMAN.

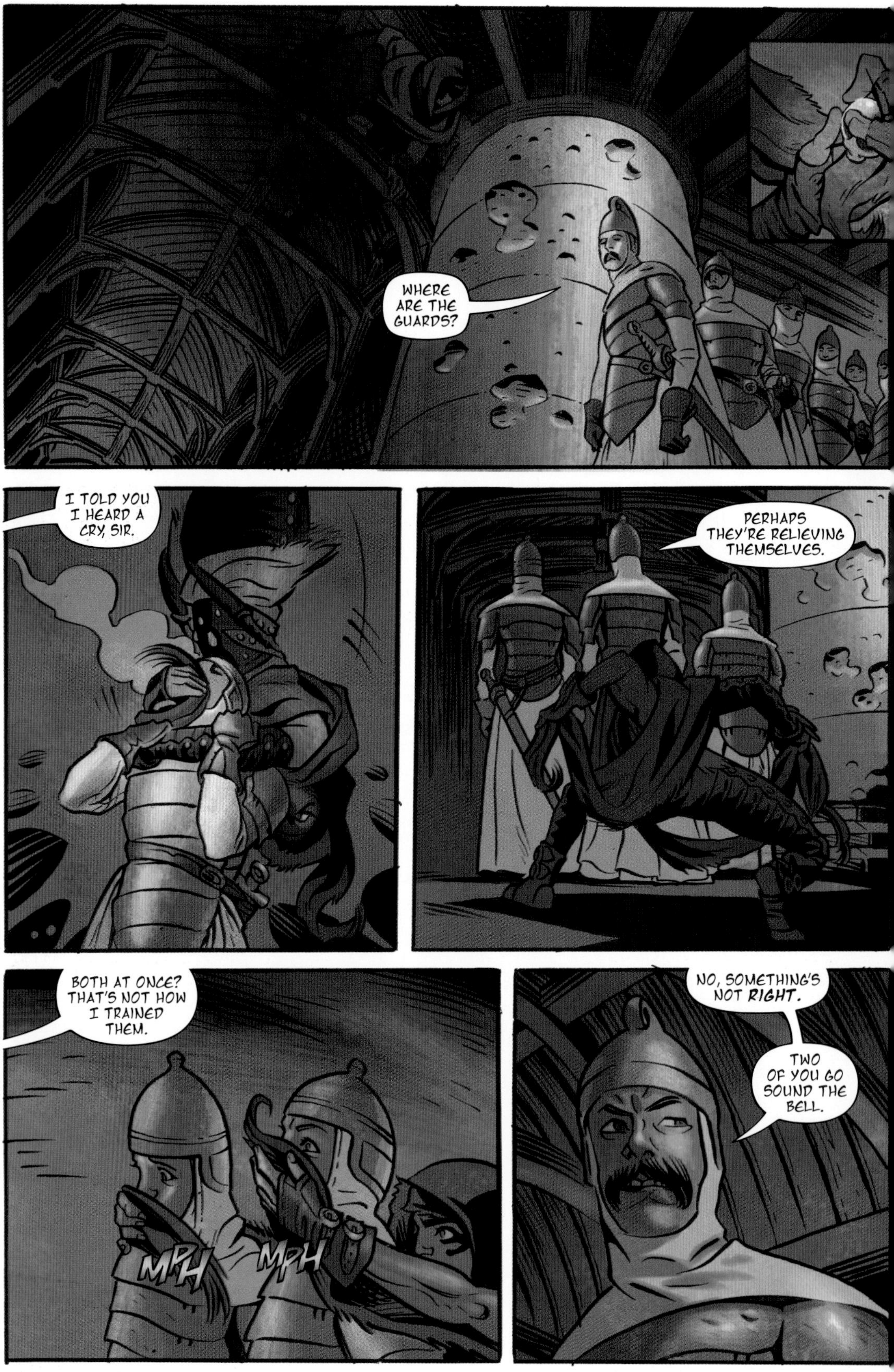

WHERE ARE THE GUARDS?
I TOLD YOU I HEARD A CRY, SIR.
PERHAPS THEY'RE RELIEVING THEMSELVES.
BOTH AT ONCE? THAT'S NOT HOW I TRAINED THEM.
MPH
MPH
NO, SOMETHING'S NOT RIGHT.
TWO OF YOU GO SOUND THE BELL.

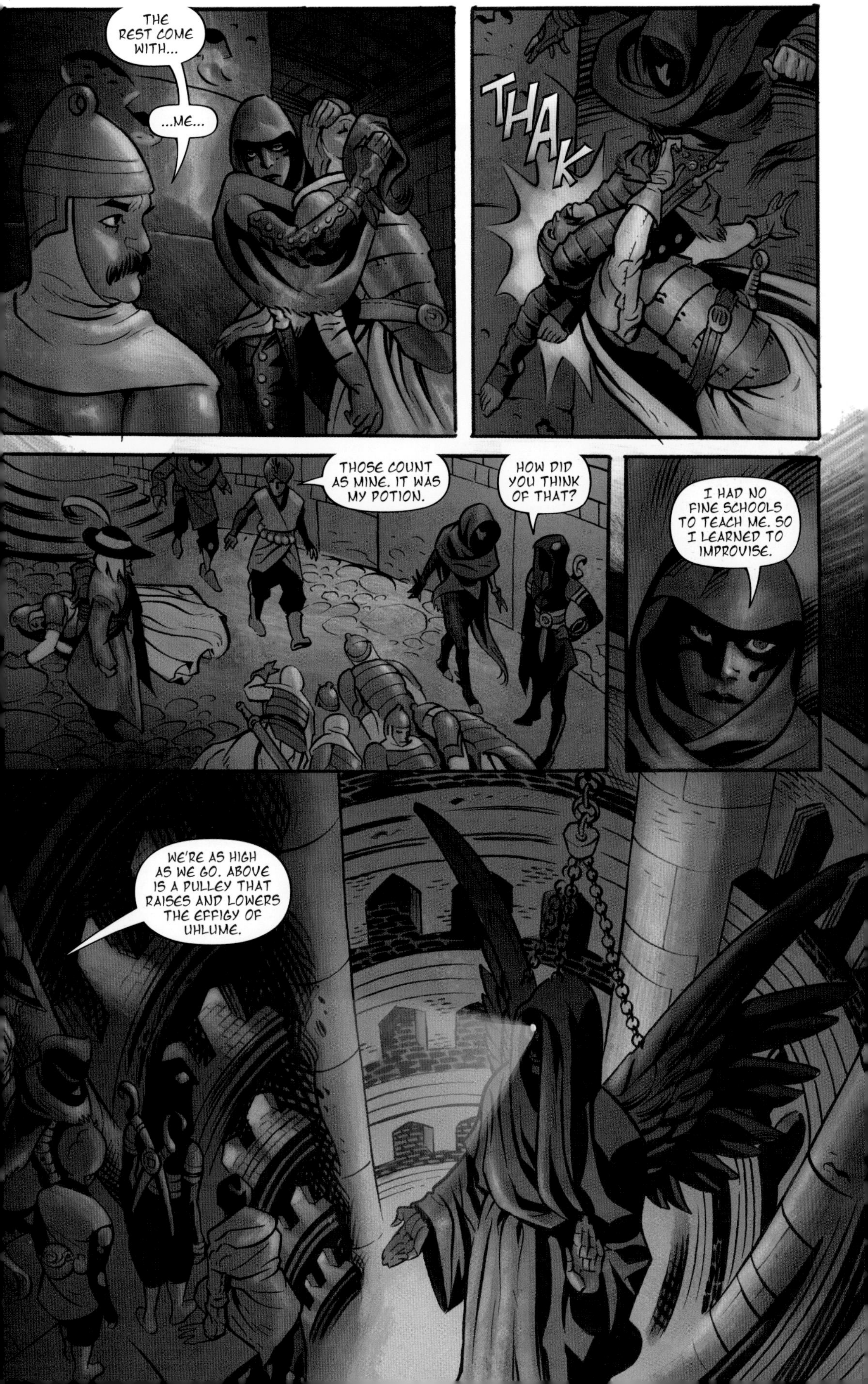
THE REST COME WITH...
...ME...
THAK
THOSE COUNT AS MINE. IT WAS MY POTION.
HOW DID YOU THINK OF THAT?
I HAD NO FINE SCHOOLS TO TEACH ME. SO I LEARNED TO IMPROVISE.
WE'RE AS HIGH AS WE GO. ABOVE IS A PULLEY THAT RAISES AND LOWERS THE EFFIGY OF UHLUME.

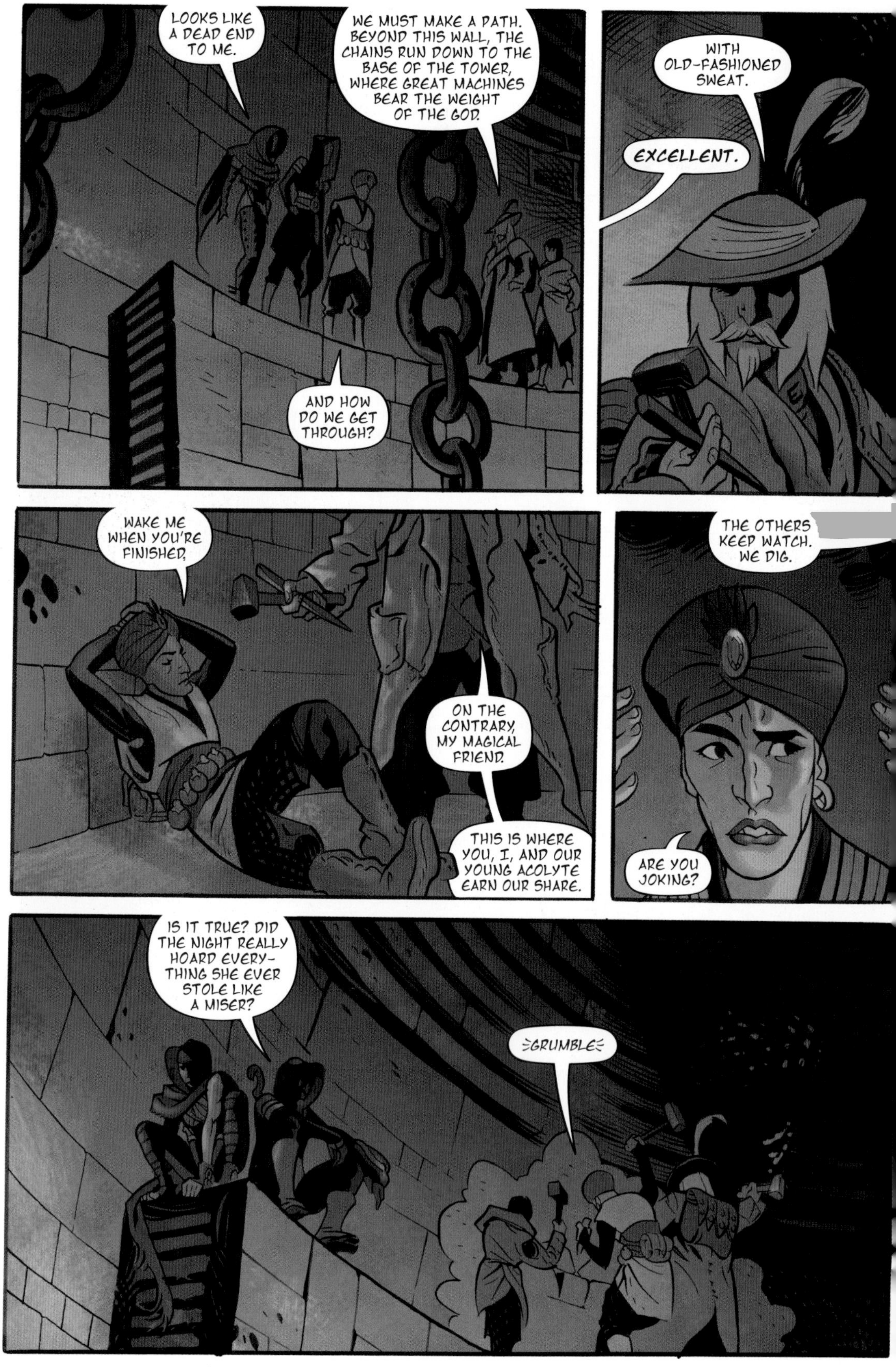
LOOKS LIKE A DEAD END TO ME.
WE MUST MAKE A PATH. BEYOND THIS WALL, THE CHAINS RUN DOWN TO THE BASE OF THE TOWER, WHERE GREAT MACHINES BEAR THE WEIGHT OF THE GOD.
AND HOW DO WE GET THROUGH?
WITH OLD-FASHIONED SWEAT.
EXCELLENT.
WAKE ME WHEN YOU'RE FINISHED.
ON THE CONTRARY, MY MAGICAL FRIEND.
THIS IS WHERE YOU, I, AND OUR YOUNG ACOLYTE EARN OUR SHARE.
THE OTHERS KEEP WATCH. WE DIG.
ARE YOU JOKING?
IS IT TRUE? DID THE NIGHT REALLY HOARD EVERY-THING SHE EVER STOLE LIKE A MISER?
GRUMBLE

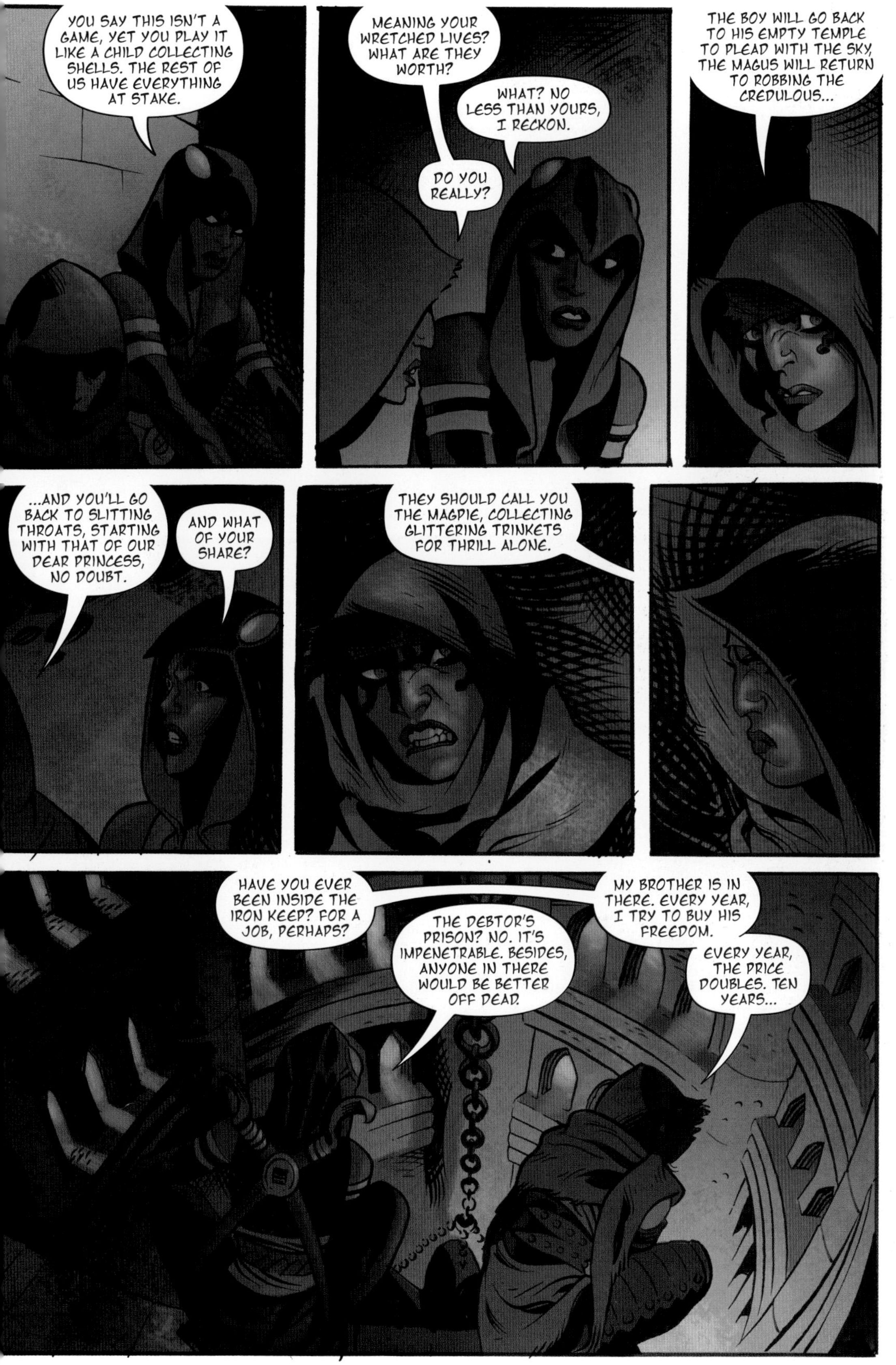
YOU SAY THIS ISN'T A GAME, YET YOU PLAY IT LIKE A CHILD COLLECTING SHELLS. THE REST OF US HAVE EVERYTHING AT STAKE.
MEANING YOUR WRETCHED LIVES? WHAT ARE THEY WORTH?
WHAT? NO LESS THAN YOURS, I RECKON.
DO YOU REALLY?
THE BOY WILL GO BACK TO HIS EMPTY TEMPLE TO PLEAD WITH THE SKY, THE MAGUS WILL RETURN TO ROBBING THE CREDULOUS...
...AND YOU'LL GO BACK TO SLITTING THROATS, STARTING WITH THAT OF OUR DEAR PRINCESS, NO DOUBT.
AND WHAT OF YOUR SHARE?
THEY SHOULD CALL YOU THE MAGPIE, COLLECTING GLITTERING TRINKETS FOR THRILL ALONE.
HAVE YOU EVER BEEN INSIDE THE IRON KEEP? FOR A JOB, PERHAPS?
THE DEBTOR'S PRISON? NO. IT'S IMPENETRABLE. BESIDES, ANYONE IN THERE WOULD BE BETTER OFF DEAD.
MY BROTHER IS IN THERE. EVERY YEAR, I TRY TO BUY HIS FREEDOM.
EVERY YEAR, THE PRICE DOUBLES. TEN YEARS...

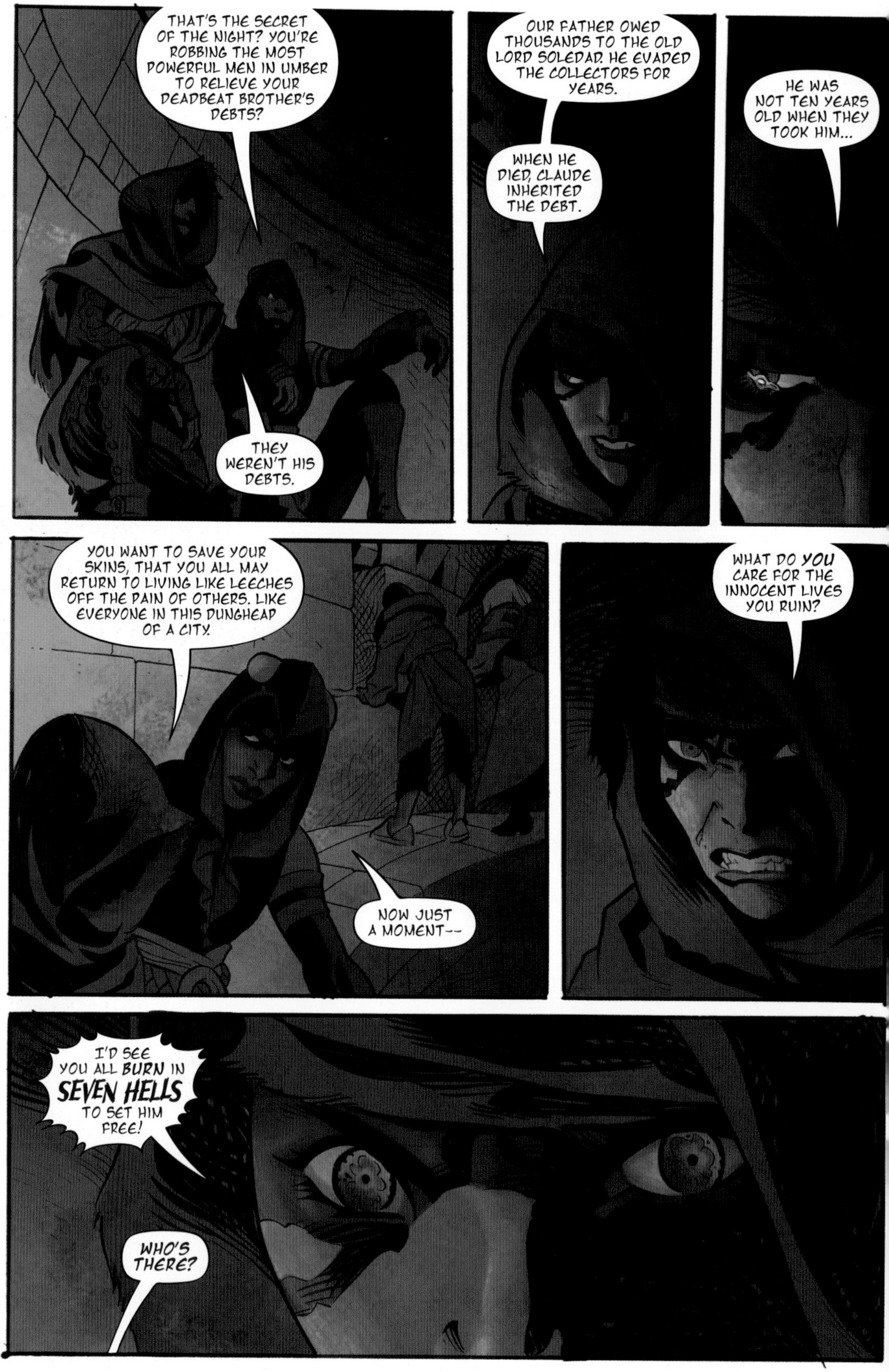
THAT'S THE SECRET OF THE NIGHT? YOU'RE ROBBING THE MOST POWERFUL MEN IN UMBER TO RELIEVE YOUR DEADBEAT BROTHER'S DEBTS?
THEY WEREN'T HIS DEBTS.
OUR FATHER OWED THOUSANDS TO THE OLD LORD SOLEDAD. HE EVADED THE COLLECTORS FOR YEARS.
WHEN HE DIED, CLAUDE INHERITED THE DEBT.
HE WAS NOT TEN YEARS OLD WHEN THEY TOOK HIM...
YOU WANT TO SAVE YOUR SKINS, THAT YOU ALL MAY RETURN TO LIVING LIKE LEECHES OFF THE PAIN OF OTHERS. LIKE EVERYONE IN THIS DUNGHEAP OF A CITY.
NOW JUST A MOMENT--
WHAT DO YOU CARE FOR THE INNOCENT LIVES YOU RUIN?
I'D SEE YOU ALL BURN IN SEVEN HELLS TO SET HIM FREE!
WHO'S THERE?

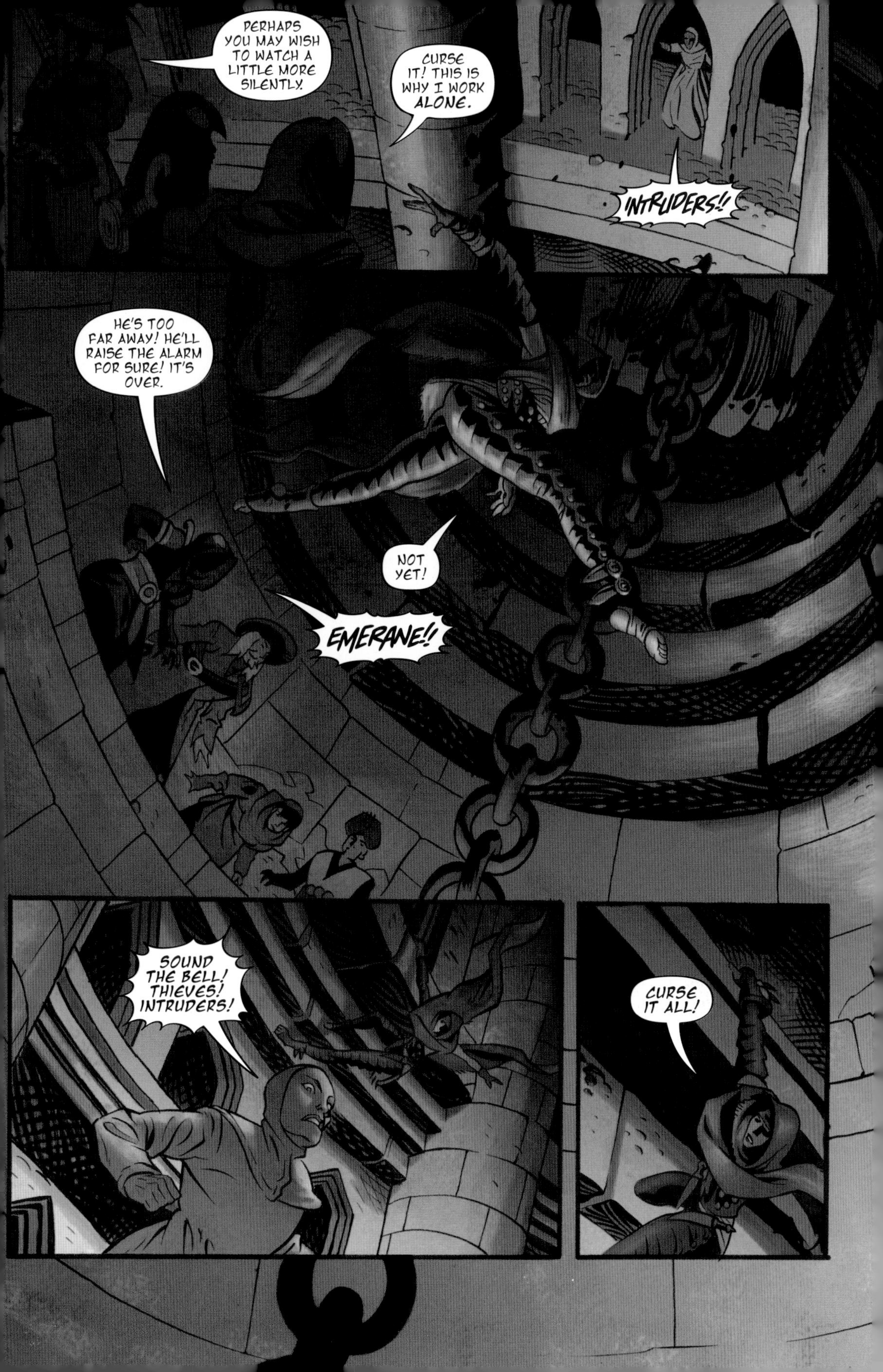
PERHAPS YOU MAY WISH TO WATCH A LITTLE MORE SILENTLY.
CURSE IT! THIS IS WHY I WORK ALONE.
INTRUDERS!!
HE'S TOO FAR AWAY! HE'LL RAISE THE ALARM FOR SURE! IT'S OVER.
NOT YET!
EMERANE!!
SOUND THE BELL! THIEVES! INTRUDERS!
CURSE IT ALL!

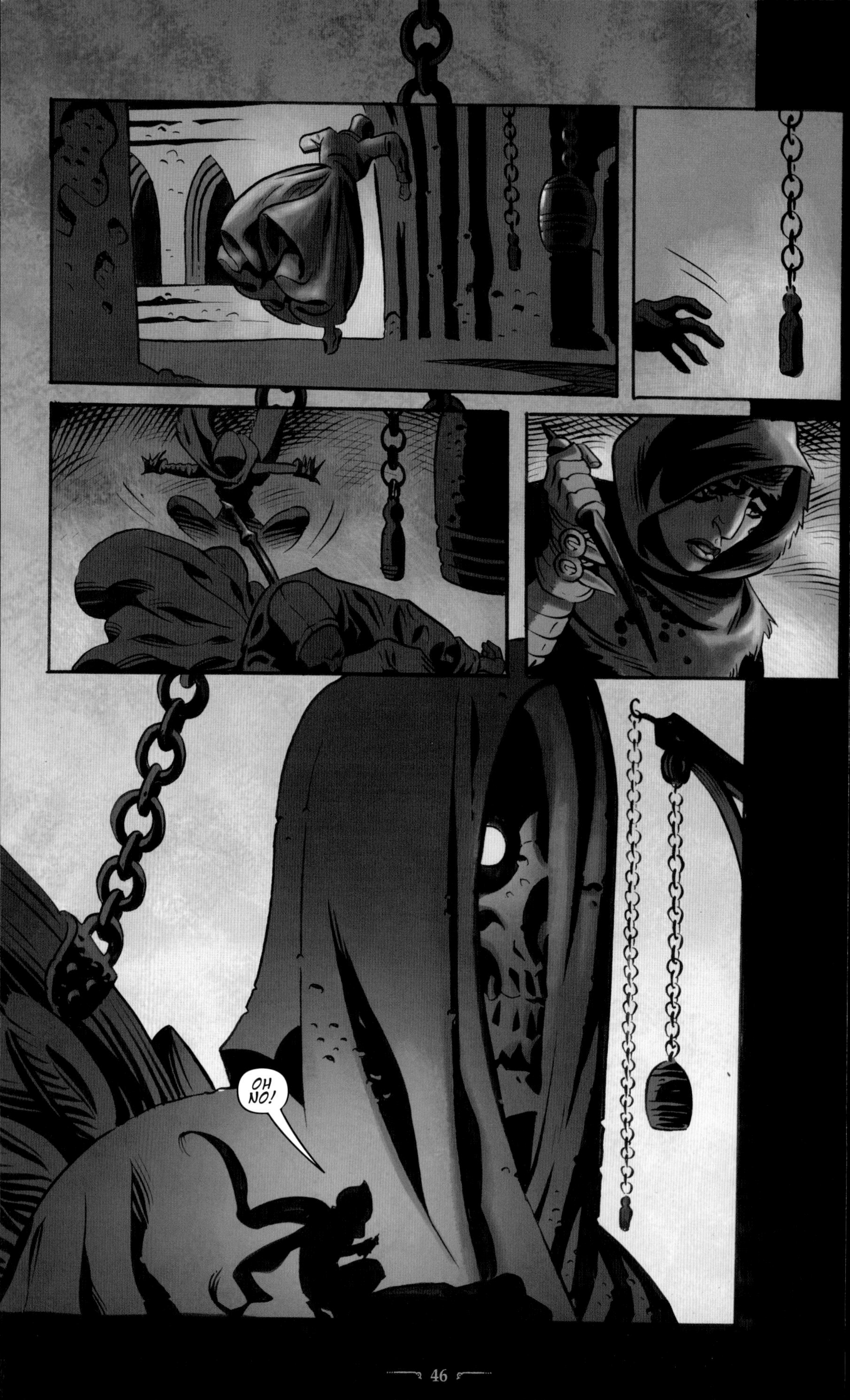
OH NO!

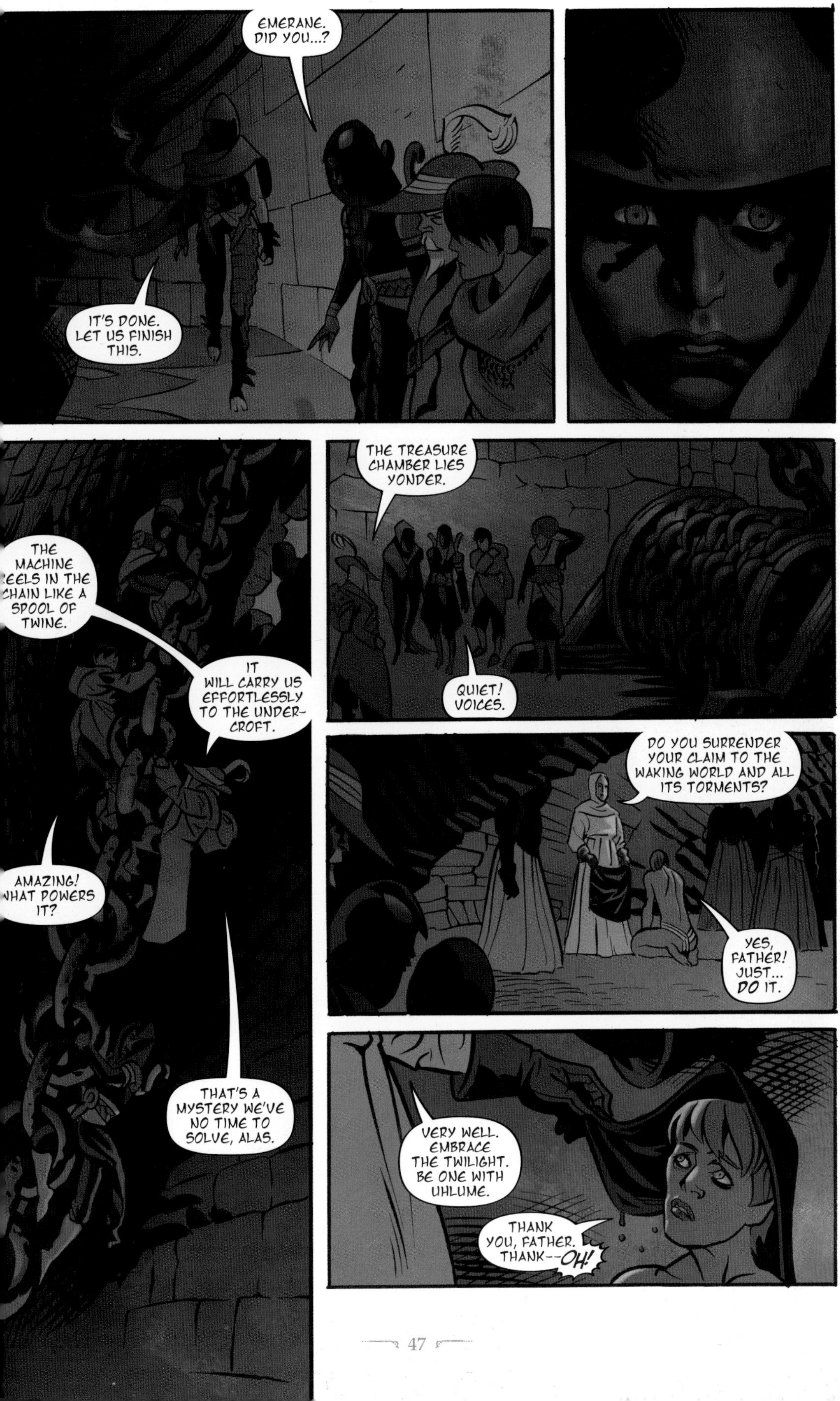

EMERANE. DID YOU...?
IT'S DONE. LET US FINISH THIS.
THE MACHINE REELS IN THE CHAIN LIKE A SPOOL OF TWINE.
IT WILL CARRY US EFFORTLESSLY TO THE UNDERCROFT.
AMAZING! WHAT POWERS IT?
THAT'S A MYSTERY WE'VE NO TIME TO SOLVE, ALAS.
THE TREASURE CHAMBER LIES YONDER.
QUIET! VOICES.
DO YOU SURRENDER YOUR CLAIM TO THE WAKING WORLD AND ALL ITS TORMENTS?
YES, FATHER! JUST... DO IT.
VERY WELL. EMBRACE THE TWILIGHT. BE ONE WITH UHLUME.
THANK YOU, FATHER. THANK--OH!

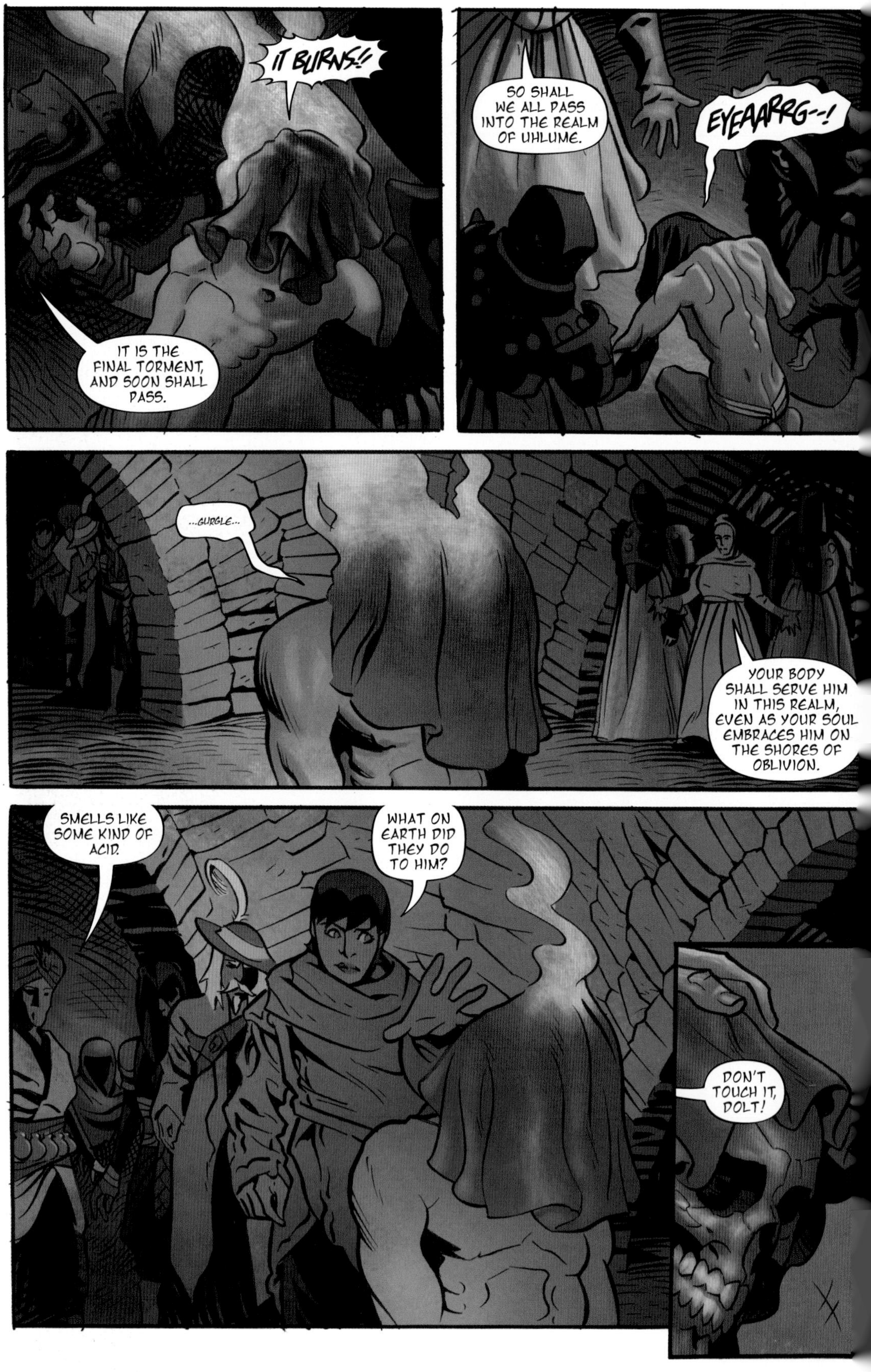
IT BURNS!!
IT IS THE FINAL TORMENT, AND SOON SHALL PASS.
SO SHALL WE ALL PASS INTO THE REALM OF UHLUME.
EYEAARRG--!
...GURGLE...
YOUR BODY SHALL SERVE HIM IN THIS REALM, EVEN AS YOUR SOUL EMBRACES HIM ON THE SHORES OF OBLIVION.
SMELLS LIKE SOME KIND OF ACID.
WHAT ON EARTH DID THEY DO TO HIM?
DON'T TOUCH IT, DOLT!

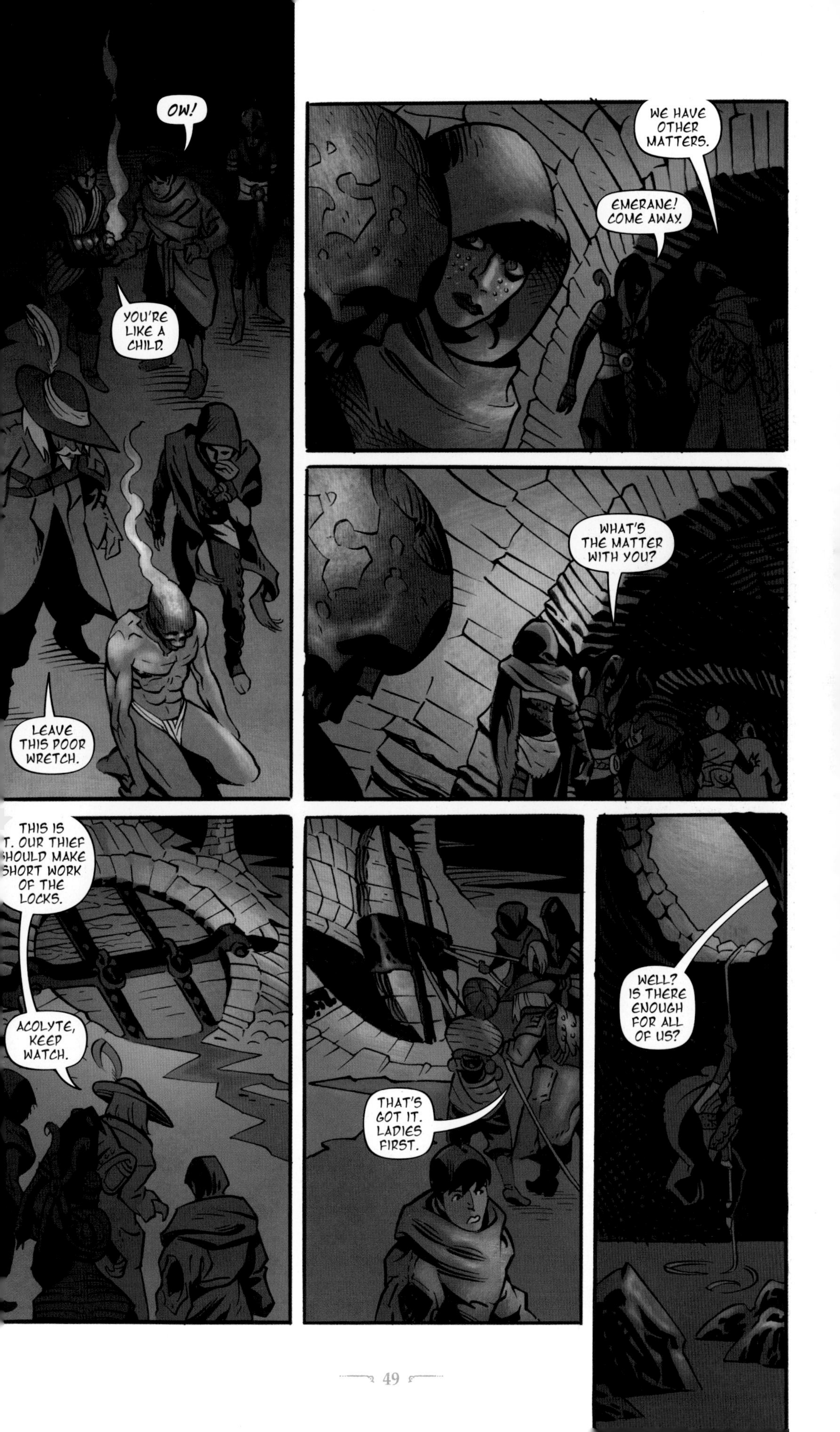

OW!
YOU'RE LIKE A CHILD.
LEAVE THIS POOR WRETCH.
WE HAVE OTHER MATTERS.
EMERANE! COME AWAY.
WHAT'S THE MATTER WITH YOU?
THIS IS IT. OUR THIEF SHOULD MAKE SHORT WORK OF THE LOCKS.
ACOLYTE, KEEP WATCH.
THAT'S GOT IT. LADIES FIRST.
WELL? IS THERE ENOUGH FOR ALL OF US?

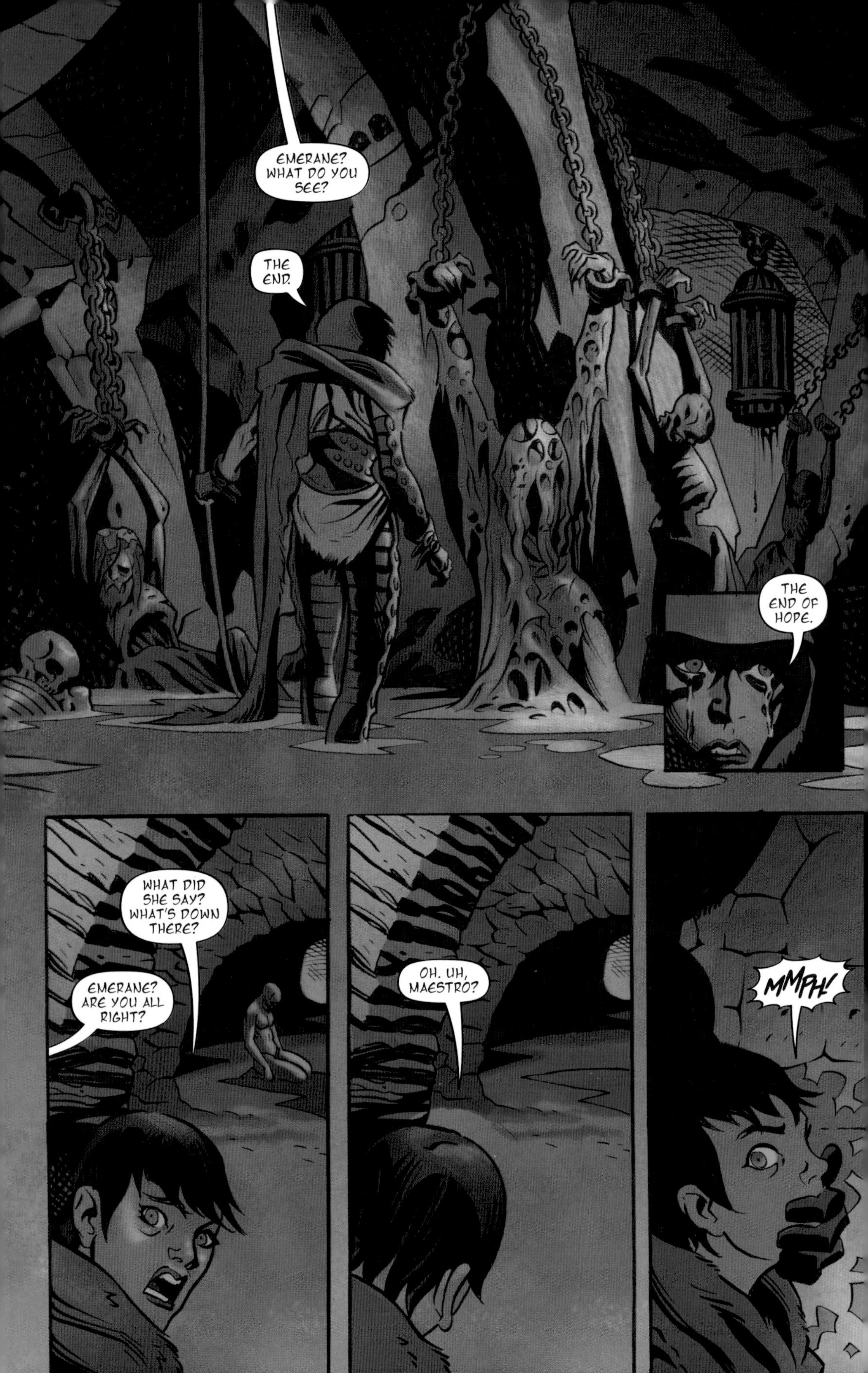
EMERANE? WHAT DO YOU SEE?
THE END.
THE END OF HOPE.
WHAT DID SHE SAY? WHAT'S DOWN THERE?
EMERANE? ARE YOU ALL RIGHT?
OH. UH, MAESTRO?
MMPH!

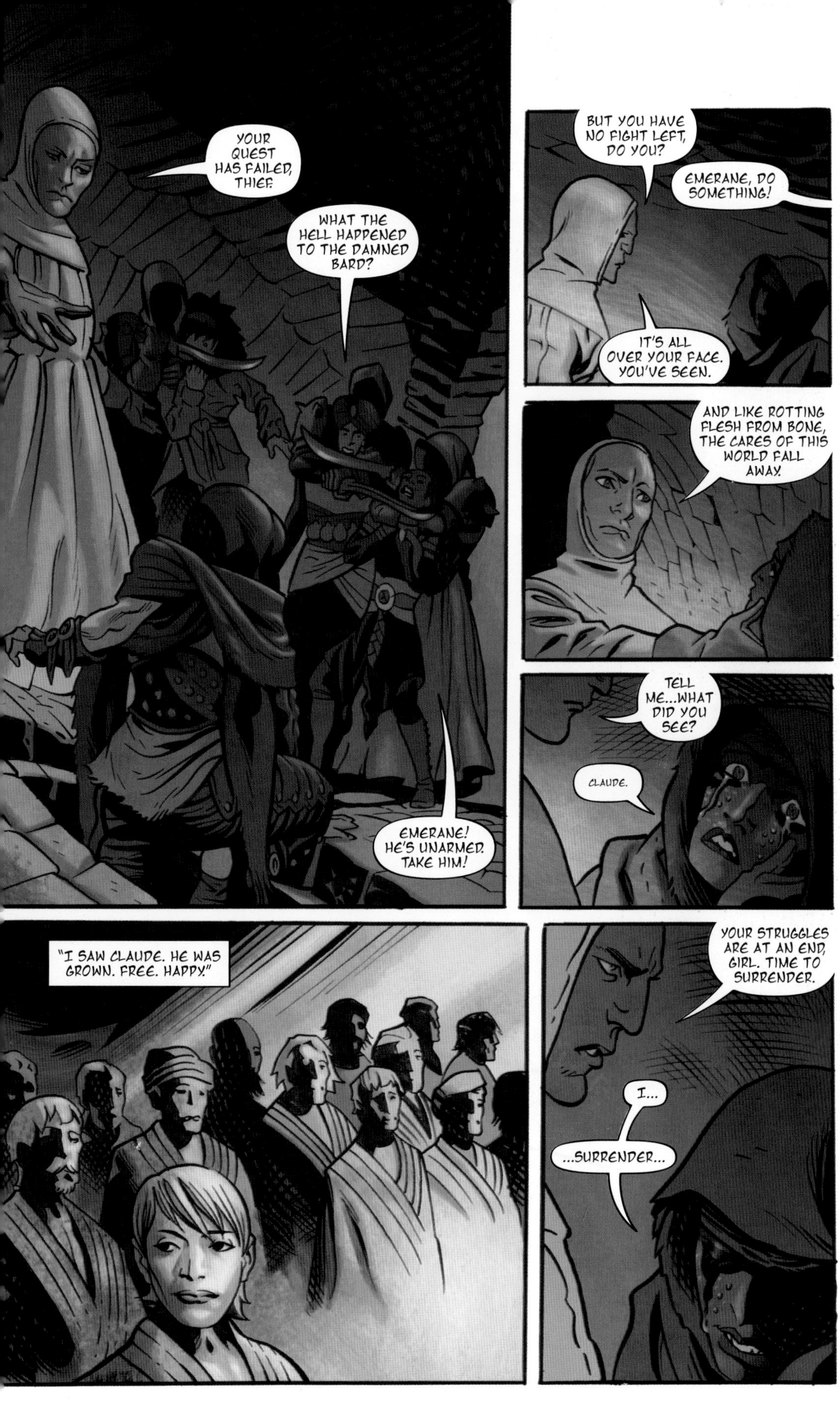
YOUR QUEST HAS FAILED, THIEF.
WHAT THE HELL HAPPENED TO THE DAMNED BARD?
EMERANE! HE'S UNARMED. TAKE HIM!
BUT YOU HAVE NO FIGHT LEFT, DO YOU?
EMERANE, DO SOMETHING!
IT'S ALL OVER YOUR FACE. YOU'VE SEEN.
AND LIKE ROTTING FLESH FROM BONE, THE CARES OF THIS WORLD FALL AWAY.
TELL ME...WHAT DID YOU SEE?
CLAUDE.
"I SAW CLAUDE. HE WAS GROWN. FREE. HAPPY."
YOUR STRUGGLES ARE AT AN END, GIRL. TIME TO SURRENDER.
I...
...SURRENDER...

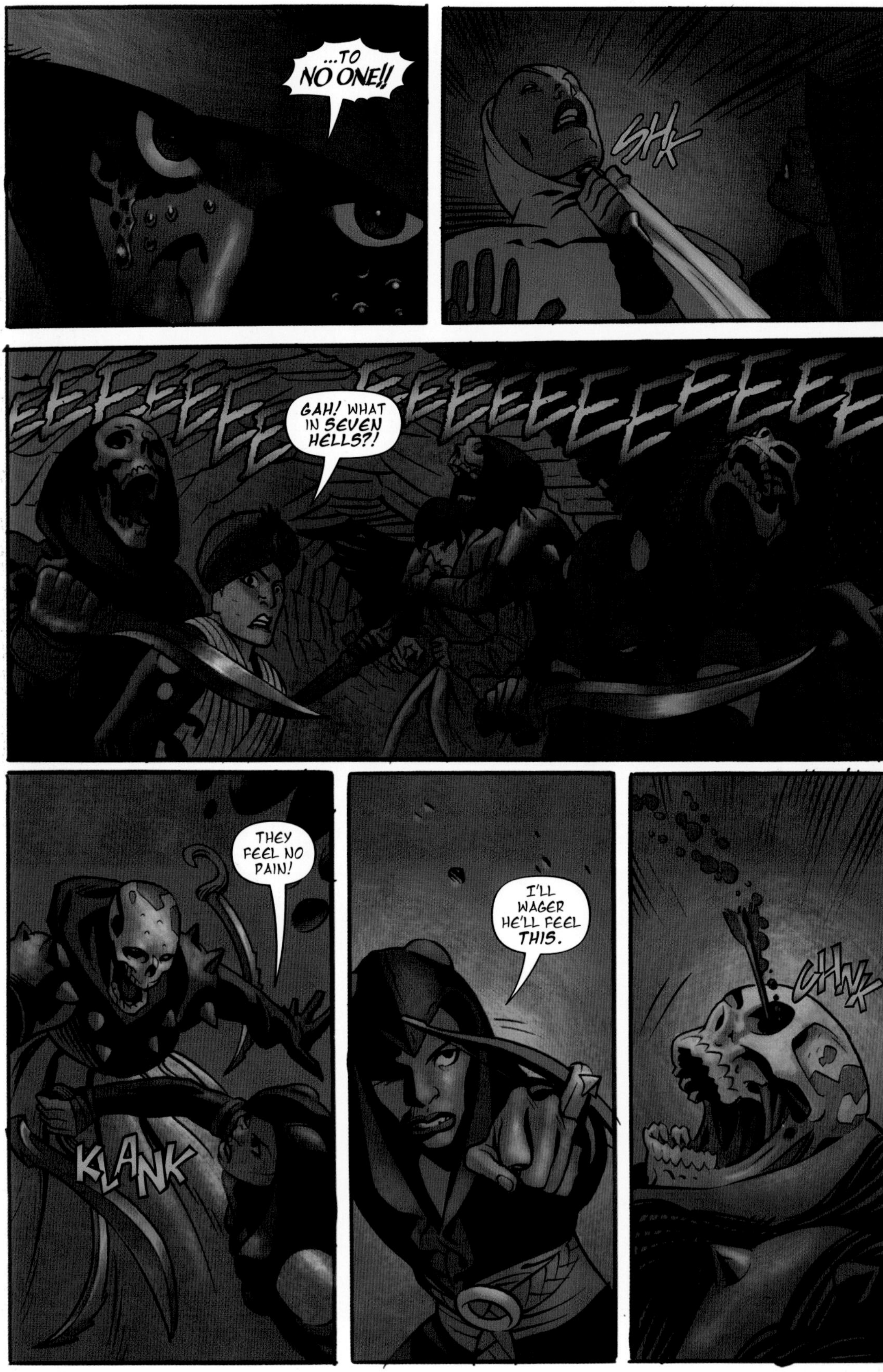
...TO NO ONE!!
SHK
EEEEEEEEEEEEEEEEEEEEE
GAH! WHAT IN SEVEN HELLS?!
THEY FEEL NO PAIN!
KLANK
I'LL WAGER HE'LL FEEL THIS.
CHNK

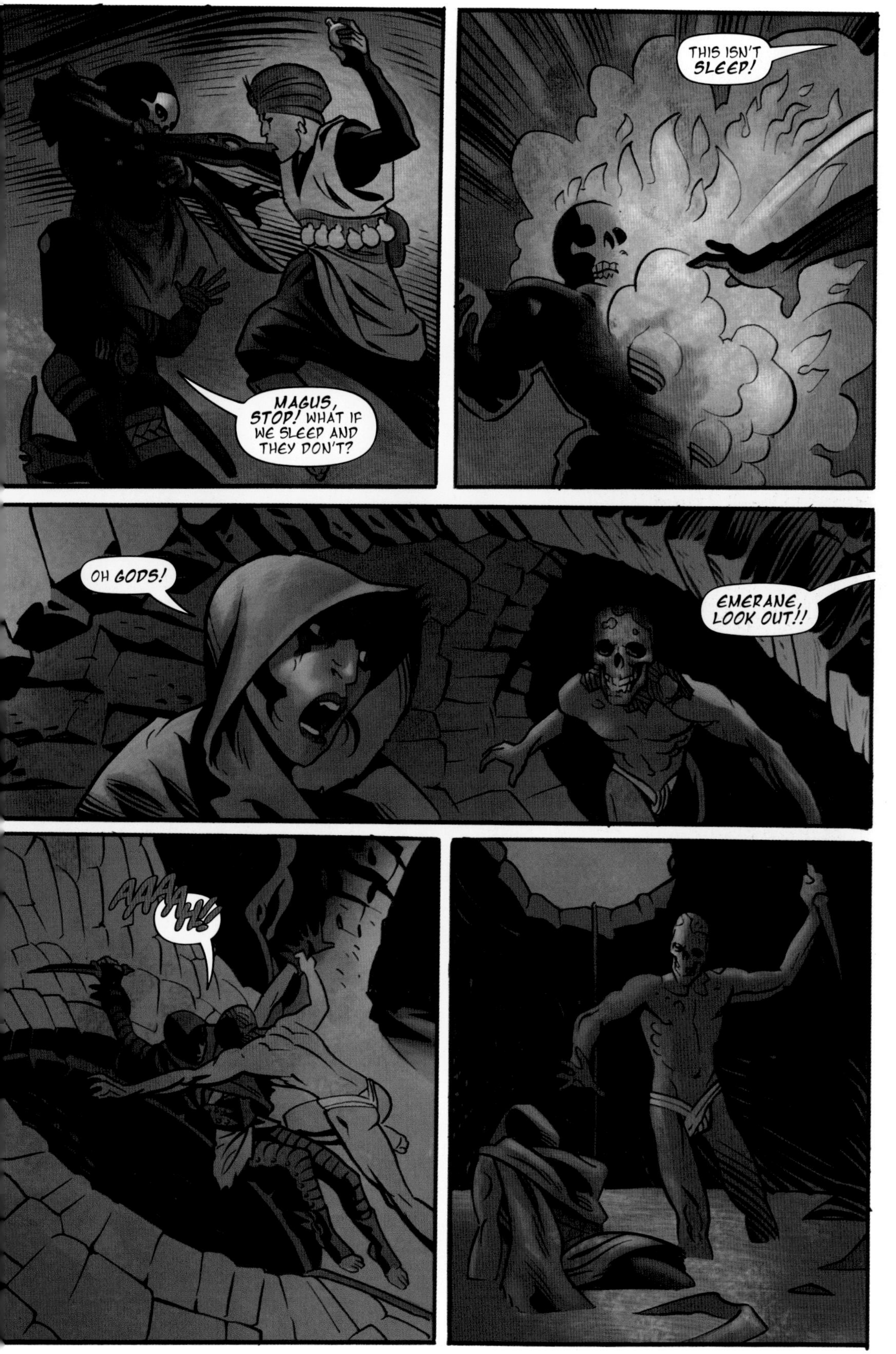
MAGUS, STOP! WHAT IF WE SLEEP AND THEY DON'T?
THIS ISN'T SLEEP!
OH GODS!
EMERANE, LOOK OUT!!
AAAAAHH!!

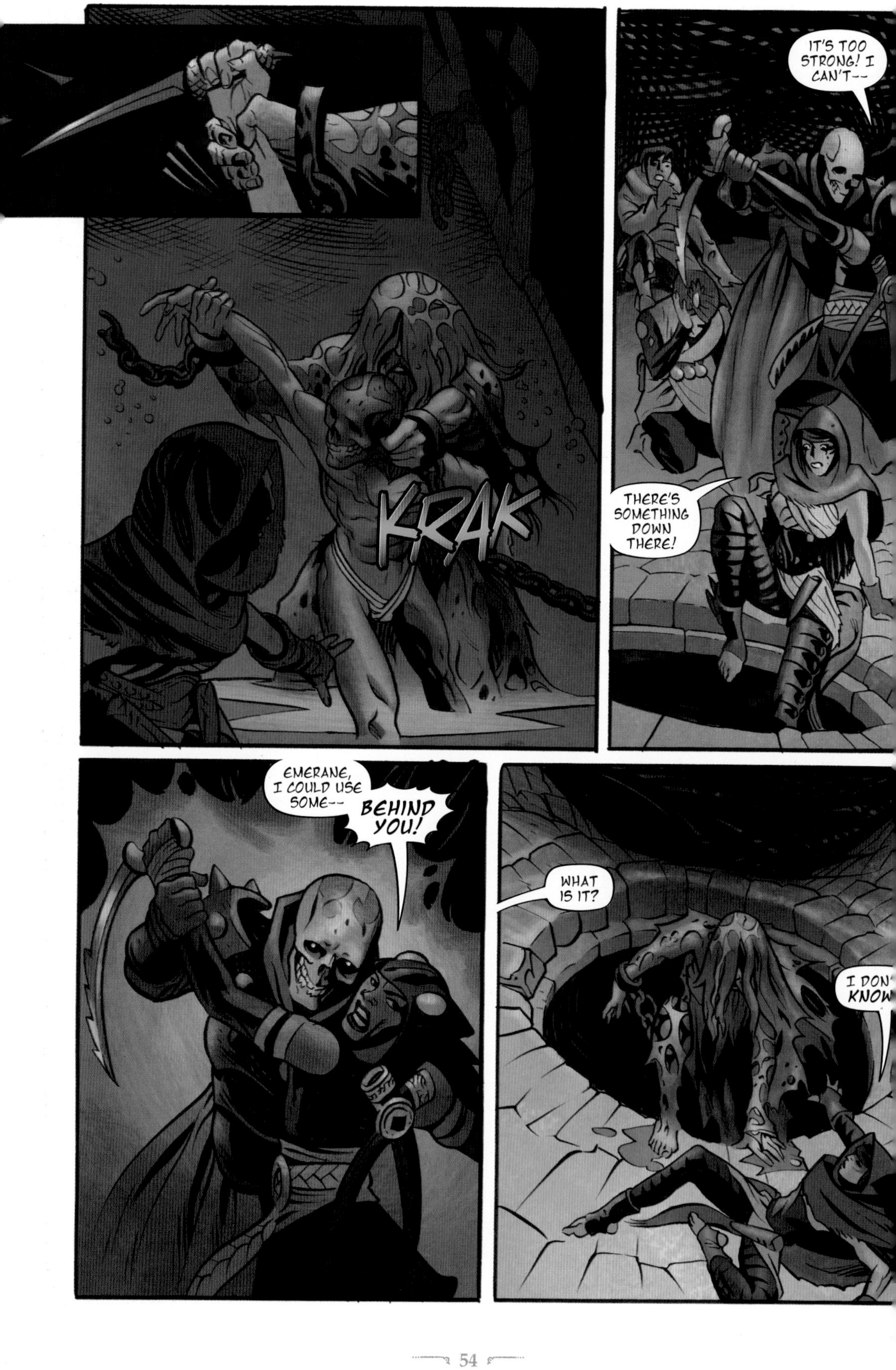
KRAK
IT'S TOO STRONG! I CAN'T--
THERE'S SOMETHING DOWN THERE!
EMERANE, I COULD USE SOME--
BEHIND YOU!
WHAT IS IT?
I DON'T KNOW

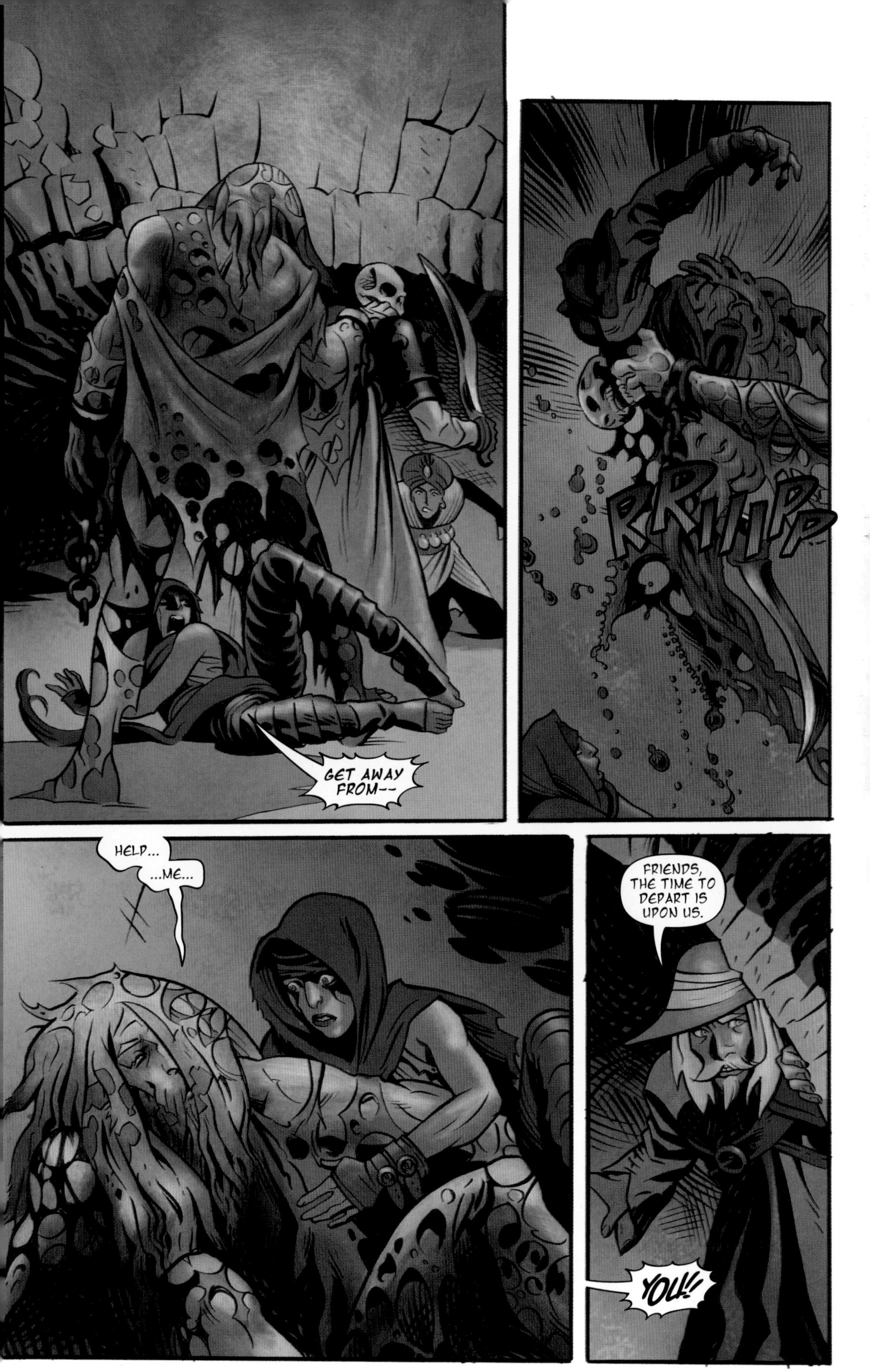
GET AWAY FROM--
RRIIPP
HELP...
...ME...
FRIENDS, THE TIME TO DEPART IS UPON US.
YOU!!

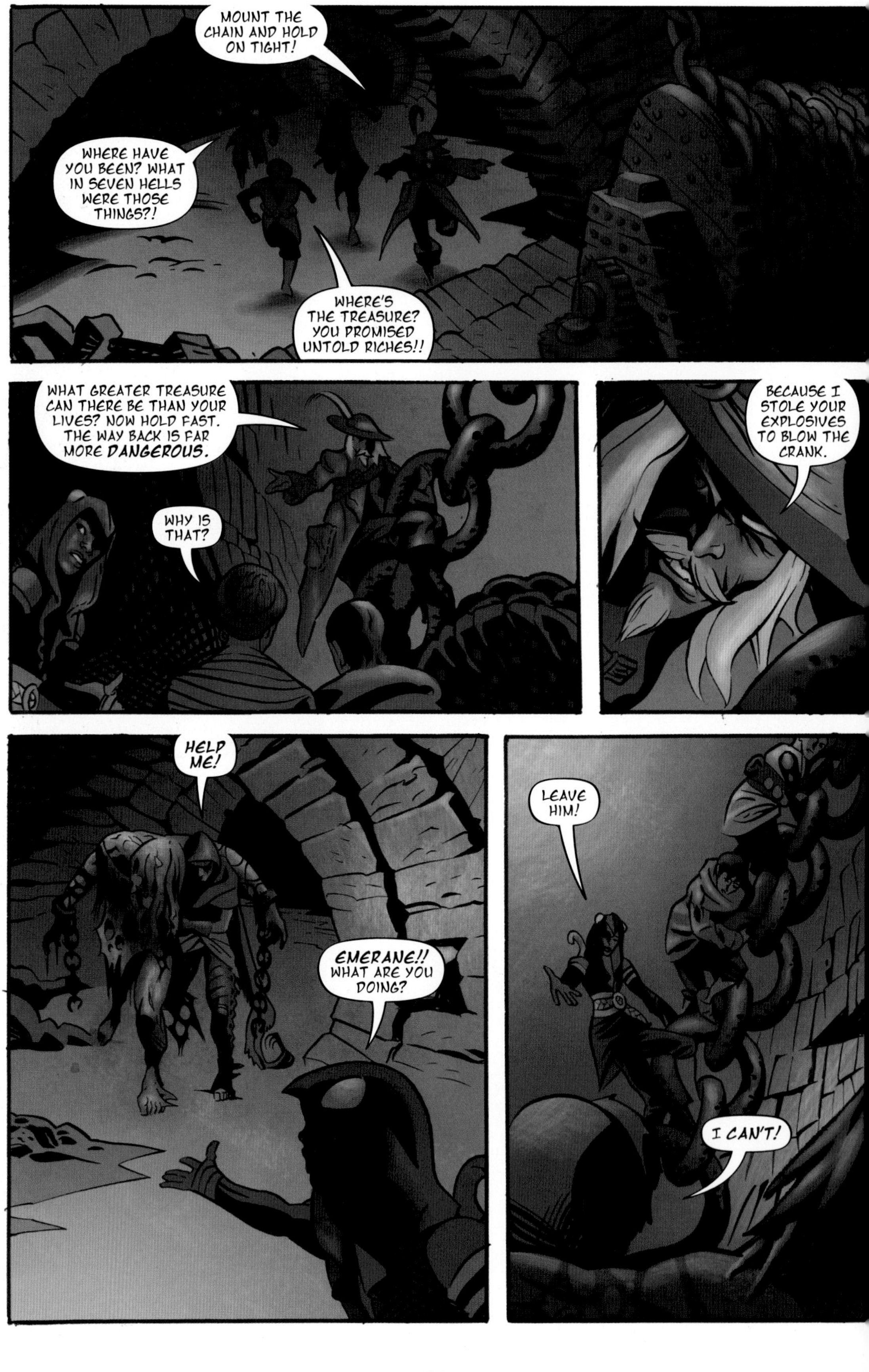
MOUNT THE CHAIN AND HOLD ON TIGHT!
WHERE HAVE YOU BEEN? WHAT IN SEVEN HELLS WERE THOSE THINGS?!
WHERE'S THE TREASURE? YOU PROMISED UNTOLD RICHES!!
WHAT GREATER TREASURE CAN THERE BE THAN YOUR LIVES? NOW HOLD FAST. THE WAY BACK IS FAR MORE DANGEROUS.
WHY IS THAT?
BECAUSE I STOLE YOUR EXPLOSIVES TO BLOW THE CRANK.
HELP ME!
EMERANE!! WHAT ARE YOU DOING?
LEAVE HIM!
I CAN'T!

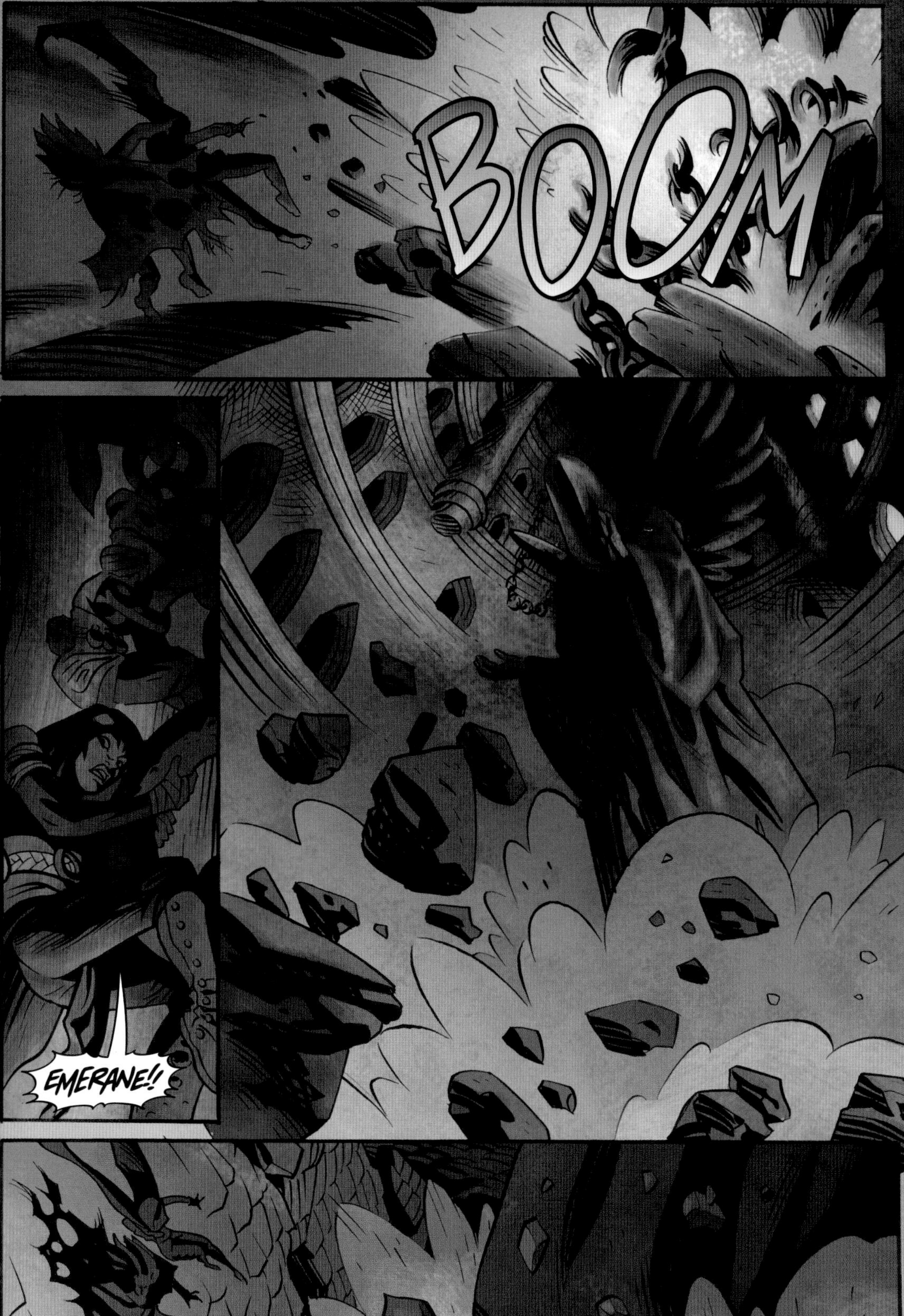
BOOM
EMERANE!!

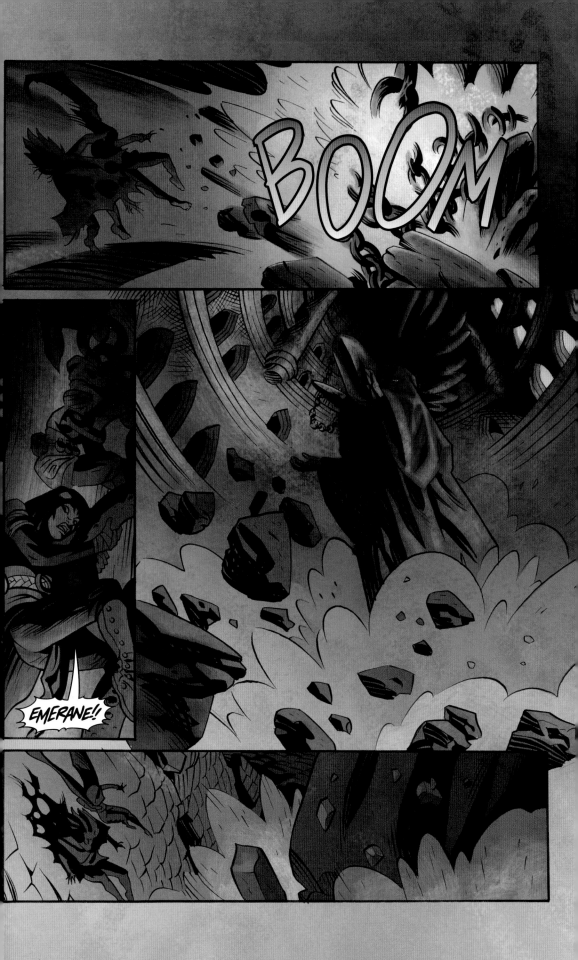

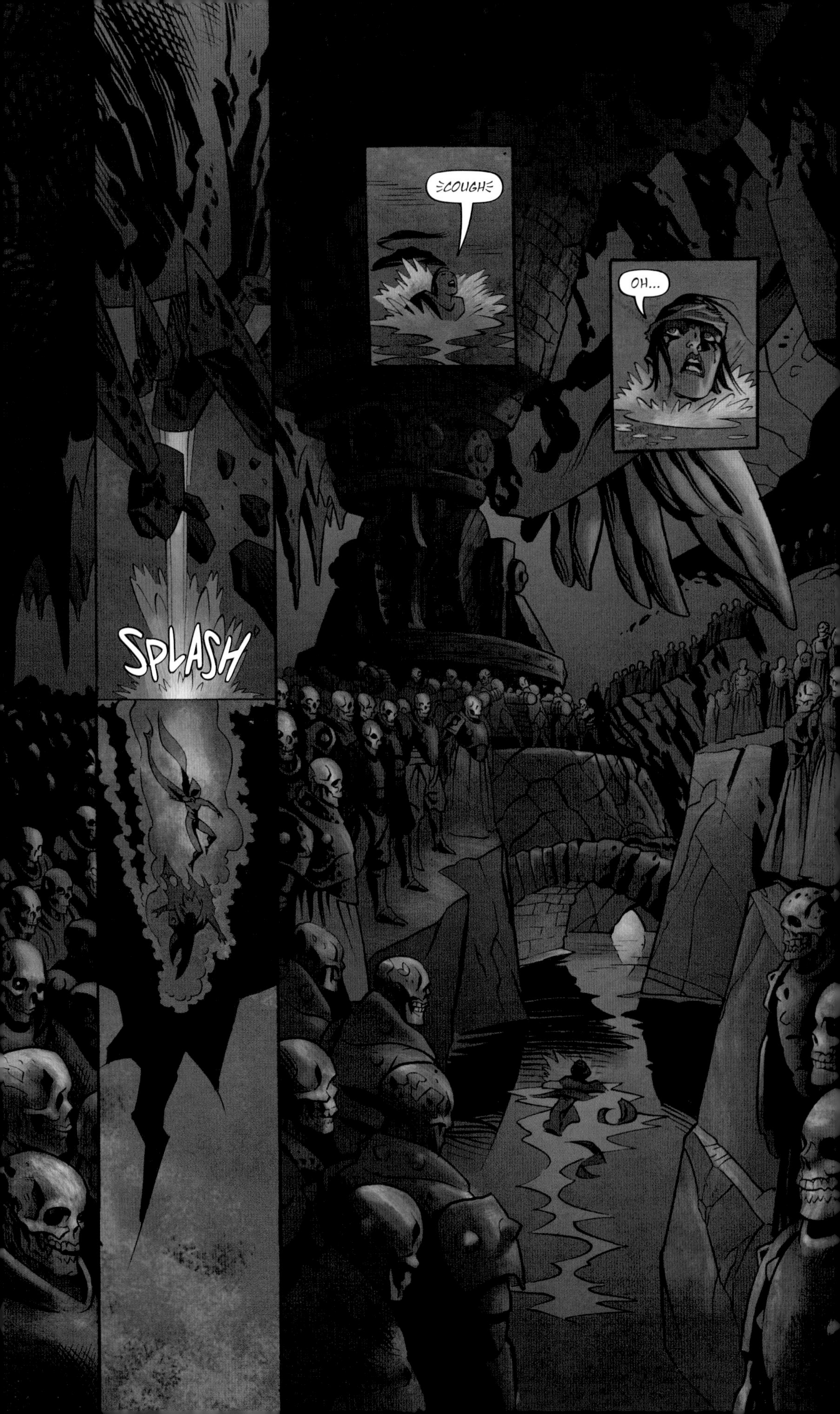
SPLASH
COUGH
OH...

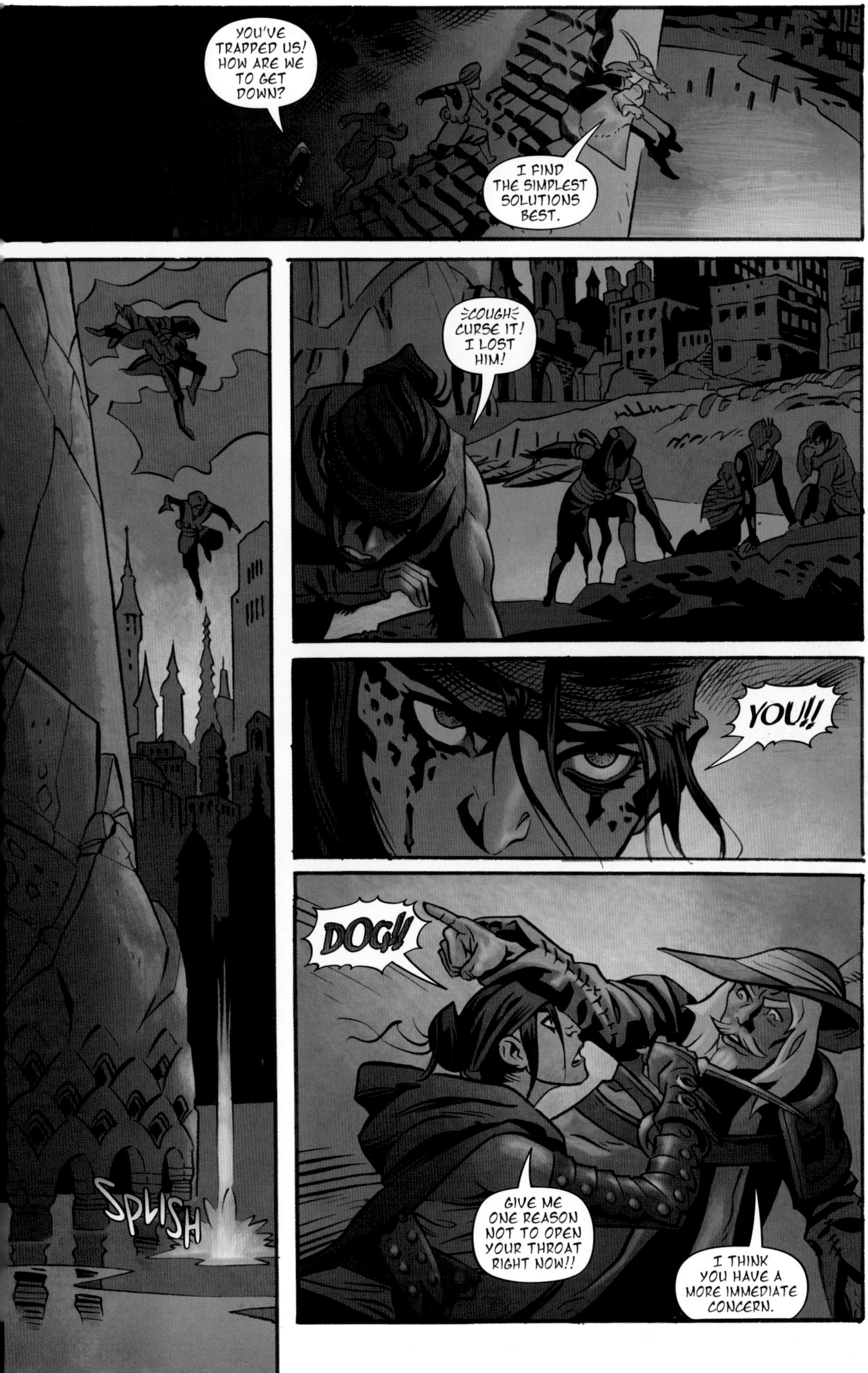
YOU'VE TRAPPED US! HOW ARE WE TO GET DOWN?
I FIND THE SIMPLEST SOLUTIONS BEST.
SPLISH
COUGH CURSE IT! I LOST HIM!
YOU!!
DOG!!
GIVE ME ONE REASON NOT TO OPEN YOUR THROAT RIGHT NOW!!
I THINK YOU HAVE A MORE IMMEDIATE CONCERN.

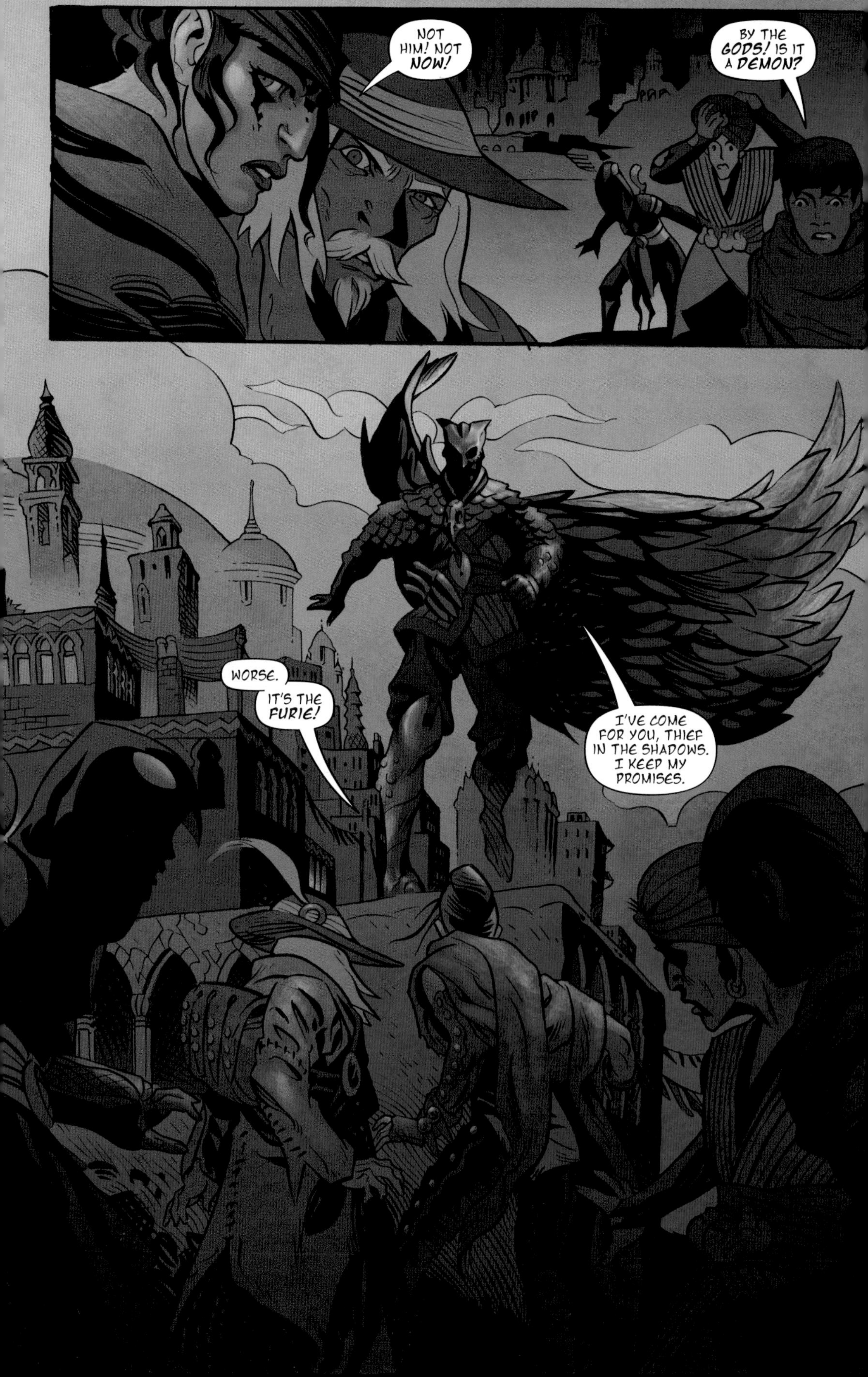
NOT HIM! NOT NOW!
BY THE GODS! IS IT A DEMON?
WORSE.
IT'S THE FURIE!
I'VE COME FOR YOU, THIEF IN THE SHADOWS. I KEEP MY PROMISES.

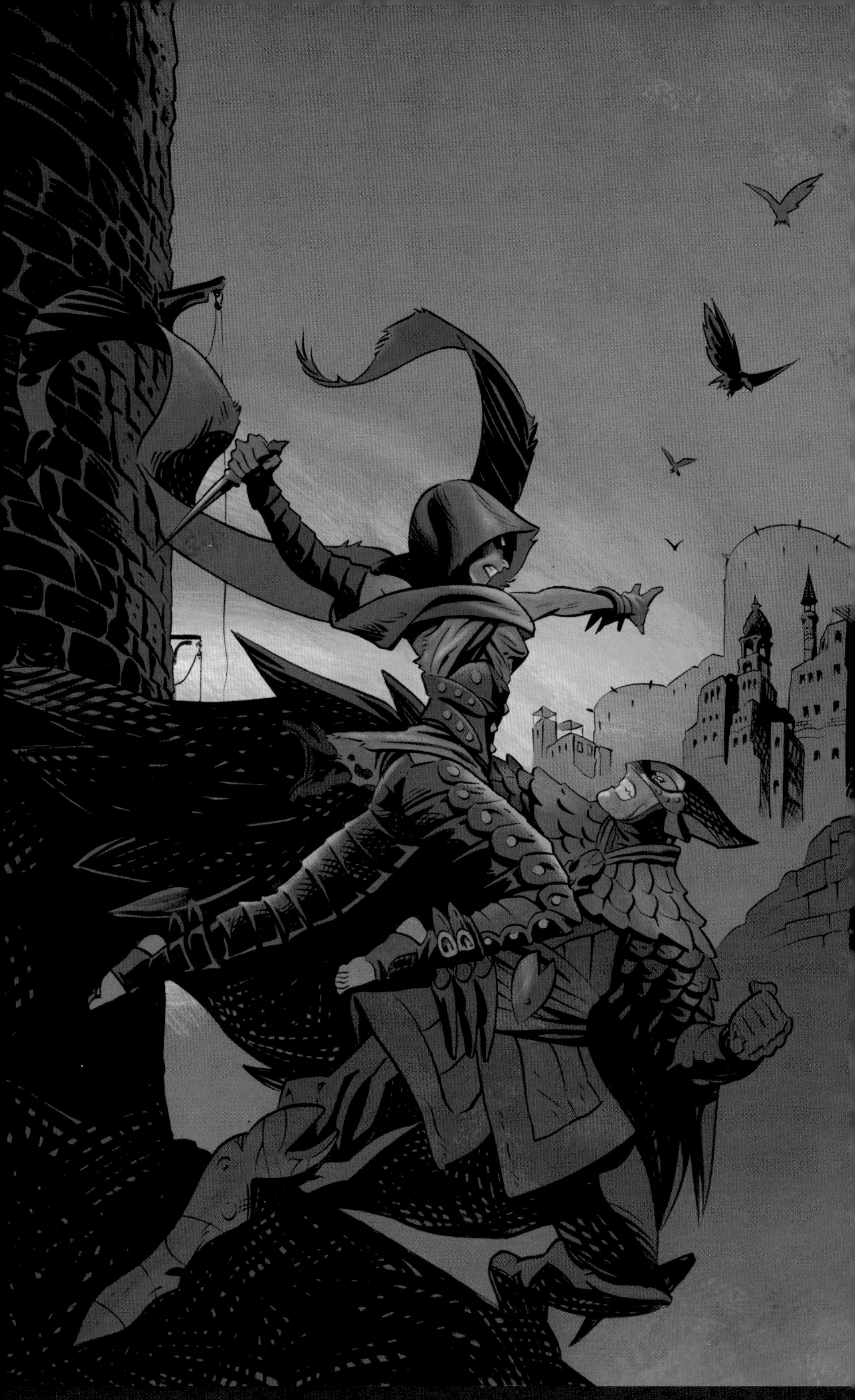

Chapter 3

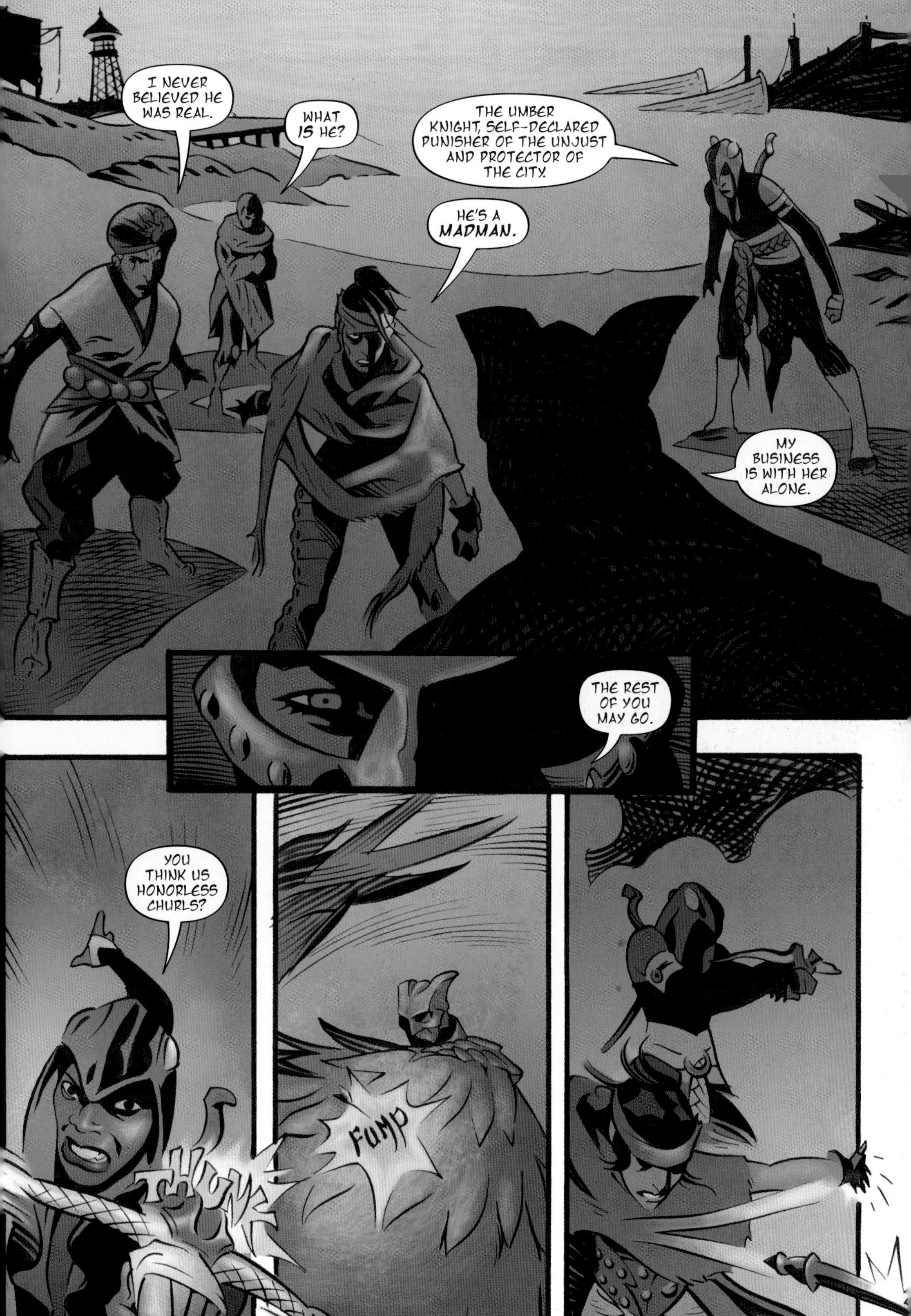
I NEVER BELIEVED HE WAS REAL.
WHAT IS HE?
THE UMBER KNIGHT, SELF-DECLARED PUNISHER OF THE UNJUST AND PROTECTOR OF THE CITY.
HE'S A MADMAN.
MY BUSINESS IS WITH HER ALONE.
THE REST OF YOU MAY GO.
YOU THINK US HONORLESS CHURLS?
THUNK
FUMP

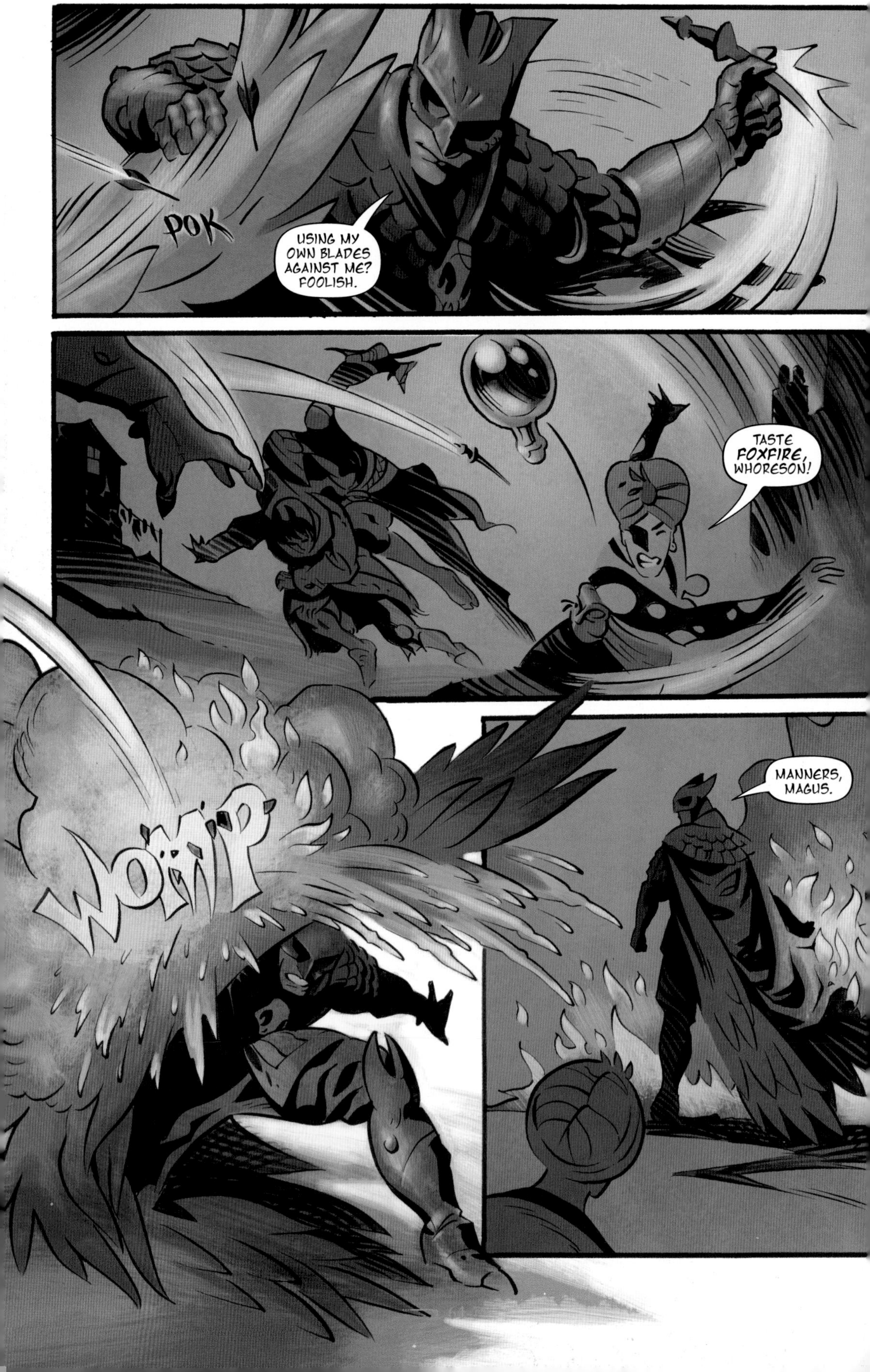
POK
USING MY OWN BLADES AGAINST ME? FOOLISH.
TASTE FOXFIRE, WHORESON!
WOMP
MANNERS, MAGUS.

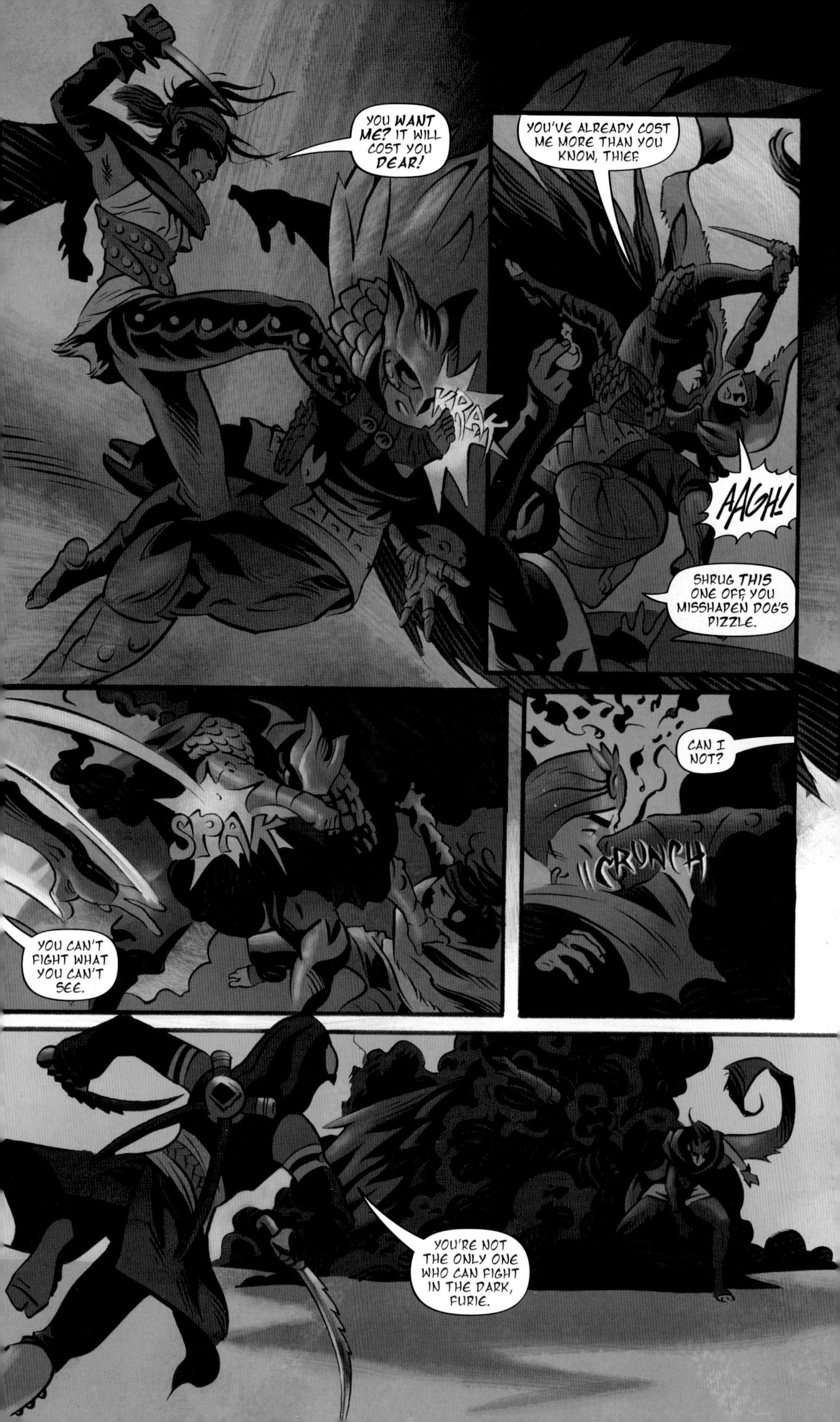
YOU WANT ME? IT WILL COST YOU DEAR!
KRRAK
YOU'VE ALREADY COST ME MORE THAN YOU KNOW, THIEF.
AAGH!
SHRUG THIS ONE OFF, YOU MISSHAPEN DOG'S PIZZLE.
SPAK
YOU CAN'T FIGHT WHAT YOU CAN'T SEE.
CAN I NOT?
CRUNCH
YOU'RE NOT THE ONLY ONE WHO CAN FIGHT IN THE DARK, FURIE.

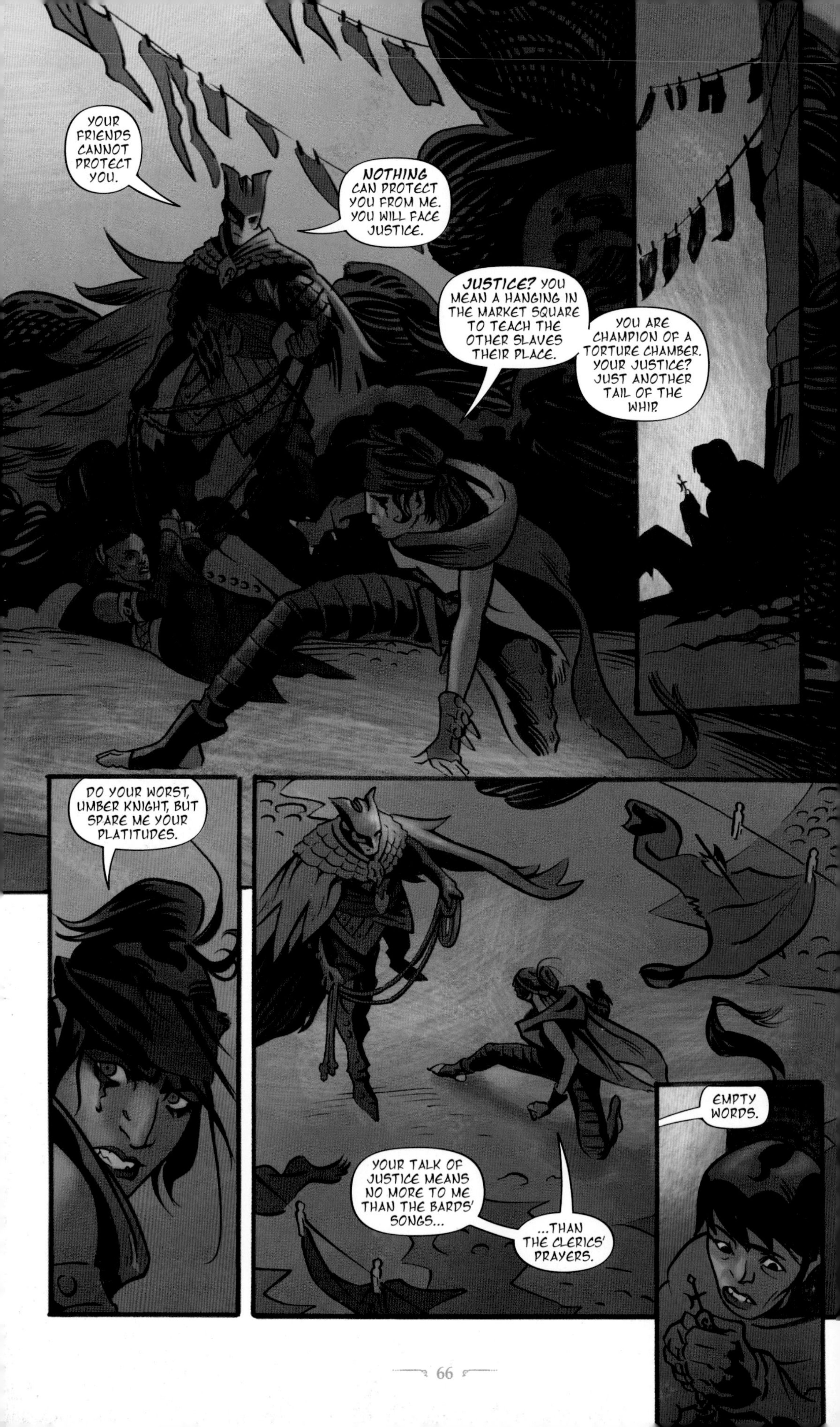
YOUR FRIENDS CANNOT PROTECT YOU.
NOTHING CAN PROTECT YOU FROM ME. YOU WILL FACE JUSTICE.
JUSTICE? YOU MEAN A HANGING IN THE MARKET SQUARE TO TEACH THE OTHER SLAVES THEIR PLACE.
YOU ARE CHAMPION OF A TORTURE CHAMBER. YOUR JUSTICE? JUST ANOTHER TAIL OF THE WHIP.
DO YOUR WORST, UMBER KNIGHT, BUT SPARE ME YOUR PLATITUDES.
YOUR TALK OF JUSTICE MEANS NO MORE TO ME THAN THE BARDS' SONGS...
...THAN THE CLERICS' PRAYERS.
EMPTY WORDS.

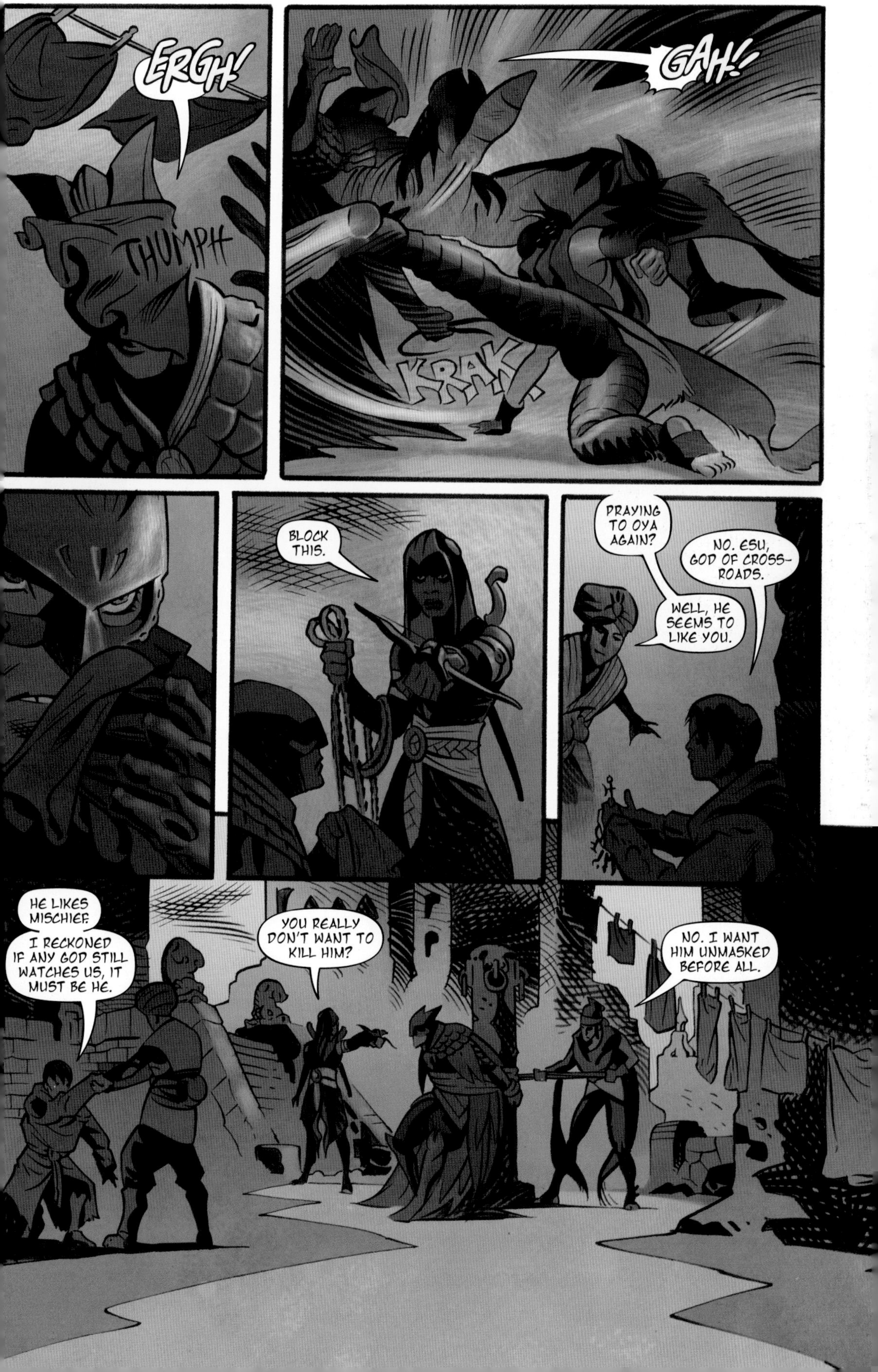
ERGH!
THUMPH
GAH!!
KRAK!
BLOCK THIS.
PRAYING TO OYA AGAIN?
NO. ESU, GOD OF CROSS-ROADS.
WELL, HE SEEMS TO LIKE YOU.
HE LIKES MISCHIEF.
I RECKONED IF ANY GOD STILL WATCHES US, IT MUST BE HE.
YOU REALLY DON'T WANT TO KILL HIM?
NO. I WANT HIM UNMASKED BEFORE ALL.

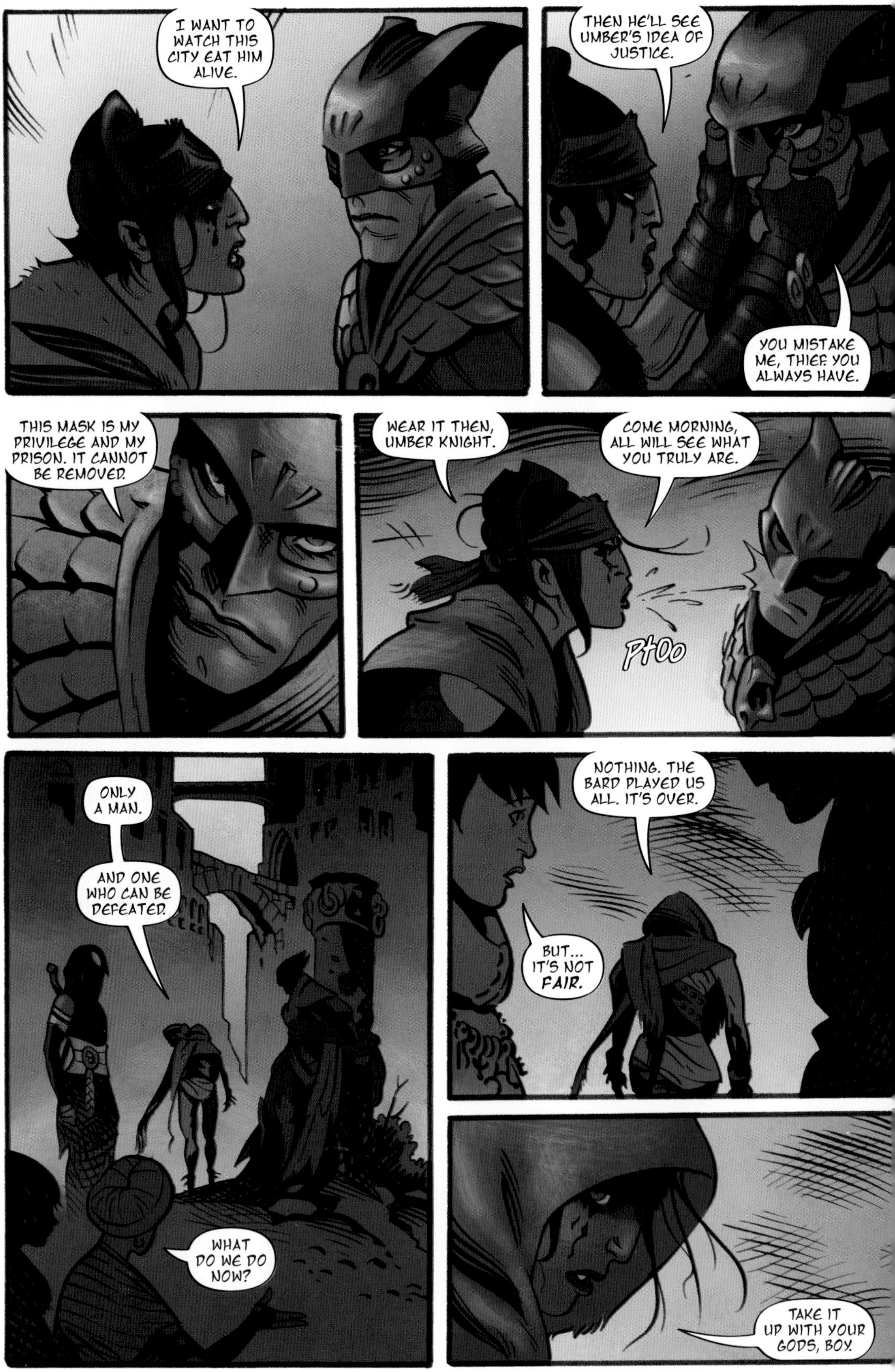

I WANT TO WATCH THIS CITY EAT HIM ALIVE.
THEN HE'LL SEE UMBER'S IDEA OF JUSTICE.
YOU MISTAKE ME, THIEF. YOU ALWAYS HAVE.
THIS MASK IS MY PRIVILEGE AND MY PRISON. IT CANNOT BE REMOVED.
WEAR IT THEN, UMBER KNIGHT.
COME MORNING, ALL WILL SEE WHAT YOU TRULY ARE.
PTOO
ONLY A MAN.
AND ONE WHO CAN BE DEFEATED.
WHAT DO WE DO NOW?
NOTHING. THE BARD PLAYED US ALL. IT'S OVER.
BUT... IT'S NOT FAIR.
TAKE IT UP WITH YOUR GODS, BOY.

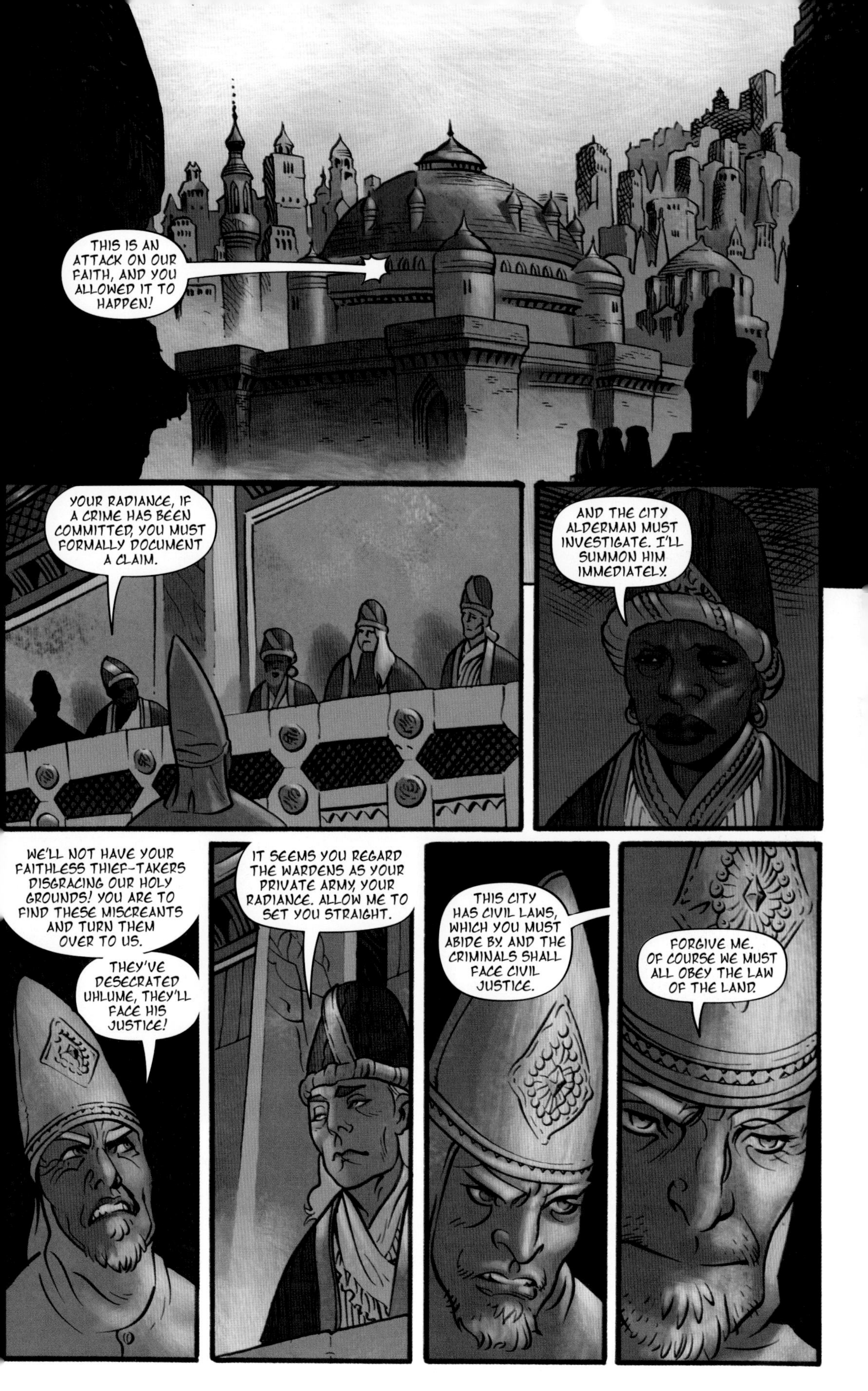
THIS IS AN ATTACK ON OUR FAITH, AND YOU ALLOWED IT TO HAPPEN!
YOUR RADIANCE, IF A CRIME HAS BEEN COMMITTED, YOU MUST FORMALLY DOCUMENT A CLAIM.
AND THE CITY ALDERMAN MUST INVESTIGATE. I'LL SUMMON HIM IMMEDIATELY.
WE'LL NOT HAVE YOUR FAITHLESS THIEF-TAKERS DISGRACING OUR HOLY GROUNDS! YOU ARE TO FIND THESE MISCREANTS AND TURN THEM OVER TO US.
THEY'VE DESECRATED UHLUME, THEY'LL FACE HIS JUSTICE!
IT SEEMS YOU REGARD THE WARDENS AS YOUR PRIVATE ARMY, YOUR RADIANCE. ALLOW ME TO SET YOU STRAIGHT.
THIS CITY HAS CIVIL LAWS, WHICH YOU MUST ABIDE BY. AND THE CRIMINALS SHALL FACE CIVIL JUSTICE.
FORGIVE ME. OF COURSE WE MUST ALL OBEY THE LAW OF THE LAND.

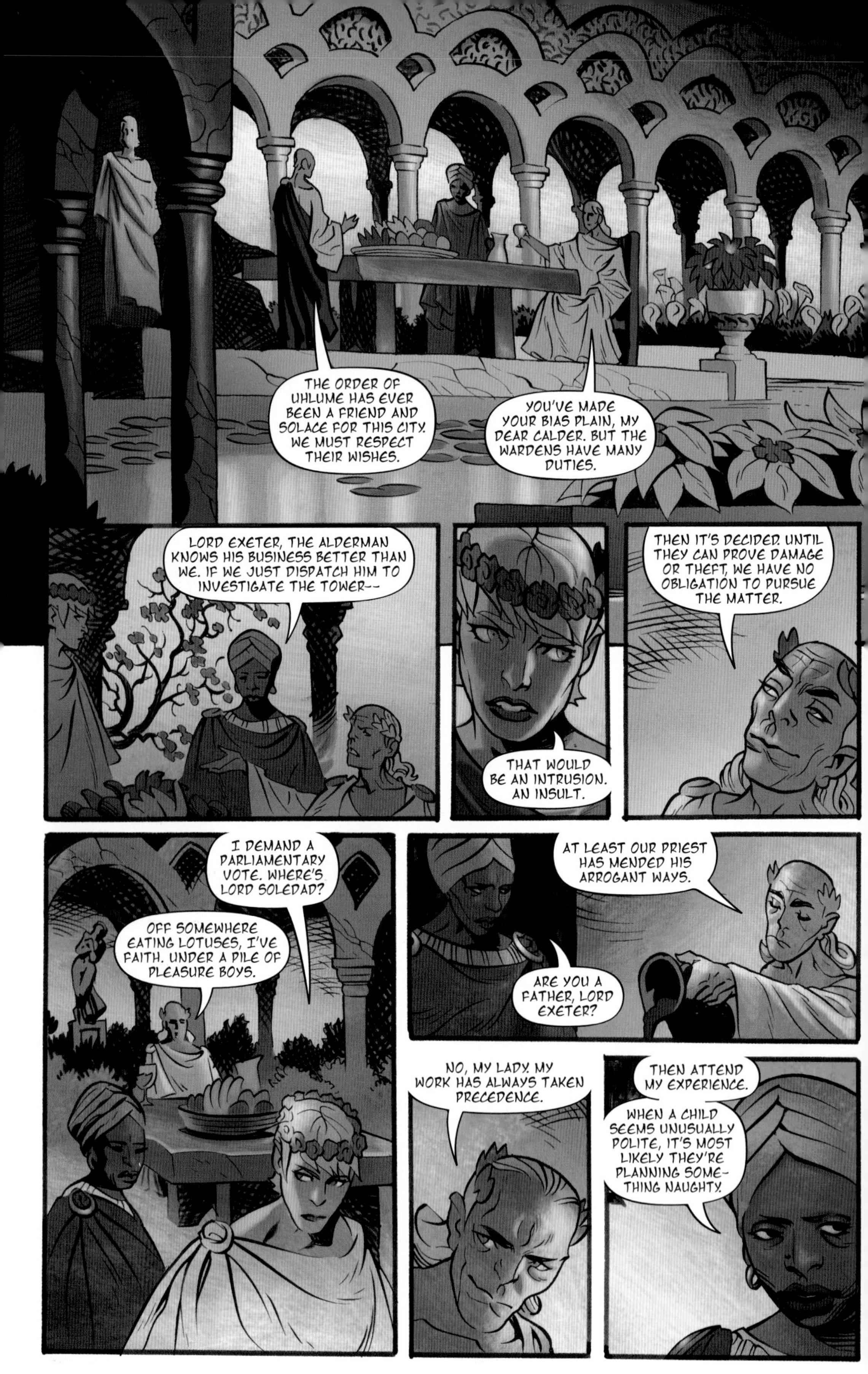
THE ORDER OF UHLUME HAS EVER BEEN A FRIEND AND SOLACE FOR THIS CITY. WE MUST RESPECT THEIR WISHES.
YOU'VE MADE YOUR BIAS PLAIN, MY DEAR CALDER. BUT THE WARDENS HAVE MANY DUTIES.
LORD EXETER, THE ALDERMAN KNOWS HIS BUSINESS BETTER THAN WE. IF WE JUST DISPATCH HIM TO INVESTIGATE THE TOWER--
THAT WOULD BE AN INTRUSION. AN INSULT.
THEN IT'S DECIDED. UNTIL THEY CAN PROVE DAMAGE OR THEFT, WE HAVE NO OBLIGATION TO PURSUE THE MATTER.
I DEMAND A PARLIAMENTARY VOTE. WHERE'S LORD SOLEDAD?
OFF SOMEWHERE EATING LOTUSES, I'VE FAITH. UNDER A PILE OF PLEASURE BOYS.
AT LEAST OUR PRIEST HAS MENDED HIS ARROGANT WAYS.
ARE YOU A FATHER, LORD EXETER?
NO, MY LADY. MY WORK HAS ALWAYS TAKEN PRECEDENCE.
THEN ATTEND MY EXPERIENCE.
WHEN A CHILD SEEMS UNUSUALLY POLITE, IT'S MOST LIKELY THEY'RE PLANNING SOME-THING NAUGHTY.

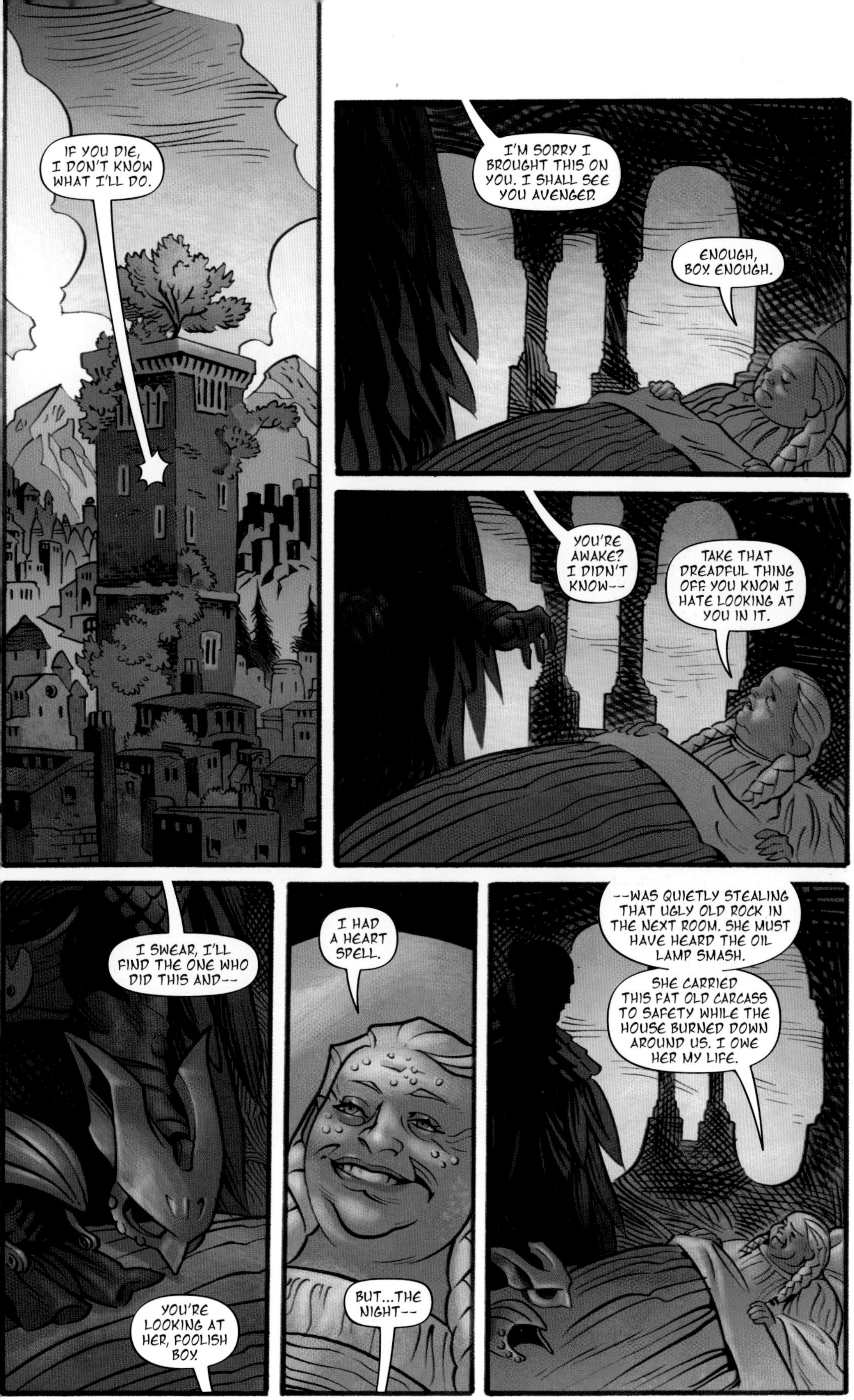
IF YOU DIE, I DON'T KNOW WHAT I'LL DO.
I'M SORRY I BROUGHT THIS ON YOU. I SHALL SEE YOU AVENGED.
ENOUGH, BOY. ENOUGH.
YOU'RE AWAKE? I DIDN'T KNOW--
TAKE THAT DREADFUL THING OFF. YOU KNOW I HATE LOOKING AT YOU IN IT.
I SWEAR, I'LL FIND THE ONE WHO DID THIS AND--
YOU'RE LOOKING AT HER, FOOLISH BOY.
I HAD A HEART SPELL.
BUT...THE NIGHT--
--WAS QUIETLY STEALING THAT UGLY OLD ROCK IN THE NEXT ROOM. SHE MUST HAVE HEARD THE OIL LAMP SMASH.
SHE CARRIED THIS FAT OLD CARCASS TO SAFETY WHILE THE HOUSE BURNED DOWN AROUND US. I OWE HER MY LIFE.

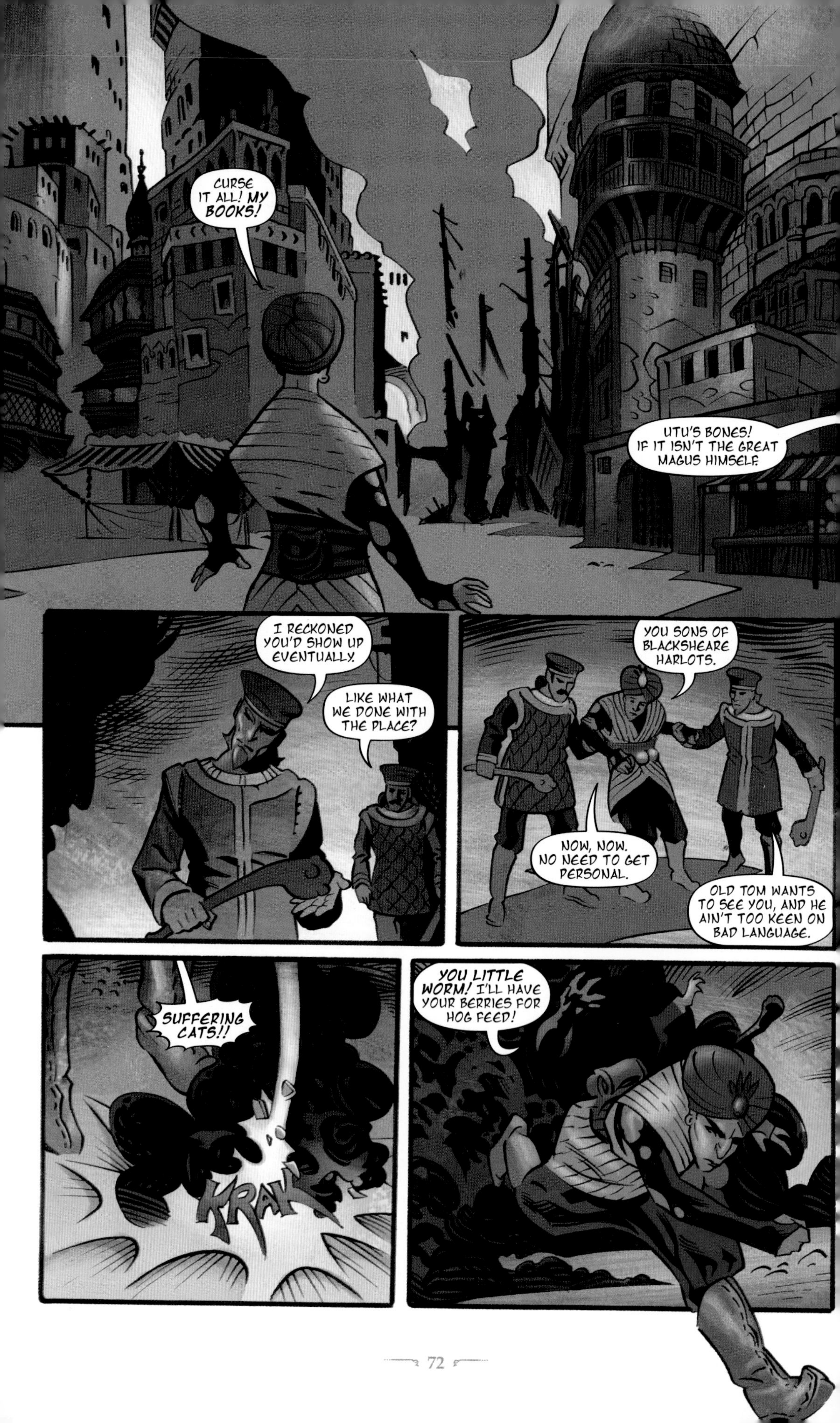
CURSE IT ALL! MY BOOKS!
UTU'S BONES! IF IT ISN'T THE GREAT MAGUS HIMSELF.
I RECKONED YOU'D SHOW UP EVENTUALLY.
LIKE WHAT WE DONE WITH THE PLACE?
YOU SONS OF BLACKSHEARE HARLOTS.
NOW, NOW. NO NEED TO GET PERSONAL.
OLD TOM WANTS TO SEE YOU, AND HE AIN'T TOO KEEN ON BAD LANGUAGE.
SUFFERING CATS!!
KRAK
YOU LITTLE WORM! I'LL HAVE YOUR BERRIES FOR HOG FEED!

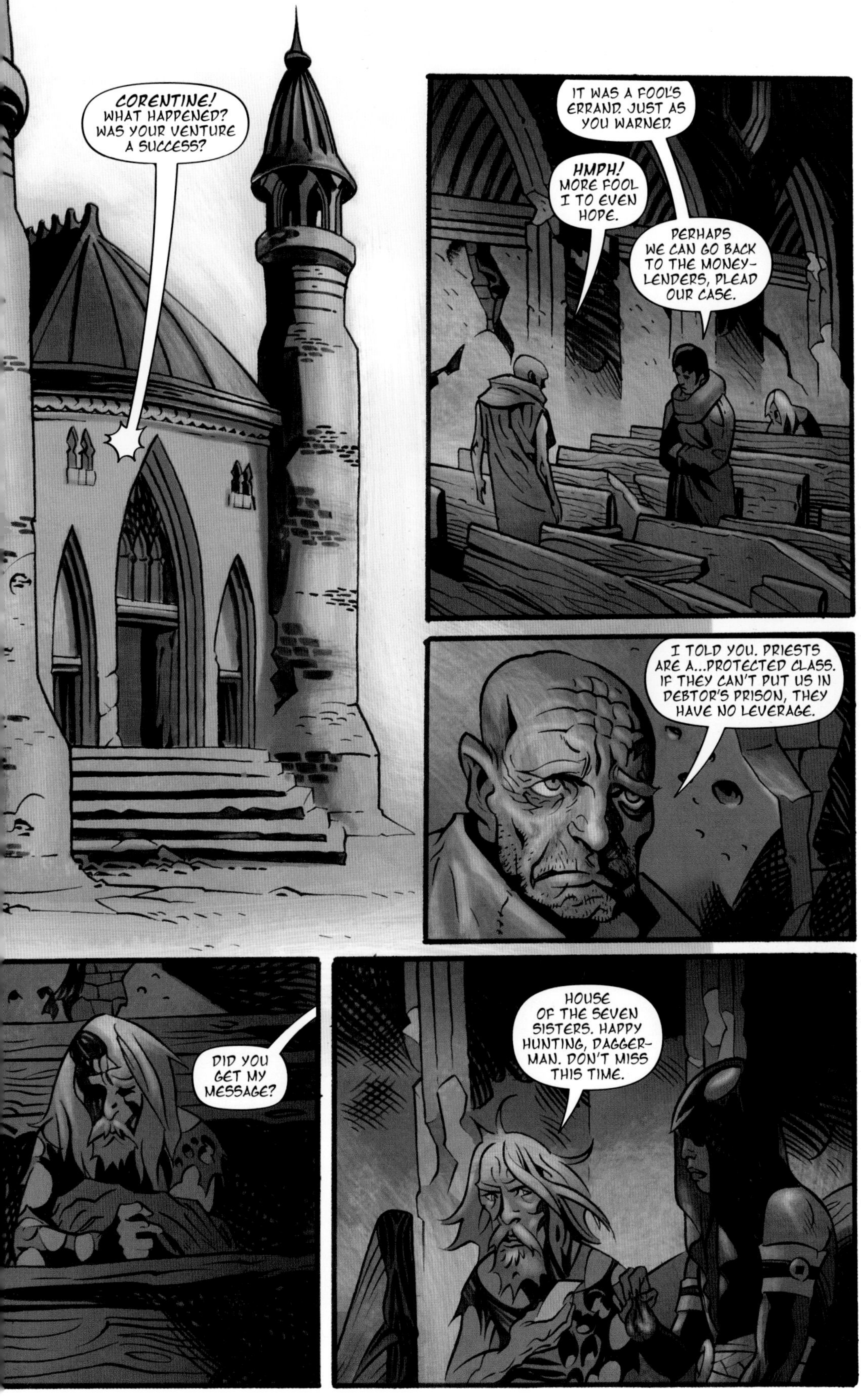

CORENTINE! WHAT HAPPENED? WAS YOUR VENTURE A SUCCESS?
IT WAS A FOOL'S ERRAND. JUST AS YOU WARNED.
HMPH! MORE FOOL I TO EVEN HOPE.
PERHAPS WE CAN GO BACK TO THE MONEY-LENDERS, PLEAD OUR CASE.
I TOLD YOU. PRIESTS ARE A...PROTECTED CLASS. IF THEY CAN'T PUT US IN DEBTOR'S PRISON, THEY HAVE NO LEVERAGE.
DID YOU GET MY MESSAGE?
HOUSE OF THE SEVEN SISTERS. HAPPY HUNTING, DAGGER-MAN. DON'T MISS THIS TIME.

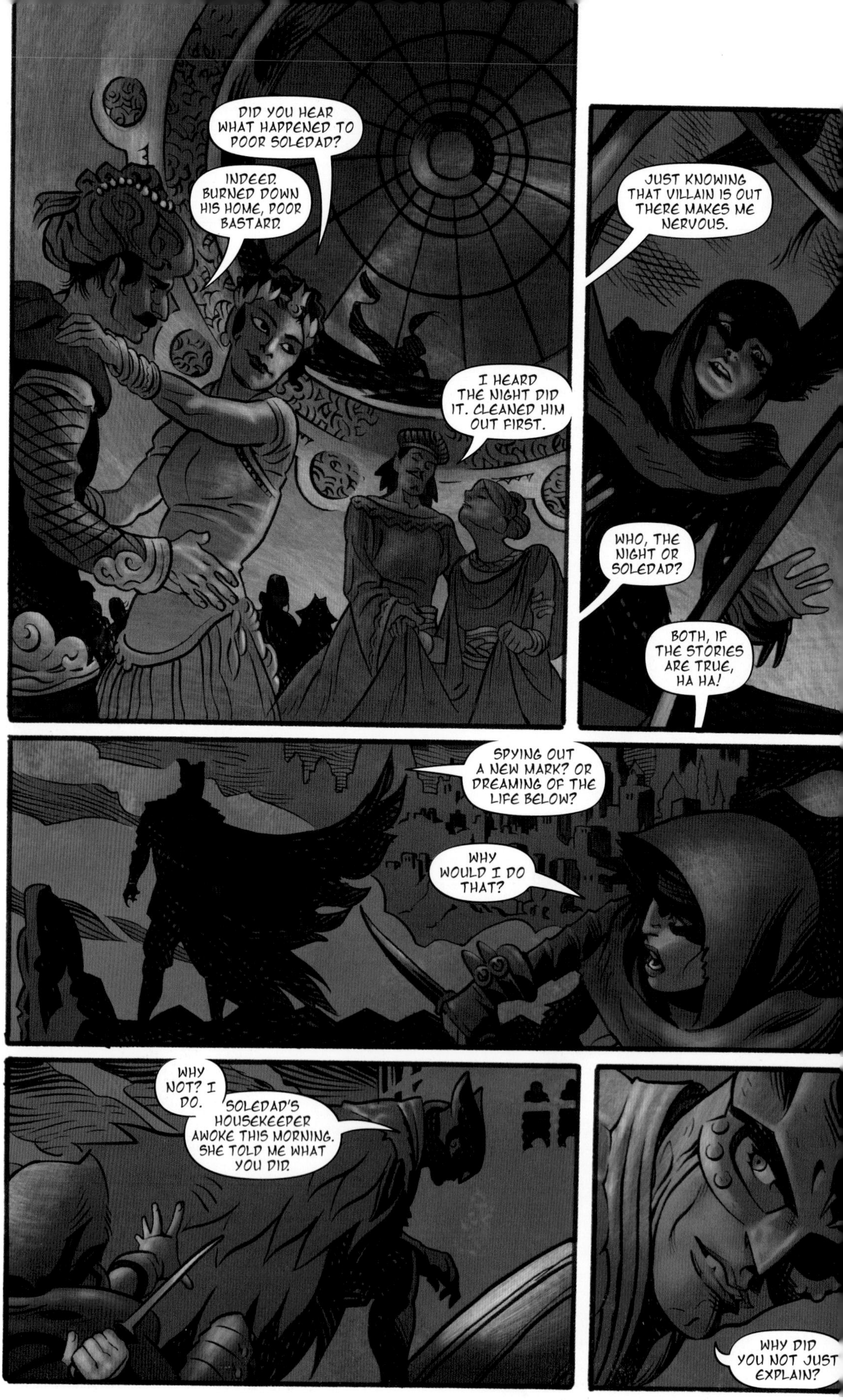
DID YOU HEAR WHAT HAPPENED TO POOR SOLEDAD?
INDEED. BURNED DOWN HIS HOME, POOR BASTARD.
I HEARD THE NIGHT DID IT. CLEANED HIM OUT FIRST.
JUST KNOWING THAT VILLAIN IS OUT THERE MAKES ME NERVOUS.
WHO, THE NIGHT OR SOLEDAD?
BOTH, IF THE STORIES ARE TRUE, HA HA!
SPYING OUT A NEW MARK? OR DREAMING OF THE LIFE BELOW?
WHY WOULD I DO THAT?
WHY NOT? I DO.
SOLEDAD'S HOUSEKEEPER AWOKE THIS MORNING. SHE TOLD ME WHAT YOU DID.
WHY DID YOU NOT JUST EXPLAIN?

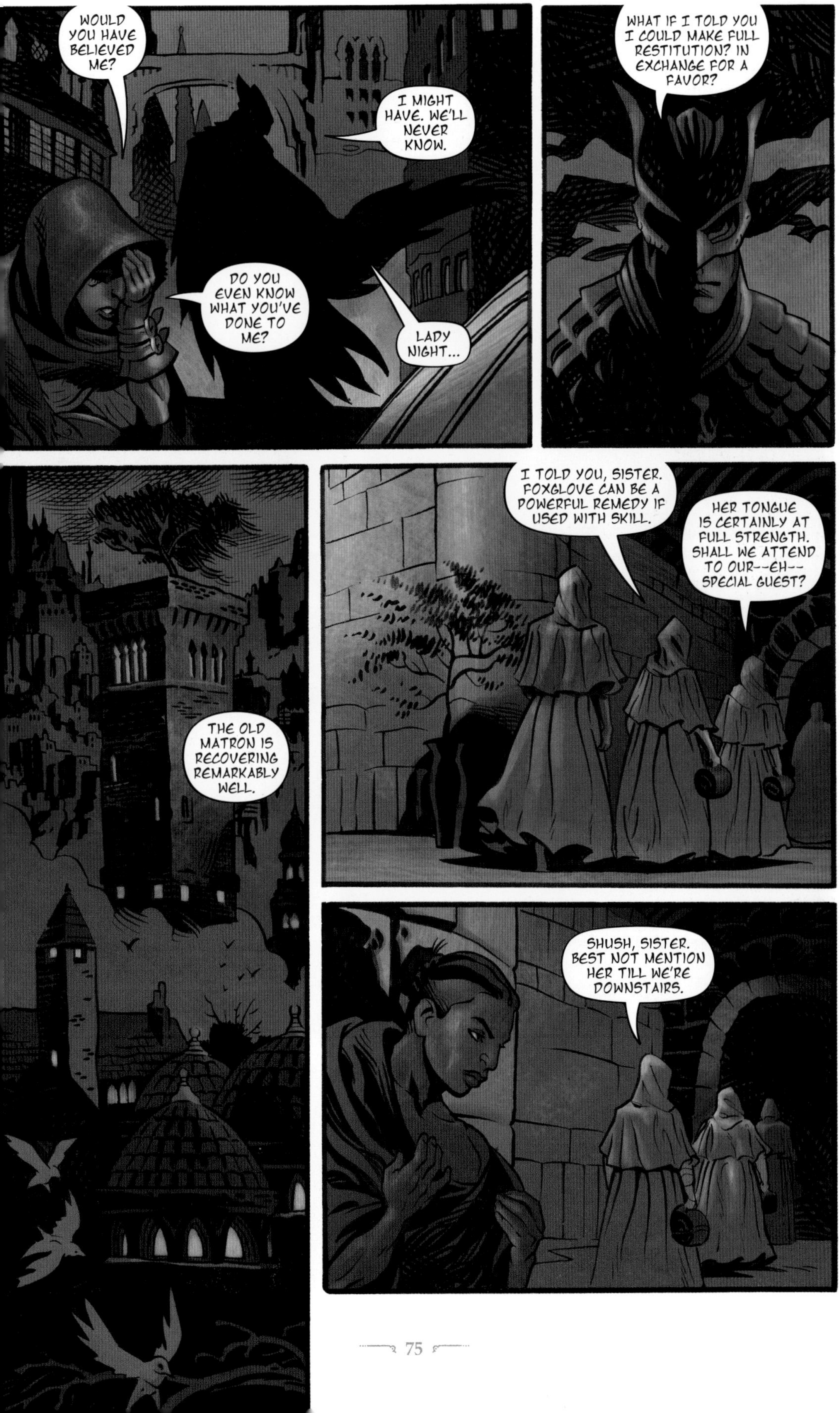
WOULD YOU HAVE BELIEVED ME?
I MIGHT HAVE. WE'LL NEVER KNOW.
DO YOU EVEN KNOW WHAT YOU'VE DONE TO ME?
LADY NIGHT...
WHAT IF I TOLD YOU I COULD MAKE FULL RESTITUTION? IN EXCHANGE FOR A FAVOR?
THE OLD MATRON IS RECOVERING REMARKABLY WELL.
I TOLD YOU, SISTER. FOXGLOVE CAN BE A POWERFUL REMEDY IF USED WITH SKILL.
HER TONGUE IS CERTAINLY AT FULL STRENGTH. SHALL WE ATTEND TO OUR--EH-- SPECIAL GUEST?
SHUSH, SISTER. BEST NOT MENTION HER TILL WE'RE DOWNSTAIRS.

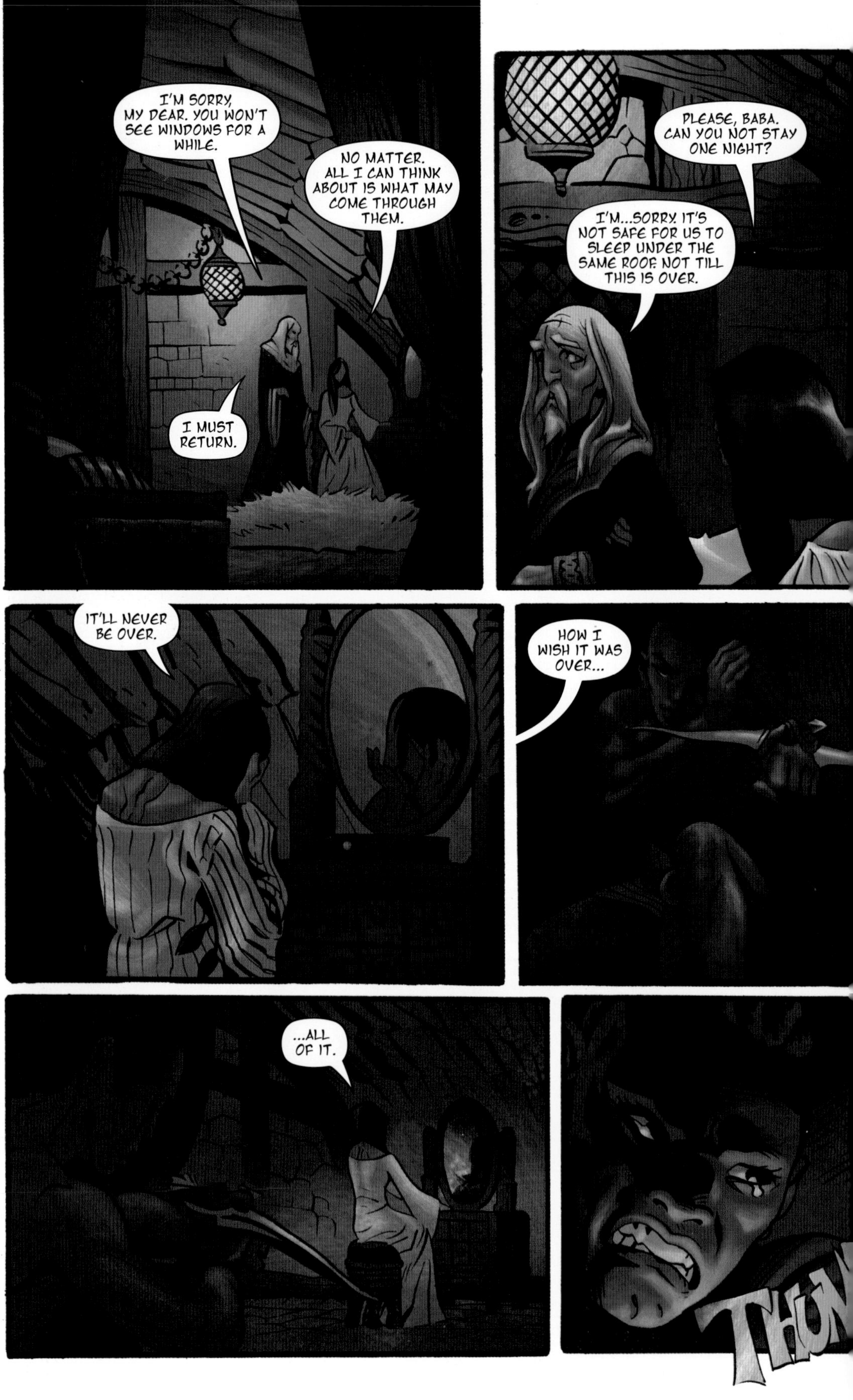
I'M SORRY, MY DEAR. YOU WON'T SEE WINDOWS FOR A WHILE.
NO MATTER. ALL I CAN THINK ABOUT IS WHAT MAY COME THROUGH THEM.
I MUST RETURN.
PLEASE, BABA. CAN YOU NOT STAY ONE NIGHT?
I'M...SORRY. IT'S NOT SAFE FOR US TO SLEEP UNDER THE SAME ROOF. NOT TILL THIS IS OVER.
IT'LL NEVER BE OVER.
HOW I WISH IT WAS OVER...
...ALL OF IT.
THUN

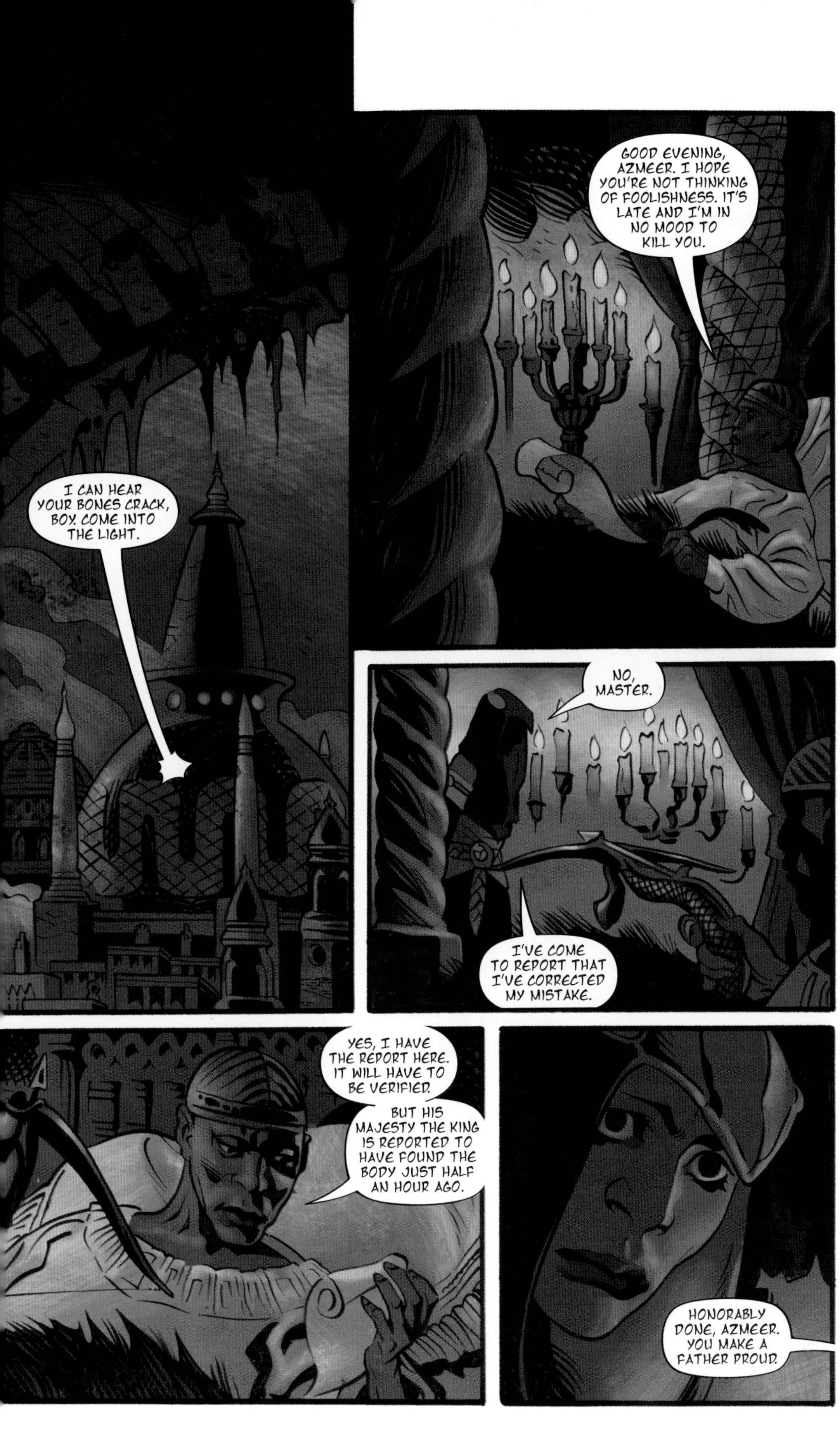
I CAN HEAR YOUR BONES CRACK, BOY. COME INTO THE LIGHT.
GOOD EVENING, AZMEER. I HOPE YOU'RE NOT THINKING OF FOOLISHNESS. IT'S LATE AND I'M IN NO MOOD TO KILL YOU.
NO, MASTER.
I'VE COME TO REPORT THAT I'VE CORRECTED MY MISTAKE.
YES, I HAVE THE REPORT HERE. IT WILL HAVE TO BE VERIFIED.
BUT HIS MAJESTY THE KING IS REPORTED TO HAVE FOUND THE BODY JUST HALF AN HOUR AGO.
HONORABLY DONE, AZMEER. YOU MAKE A FATHER PROUD.

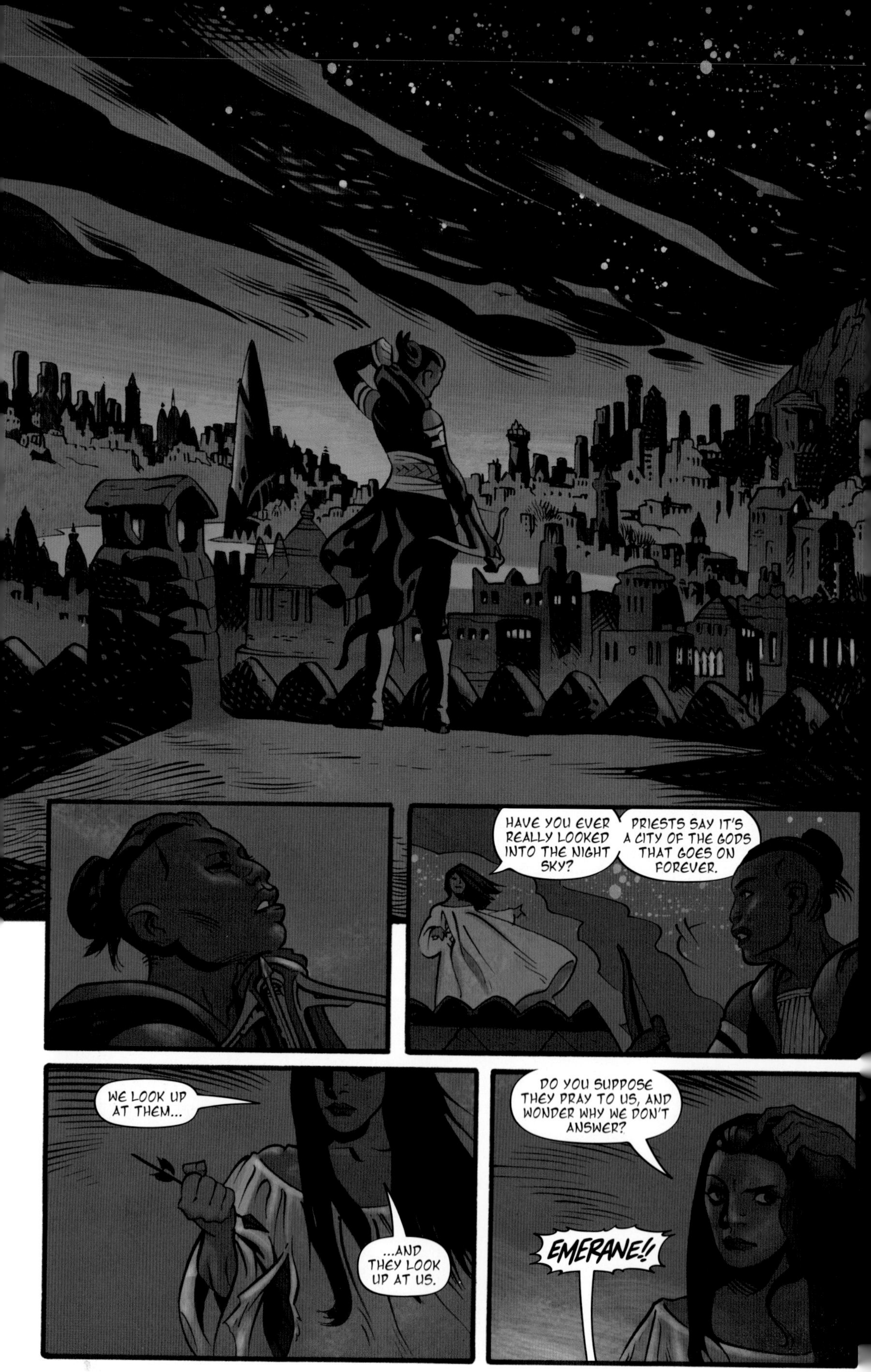
HAVE YOU EVER REALLY LOOKED INTO THE NIGHT SKY?
PRIESTS SAY IT'S A CITY OF THE GODS THAT GOES ON FOREVER.
WE LOOK UP AT THEM...
...AND THEY LOOK UP AT US.
DO YOU SUPPOSE THEY PRAY TO US, AND WONDER WHY WE DON'T ANSWER?
EMERANE!!

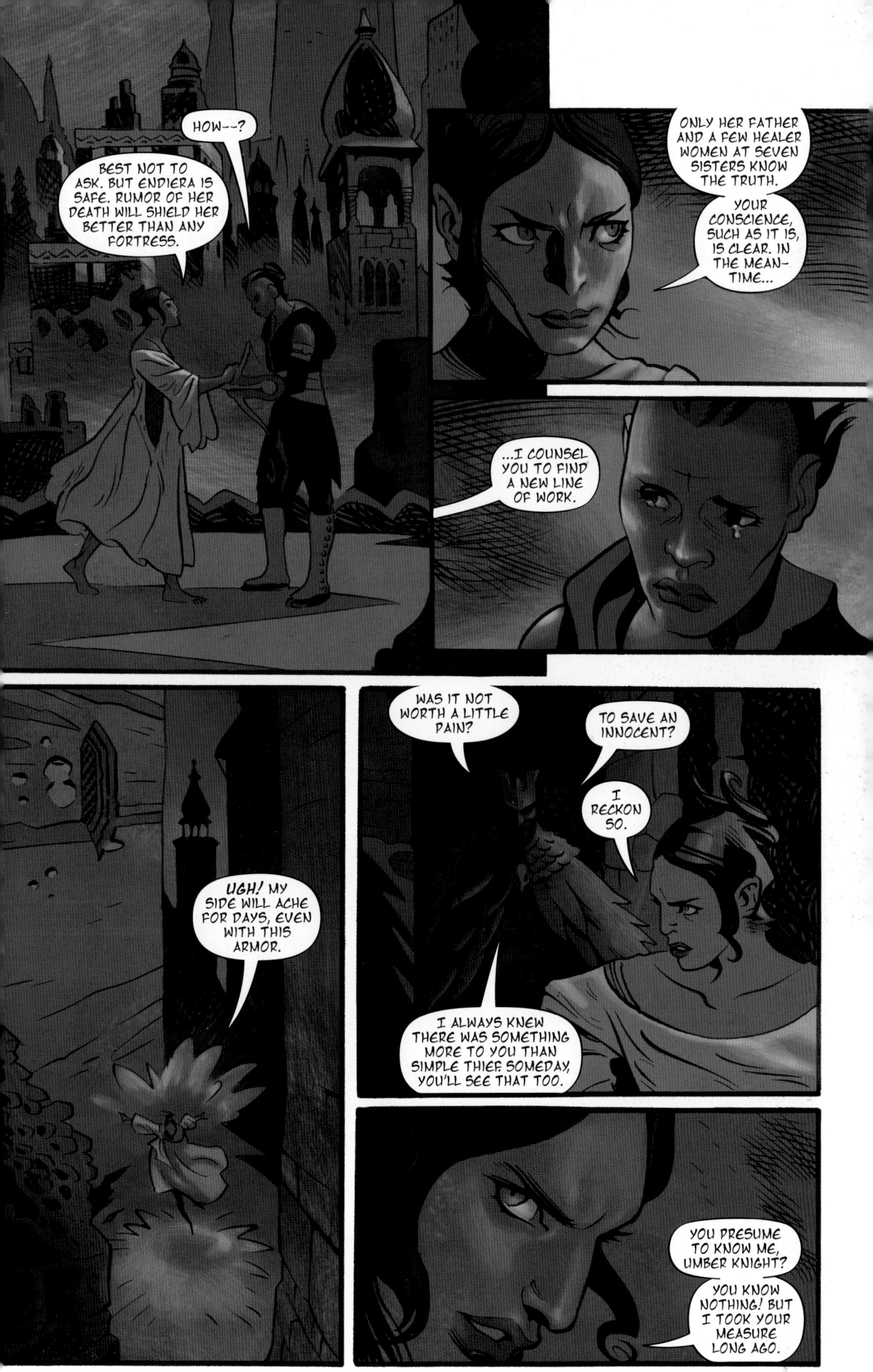
HOW--?
BEST NOT TO ASK. BUT ENDIERA IS SAFE. RUMOR OF HER DEATH WILL SHIELD HER BETTER THAN ANY FORTRESS.
ONLY HER FATHER AND A FEW HEALER WOMEN AT SEVEN SISTERS KNOW THE TRUTH.
YOUR CONSCIENCE, SUCH AS IT IS, IS CLEAR. IN THE MEAN-TIME...
...I COUNSEL YOU TO FIND A NEW LINE OF WORK.
UGH! MY SIDE WILL ACHE FOR DAYS, EVEN WITH THIS ARMOR.
WAS IT NOT WORTH A LITTLE PAIN?
TO SAVE AN INNOCENT?
I RECKON SO.
I ALWAYS KNEW THERE WAS SOMETHING MORE TO YOU THAN SIMPLE THIEF. SOMEDAY, YOU'LL SEE THAT TOO.
YOU PRESUME TO KNOW ME, UMBER KNIGHT?
YOU KNOW NOTHING! BUT I TOOK YOUR MEASURE LONG AGO.

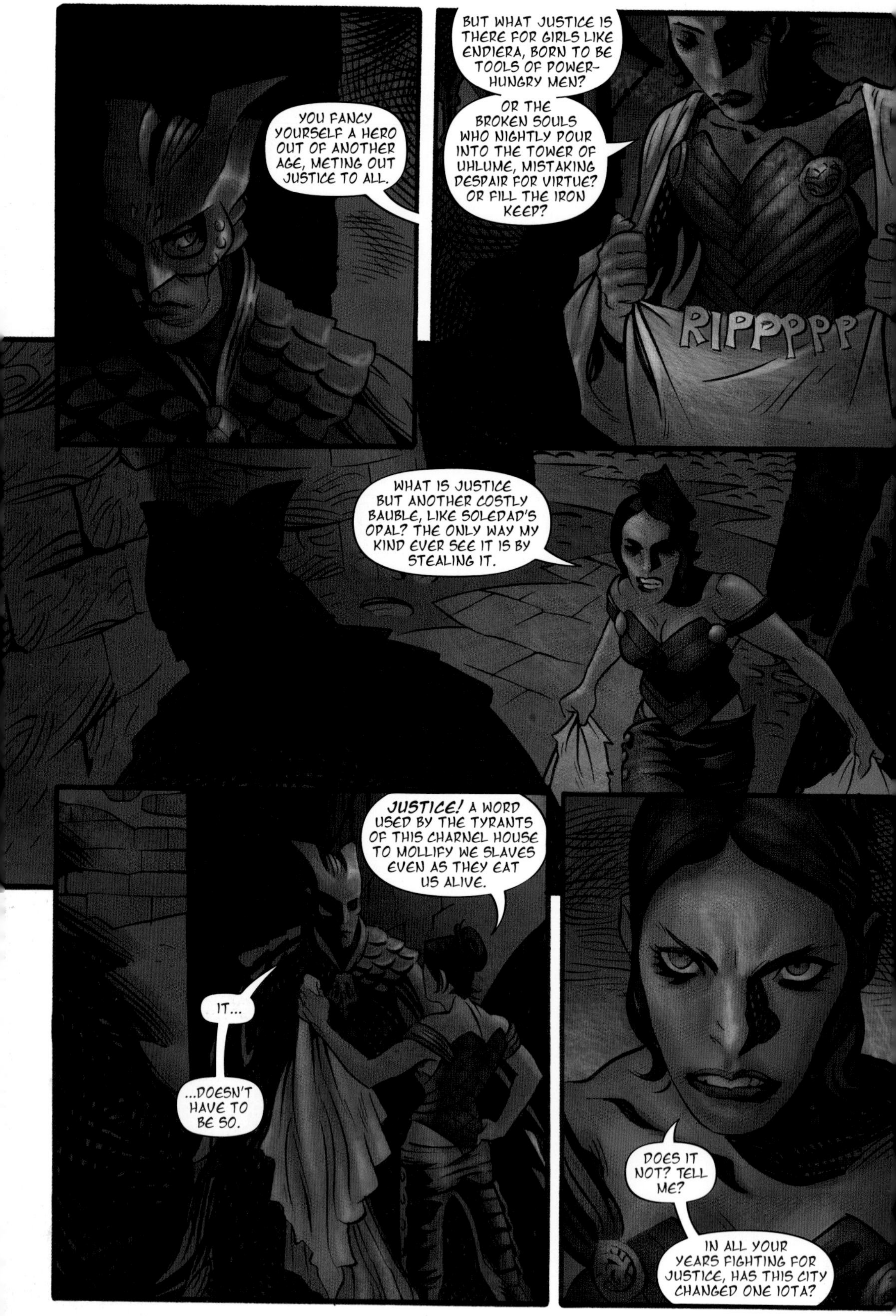
YOU FANCY YOURSELF A HERO OUT OF ANOTHER AGE, METING OUT JUSTICE TO ALL.
BUT WHAT JUSTICE IS THERE FOR GIRLS LIKE ENDIERA, BORN TO BE TOOLS OF POWER-HUNGRY MEN?
OR THE BROKEN SOULS WHO NIGHTLY POUR INTO THE TOWER OF UHLUME, MISTAKING DESPAIR FOR VIRTUE? OR FILL THE IRON KEEP?
RIPPPPPP
WHAT IS JUSTICE BUT ANOTHER COSTLY BAUBLE, LIKE SOLEDAD'S OPAL? THE ONLY WAY MY KIND EVER SEE IT IS BY STEALING IT.
JUSTICE! A WORD USED BY THE TYRANTS OF THIS CHARNEL HOUSE TO MOLLIFY WE SLAVES EVEN AS THEY EAT US ALIVE.
IT...
...DOESN'T HAVE TO BE SO.
DOES IT NOT? TELL ME?
IN ALL YOUR YEARS FIGHTING FOR JUSTICE, HAS THIS CITY CHANGED ONE IOTA?

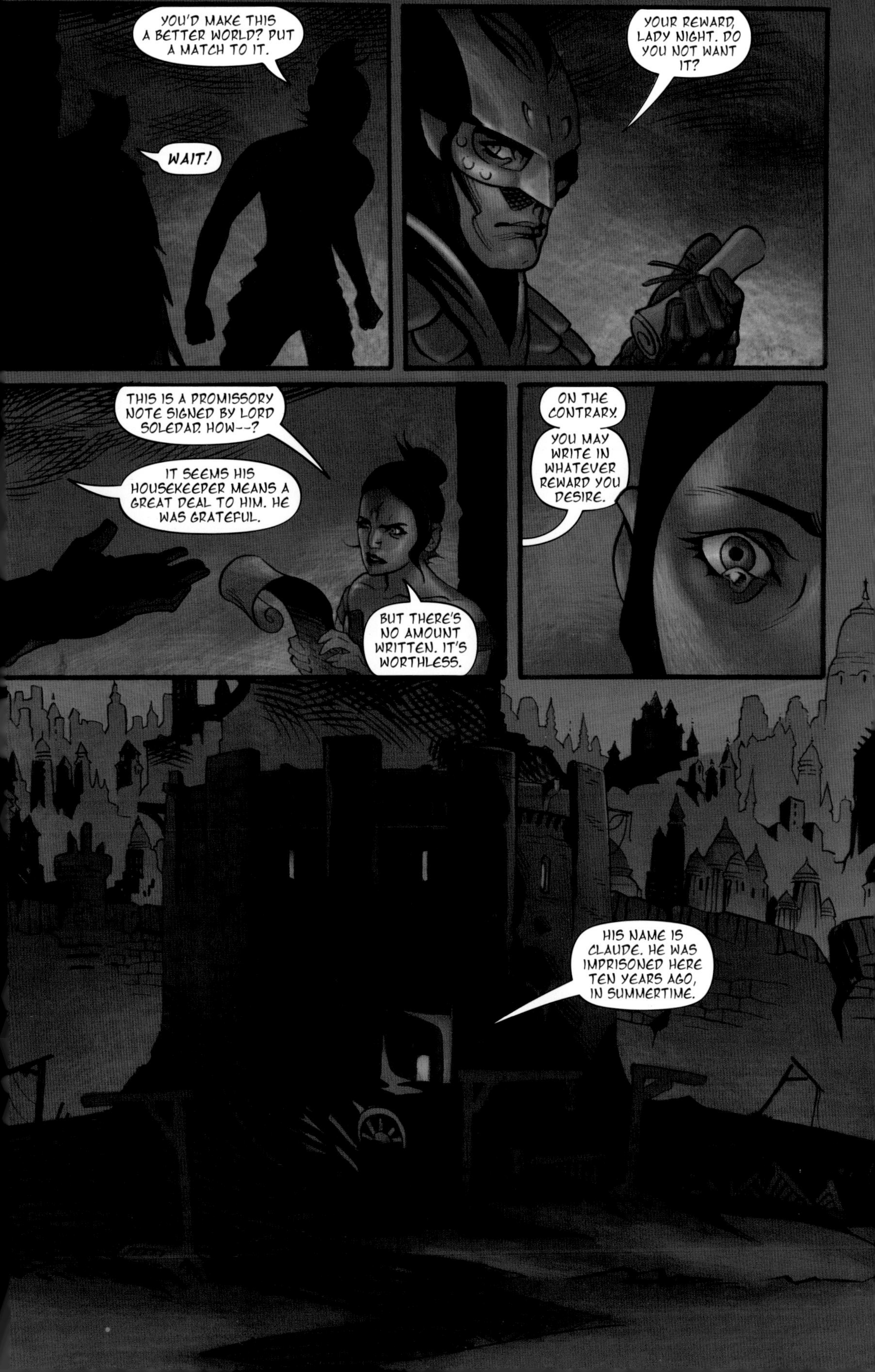

YOU'D MAKE THIS A BETTER WORLD? PUT A MATCH TO IT.
WAIT!
YOUR REWARD, LADY NIGHT. DO YOU NOT WANT IT?
THIS IS A PROMISSORY NOTE SIGNED BY LORD SOLEDAD. HOW--?
IT SEEMS HIS HOUSEKEEPER MEANS A GREAT DEAL TO HIM. HE WAS GRATEFUL.
BUT THERE'S NO AMOUNT WRITTEN. IT'S WORTHLESS.
ON THE CONTRARY.
YOU MAY WRITE IN WHATEVER REWARD YOU DESIRE.
HIS NAME IS CLAUDE. HE WAS IMPRISONED HERE TEN YEARS AGO, IN SUMMERTIME.

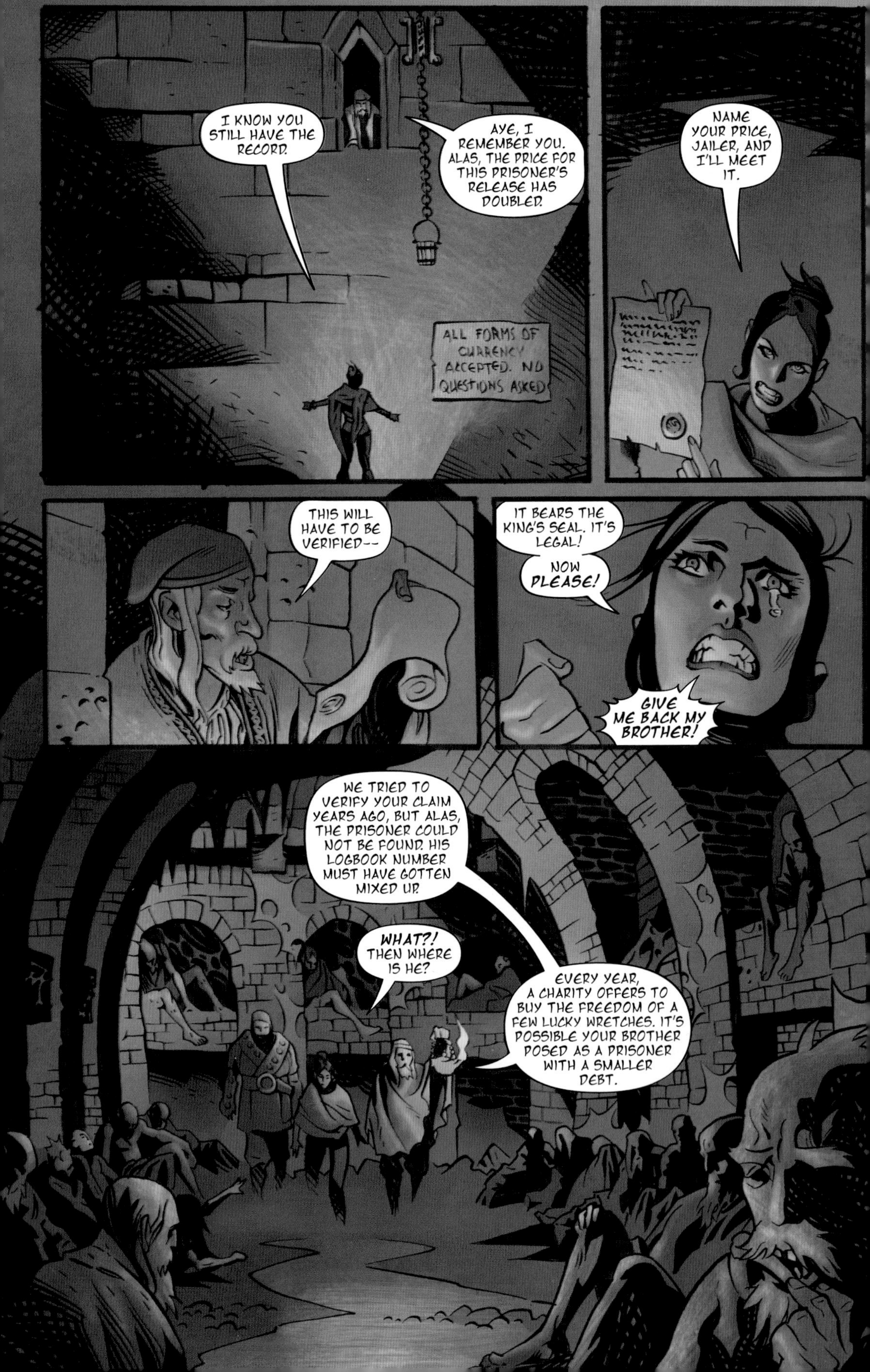
I KNOW YOU STILL HAVE THE RECORD.
AYE, I REMEMBER YOU. ALAS, THE PRICE FOR THIS PRISONER'S RELEASE HAS DOUBLED.
ALL FORMS OF CURRENCY ACCEPTED. NO QUESTIONS ASKED
NAME YOUR PRICE, JAILER, AND I'LL MEET IT.
THIS WILL HAVE TO BE VERIFIED--
IT BEARS THE KING'S SEAL. IT'S LEGAL!
NOW *PLEASE!*
GIVE ME BACK MY BROTHER!
WE TRIED TO VERIFY YOUR CLAIM YEARS AGO, BUT ALAS, THE PRISONER COULD NOT BE FOUND. HIS LOGBOOK NUMBER MUST HAVE GOTTEN MIXED UP.
WHAT?! THEN WHERE IS HE?
EVERY YEAR, A CHARITY OFFERS TO BUY THE FREEDOM OF A FEW LUCKY WRETCHES. IT'S POSSIBLE YOUR BROTHER POSED AS A PRISONER WITH A SMALLER DEBT.

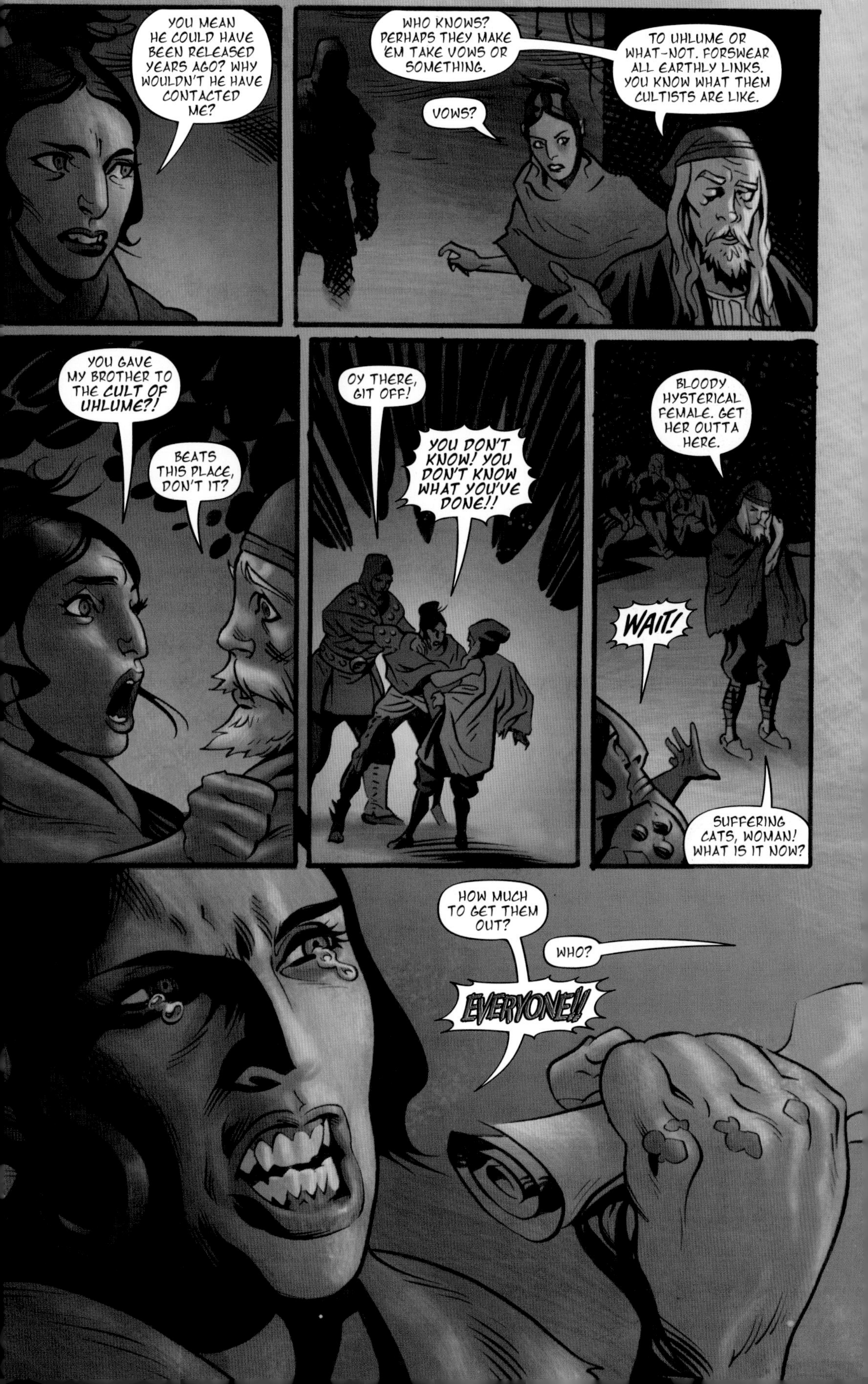

YOU MEAN HE COULD HAVE BEEN RELEASED YEARS AGO? WHY WOULDN'T HE HAVE CONTACTED ME?
WHO KNOWS? PERHAPS THEY MAKE 'EM TAKE VOWS OR SOMETHING.
VOWS?
TO UHLUME OR WHAT-NOT. FORSWEAR ALL EARTHLY LINKS. YOU KNOW WHAT THEM CULTISTS ARE LIKE.
YOU GAVE MY BROTHER TO THE CULT OF UHLUME?!
BEATS THIS PLACE, DON'T IT?
OY THERE, GIT OFF!
YOU DON'T KNOW! YOU DON'T KNOW WHAT YOU'VE DONE!!
BLOODY HYSTERICAL FEMALE. GET HER OUTTA HERE.
WAIT!
SUFFERING CATS, WOMAN! WHAT IS IT NOW?
HOW MUCH TO GET THEM OUT?
WHO?
EVERYONE!!

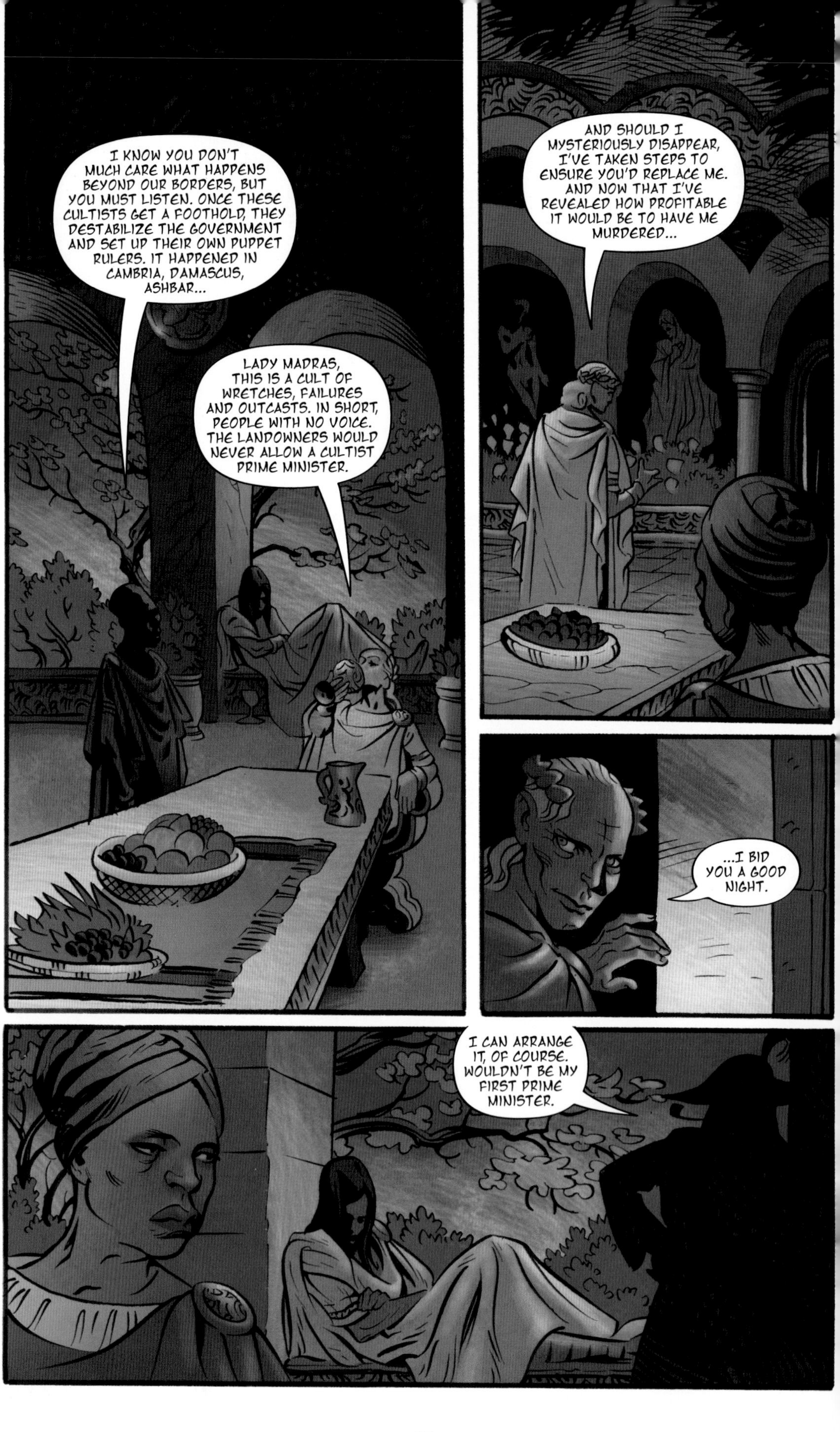
I KNOW YOU DON'T MUCH CARE WHAT HAPPENS BEYOND OUR BORDERS, BUT YOU MUST LISTEN. ONCE THESE CULTISTS GET A FOOTHOLD, THEY DESTABILIZE THE GOVERNMENT AND SET UP THEIR OWN PUPPET RULERS. IT HAPPENED IN CAMBRIA, DAMASCUS, ASHBAR...
LADY MADRAS, THIS IS A CULT OF WRETCHES, FAILURES AND OUTCASTS. IN SHORT, PEOPLE WITH NO VOICE. THE LANDOWNERS WOULD NEVER ALLOW A CULTIST PRIME MINISTER.
AND SHOULD I MYSTERIOUSLY DISAPPEAR, I'VE TAKEN STEPS TO ENSURE YOU'D REPLACE ME. AND NOW THAT I'VE REVEALED HOW PROFITABLE IT WOULD BE TO HAVE ME MURDERED...
...I BID YOU A GOOD NIGHT.
I CAN ARRANGE IT, OF COURSE. WOULDN'T BE MY FIRST PRIME MINISTER.

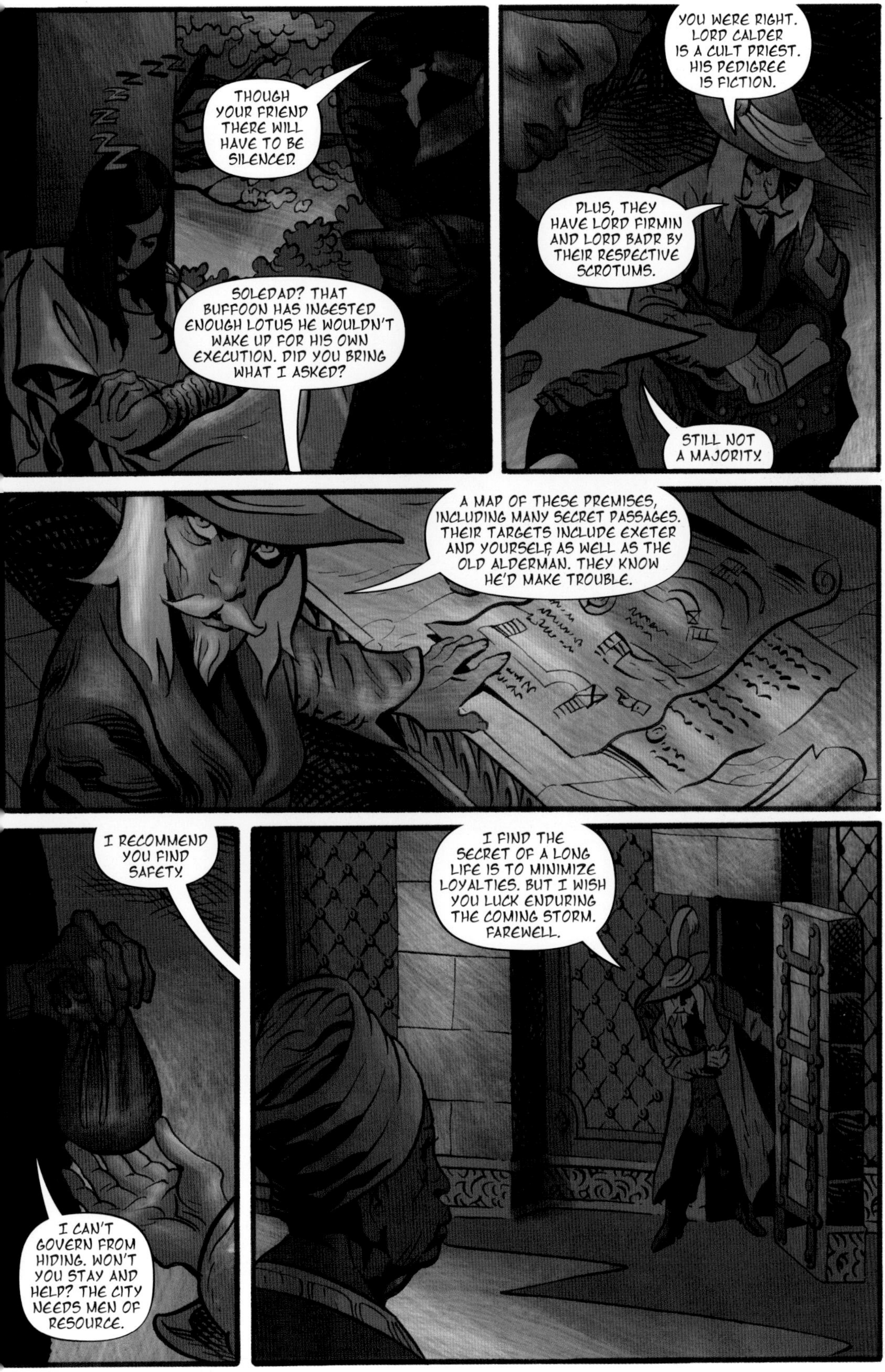
THOUGH YOUR FRIEND THERE WILL HAVE TO BE SILENCED.
SOLEDAD? THAT BUFFOON HAS INGESTED ENOUGH LOTUS HE WOULDN'T WAKE UP FOR HIS OWN EXECUTION. DID YOU BRING WHAT I ASKED?
YOU WERE RIGHT. LORD CALDER IS A CULT PRIEST. HIS PEDIGREE IS FICTION.
PLUS, THEY HAVE LORD FIRMIN AND LORD BADR BY THEIR RESPECTIVE SCROTUMS.
STILL NOT A MAJORITY.
A MAP OF THESE PREMISES, INCLUDING MANY SECRET PASSAGES. THEIR TARGETS INCLUDE EXETER AND YOURSELF, AS WELL AS THE OLD ALDERMAN. THEY KNOW HE'D MAKE TROUBLE.
I RECOMMEND YOU FIND SAFETY.
I CAN'T GOVERN FROM HIDING. WON'T YOU STAY AND HELP? THE CITY NEEDS MEN OF RESOURCE.
I FIND THE SECRET OF A LONG LIFE IS TO MINIMIZE LOYALTIES. BUT I WISH YOU LUCK ENDURING THE COMING STORM. FAREWELL.

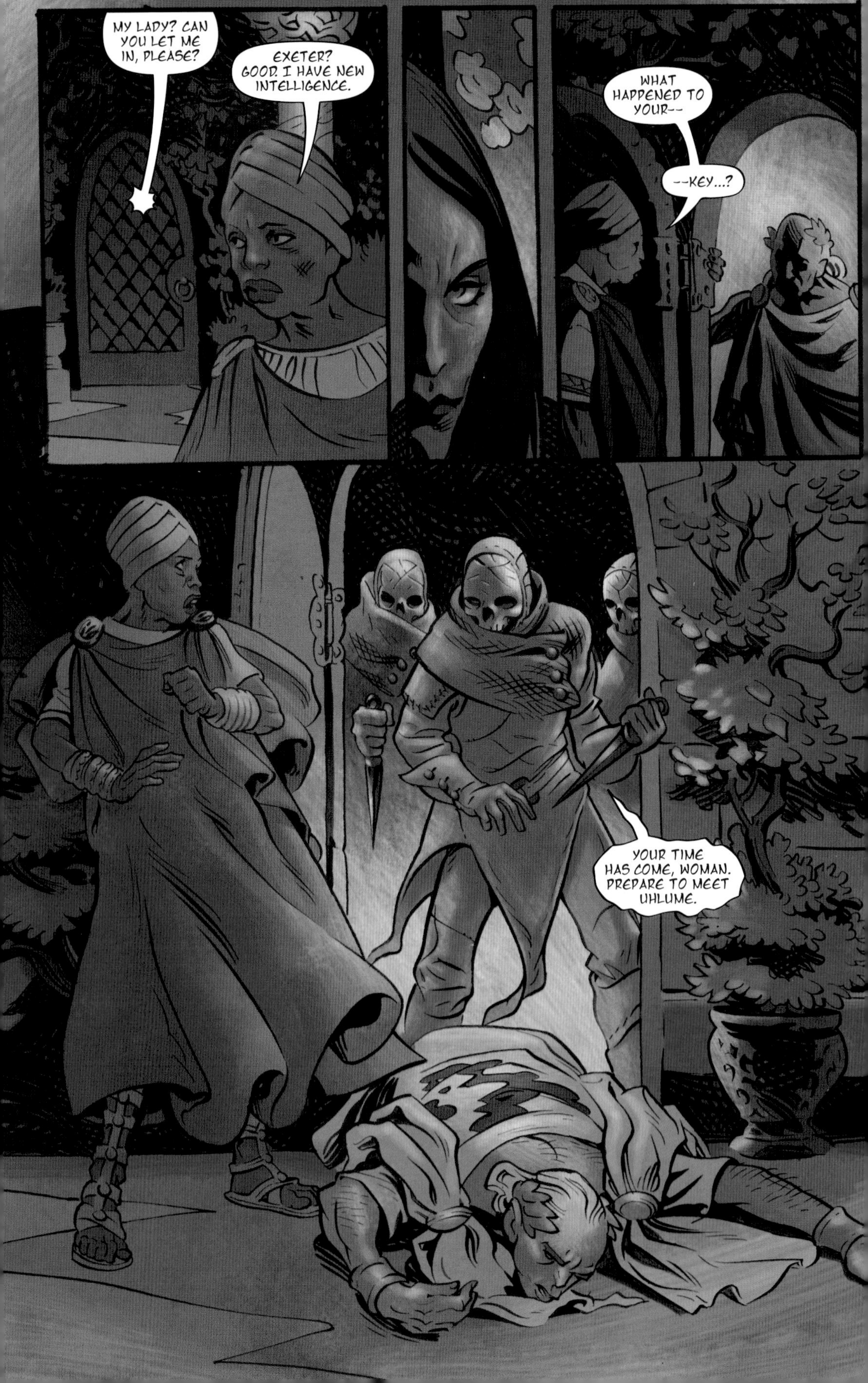
MY LADY? CAN YOU LET ME IN, PLEASE?
EXETER? GOOD. I HAVE NEW INTELLIGENCE.
WHAT HAPPENED TO YOUR--
--KEY...?
YOUR TIME HAS COME, WOMAN. PREPARE TO MEET UHLUME.

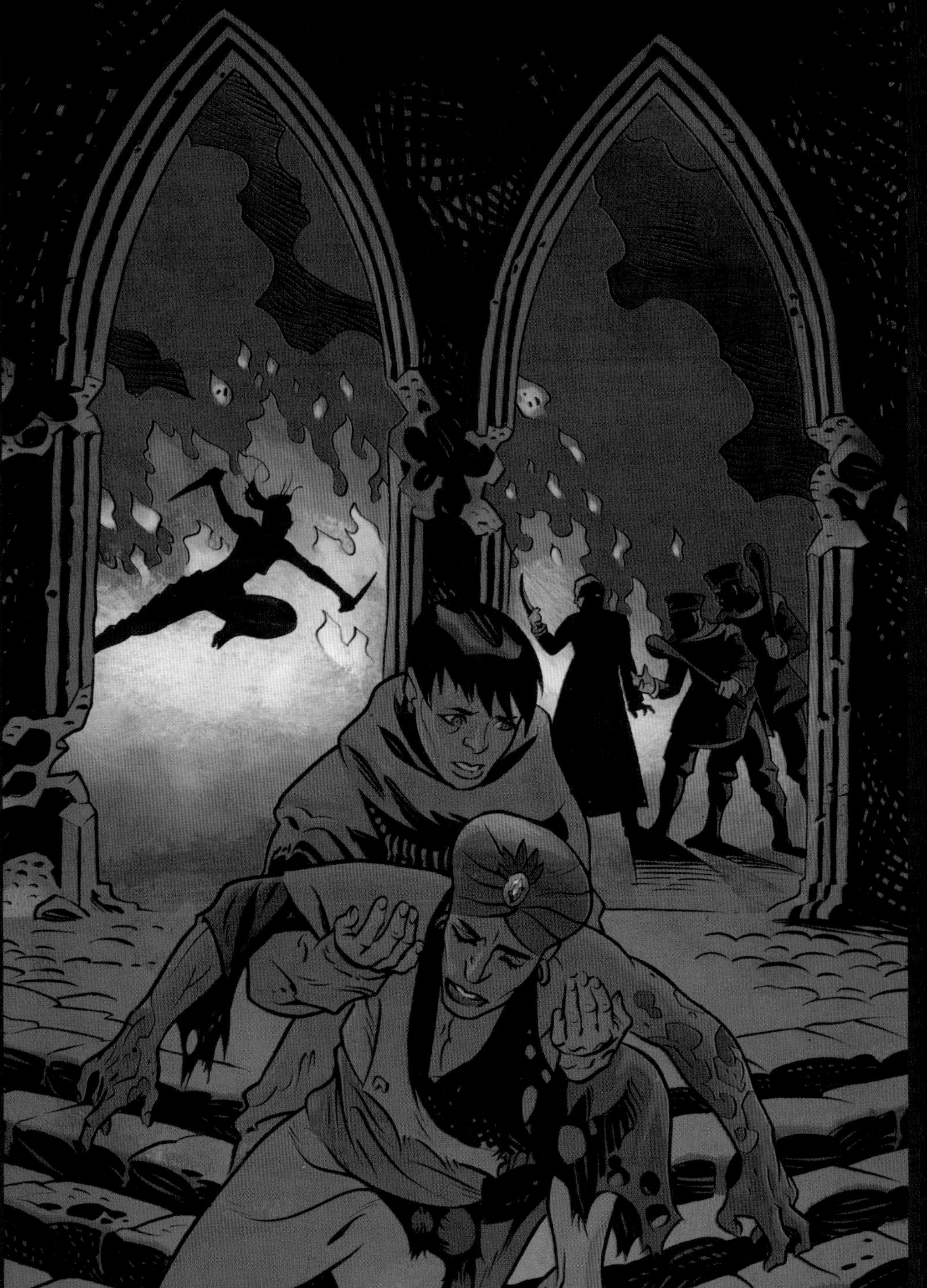

Chapter 4

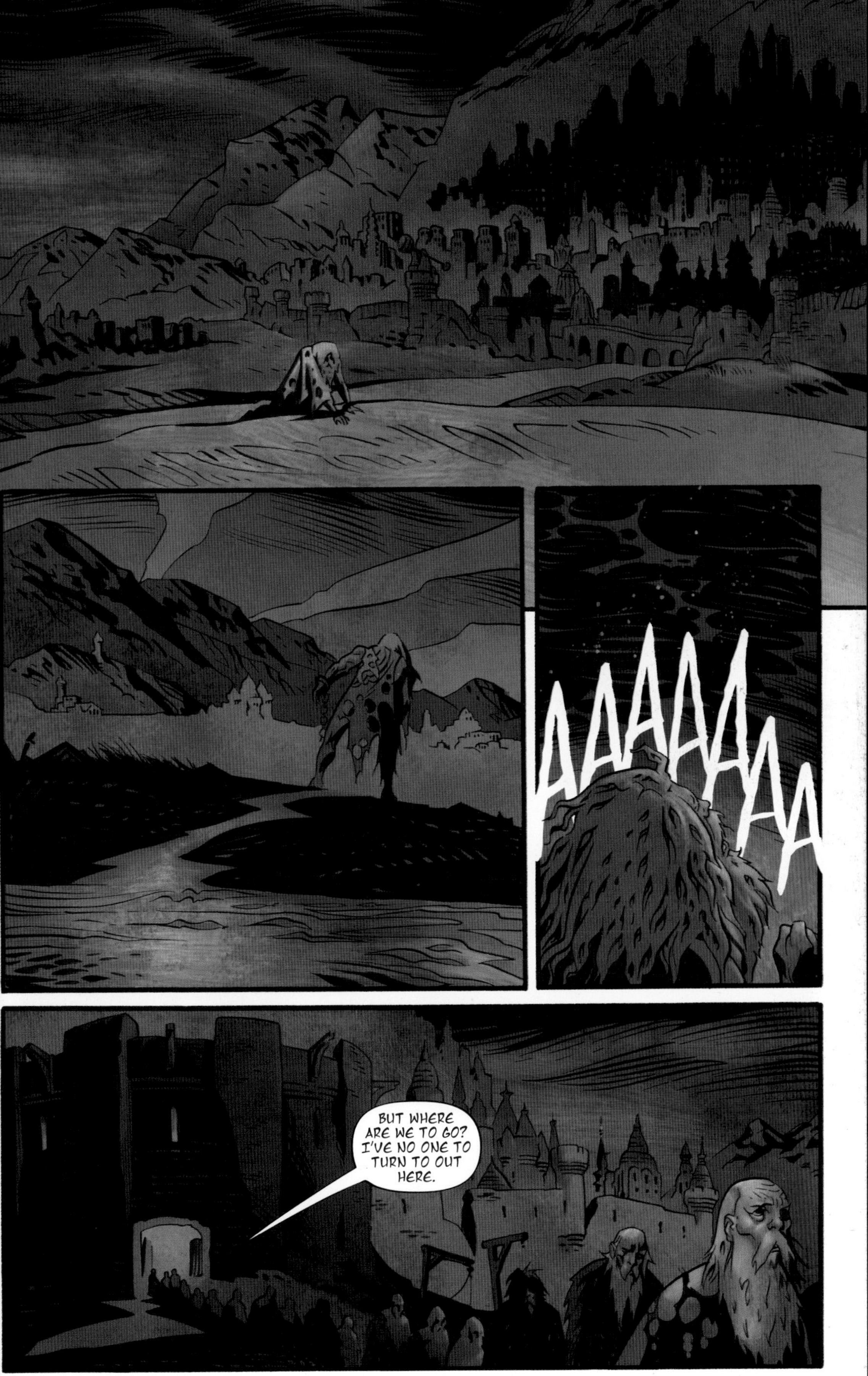
AAAAAAA
BUT WHERE ARE WE TO GO? I'VE NO ONE TO TURN TO OUT HERE.

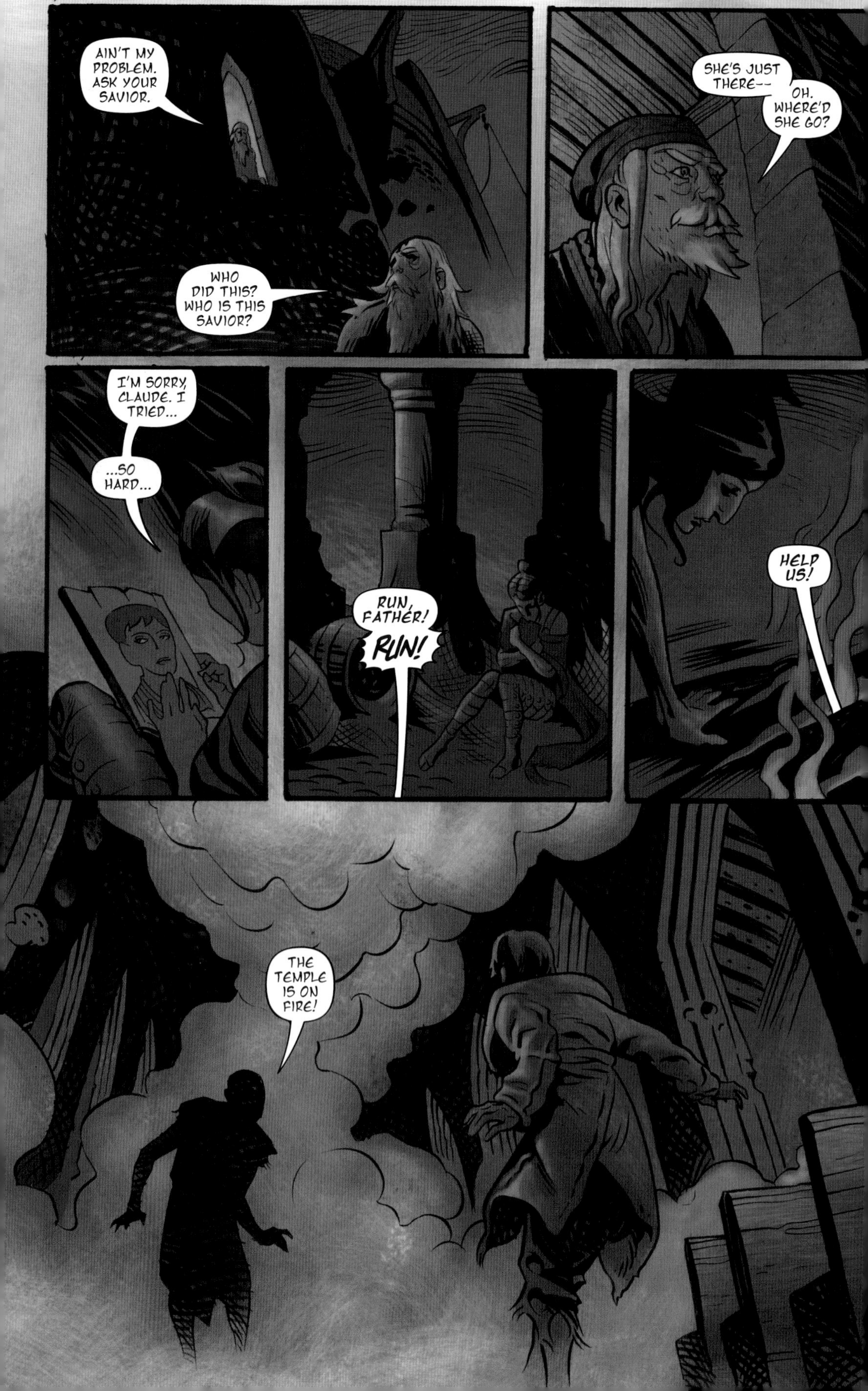

AIN'T MY PROBLEM. ASK YOUR SAVIOR.
WHO DID THIS? WHO IS THIS SAVIOR?
SHE'S JUST THERE--
OH. WHERE'D SHE GO?
I'M SORRY, CLAUDE. I TRIED...
...SO HARD...
RUN, FATHER!
RUN!
HELP US!
THE TEMPLE IS ON FIRE!

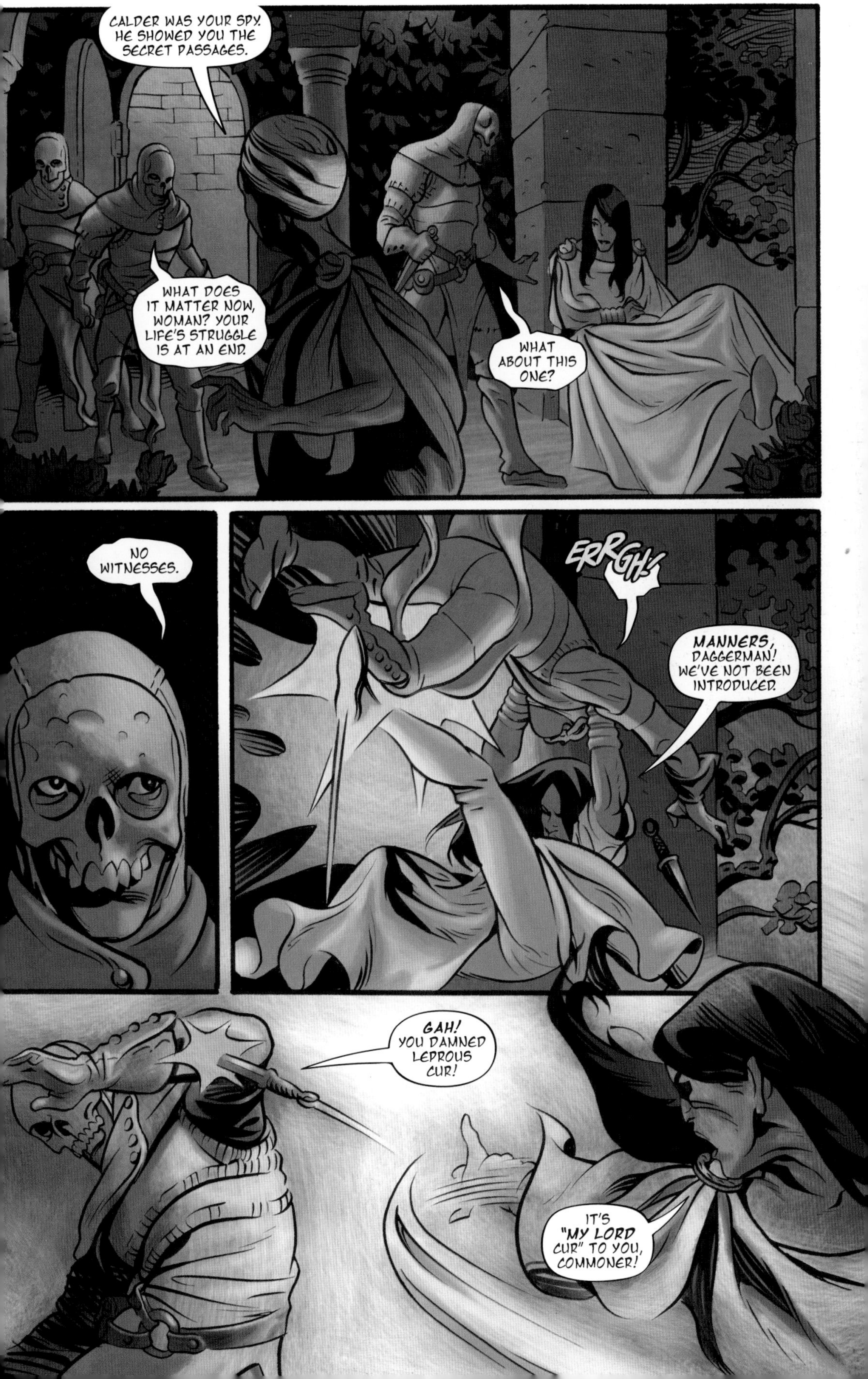
CALDER WAS YOUR SPY. HE SHOWED YOU THE SECRET PASSAGES.
WHAT DOES IT MATTER NOW, WOMAN? YOUR LIFE'S STRUGGLE IS AT AN END.
WHAT ABOUT THIS ONE?
NO WITNESSES.
ERRGH!
MANNERS, DAGGERMAN! WE'VE NOT BEEN INTRODUCED.
GAH! YOU DAMNED LEPROUS CUR!
IT'S "MY LORD CUR" TO YOU, COMMONER!

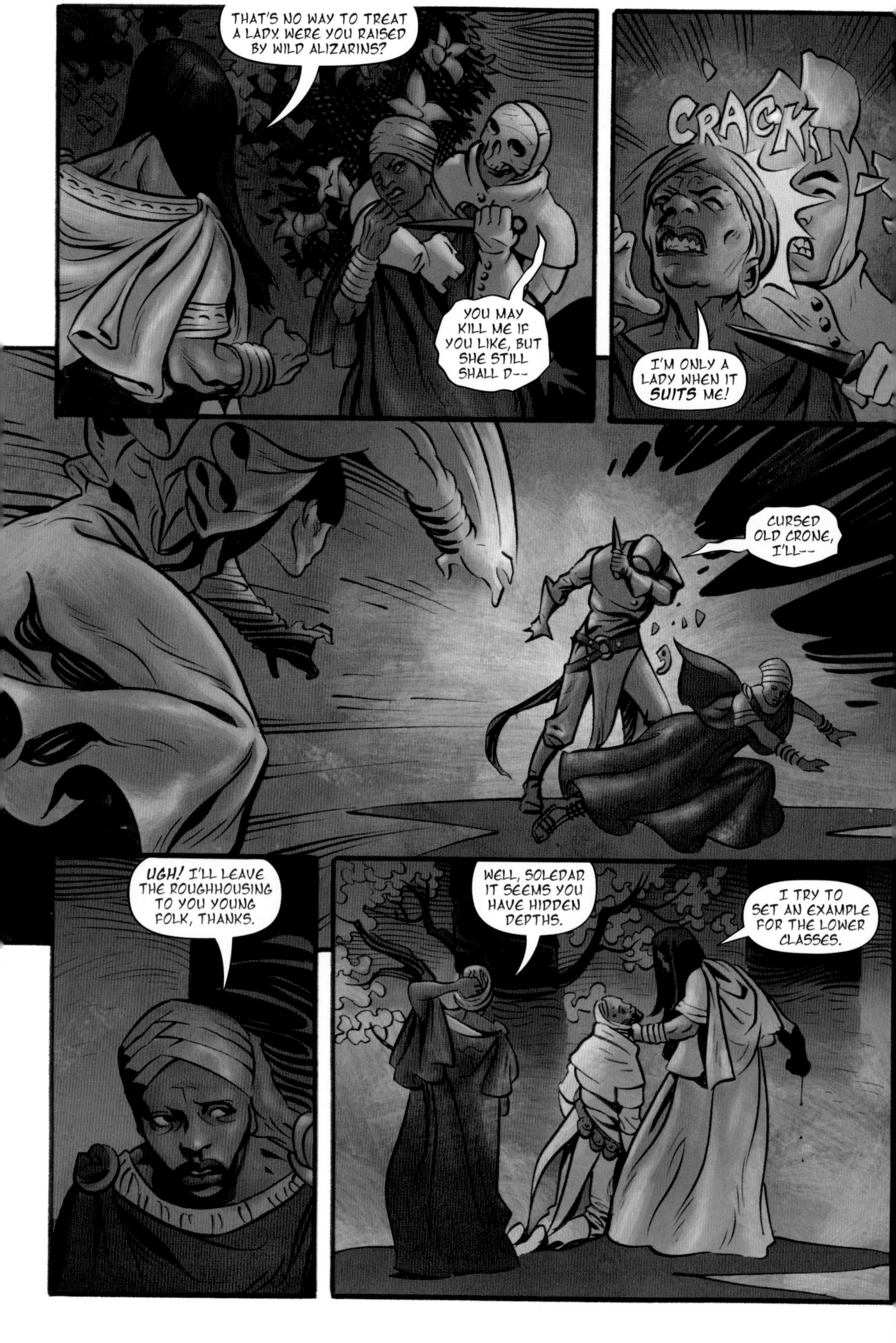
THAT'S NO WAY TO TREAT A LADY. WERE YOU RAISED BY WILD ALIZARINS?
YOU MAY KILL ME IF YOU LIKE, BUT SHE STILL SHALL D--
CRACK
I'M ONLY A LADY WHEN IT SUITS ME!
CURSED OLD CRONE, I'LL--
UGH! I'LL LEAVE THE ROUGHHOUSING TO YOU YOUNG FOLK, THANKS.
WELL, SOLEDAD. IT SEEMS YOU HAVE HIDDEN DEPTHS.
I TRY TO SET AN EXAMPLE FOR THE LOWER CLASSES.

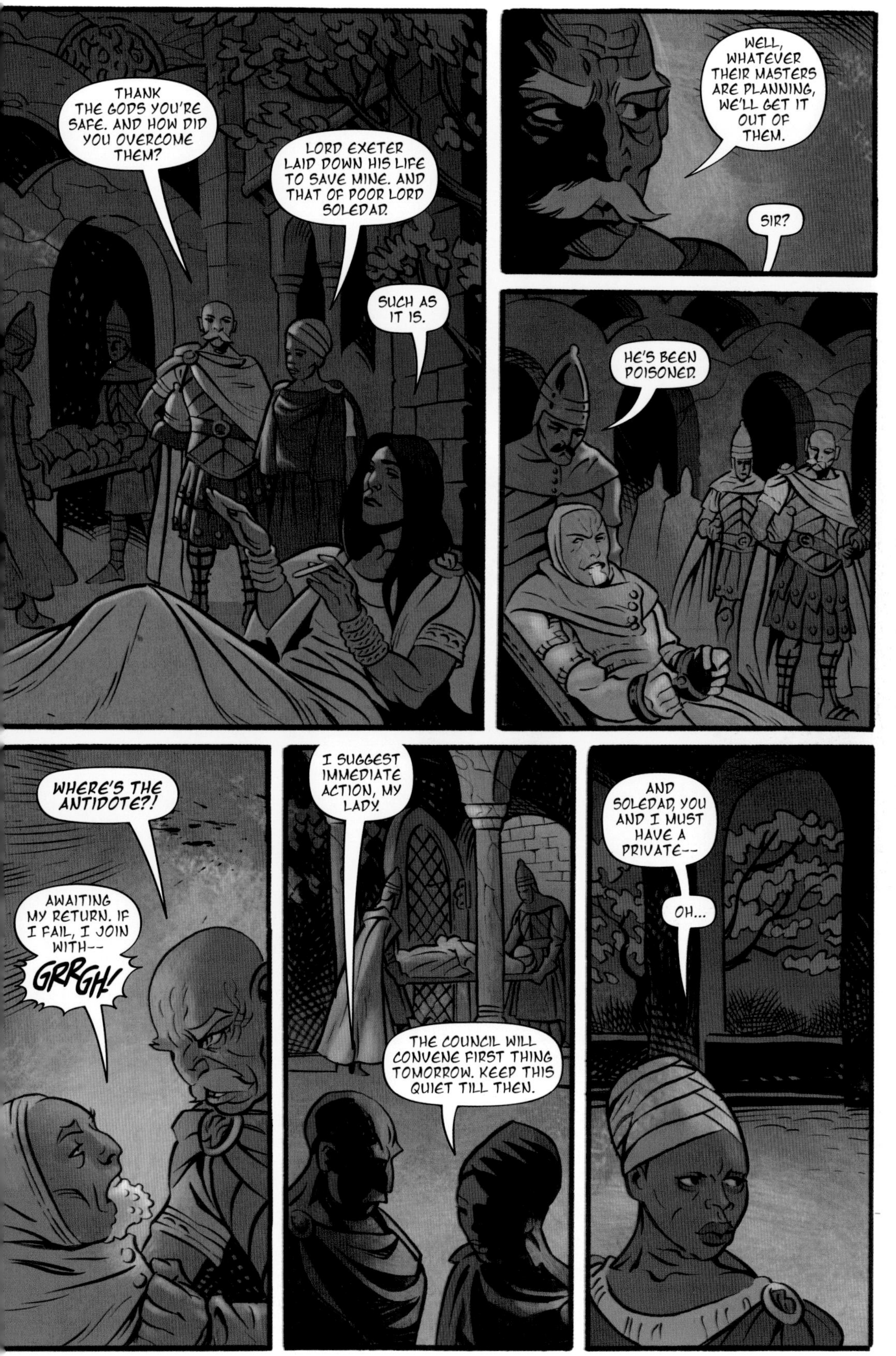
THANK THE GODS YOU'RE SAFE. AND HOW DID YOU OVERCOME THEM?
LORD EXETER LAID DOWN HIS LIFE TO SAVE MINE. AND THAT OF POOR LORD SOLEDAD.
SUCH AS IT IS.
WELL, WHATEVER THEIR MASTERS ARE PLANNING, WE'LL GET IT OUT OF THEM.
SIR?
HE'S BEEN POISONED.
WHERE'S THE ANTIDOTE?!
AWAITING MY RETURN. IF I FAIL, I JOIN WITH--
GRRGH!
I SUGGEST IMMEDIATE ACTION, MY LADY.
THE COUNCIL WILL CONVENE FIRST THING TOMORROW. KEEP THIS QUIET TILL THEN.
AND SOLEDAD, YOU AND I MUST HAVE A PRIVATE--
OH...

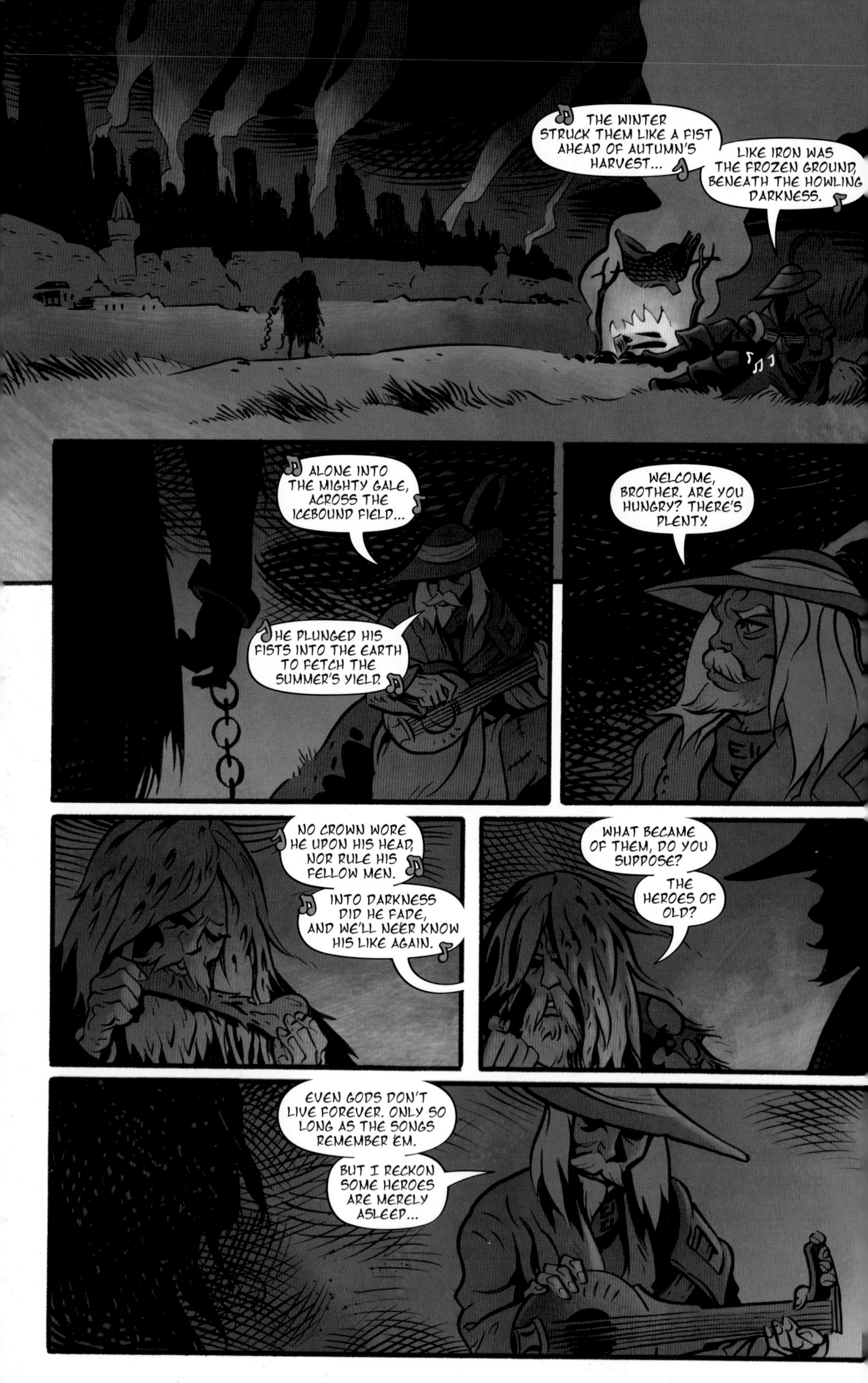
THE WINTER STRUCK THEM LIKE A FIST AHEAD OF AUTUMN'S HARVEST...
LIKE IRON WAS THE FROZEN GROUND, BENEATH THE HOWLING DARKNESS.
ALONE INTO THE MIGHTY GALE, ACROSS THE ICEBOUND FIELD...
HE PLUNGED HIS FISTS INTO THE EARTH TO FETCH THE SUMMER'S YIELD.
WELCOME, BROTHER. ARE YOU HUNGRY? THERE'S PLENTY.
NO CROWN WORE HE UPON HIS HEAD, NOR RULE HIS FELLOW MEN.
INTO DARKNESS DID HE FADE, AND WE'LL NE'ER KNOW HIS LIKE AGAIN.
WHAT BECAME OF THEM, DO YOU SUPPOSE?
THE HEROES OF OLD?
EVEN GODS DON'T LIVE FOREVER. ONLY SO LONG AS THE SONGS REMEMBER 'EM.
BUT I RECKON SOME HEROES ARE MERELY ASLEEP...

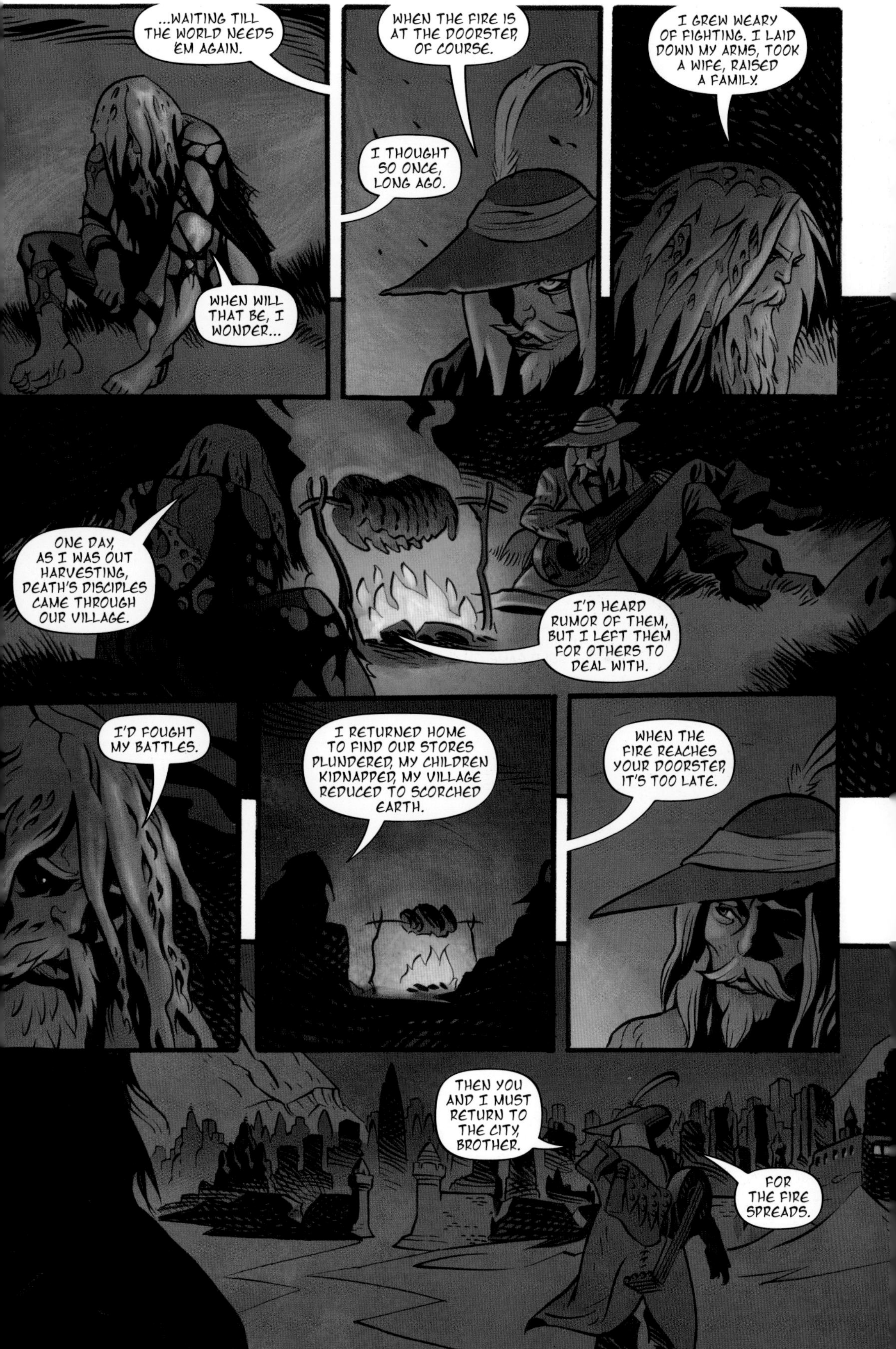
...WAITING TILL THE WORLD NEEDS 'EM AGAIN.
WHEN WILL THAT BE, I WONDER...
WHEN THE FIRE IS AT THE DOORSTEP, OF COURSE.
I THOUGHT SO ONCE, LONG AGO.
I GREW WEARY OF FIGHTING. I LAID DOWN MY ARMS, TOOK A WIFE, RAISED A FAMILY.
ONE DAY, AS I WAS OUT HARVESTING, DEATH'S DISCIPLES CAME THROUGH OUR VILLAGE.
I'D HEARD RUMOR OF THEM, BUT I LEFT THEM FOR OTHERS TO DEAL WITH.
I'D FOUGHT MY BATTLES.
I RETURNED HOME TO FIND OUR STORES PLUNDERED, MY CHILDREN KIDNAPPED, MY VILLAGE REDUCED TO SCORCHED EARTH.
WHEN THE FIRE REACHES YOUR DOORSTEP, IT'S TOO LATE.
THEN YOU AND I MUST RETURN TO THE CITY, BROTHER.
FOR THE FIRE SPREADS.

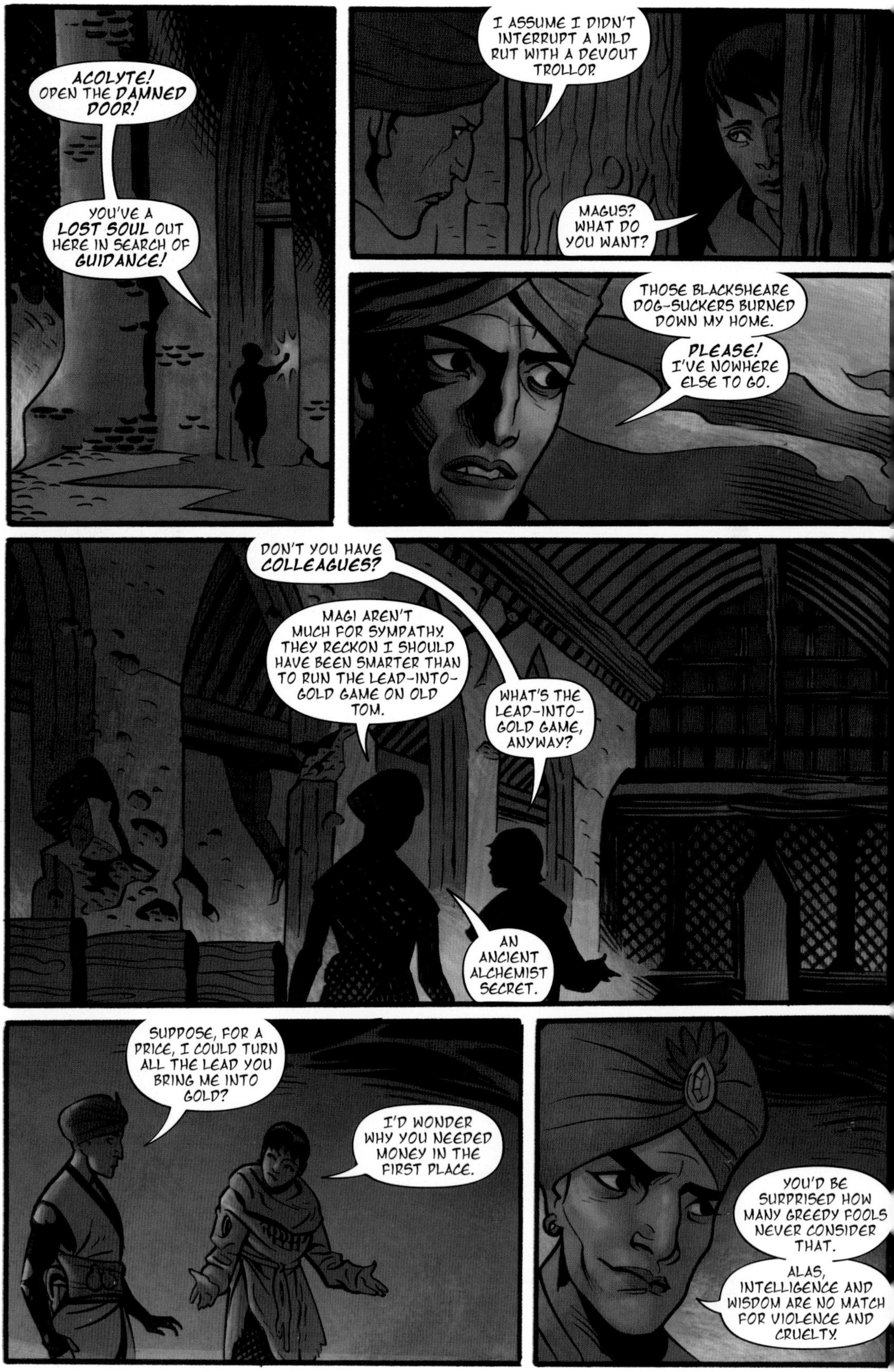
ACOLYTE! OPEN THE DAMNED DOOR!
YOU'VE A LOST SOUL OUT HERE IN SEARCH OF GUIDANCE!
I ASSUME I DIDN'T INTERRUPT A WILD RUT WITH A DEVOUT TROLLOP.
MAGUS? WHAT DO YOU WANT?
THOSE BLACKSHEARE DOG-SUCKERS BURNED DOWN MY HOME.
PLEASE! I'VE NOWHERE ELSE TO GO.
DON'T YOU HAVE COLLEAGUES?
MAGI AREN'T MUCH FOR SYMPATHY. THEY RECKON I SHOULD HAVE BEEN SMARTER THAN TO RUN THE LEAD-INTO-GOLD GAME ON OLD TOM.
WHAT'S THE LEAD-INTO-GOLD GAME, ANYWAY?
AN ANCIENT ALCHEMIST SECRET.
SUPPOSE, FOR A PRICE, I COULD TURN ALL THE LEAD YOU BRING ME INTO GOLD?
I'D WONDER WHY YOU NEEDED MONEY IN THE FIRST PLACE.
YOU'D BE SURPRISED HOW MANY GREEDY FOOLS NEVER CONSIDER THAT.
ALAS, INTELLIGENCE AND WISDOM ARE NO MATCH FOR VIOLENCE AND CRUELTY.

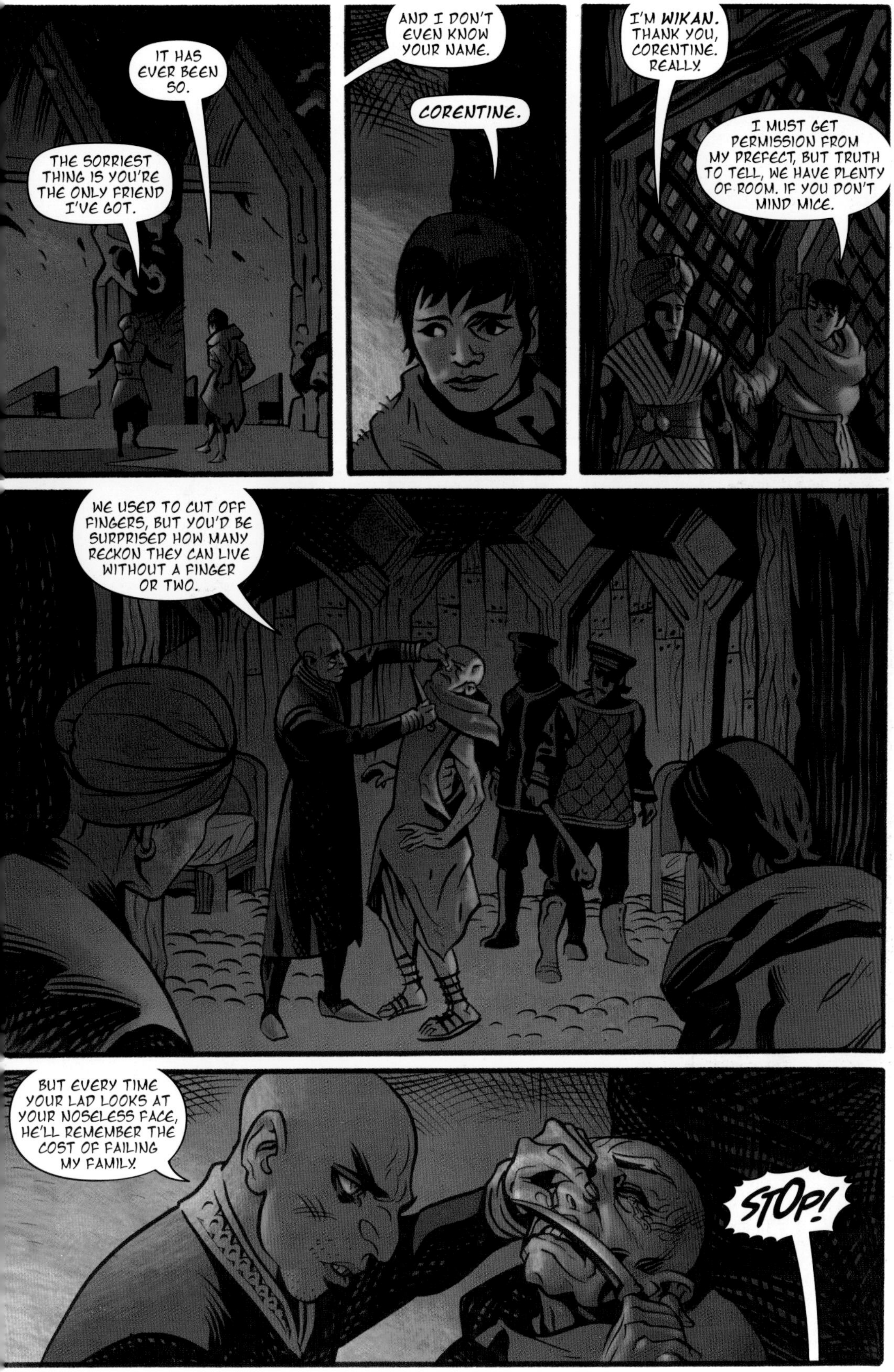
IT HAS EVER BEEN SO.
THE SORRIEST THING IS YOU'RE THE ONLY FRIEND I'VE GOT.
AND I DON'T EVEN KNOW YOUR NAME.
CORENTINE.
I'M WIKAN. THANK YOU, CORENTINE. REALLY.
I MUST GET PERMISSION FROM MY PREFECT, BUT TRUTH TO TELL, WE HAVE PLENTY OF ROOM. IF YOU DON'T MIND MICE.
WE USED TO CUT OFF FINGERS, BUT YOU'D BE SURPRISED HOW MANY RECKON THEY CAN LIVE WITHOUT A FINGER OR TWO.
BUT EVERY TIME YOUR LAD LOOKS AT YOUR NOSELESS FACE, HE'LL REMEMBER THE COST OF FAILING MY FAMILY.
STOP!

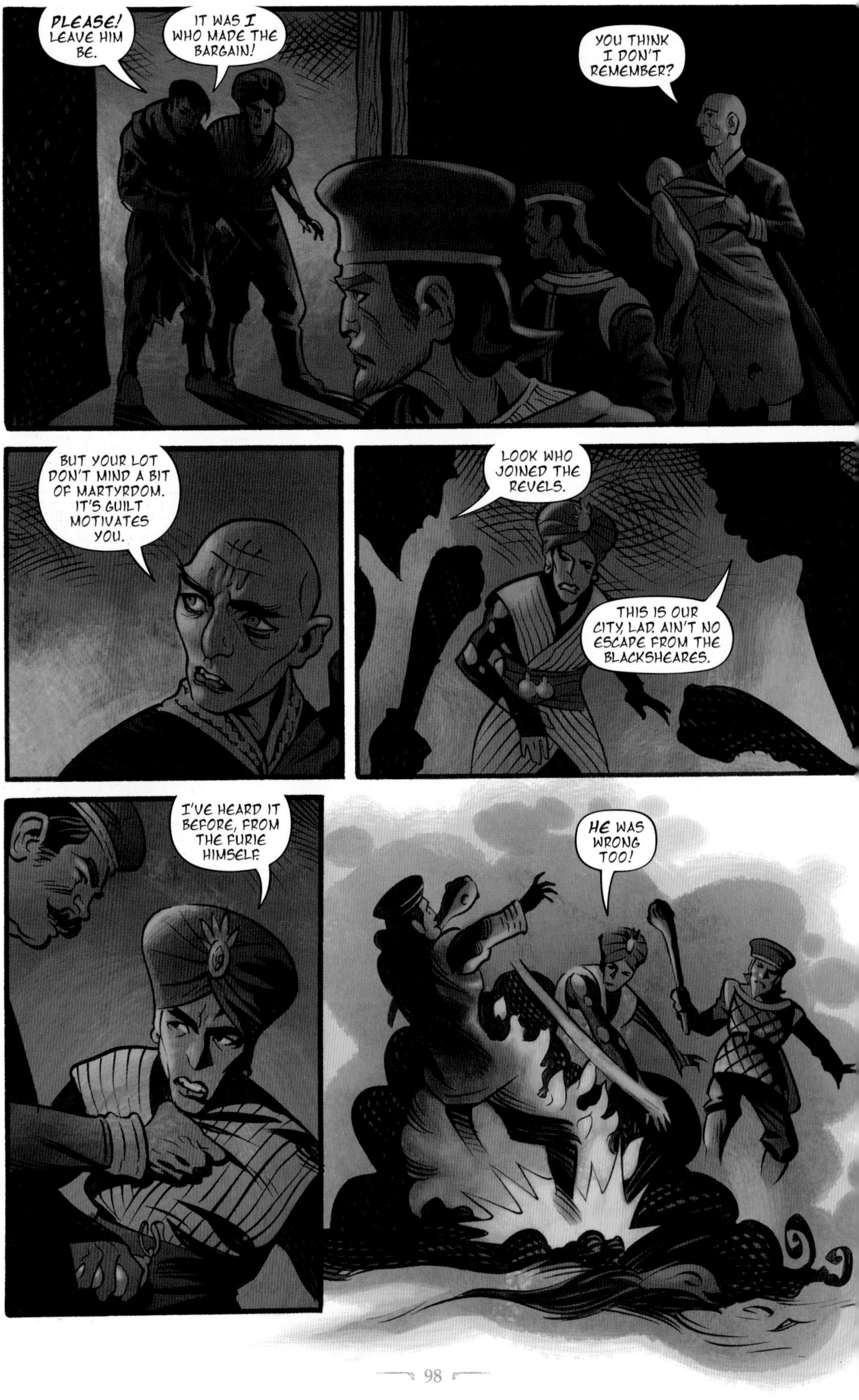

PLEASE! LEAVE HIM BE.
IT WAS I WHO MADE THE BARGAIN!
YOU THINK I DON'T REMEMBER?
BUT YOUR LOT DON'T MIND A BIT OF MARTYRDOM. IT'S GUILT MOTIVATES YOU.
LOOK WHO JOINED THE REVELS.
THIS IS OUR CITY, LAD. AIN'T NO ESCAPE FROM THE BLACKSHEARES.
I'VE HEARD IT BEFORE, FROM THE FURIE HIMSELF.
HE WAS WRONG TOO!

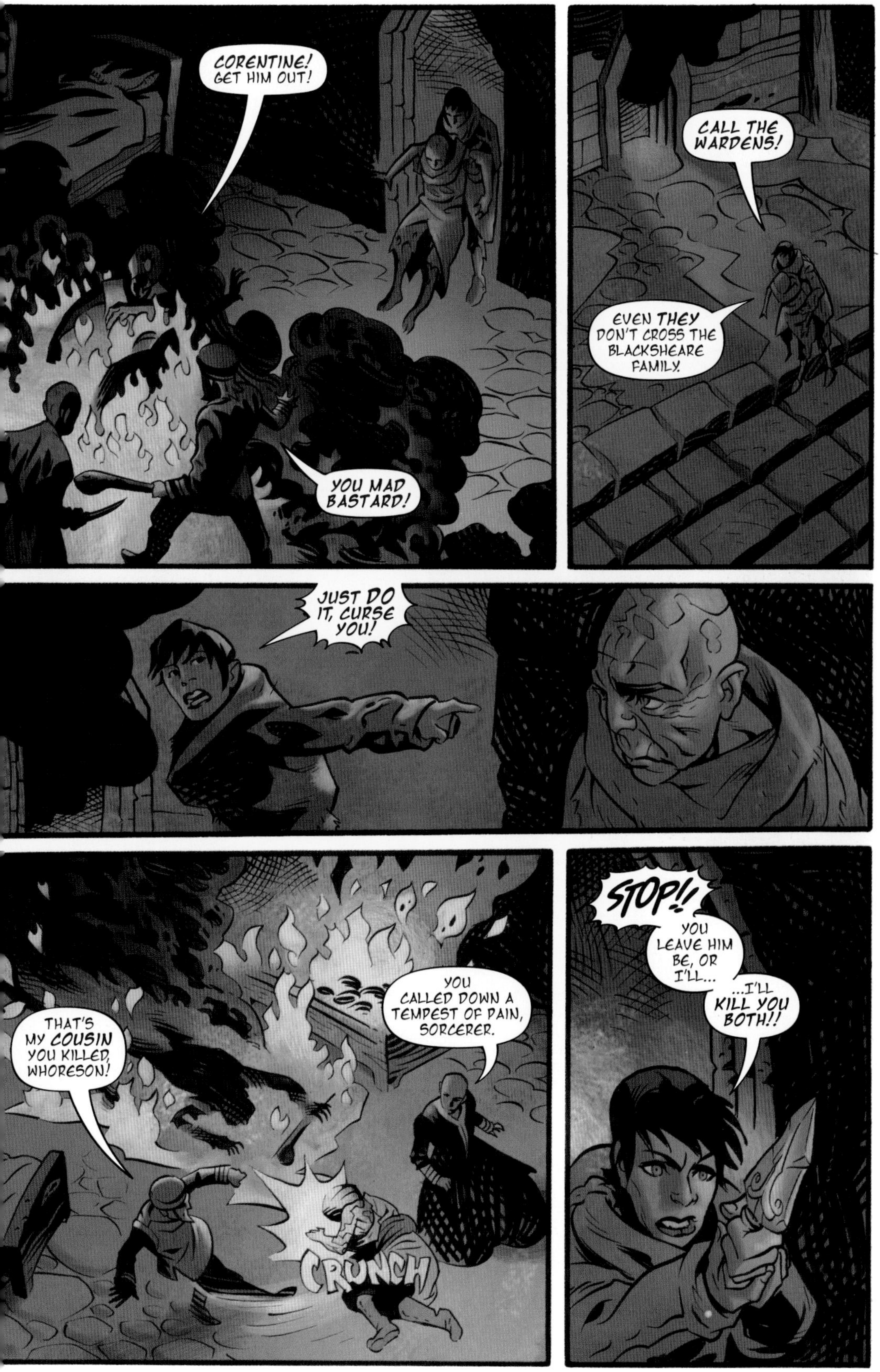
CORENTINE! GET HIM OUT!
YOU MAD BASTARD!
CALL THE WARDENS!
EVEN THEY DON'T CROSS THE BLACKSHEARE FAMILY.
JUST DO IT, CURSE YOU!
THAT'S MY COUSIN YOU KILLED, WHORESON!
YOU CALLED DOWN A TEMPEST OF PAIN, SORCERER.
CRUNCH
STOP!!
YOU LEAVE HIM BE, OR I'LL...
...I'LL KILL YOU BOTH!!

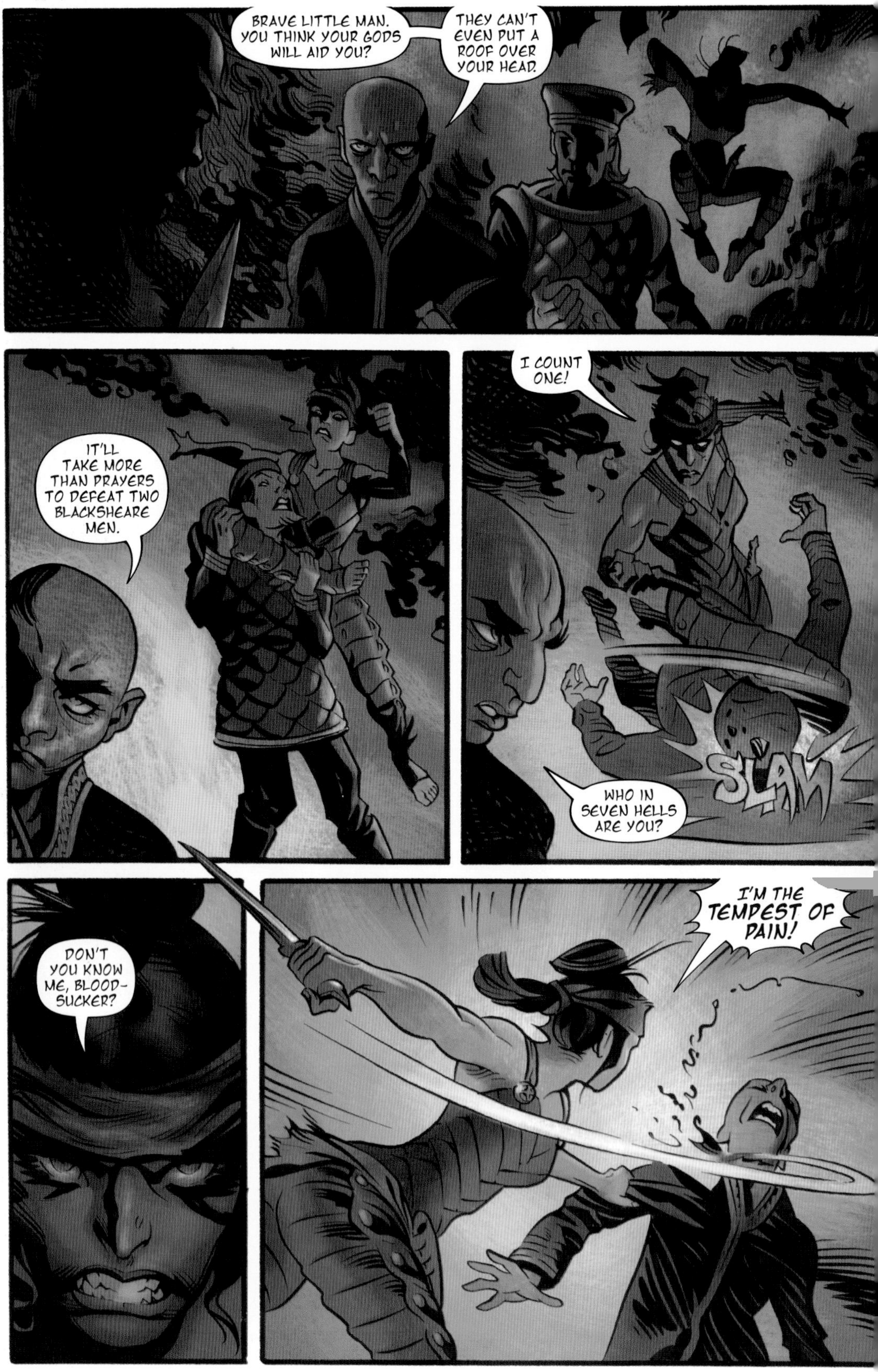
BRAVE LITTLE MAN. YOU THINK YOUR GODS WILL AID YOU?
THEY CAN'T EVEN PUT A ROOF OVER YOUR HEAD.
IT'LL TAKE MORE THAN PRAYERS TO DEFEAT TWO BLACKSHEARE MEN.
I COUNT ONE!
SLAM
WHO IN SEVEN HELLS ARE YOU?
DON'T YOU KNOW ME, BLOOD-SUCKER?
I'M THE TEMPEST OF PAIN!

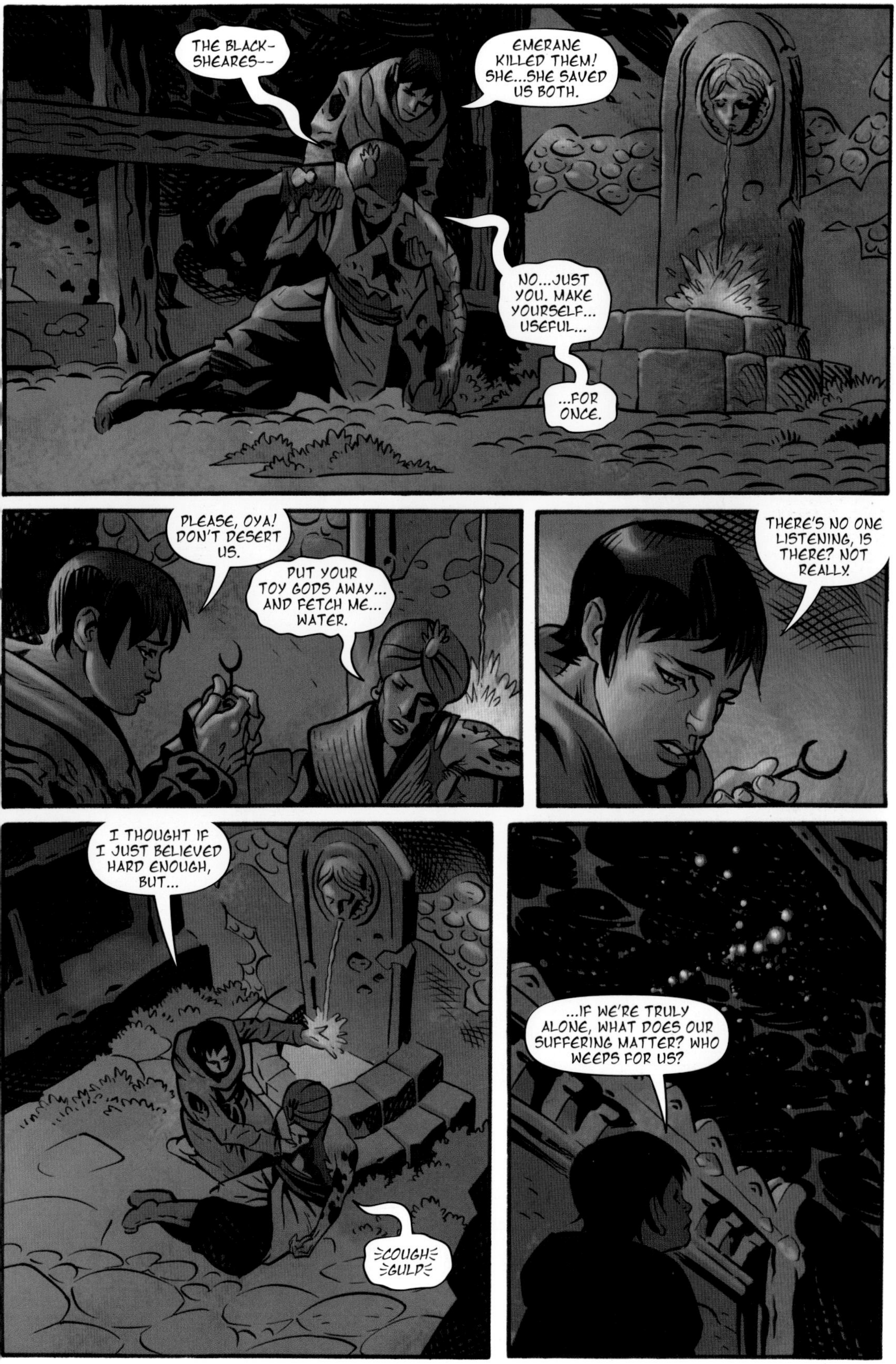
THE BLACK-SHEARES--
EMERANE KILLED THEM! SHE...SHE SAVED US BOTH.
NO...JUST YOU. MAKE YOURSELF... USEFUL...
...FOR ONCE.
PLEASE, OYA! DON'T DESERT US.
PUT YOUR TOY GODS AWAY... AND FETCH ME... WATER.
THERE'S NO ONE LISTENING, IS THERE? NOT REALLY.
I THOUGHT IF I JUST BELIEVED HARD ENOUGH, BUT...
COUGH GULP
...IF WE'RE TRULY ALONE, WHAT DOES OUR SUFFERING MATTER? WHO WEEPS FOR US?

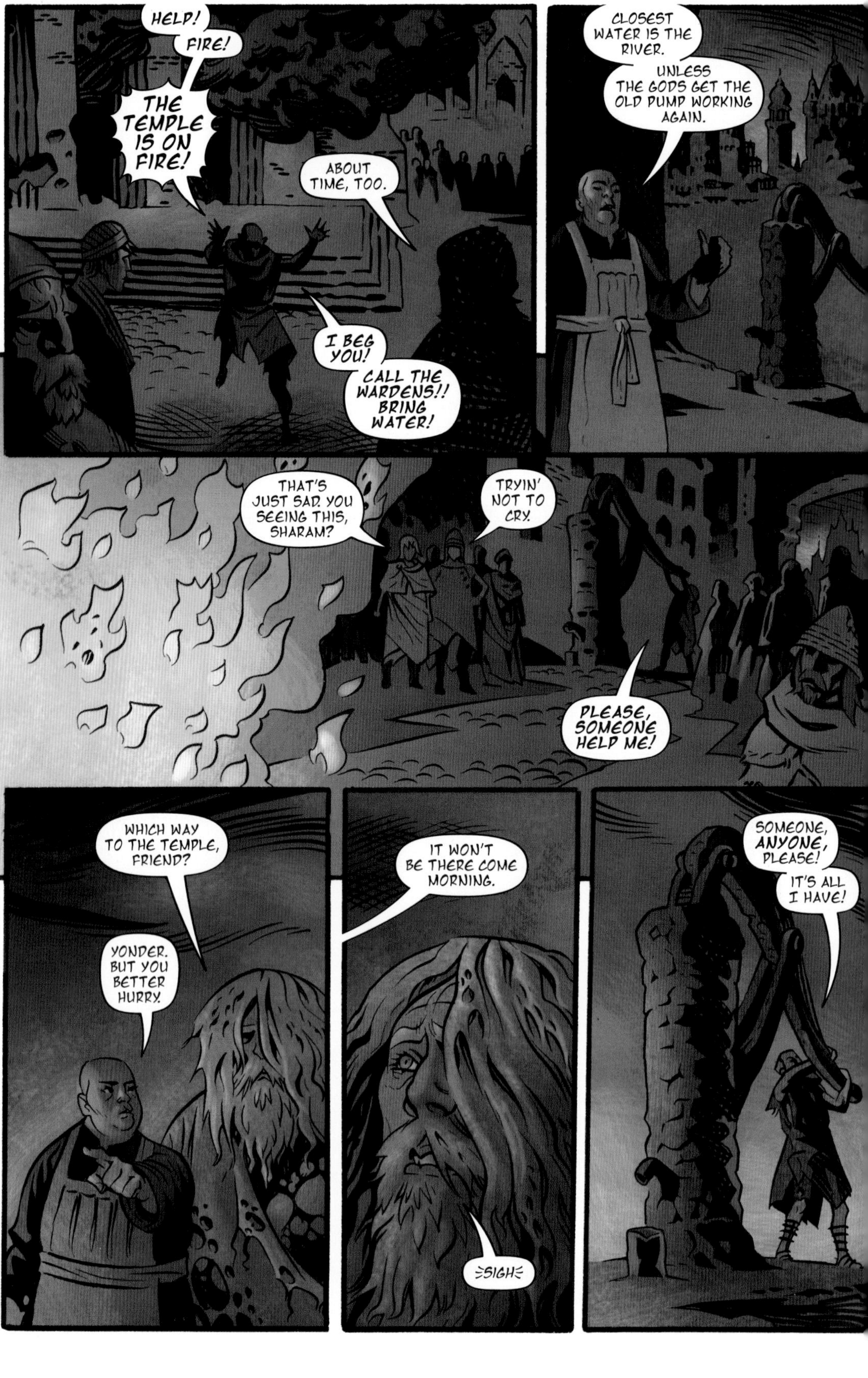
HELP!
FIRE!
THE TEMPLE IS ON FIRE!
ABOUT TIME, TOO.
I BEG YOU!
CALL THE WARDENS!! BRING WATER!
CLOSEST WATER IS THE RIVER.
UNLESS THE GODS GET THE OLD PUMP WORKING AGAIN.
THAT'S JUST SAD. YOU SEEING THIS, SHARAM?
TRYIN' NOT TO CRY.
PLEASE, SOMEONE HELP ME!
WHICH WAY TO THE TEMPLE, FRIEND?
YONDER. BUT YOU BETTER HURRY.
IT WON'T BE THERE COME MORNING.
SIGH
SOMEONE, ANYONE, PLEASE!
IT'S ALL I HAVE!

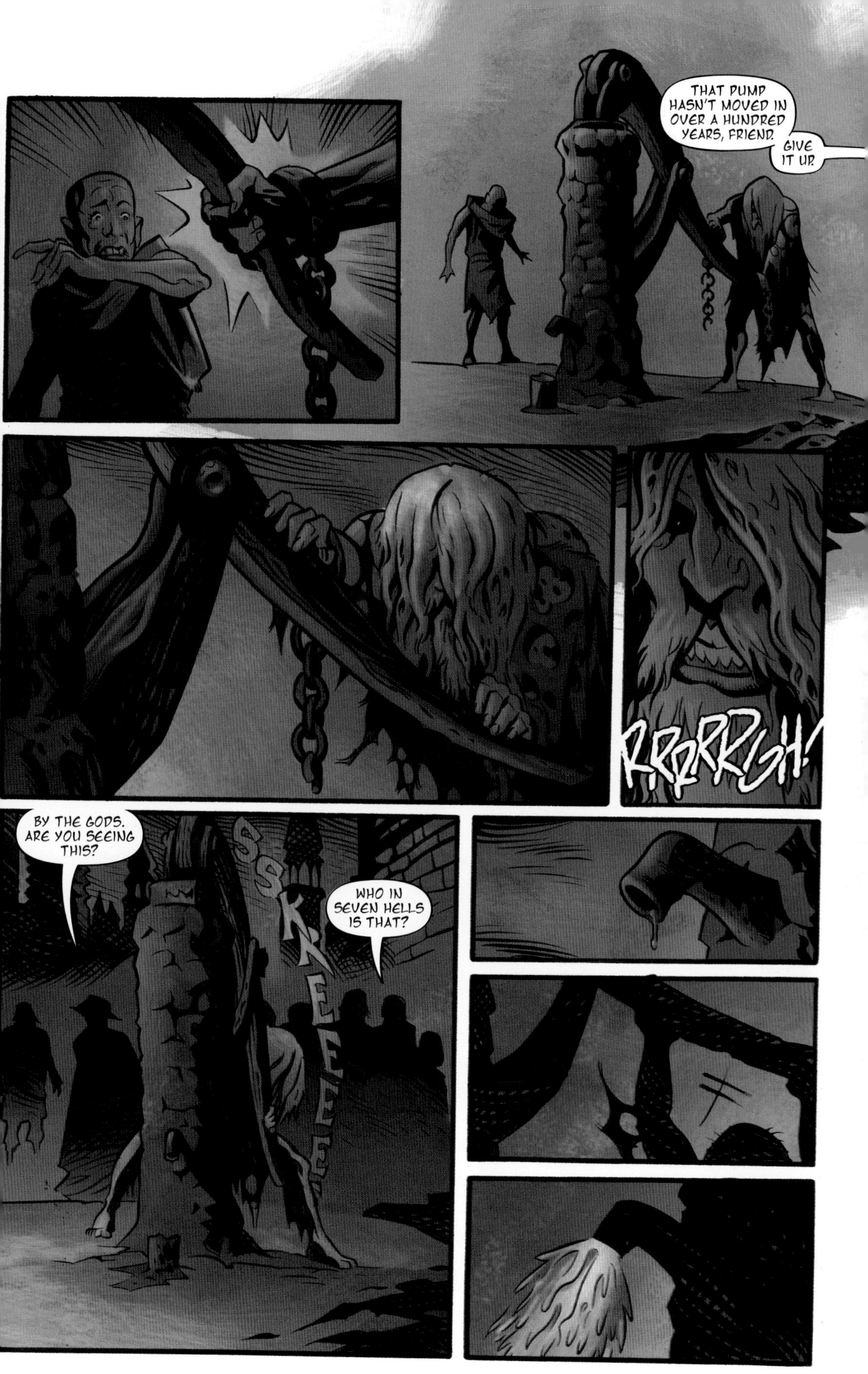
THAT PUMP HASN'T MOVED IN OVER A HUNDRED YEARS, FRIEND.
GIVE IT UP.
RRRRRGH!
BY THE GODS. ARE YOU SEEING THIS?
SSKREEEEE
WHO IN SEVEN HELLS IS THAT?

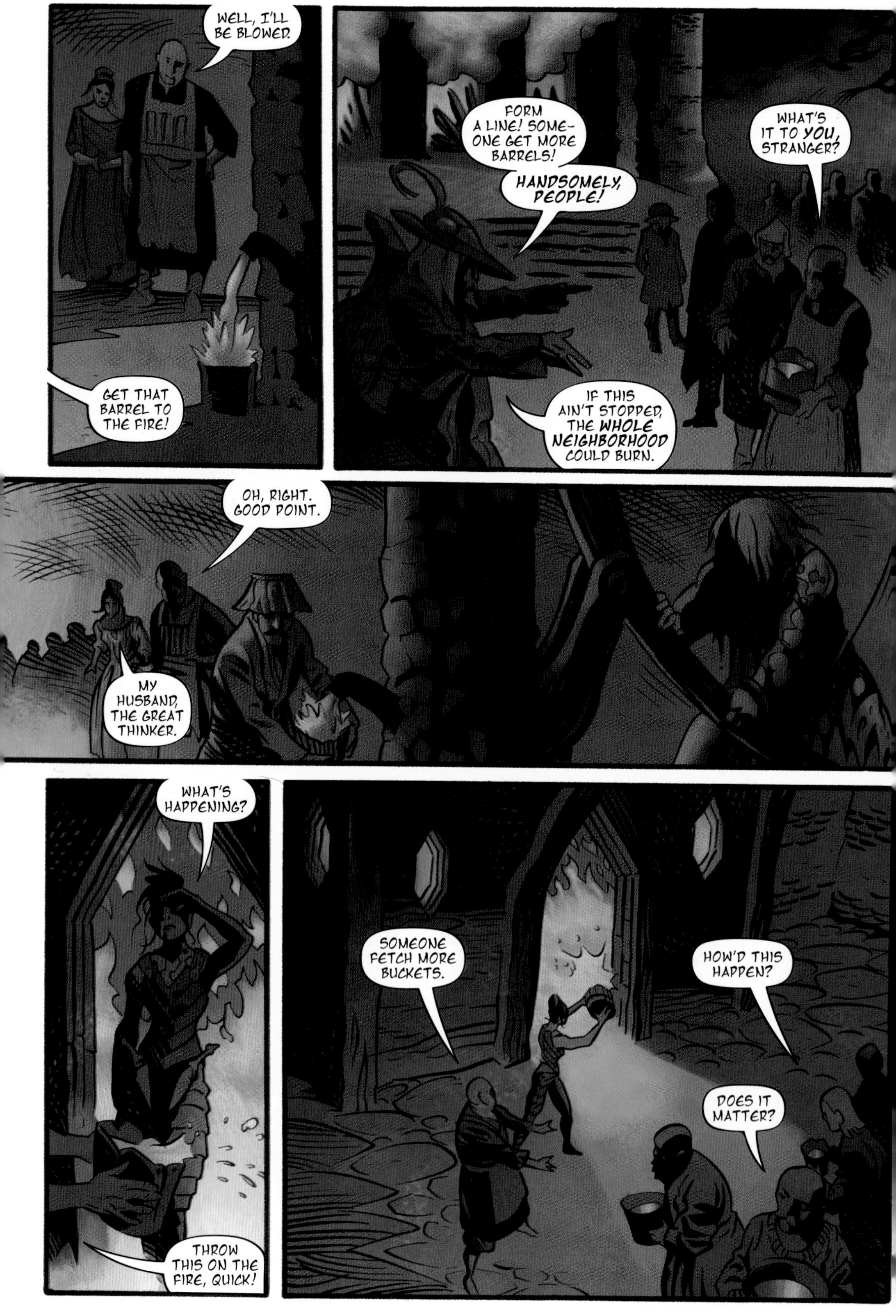
WELL, I'LL BE BLOWED.
GET THAT BARREL TO THE FIRE!
FORM A LINE! SOMEONE GET MORE BARRELS!
HANDSOMELY, PEOPLE!
WHAT'S IT TO YOU, STRANGER?
IF THIS AIN'T STOPPED, THE WHOLE NEIGHBORHOOD COULD BURN.
OH, RIGHT. GOOD POINT.
MY HUSBAND, THE GREAT THINKER.
WHAT'S HAPPENING?
THROW THIS ON THE FIRE, QUICK!
SOMEONE FETCH MORE BUCKETS.
HOW'D THIS HAPPEN?
DOES IT MATTER?

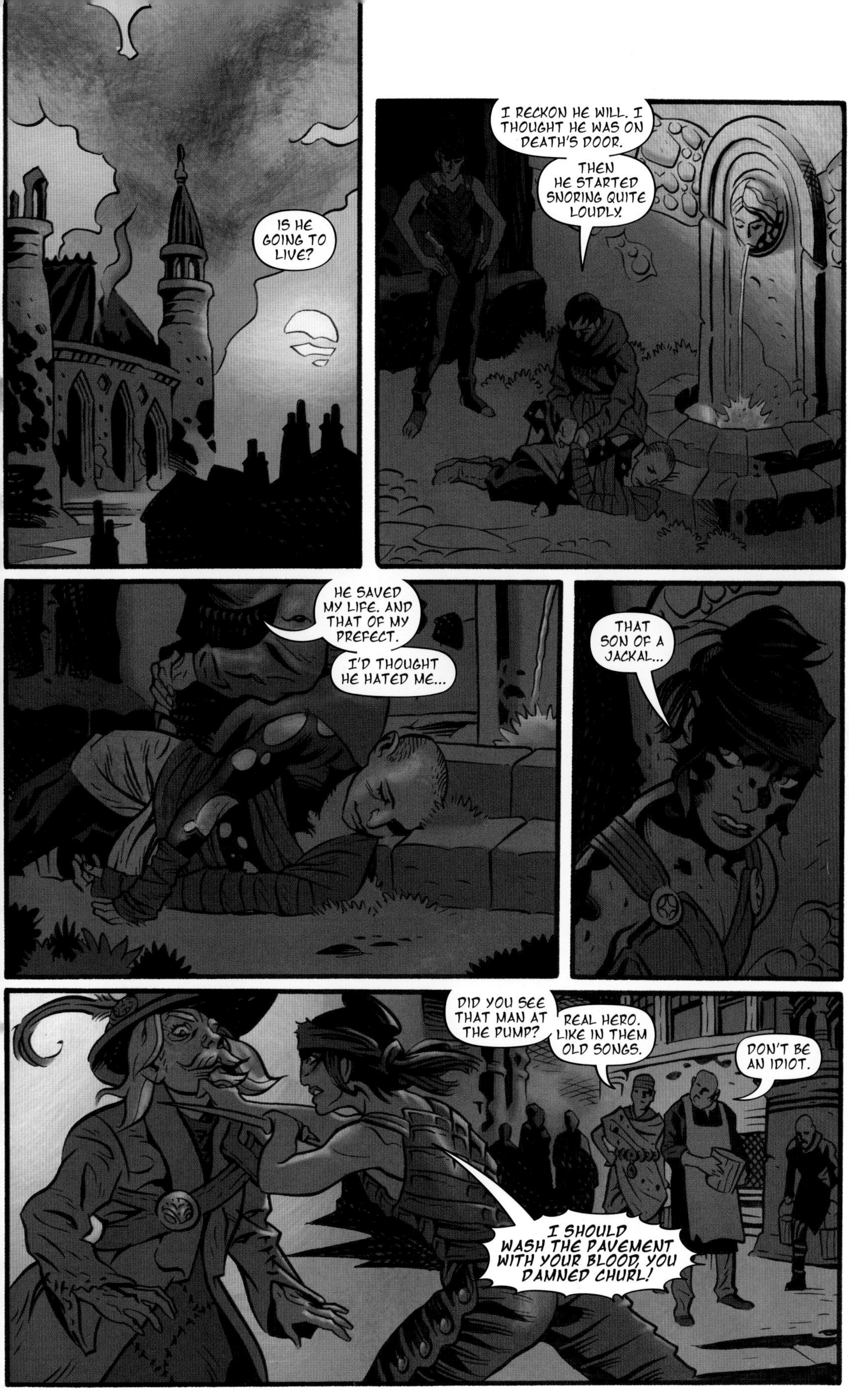
IS HE GOING TO LIVE?
I RECKON HE WILL. I THOUGHT HE WAS ON DEATH'S DOOR.
THEN HE STARTED SNORING QUITE LOUDLY.
HE SAVED MY LIFE. AND THAT OF MY PREFECT.
I'D THOUGHT HE HATED ME...
THAT SON OF A JACKAL...
DID YOU SEE THAT MAN AT THE PUMP?
REAL HERO. LIKE IN THEM OLD SONGS.
DON'T BE AN IDIOT.
I SHOULD WASH THE PAVEMENT WITH YOUR BLOOD, YOU DAMNED CHURL!

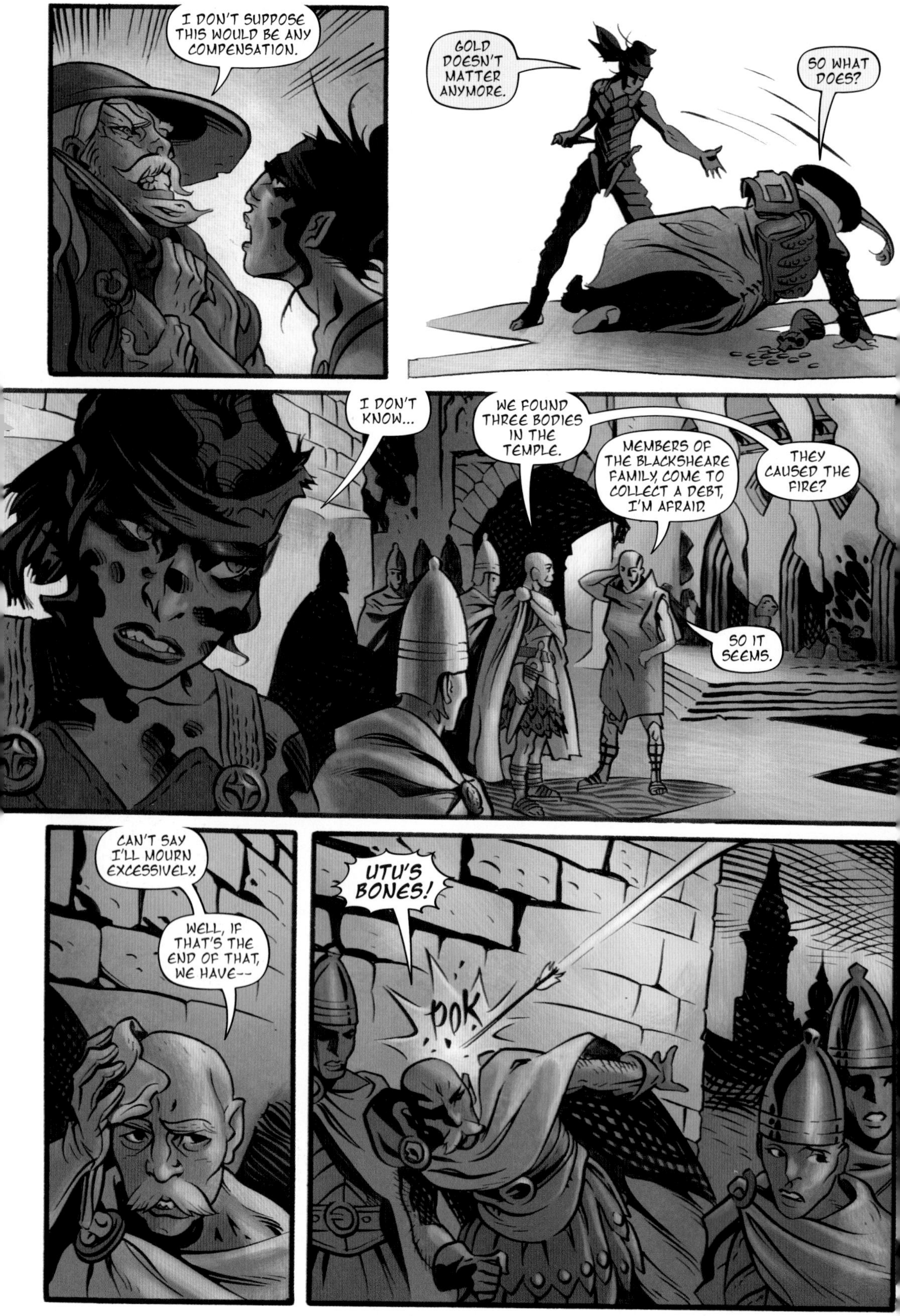
I DON'T SUPPOSE THIS WOULD BE ANY COMPENSATION.
GOLD DOESN'T MATTER ANYMORE.
SO WHAT DOES?
I DON'T KNOW...
WE FOUND THREE BODIES IN THE TEMPLE.
MEMBERS OF THE BLACKSHEARE FAMILY, COME TO COLLECT A DEBT, I'M AFRAID.
THEY CAUSED THE FIRE?
SO IT SEEMS.
CAN'T SAY I'LL MOURN EXCESSIVELY.
WELL, IF THAT'S THE END OF THAT, WE HAVE--
UTU'S BONES!
POK

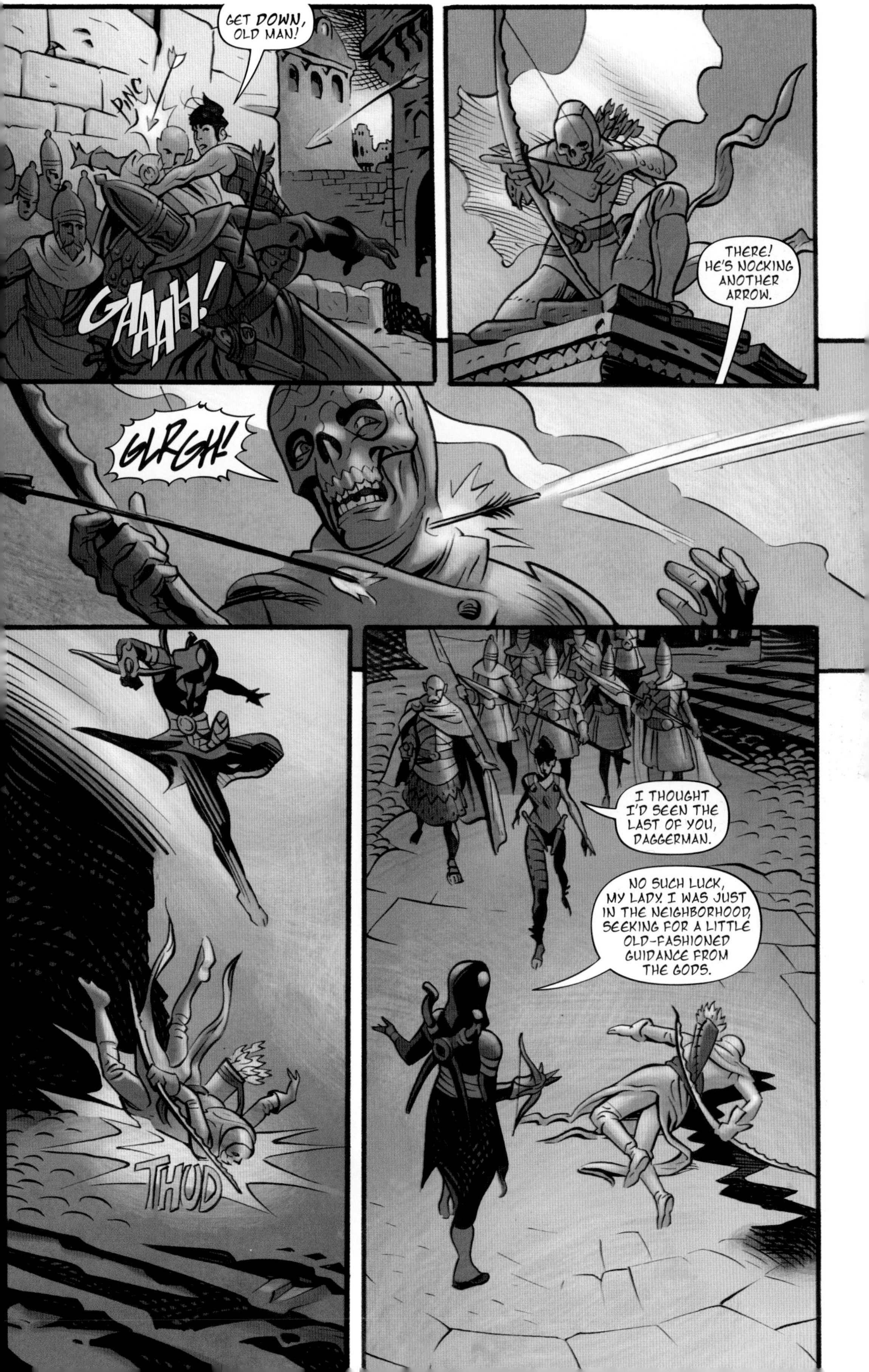
GET DOWN, OLD MAN!
PING
GAAAH!
THERE! HE'S NOCKING ANOTHER ARROW.
GLRGH!
THUD
I THOUGHT I'D SEEN THE LAST OF YOU, DAGGERMAN.
NO SUCH LUCK, MY LADY. I WAS JUST IN THE NEIGHBORHOOD, SEEKING FOR A LITTLE OLD-FASHIONED GUIDANCE FROM THE GODS.

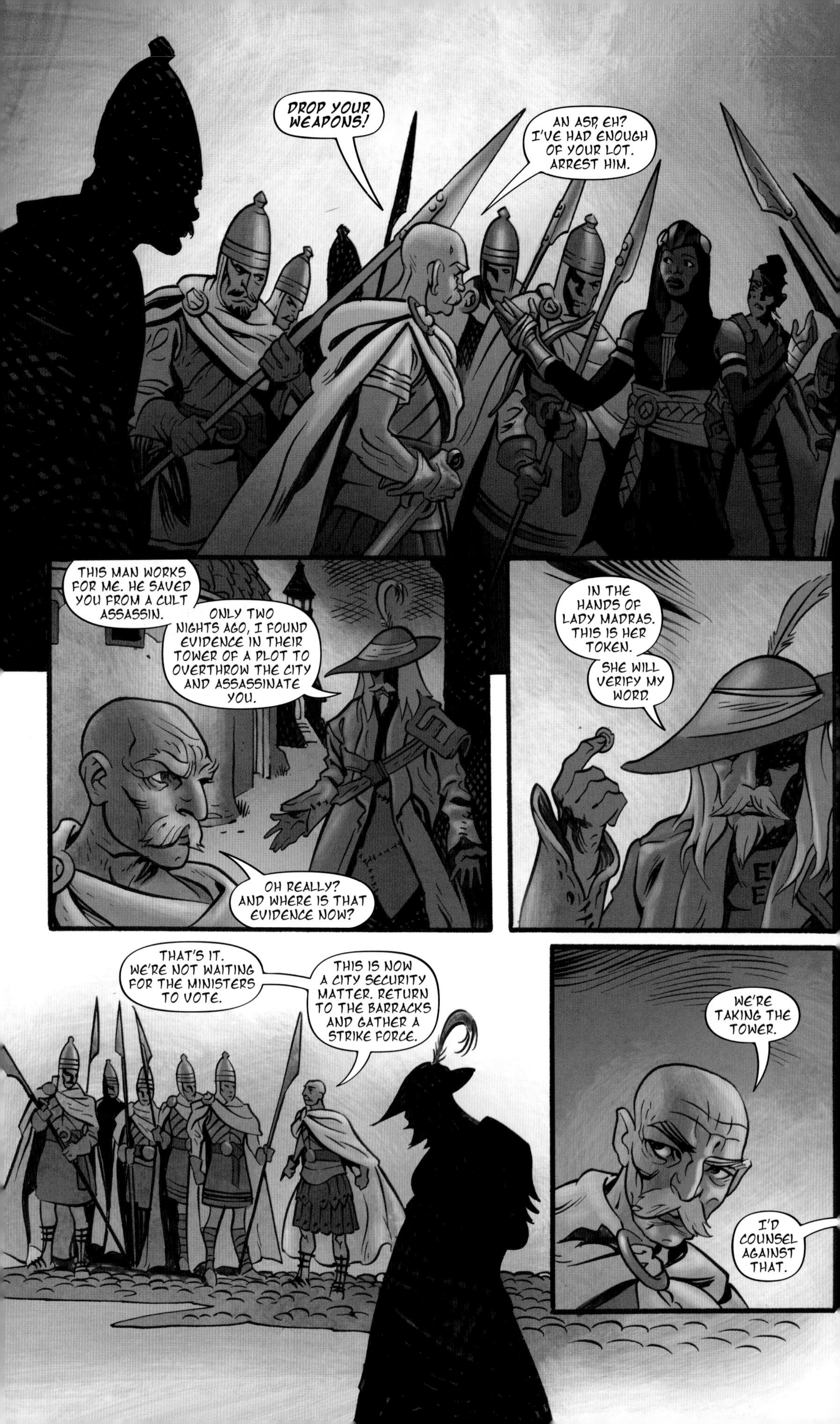
DROP YOUR WEAPONS!
AN ASP, EH? I'VE HAD ENOUGH OF YOUR LOT. ARREST HIM.
THIS MAN WORKS FOR ME. HE SAVED YOU FROM A CULT ASSASSIN.
ONLY TWO NIGHTS AGO, I FOUND EVIDENCE IN THEIR TOWER OF A PLOT TO OVERTHROW THE CITY AND ASSASSINATE YOU.
OH REALLY? AND WHERE IS THAT EVIDENCE NOW?
IN THE HANDS OF LADY MADRAS. THIS IS HER TOKEN.
SHE WILL VERIFY MY WORD.
THAT'S IT. WE'RE NOT WAITING FOR THE MINISTERS TO VOTE.
THIS IS NOW A CITY SECURITY MATTER. RETURN TO THE BARRACKS AND GATHER A STRIKE FORCE.
WE'RE TAKING THE TOWER.
I'D COUNSEL AGAINST THAT.

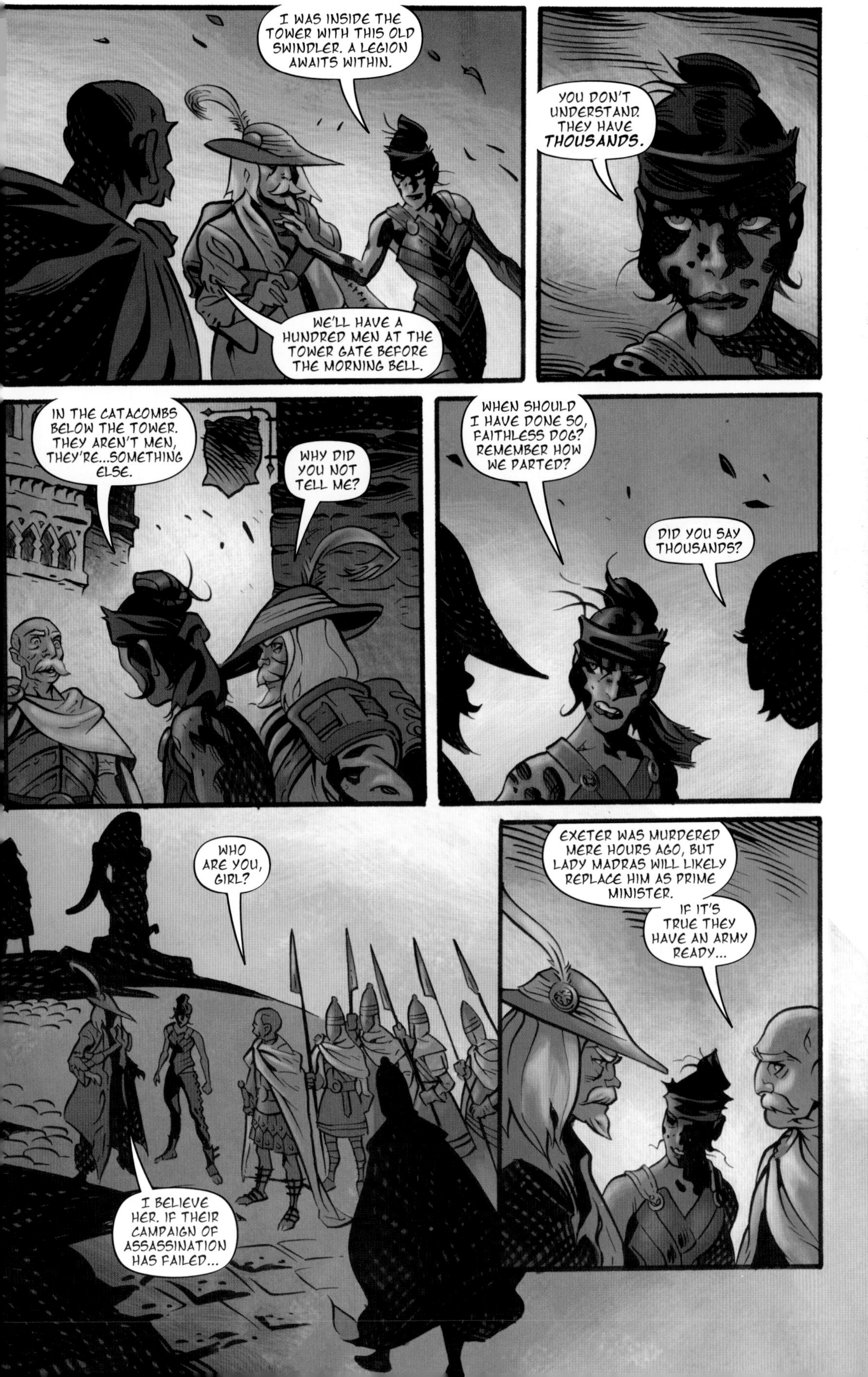
I WAS INSIDE THE TOWER WITH THIS OLD SWINDLER. A LEGION AWAITS WITHIN.
WE'LL HAVE A HUNDRED MEN AT THE TOWER GATE BEFORE THE MORNING BELL.
YOU DON'T UNDERSTAND. THEY HAVE *THOUSANDS*.
IN THE CATACOMBS BELOW THE TOWER. THEY AREN'T MEN, THEY'RE...SOMETHING ELSE.
WHY DID YOU NOT TELL ME?
WHEN SHOULD I HAVE DONE SO, FAITHLESS DOG? REMEMBER HOW WE PARTED?
DID YOU SAY THOUSANDS?
WHO ARE YOU, GIRL?
I BELIEVE HER. IF THEIR CAMPAIGN OF ASSASSINATION HAS FAILED...
EXETER WAS MURDERED MERE HOURS AGO, BUT LADY MADRAS WILL LIKELY REPLACE HIM AS PRIME MINISTER.
IF IT'S TRUE THEY HAVE AN ARMY READY...

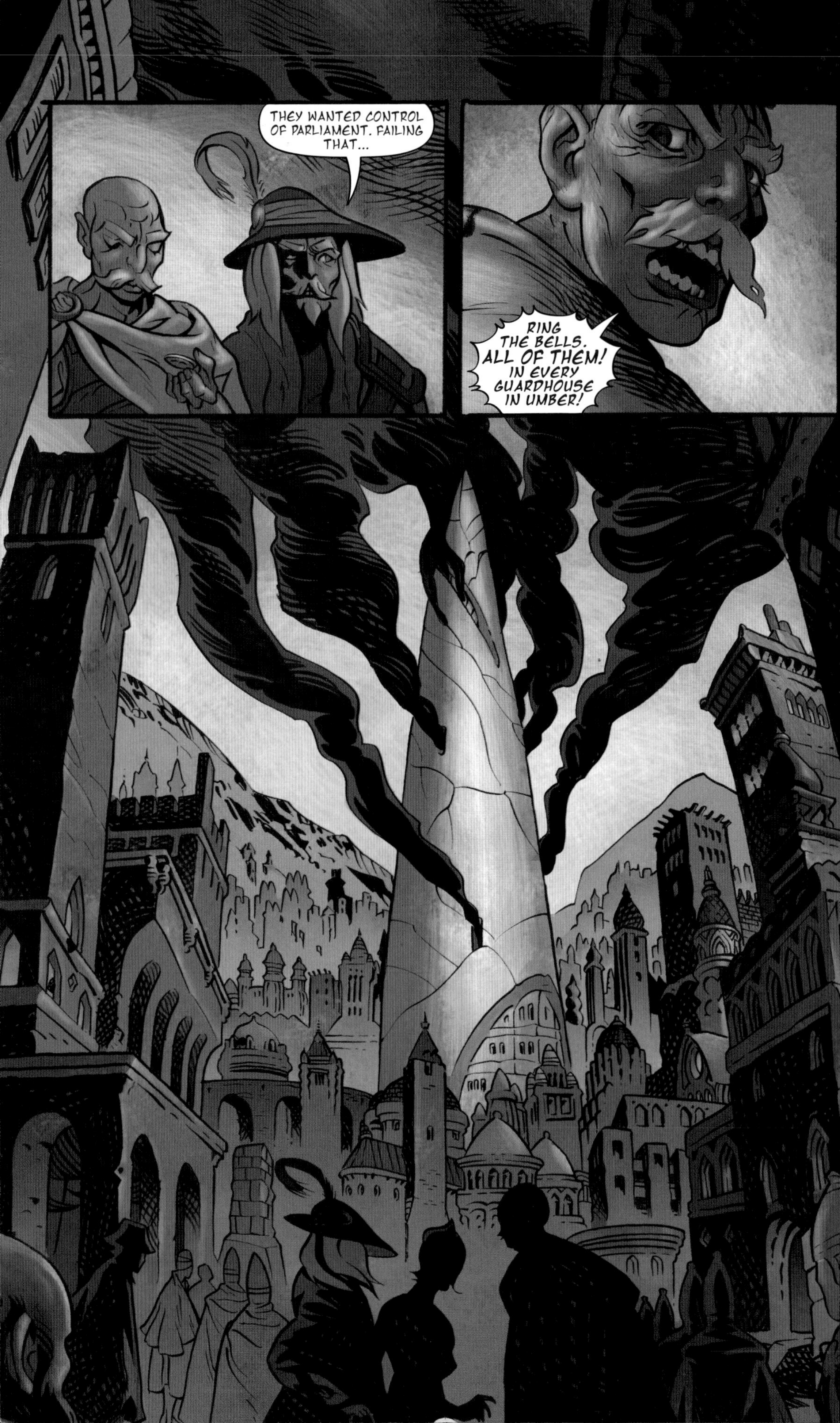
THEY WANTED CONTROL OF PARLIAMENT. FAILING THAT...
RING THE BELLS. ALL OF THEM! IN EVERY GUARDHOUSE IN UMBER!

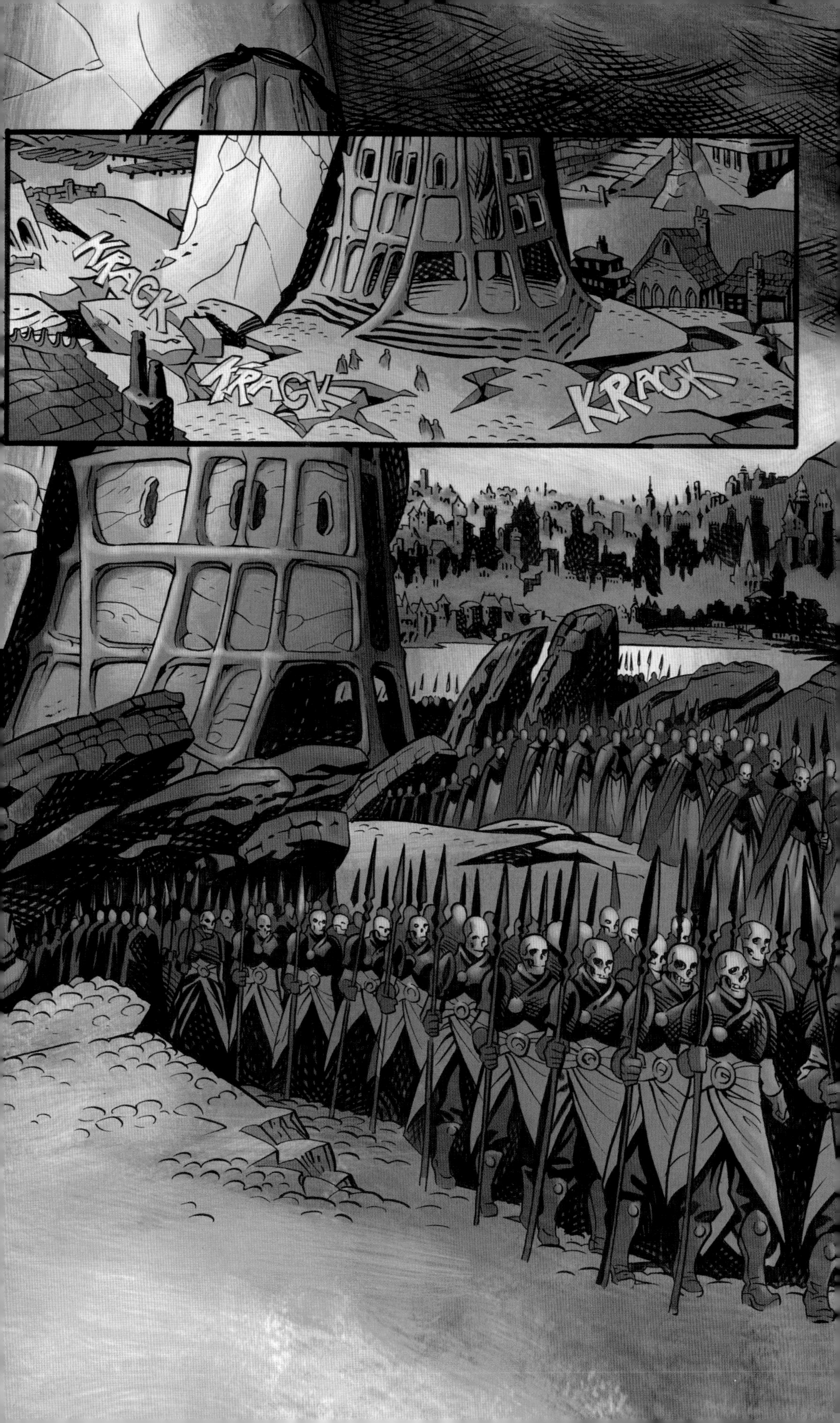
KRACK
KRACK
KRACK

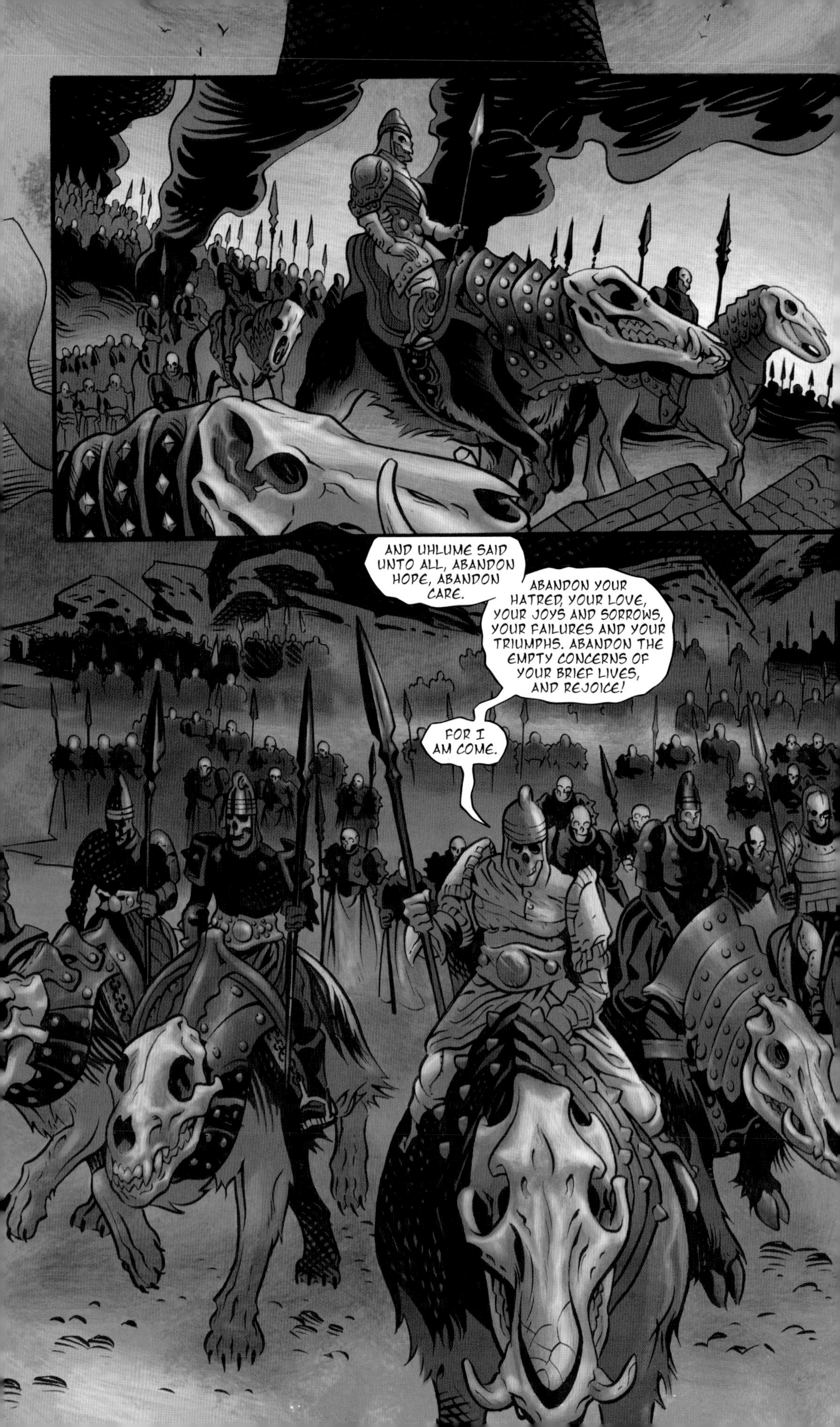
AND UHLUME SAID UNTO ALL, ABANDON HOPE, ABANDON CARE.
ABANDON YOUR HATRED, YOUR LOVE, YOUR JOYS AND SORROWS, YOUR FAILURES AND YOUR TRIUMPHS. ABANDON THE EMPTY CONCERNS OF YOUR BRIEF LIVES, AND REJOICE!
FOR I AM COME.

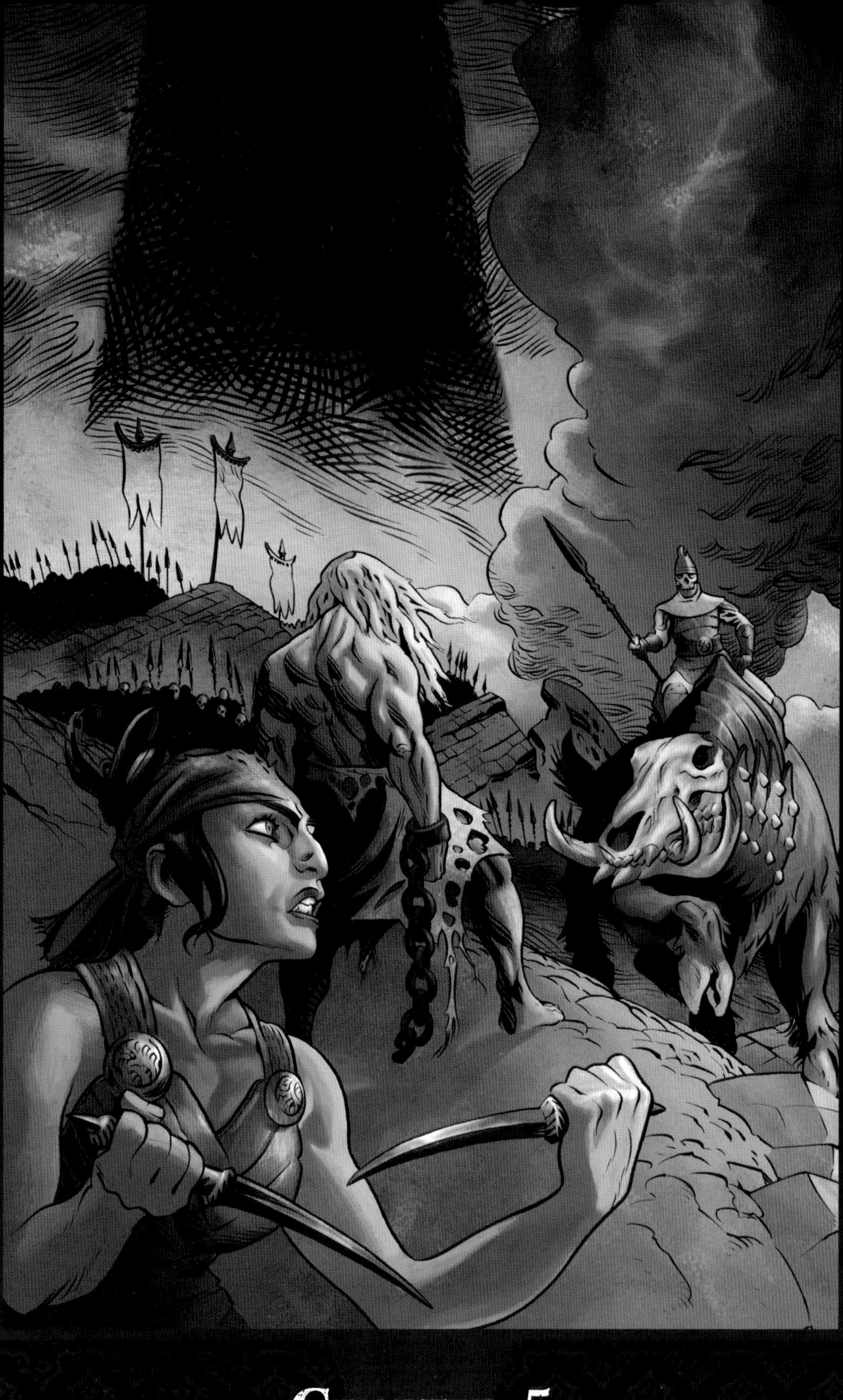

Chapter 5

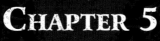

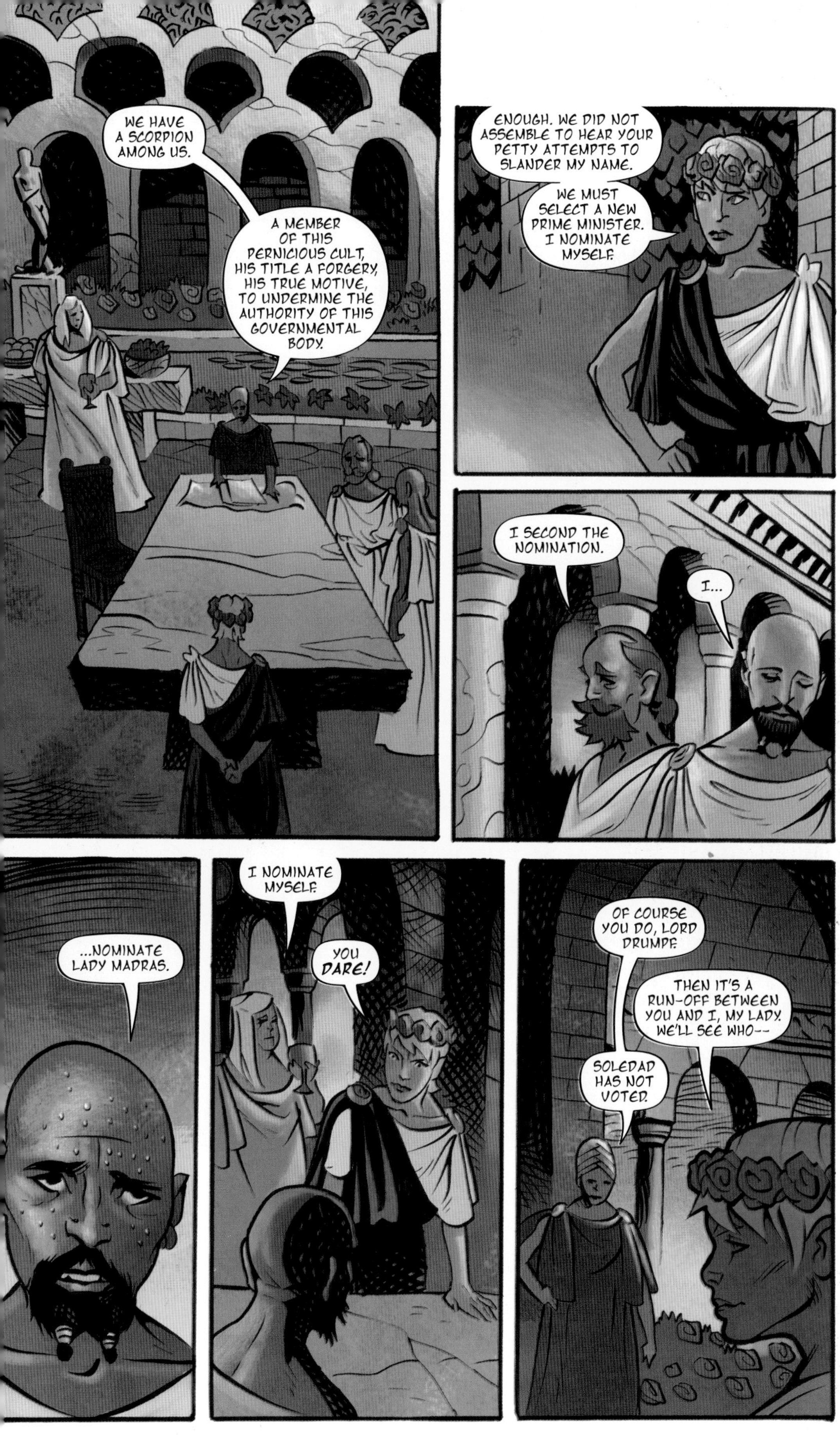
WE HAVE A SCORPION AMONG US.
A MEMBER OF THIS PERNICIOUS CULT, HIS TITLE A FORGERY, HIS TRUE MOTIVE, TO UNDERMINE THE AUTHORITY OF THIS GOVERNMENTAL BODY.
ENOUGH. WE DID NOT ASSEMBLE TO HEAR YOUR PETTY ATTEMPTS TO SLANDER MY NAME.
WE MUST SELECT A NEW PRIME MINISTER. I NOMINATE MYSELF.
I SECOND THE NOMINATION.
I...
...NOMINATE LADY MADRAS.
I NOMINATE MYSELF.
YOU *DARE!*
OF COURSE YOU DO, LORD DRUMPF.
THEN IT'S A RUN-OFF BETWEEN YOU AND I, MY LADY. WE'LL SEE WHO--
SOLEDAD HAS NOT VOTED.

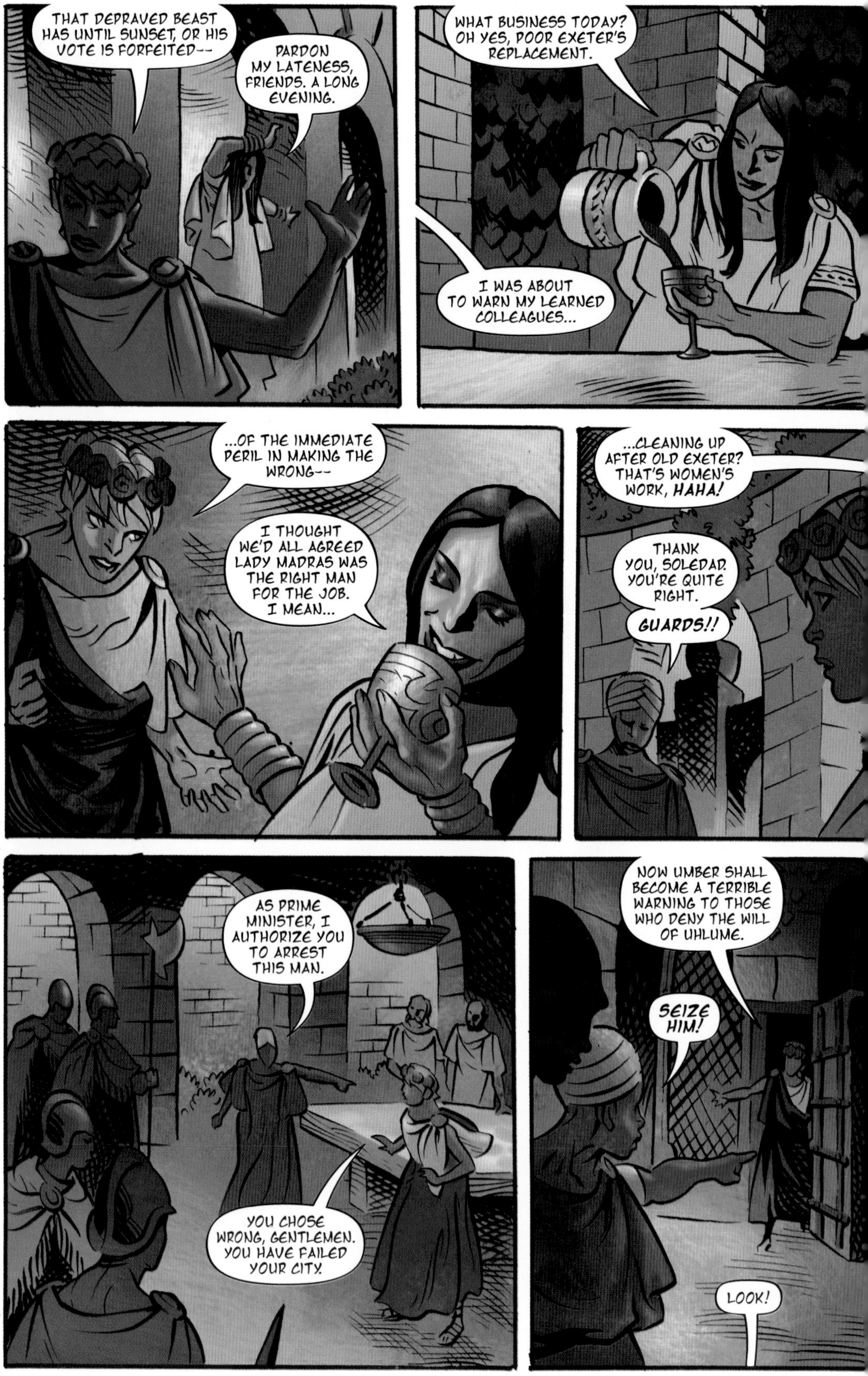
THAT DEPRAVED BEAST HAS UNTIL SUNSET, OR HIS VOTE IS FORFEITED--
PARDON MY LATENESS, FRIENDS. A LONG EVENING.
WHAT BUSINESS TODAY? OH YES, POOR EXETER'S REPLACEMENT.
I WAS ABOUT TO WARN MY LEARNED COLLEAGUES...
...OF THE IMMEDIATE PERIL IN MAKING THE WRONG--
I THOUGHT WE'D ALL AGREED LADY MADRAS WAS THE RIGHT MAN FOR THE JOB. I MEAN...
...CLEANING UP AFTER OLD EXETER? THAT'S WOMEN'S WORK, **HAHA!**
THANK YOU, SOLEDAD. YOU'RE QUITE RIGHT.
GUARDS!!
AS PRIME MINISTER, I AUTHORIZE YOU TO ARREST THIS MAN.
YOU CHOSE WRONG, GENTLEMEN. YOU HAVE FAILED YOUR CITY.
NOW UMBER SHALL BECOME A TERRIBLE WARNING TO THOSE WHO DENY THE WILL OF UHLUME.
SEIZE HIM!
LOOK!

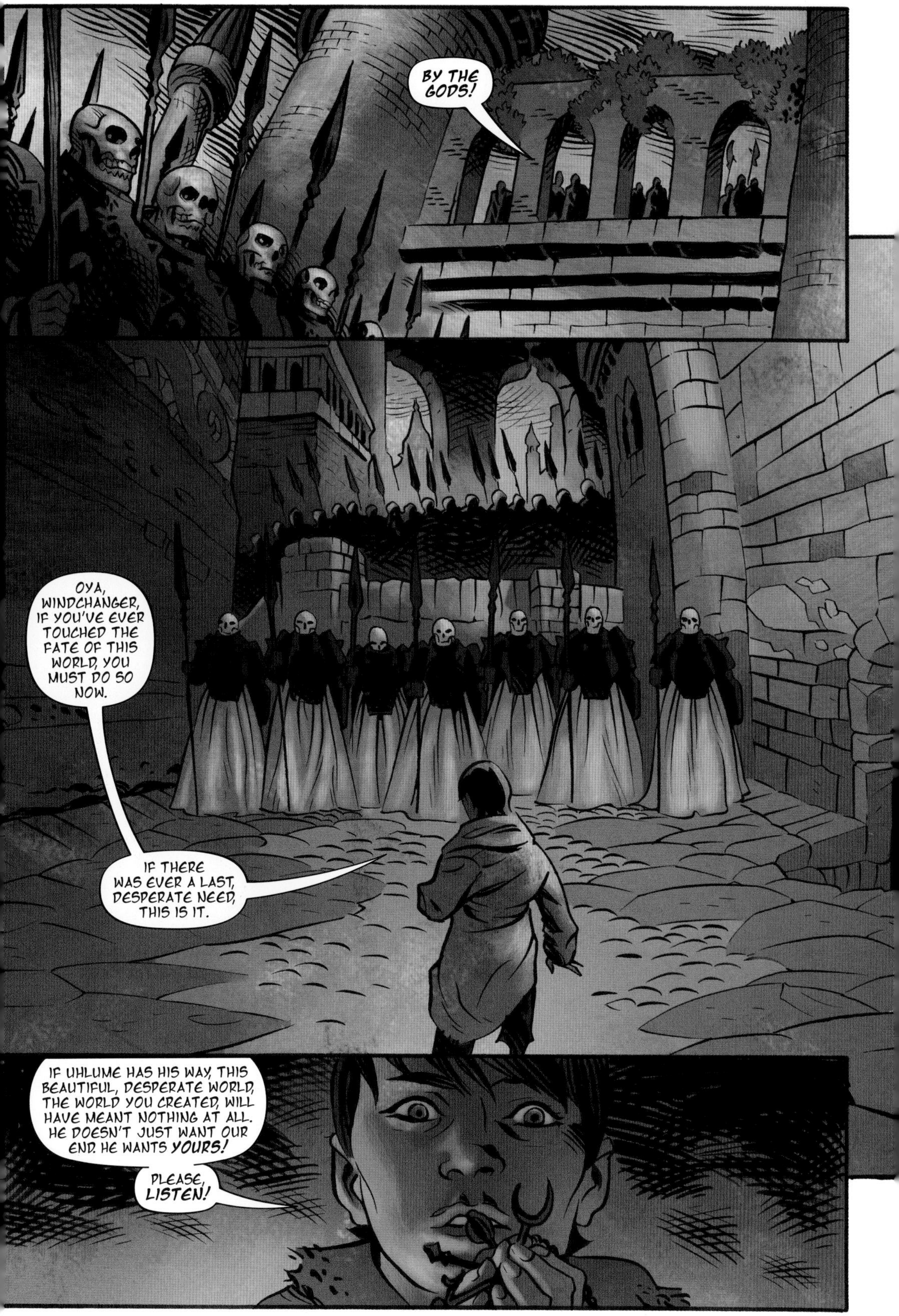
BY THE GODS!
OYA, WINDCHANGER, IF YOU'VE EVER TOUCHED THE FATE OF THIS WORLD, YOU MUST DO SO NOW.
IF THERE WAS EVER A LAST, DESPERATE NEED, THIS IS IT.
IF UHLUME HAS HIS WAY, THIS BEAUTIFUL, DESPERATE WORLD, THE WORLD YOU CREATED, WILL HAVE MEANT NOTHING AT ALL. HE DOESN'T JUST WANT OUR END. HE WANTS YOURS!
PLEASE, LISTEN!

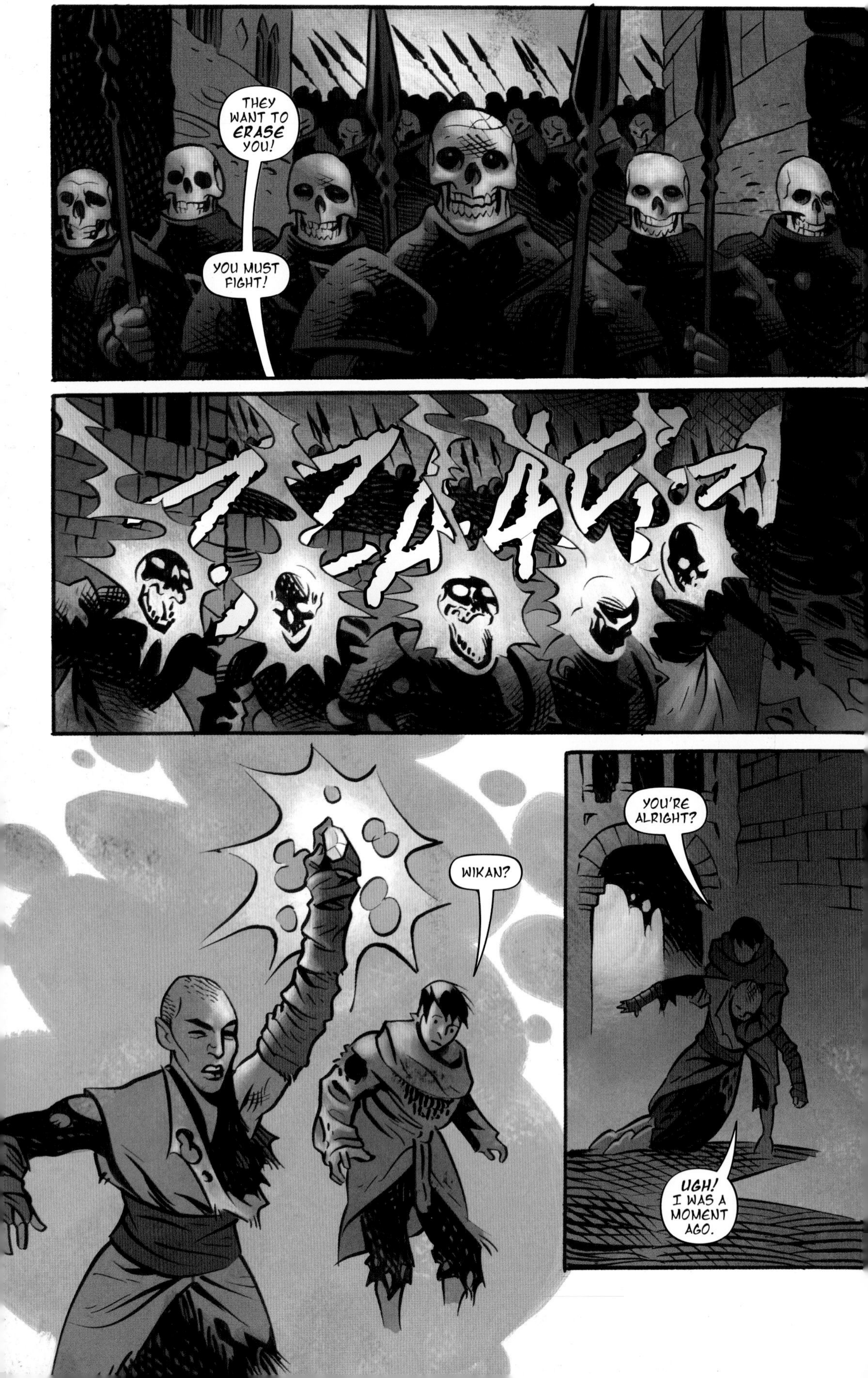
THEY WANT TO ERASE YOU!
YOU MUST FIGHT!
ZZAAK!
WIKAN?
YOU'RE ALRIGHT?
UGH! I WAS A MOMENT AGO.

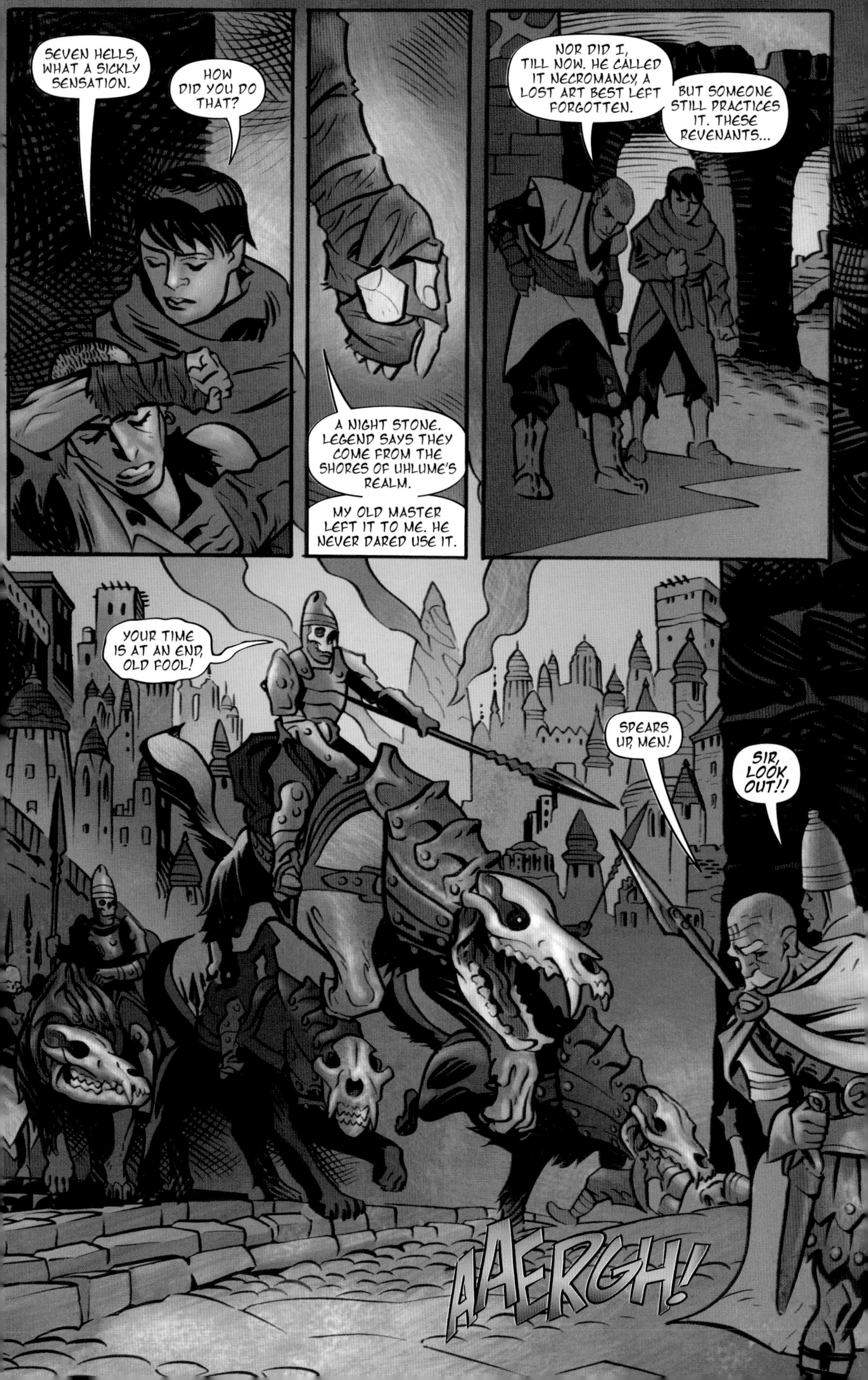
SEVEN HELLS, WHAT A SICKLY SENSATION.
HOW DID YOU DO THAT?
A NIGHT STONE. LEGEND SAYS THEY COME FROM THE SHORES OF UHLUME'S REALM.
MY OLD MASTER LEFT IT TO ME. HE NEVER DARED USE IT.
NOR DID I, TILL NOW. HE CALLED IT NECROMANCY, A LOST ART BEST LEFT FORGOTTEN.
BUT SOMEONE STILL PRACTICES IT. THESE REVENANTS...
YOUR TIME IS AT AN END, OLD FOOL!
SPEARS UP, MEN!
SIR, LOOK OUT!!
AAERGH!

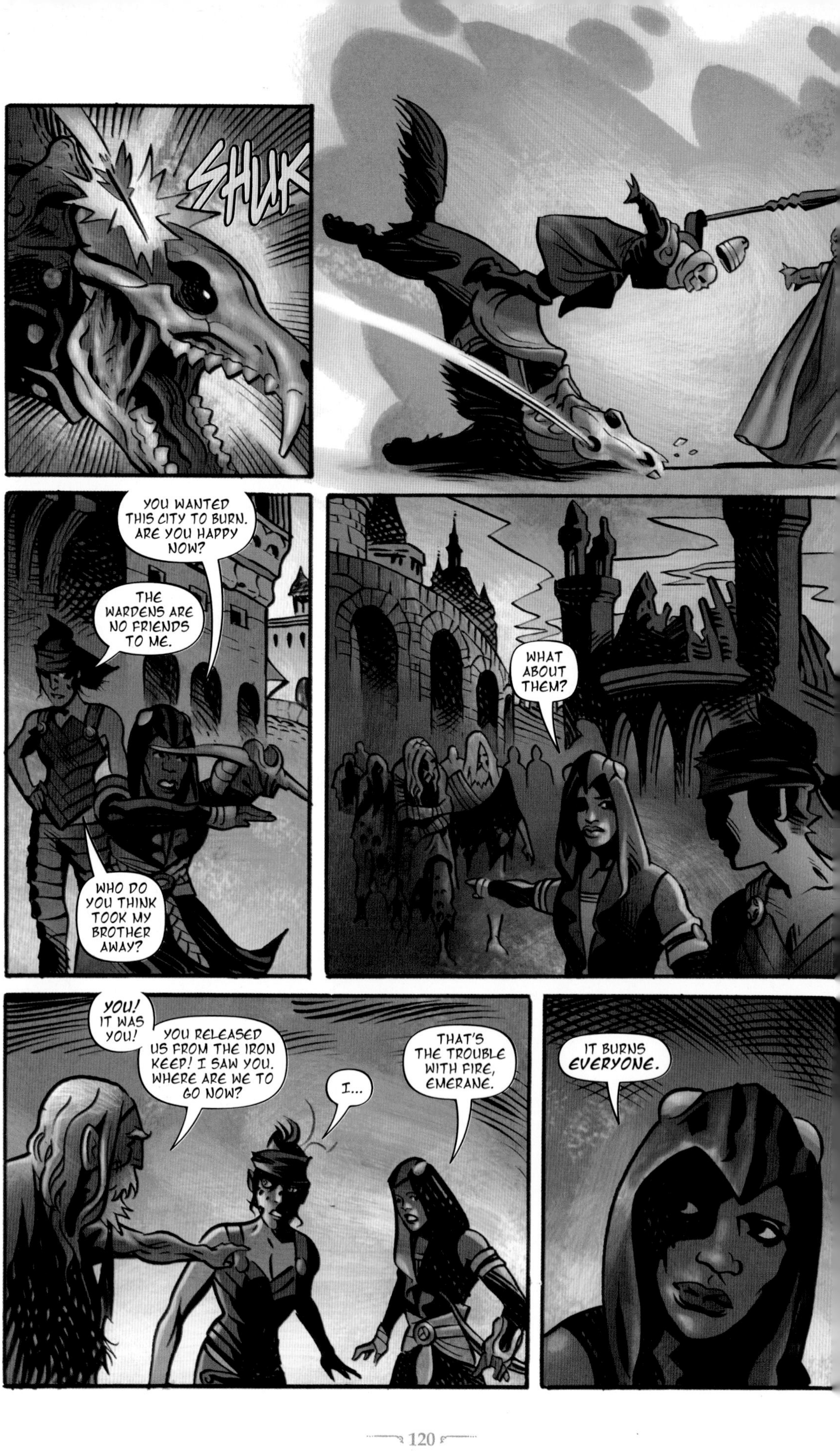
SHUK
YOU WANTED THIS CITY TO BURN. ARE YOU HAPPY NOW?
THE WARDENS ARE NO FRIENDS TO ME.
WHO DO YOU THINK TOOK MY BROTHER AWAY?
WHAT ABOUT THEM?
YOU! IT WAS YOU!
YOU RELEASED US FROM THE IRON KEEP! I SAW YOU. WHERE ARE WE TO GO NOW?
I...
THAT'S THE TROUBLE WITH FIRE, EMERANE.
IT BURNS EVERYONE.

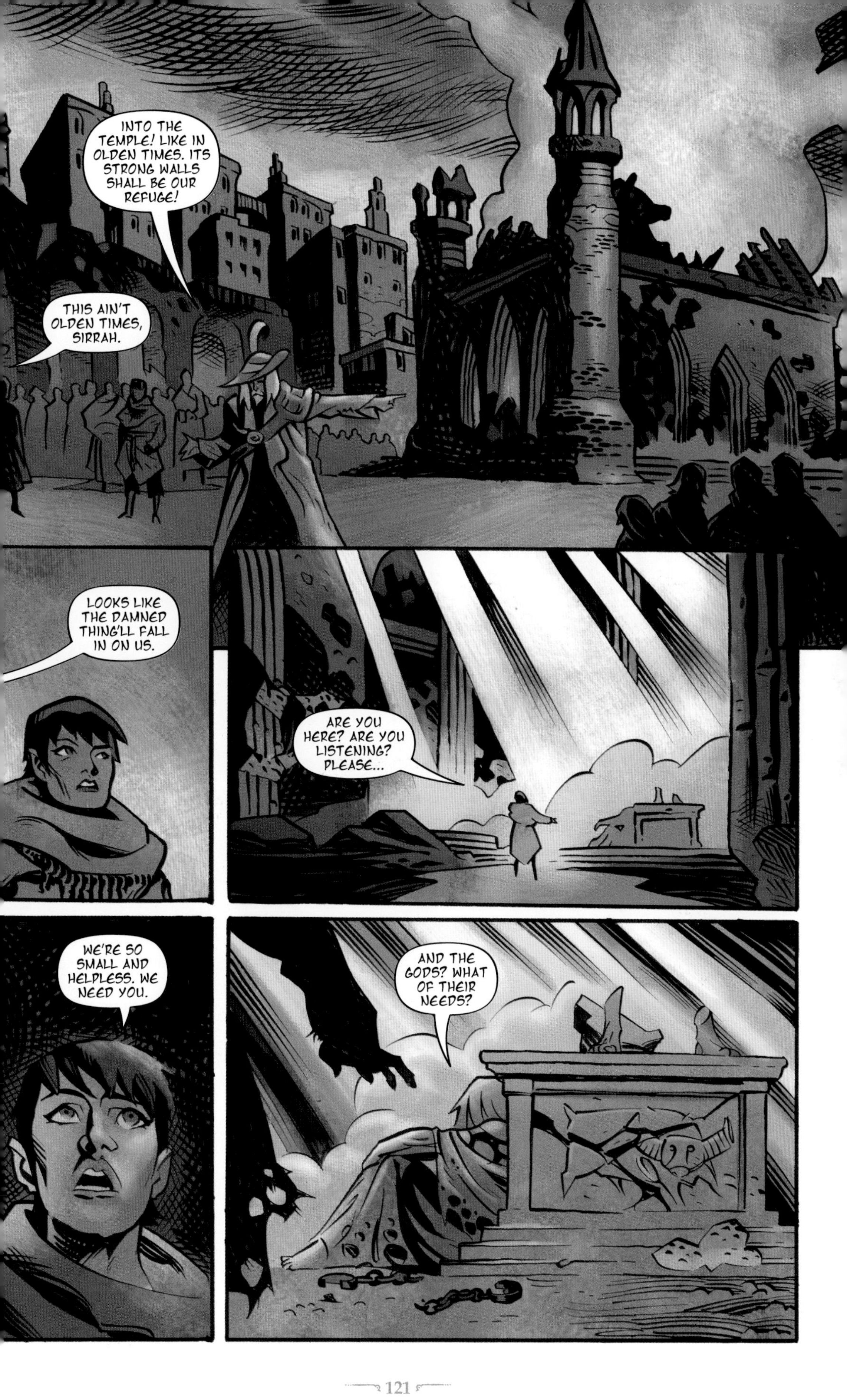
INTO THE TEMPLE! LIKE IN OLDEN TIMES. ITS STRONG WALLS SHALL BE OUR REFUGE!
THIS AIN'T OLDEN TIMES, SIRRAH.
LOOKS LIKE THE DAMNED THING'LL FALL IN ON US.
ARE YOU HERE? ARE YOU LISTENING? PLEASE...
WE'RE SO SMALL AND HELPLESS. WE NEED YOU.
AND THE GODS? WHAT OF THEIR NEEDS?

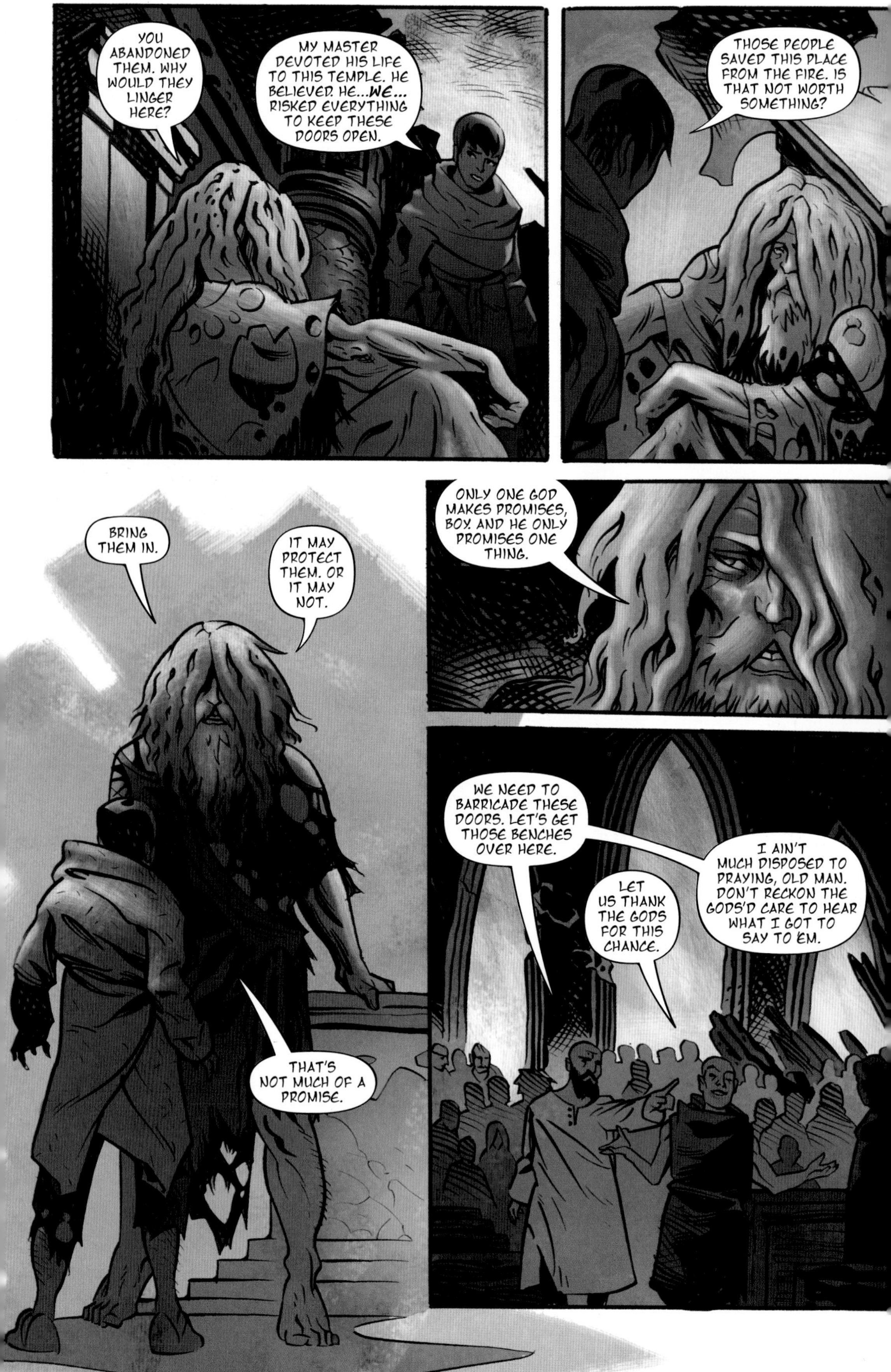
YOU ABANDONED THEM. WHY WOULD THEY LINGER HERE?
MY MASTER DEVOTED HIS LIFE TO THIS TEMPLE. HE BELIEVED. HE... **WE...** RISKED EVERYTHING TO KEEP THESE DOORS OPEN.
THOSE PEOPLE SAVED THIS PLACE FROM THE FIRE. IS THAT NOT WORTH SOMETHING?
ONLY ONE GOD MAKES PROMISES, BOY. AND HE ONLY PROMISES ONE THING.
BRING THEM IN.
IT MAY PROTECT THEM. OR IT MAY NOT.
THAT'S NOT MUCH OF A PROMISE.
WE NEED TO BARRICADE THESE DOORS. LET'S GET THOSE BENCHES OVER HERE.
LET US THANK THE GODS FOR THIS CHANCE.
I AIN'T MUCH DISPOSED TO PRAYING, OLD MAN. DON'T RECKON THE GODS'D CARE TO HEAR WHAT I GOT TO SAY TO 'EM.

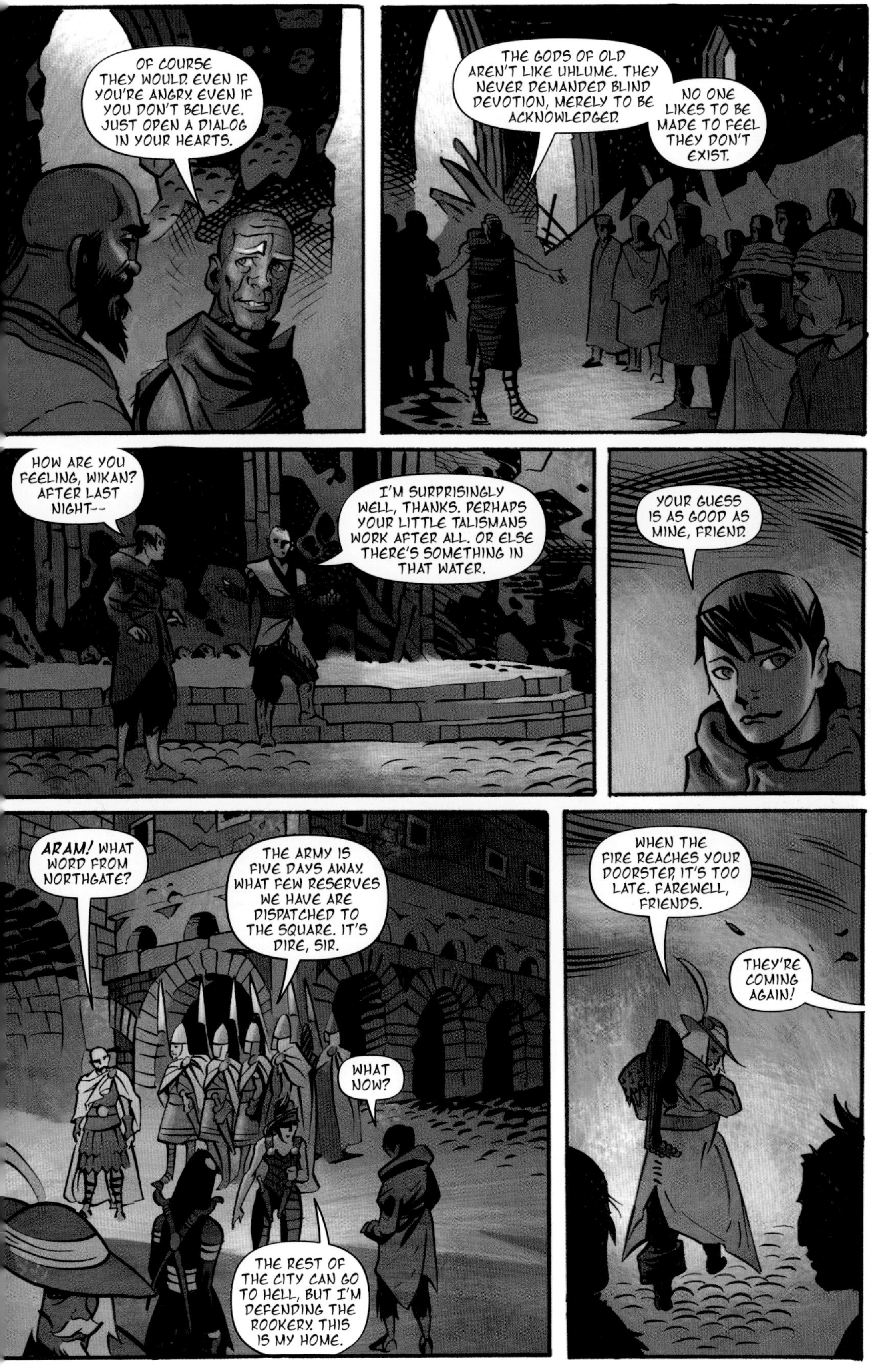
OF COURSE THEY WOULD. EVEN IF YOU'RE ANGRY. EVEN IF YOU DON'T BELIEVE. JUST OPEN A DIALOG IN YOUR HEARTS.
THE GODS OF OLD AREN'T LIKE UHLUME. THEY NEVER DEMANDED BLIND DEVOTION, MERELY TO BE ACKNOWLEDGED.
NO ONE LIKES TO BE MADE TO FEEL THEY DON'T EXIST.
HOW ARE YOU FEELING, WIKAN? AFTER LAST NIGHT--
I'M SURPRISINGLY WELL, THANKS. PERHAPS YOUR LITTLE TALISMANS WORK AFTER ALL. OR ELSE THERE'S SOMETHING IN THAT WATER.
YOUR GUESS IS AS GOOD AS MINE, FRIEND.
ARAM! WHAT WORD FROM NORTHGATE?
THE ARMY IS FIVE DAYS AWAY. WHAT FEW RESERVES WE HAVE ARE DISPATCHED TO THE SQUARE. IT'S DIRE, SIR.
WHAT NOW?
THE REST OF THE CITY CAN GO TO HELL, BUT I'M DEFENDING THE ROOKERY. THIS IS MY HOME.
WHEN THE FIRE REACHES YOUR DOORSTEP, IT'S TOO LATE. FAREWELL, FRIENDS.
THEY'RE COMING AGAIN!

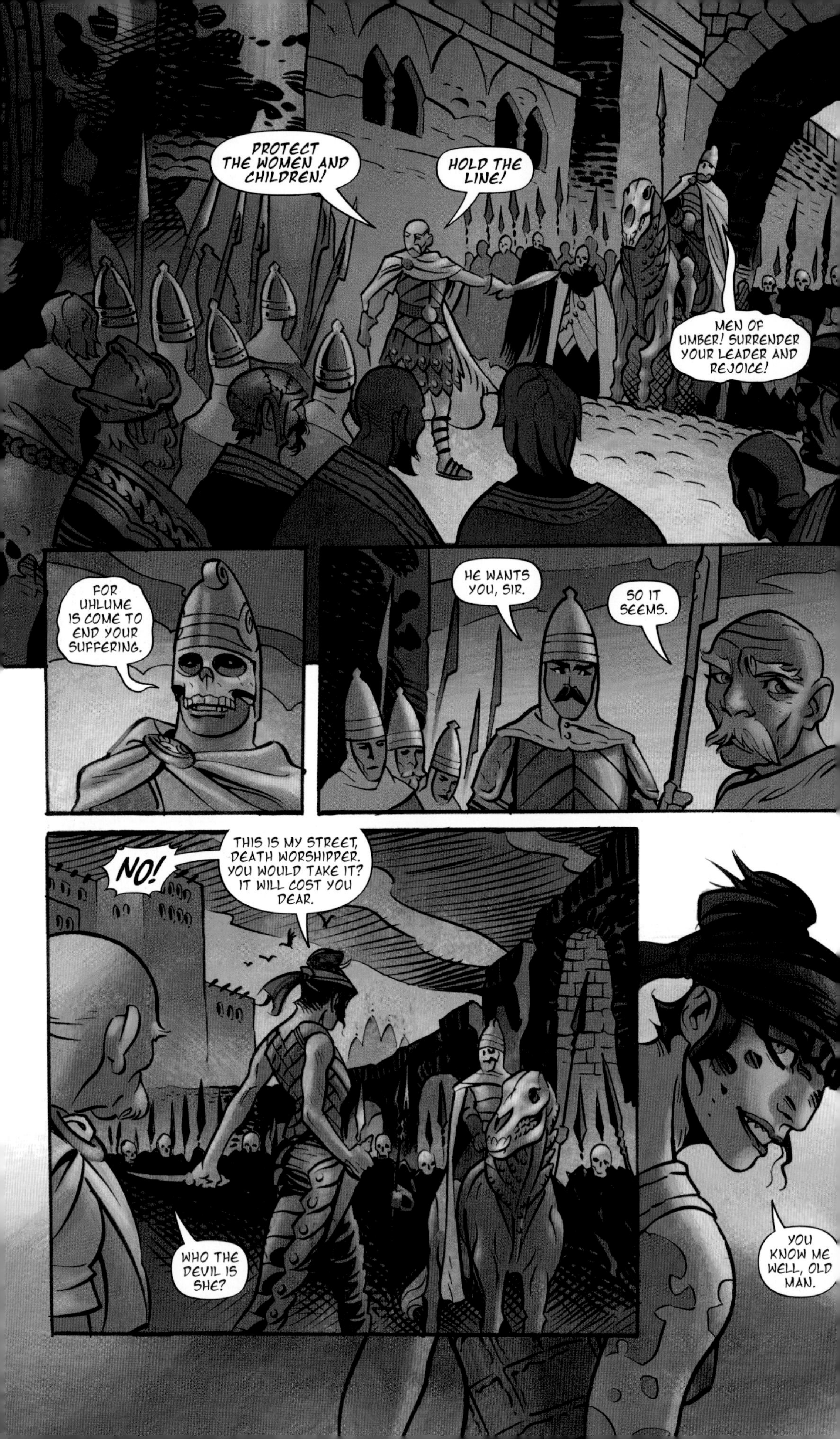
PROTECT THE WOMEN AND CHILDREN!
HOLD THE LINE!
MEN OF UMBER! SURRENDER YOUR LEADER AND REJOICE!
FOR UHLUME IS COME TO END YOUR SUFFERING.
HE WANTS YOU, SIR.
SO IT SEEMS.
NO!
THIS IS MY STREET, DEATH WORSHIPPER. YOU WOULD TAKE IT? IT WILL COST YOU DEAR.
WHO THE DEVIL IS SHE?
YOU KNOW ME WELL, OLD MAN.

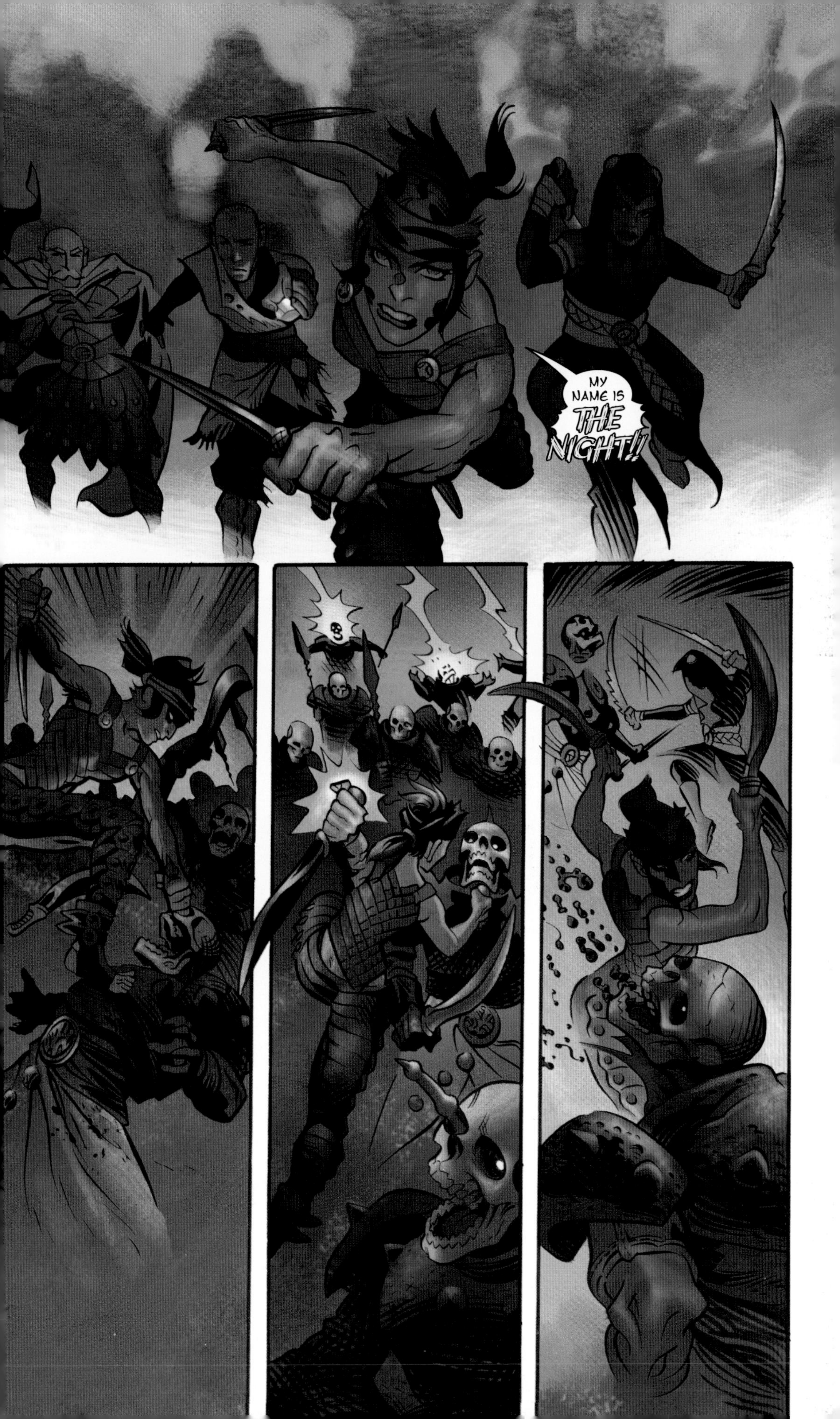
MY NAME IS THE NIGHT!!

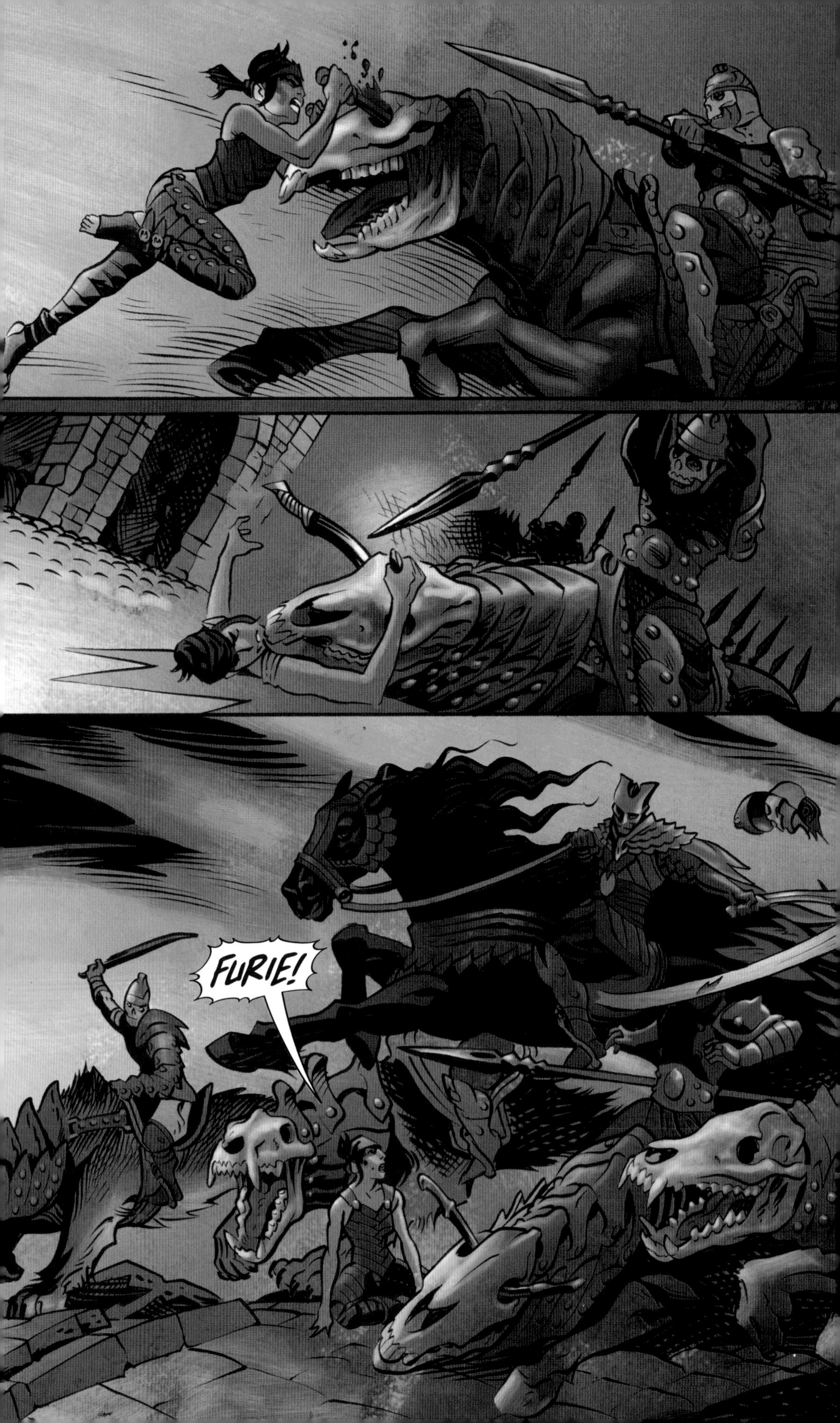
FURIE!

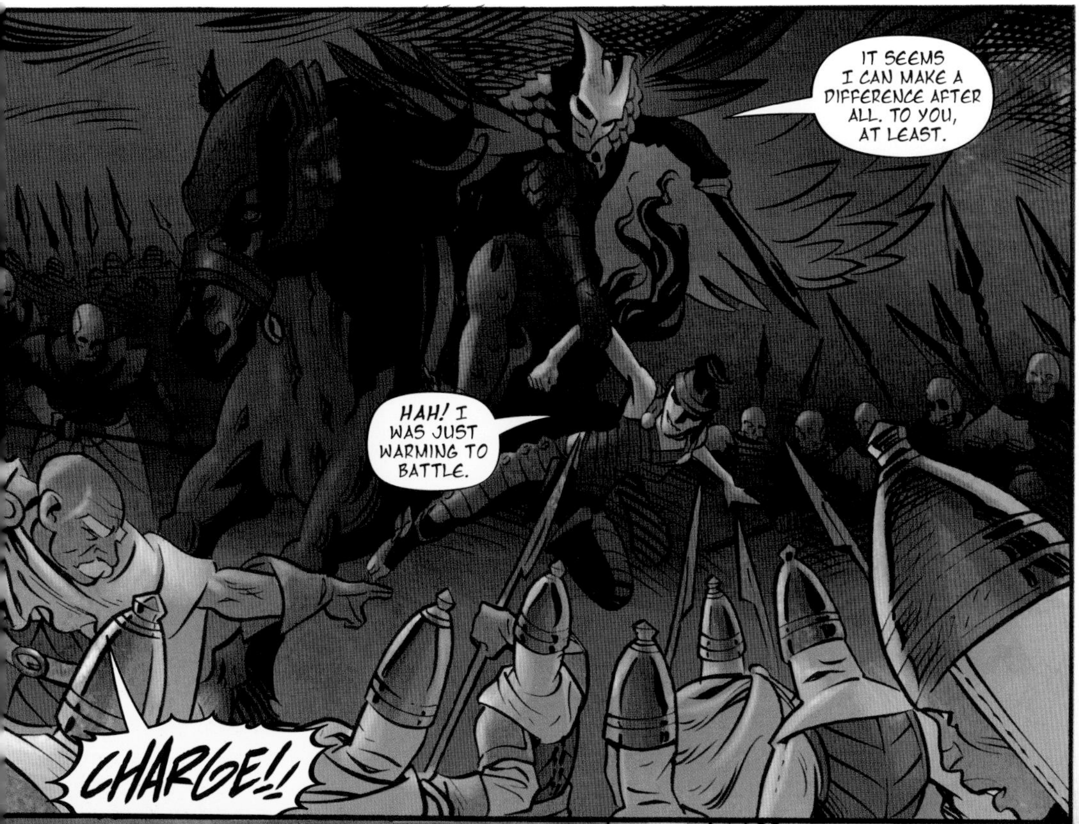
IT SEEMS I CAN MAKE A DIFFERENCE AFTER ALL. TO YOU, AT LEAST.
HAH! I WAS JUST WARMING TO BATTLE.
CHARGE!!

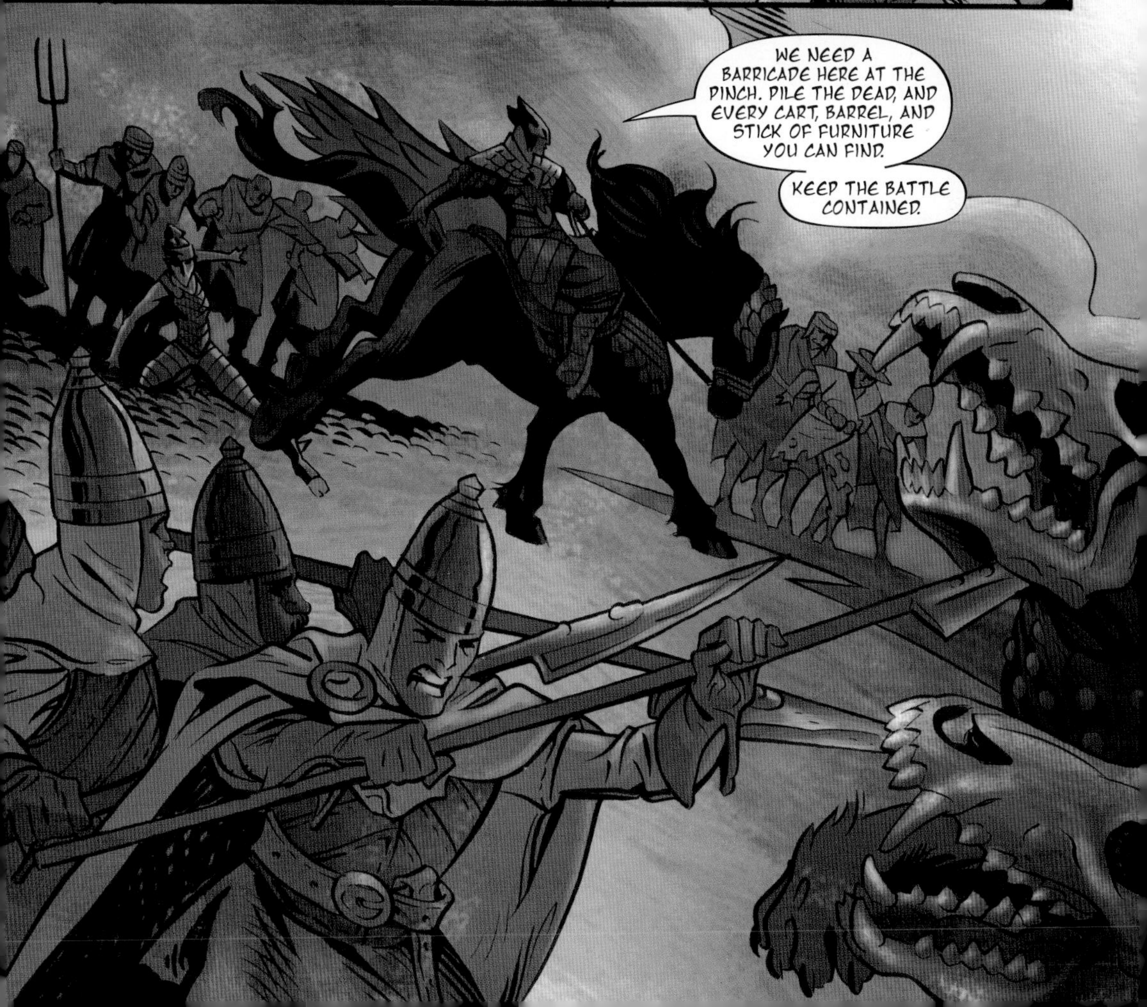
WE NEED A BARRICADE HERE AT THE PINCH. PILE THE DEAD, AND EVERY CART, BARREL, AND STICK OF FURNITURE YOU CAN FIND.
KEEP THE BATTLE CONTAINED.

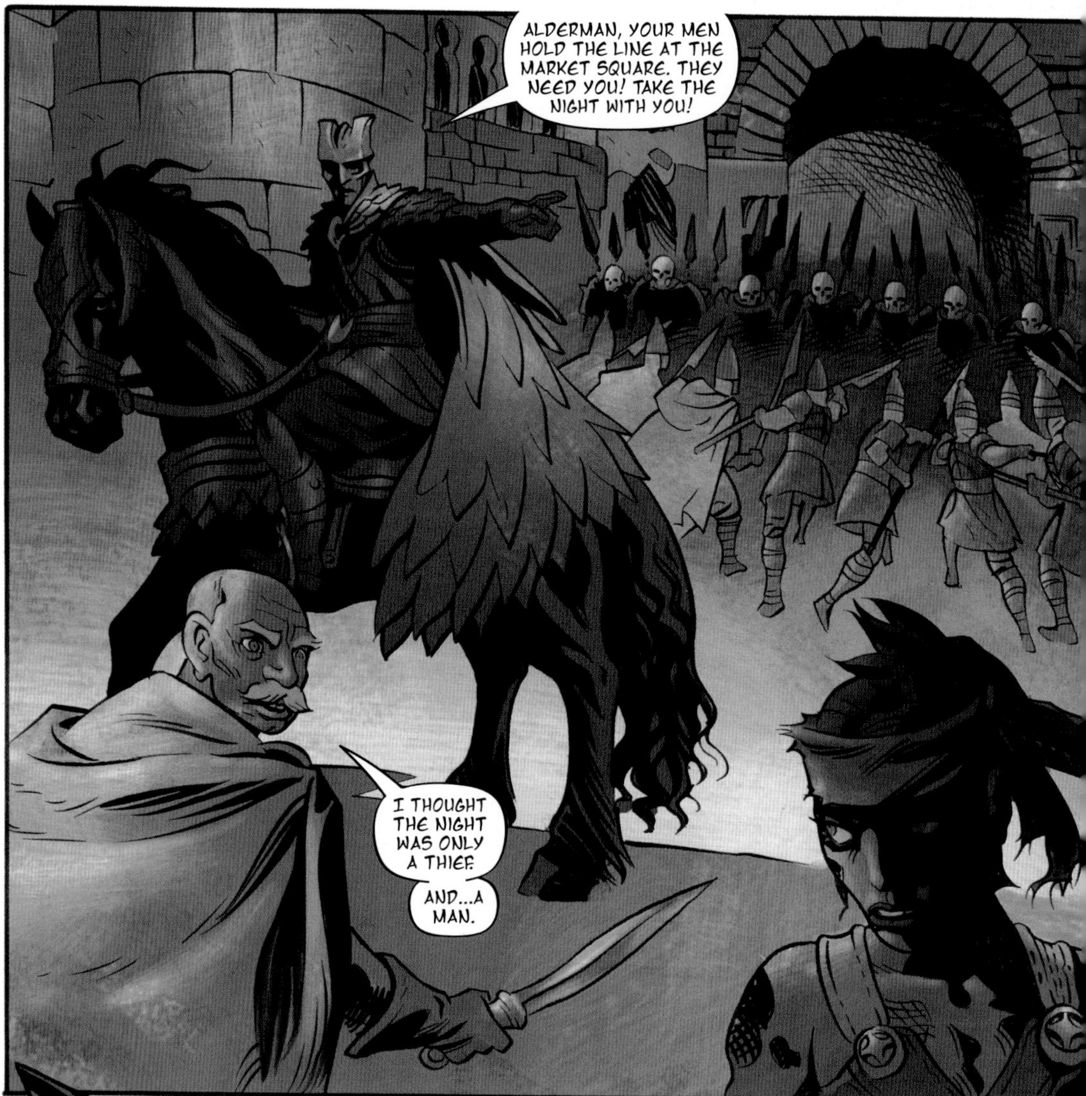
ALDERMAN, YOUR MEN HOLD THE LINE AT THE MARKET SQUARE. THEY NEED YOU! TAKE THE NIGHT WITH YOU!
I THOUGHT THE NIGHT WAS ONLY A THIEF.
AND...A MAN.

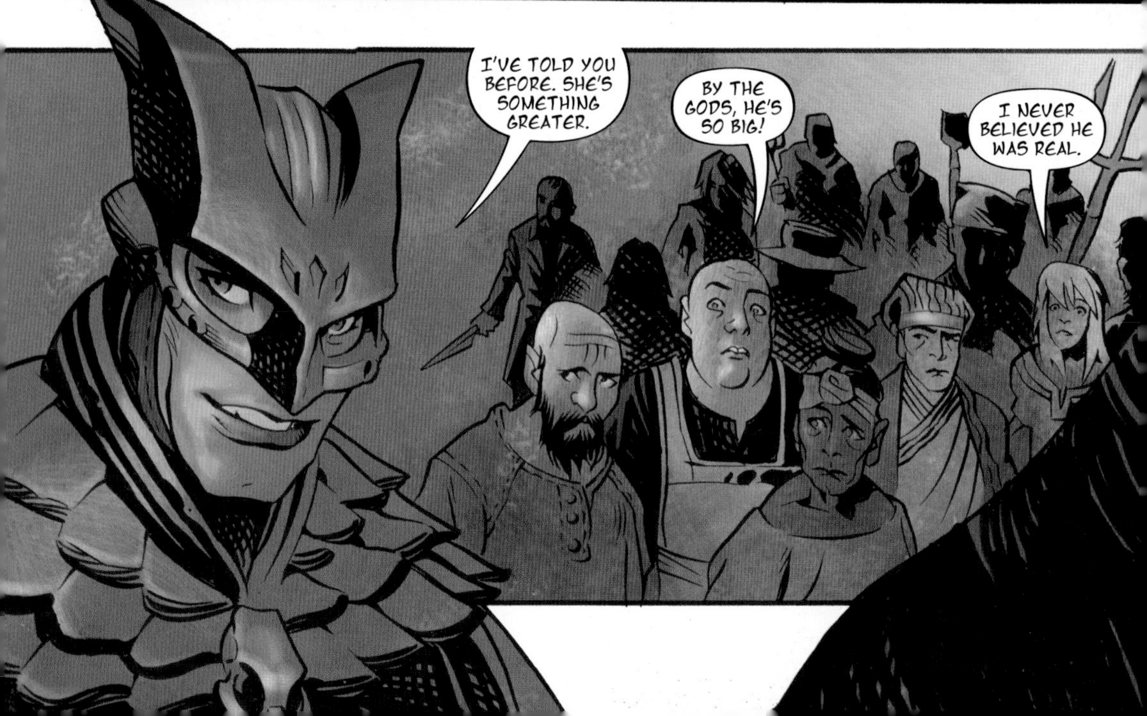
I'VE TOLD YOU BEFORE. SHE'S SOMETHING GREATER.
BY THE GODS, HE'S SO BIG!
I NEVER BELIEVED HE WAS REAL.

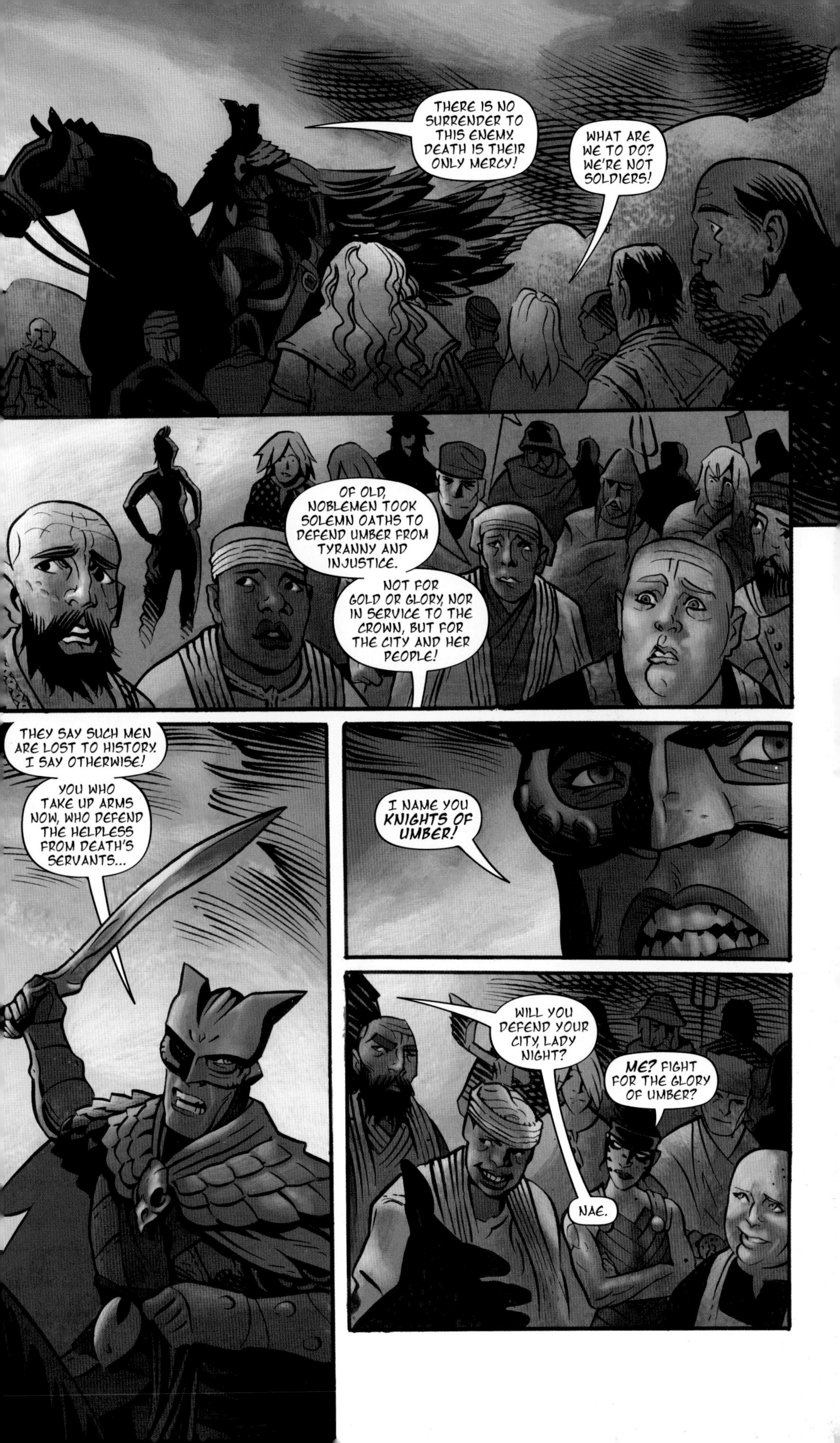
THERE IS NO SURRENDER TO THIS ENEMY. DEATH IS THEIR ONLY MERCY!
WHAT ARE WE TO DO? WE'RE NOT SOLDIERS!
OF OLD, NOBLEMEN TOOK SOLEMN OATHS TO DEFEND UMBER FROM TYRANNY AND INJUSTICE.
NOT FOR GOLD OR GLORY, NOR IN SERVICE TO THE CROWN, BUT FOR THE CITY AND HER PEOPLE!
THEY SAY SUCH MEN ARE LOST TO HISTORY. I SAY OTHERWISE!
YOU WHO TAKE UP ARMS NOW, WHO DEFEND THE HELPLESS FROM DEATH'S SERVANTS...
I NAME YOU KNIGHTS OF UMBER!
WILL YOU DEFEND YOUR CITY, LADY NIGHT?
ME? FIGHT FOR THE GLORY OF UMBER?
NAE.

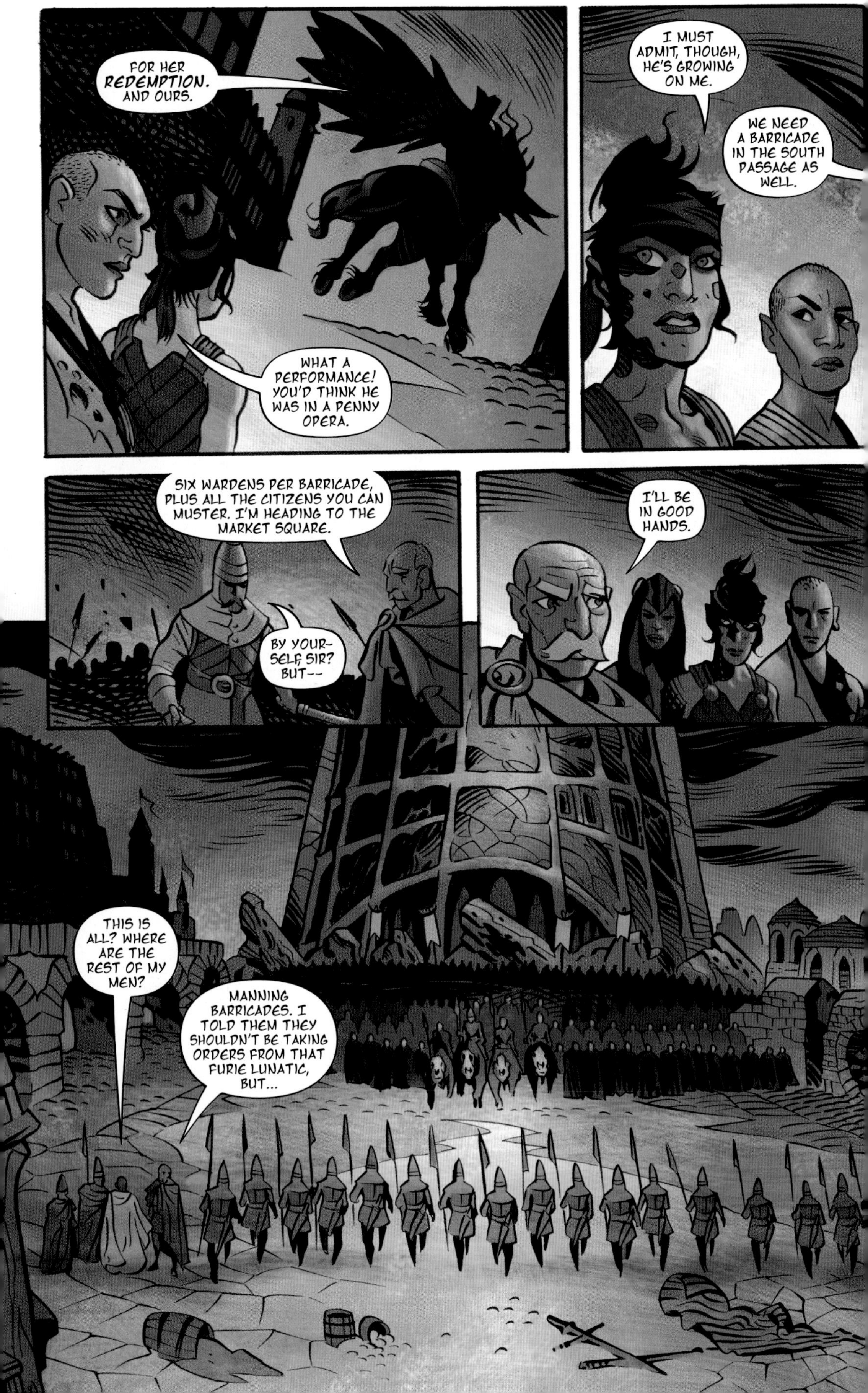
FOR HER REDEMPTION. AND OURS.
WHAT A PERFORMANCE! YOU'D THINK HE WAS IN A PENNY OPERA.
I MUST ADMIT, THOUGH, HE'S GROWING ON ME.
WE NEED A BARRICADE IN THE SOUTH PASSAGE AS WELL.
SIX WARDENS PER BARRICADE, PLUS ALL THE CITIZENS YOU CAN MUSTER. I'M HEADING TO THE MARKET SQUARE.
BY YOURSELF, SIR? BUT--
I'LL BE IN GOOD HANDS.
THIS IS ALL? WHERE ARE THE REST OF MY MEN?
MANNING BARRICADES. I TOLD THEM THEY SHOULDN'T BE TAKING ORDERS FROM THAT FURIE LUNATIC, BUT...

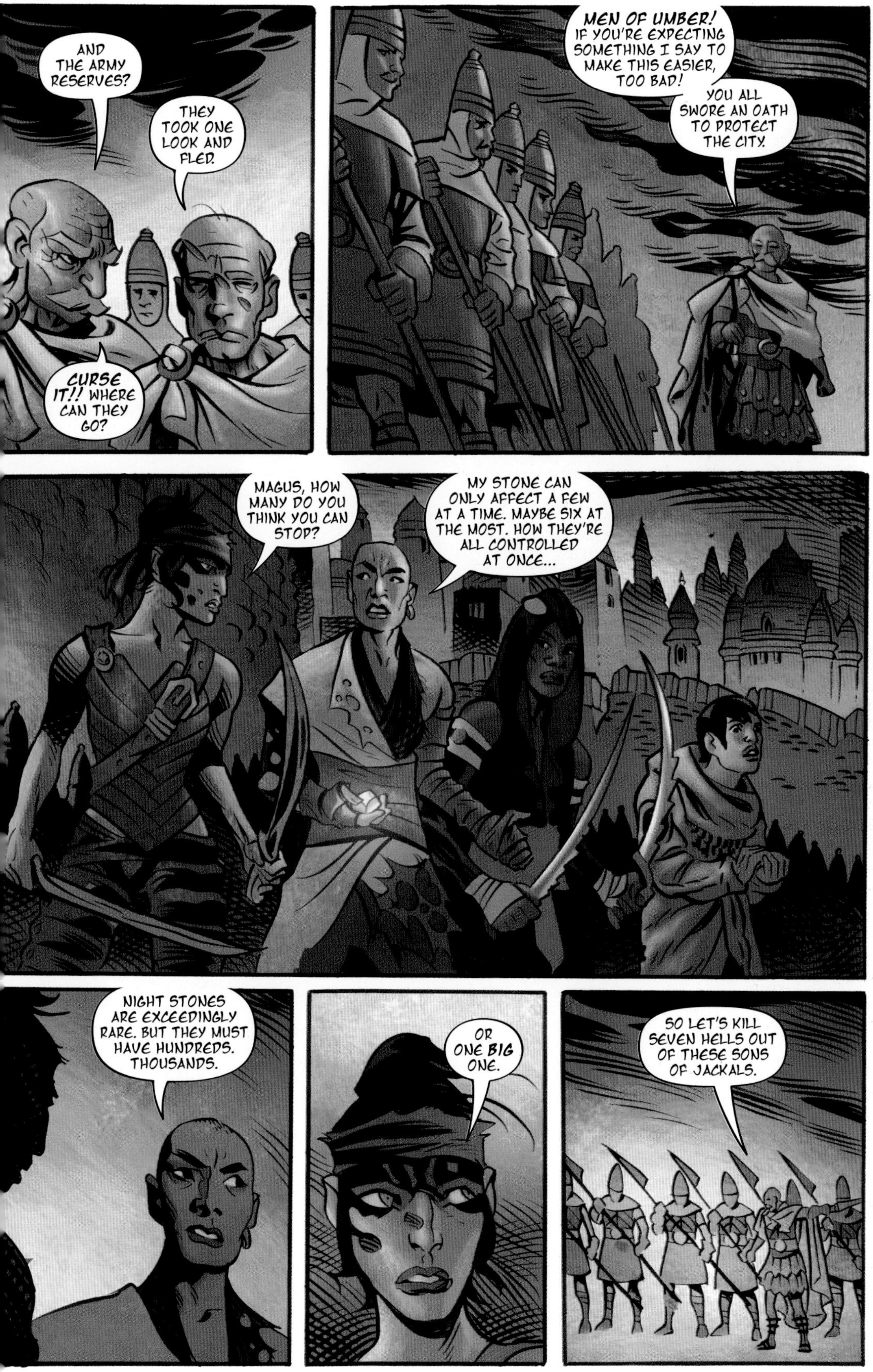
AND THE ARMY RESERVES?
THEY TOOK ONE LOOK AND FLED.
CURSE IT!! WHERE CAN THEY GO?
MEN OF UMBER! IF YOU'RE EXPECTING SOMETHING I SAY TO MAKE THIS EASIER, TOO BAD!
YOU ALL SWORE AN OATH TO PROTECT THE CITY.
MAGUS, HOW MANY DO YOU THINK YOU CAN STOP?
MY STONE CAN ONLY AFFECT A FEW AT A TIME. MAYBE SIX AT THE MOST. HOW THEY'RE ALL CONTROLLED AT ONCE...
NIGHT STONES ARE EXCEEDINGLY RARE. BUT THEY MUST HAVE HUNDREDS. THOUSANDS.
OR ONE BIG ONE.
SO LET'S KILL SEVEN HELLS OUT OF THESE SONS OF JACKALS.

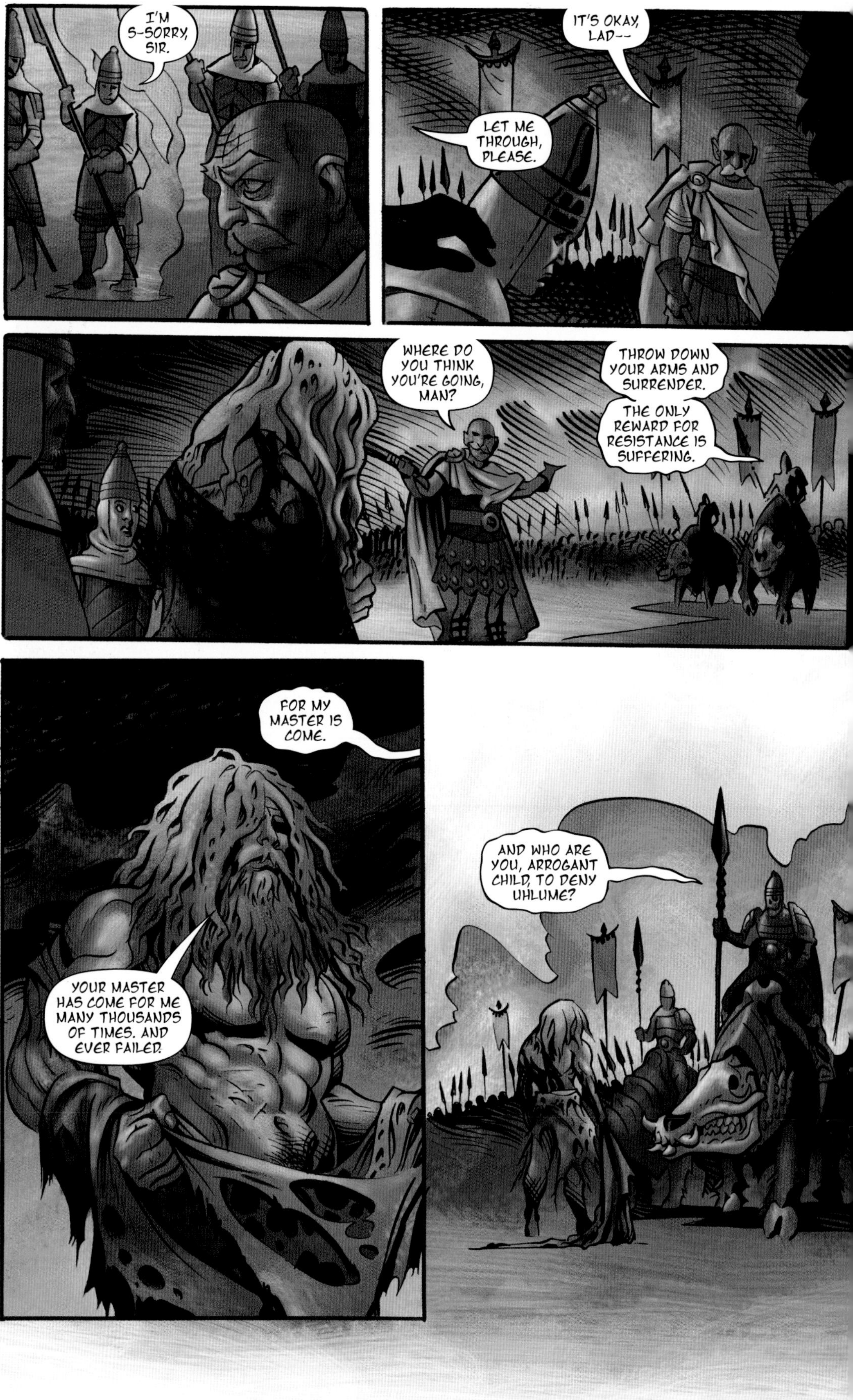
I'M S-SORRY, SIR.
IT'S OKAY, LAD--
LET ME THROUGH, PLEASE.
WHERE DO YOU THINK YOU'RE GOING, MAN?
THROW DOWN YOUR ARMS AND SURRENDER.
THE ONLY REWARD FOR RESISTANCE IS SUFFERING.
FOR MY MASTER IS COME.
AND WHO ARE YOU, ARROGANT CHILD, TO DENY UHLUME?
YOUR MASTER HAS COME FOR ME MANY THOUSANDS OF TIMES. AND EVER FAILED.

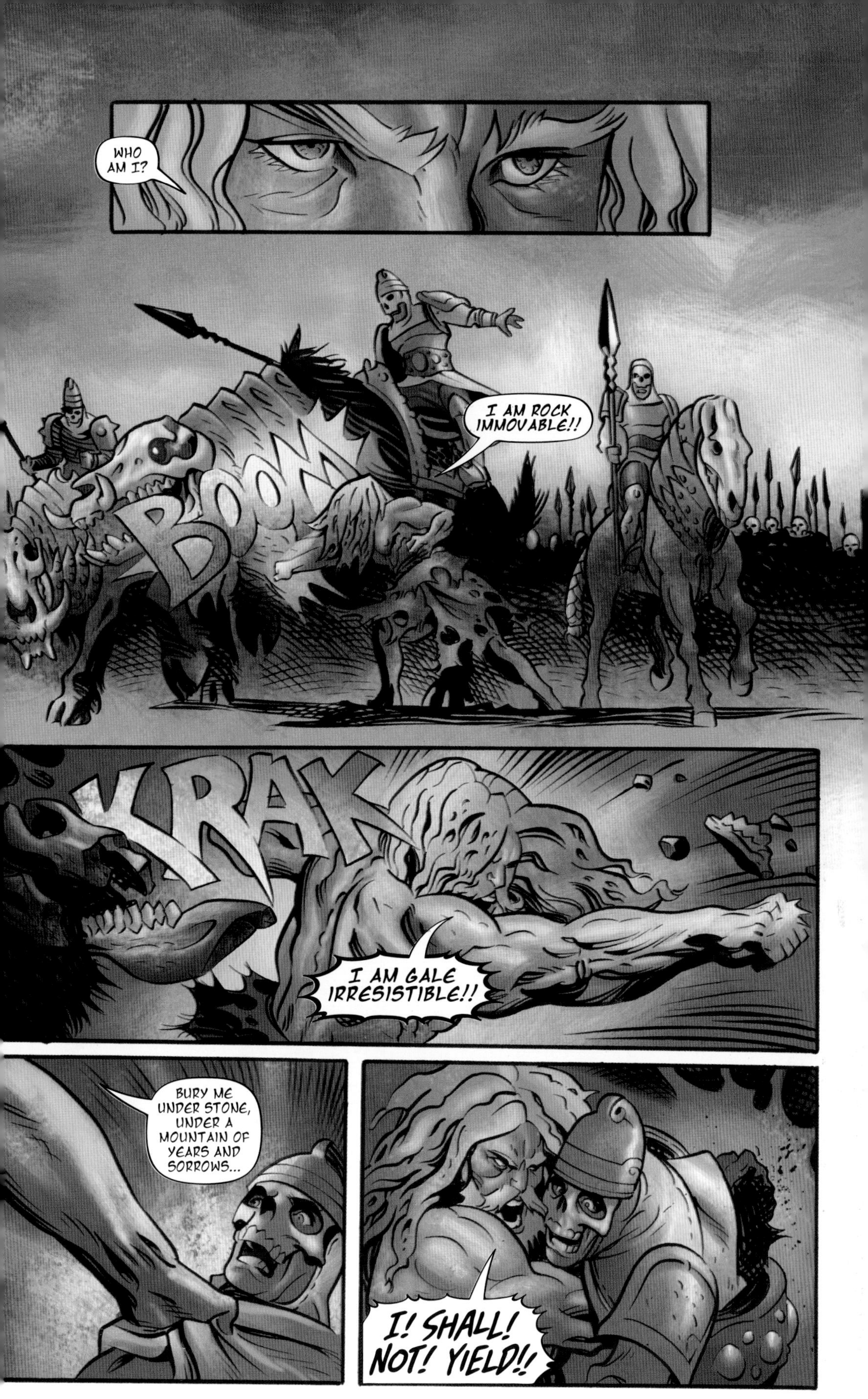
WHO AM I?
I AM ROCK IMMOVABLE!!
BOOM
KRAK
I AM GALE IRRESISTIBLE!!
BURY ME UNDER STONE, UNDER A MOUNTAIN OF YEARS AND SORROWS...
I! SHALL! NOT! YIELD!!

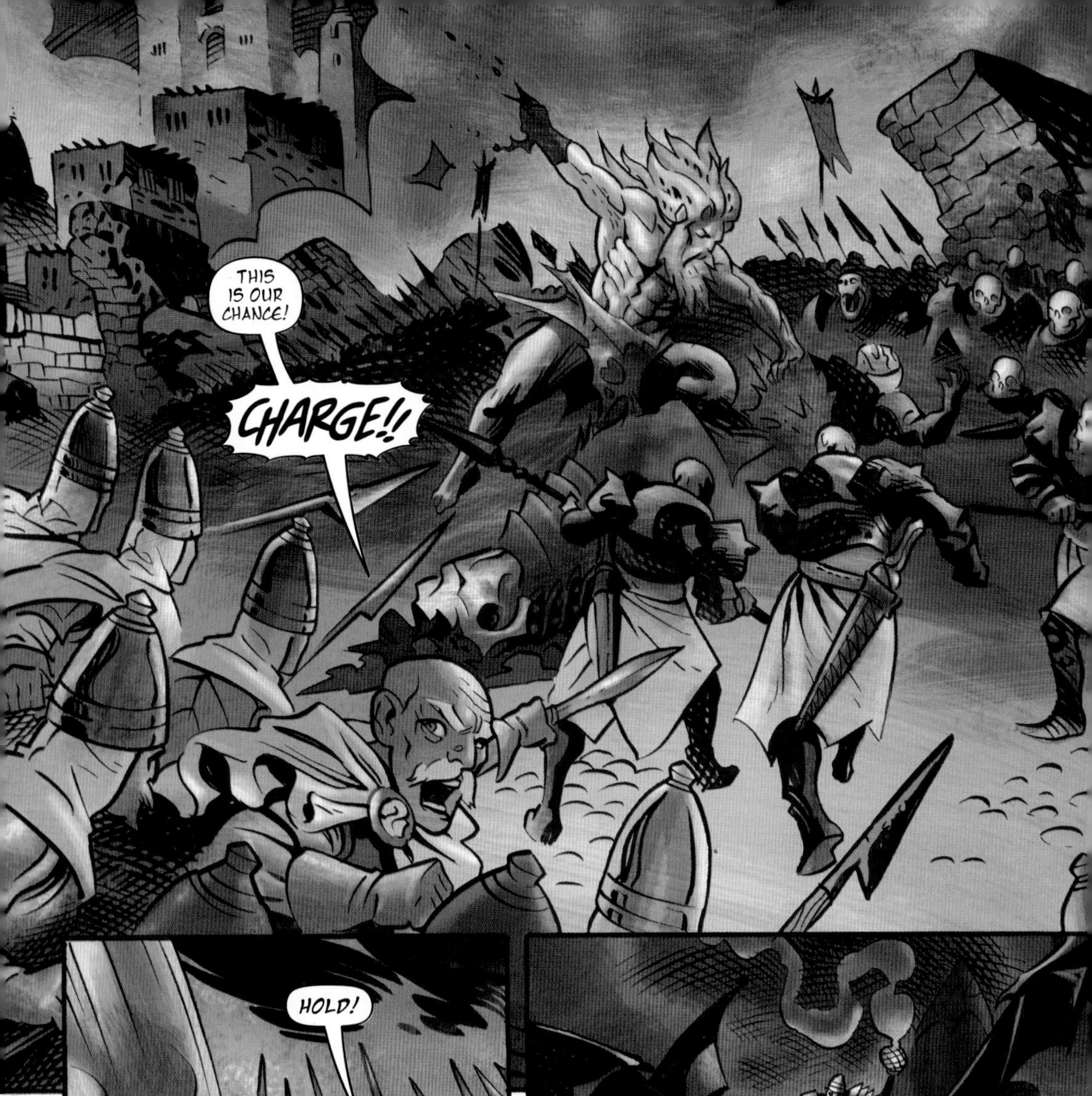
THIS IS OUR CHANCE!
CHARGE!!

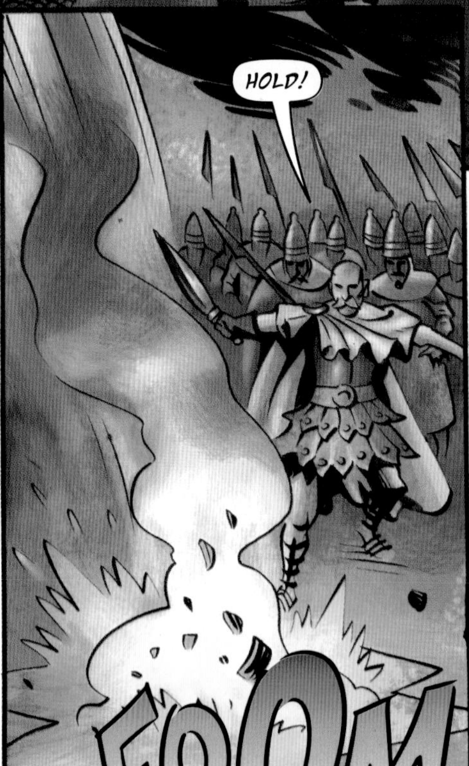
HOLD!
FOOM

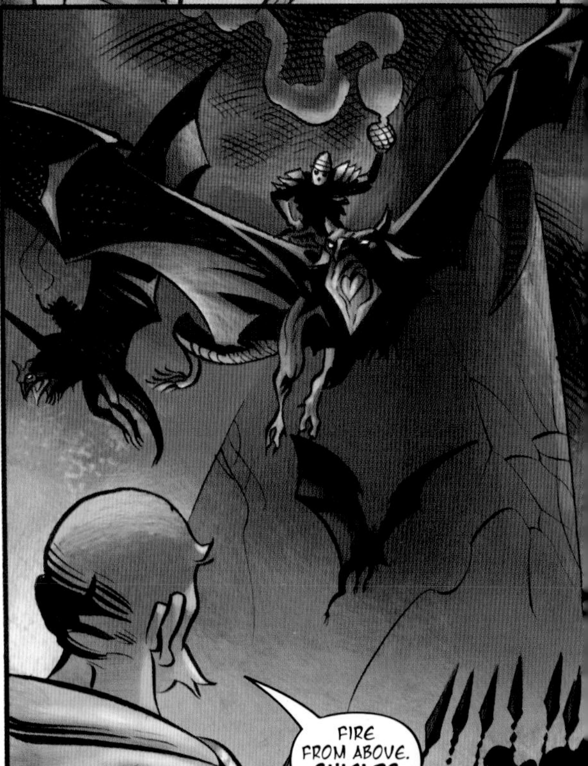
FIRE FROM ABOVE. SHIELDS UP!

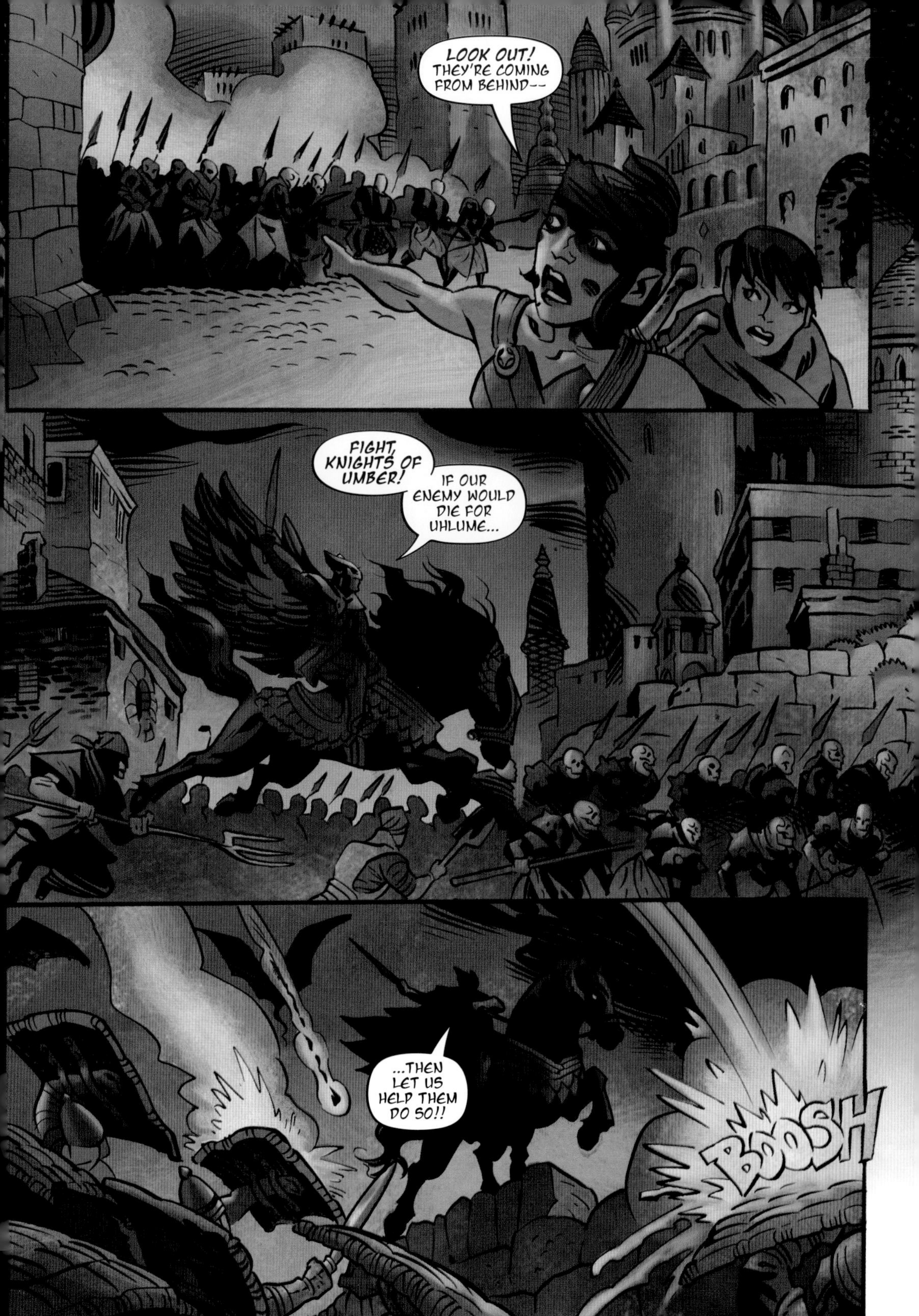
LOOK OUT! THEY'RE COMING FROM BEHIND--
FIGHT, KNIGHTS OF UMBER!
IF OUR ENEMY WOULD DIE FOR UHLUME...
...THEN LET US HELP THEM DO SO!!
BOOSH

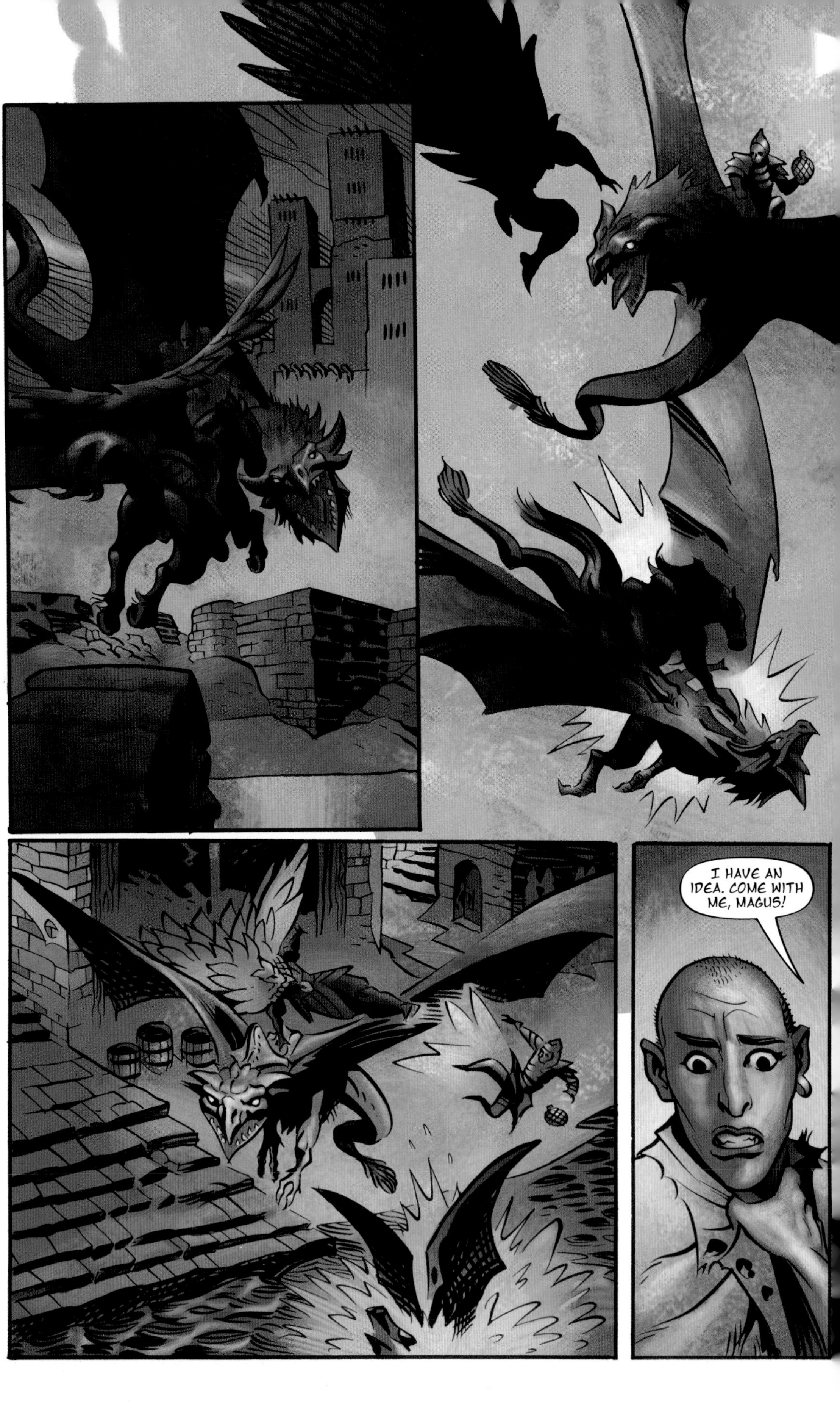
I HAVE AN IDEA. COME WITH ME, MAGUS!

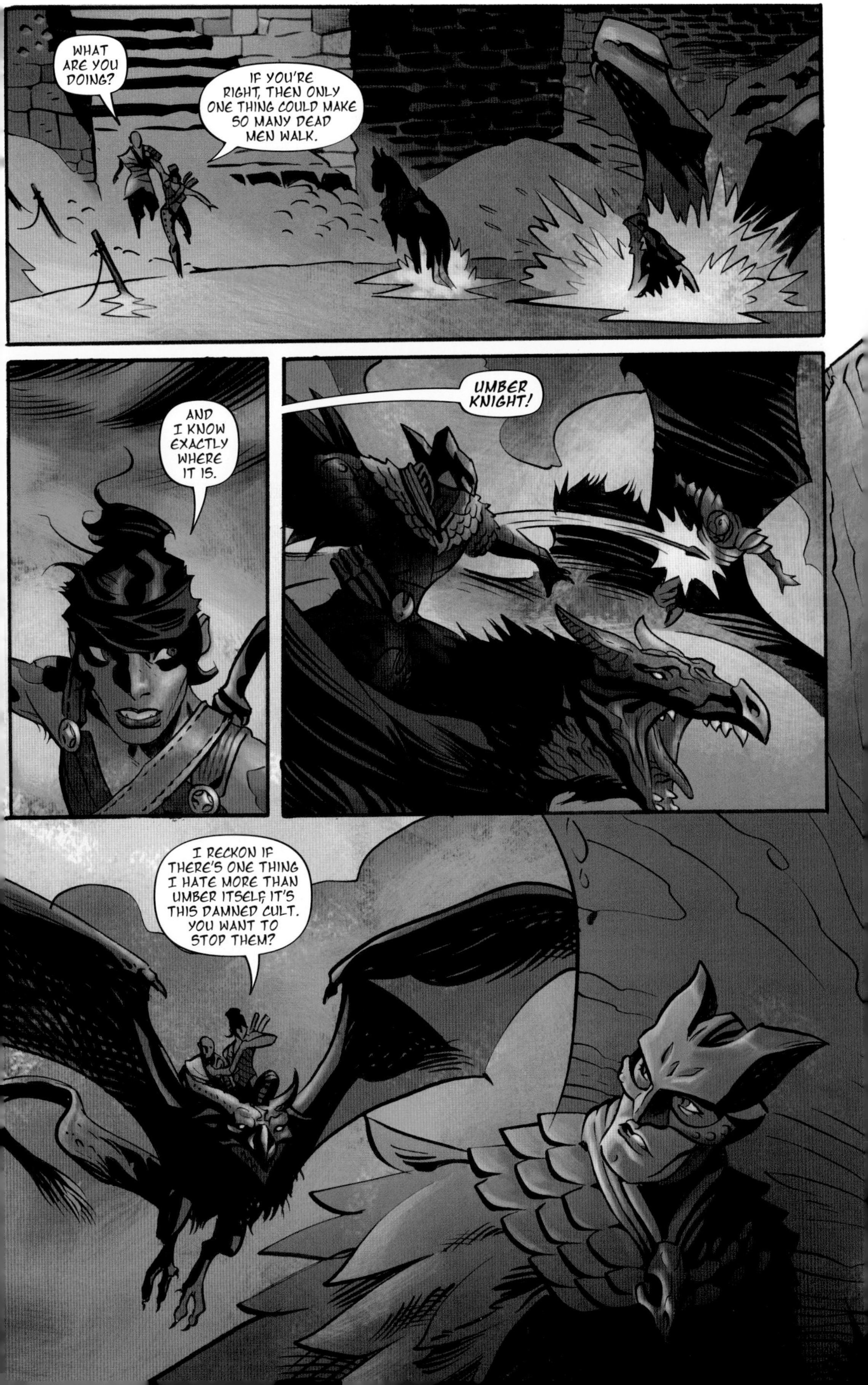
WHAT ARE YOU DOING?
IF YOU'RE RIGHT, THEN ONLY ONE THING COULD MAKE SO MANY DEAD MEN WALK.
AND I KNOW EXACTLY WHERE IT IS.
UMBER KNIGHT!
I RECKON IF THERE'S ONE THING I HATE MORE THAN UMBER ITSELF, IT'S THIS DAMNED CULT. YOU WANT TO STOP THEM?

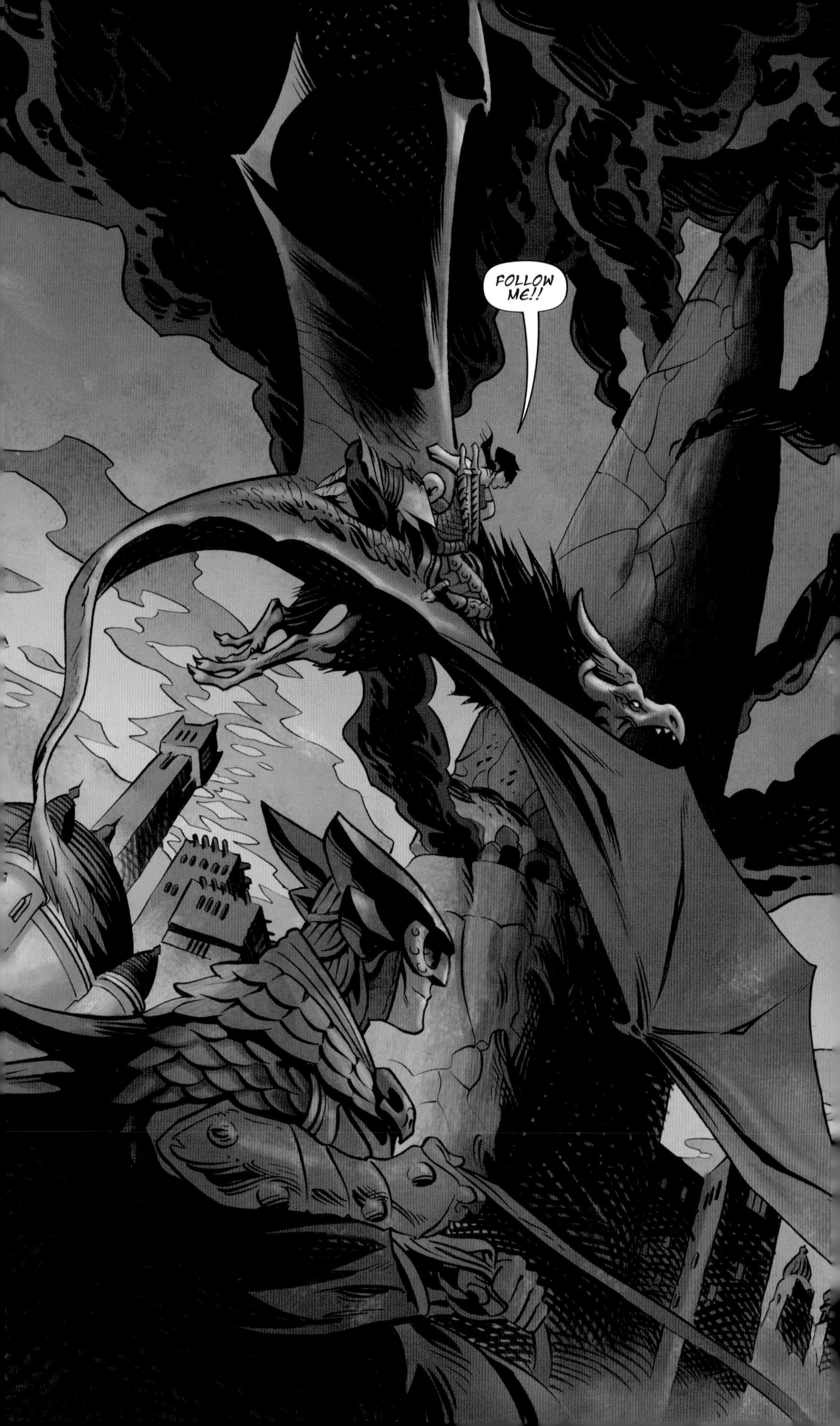
FOLLOW ME!!

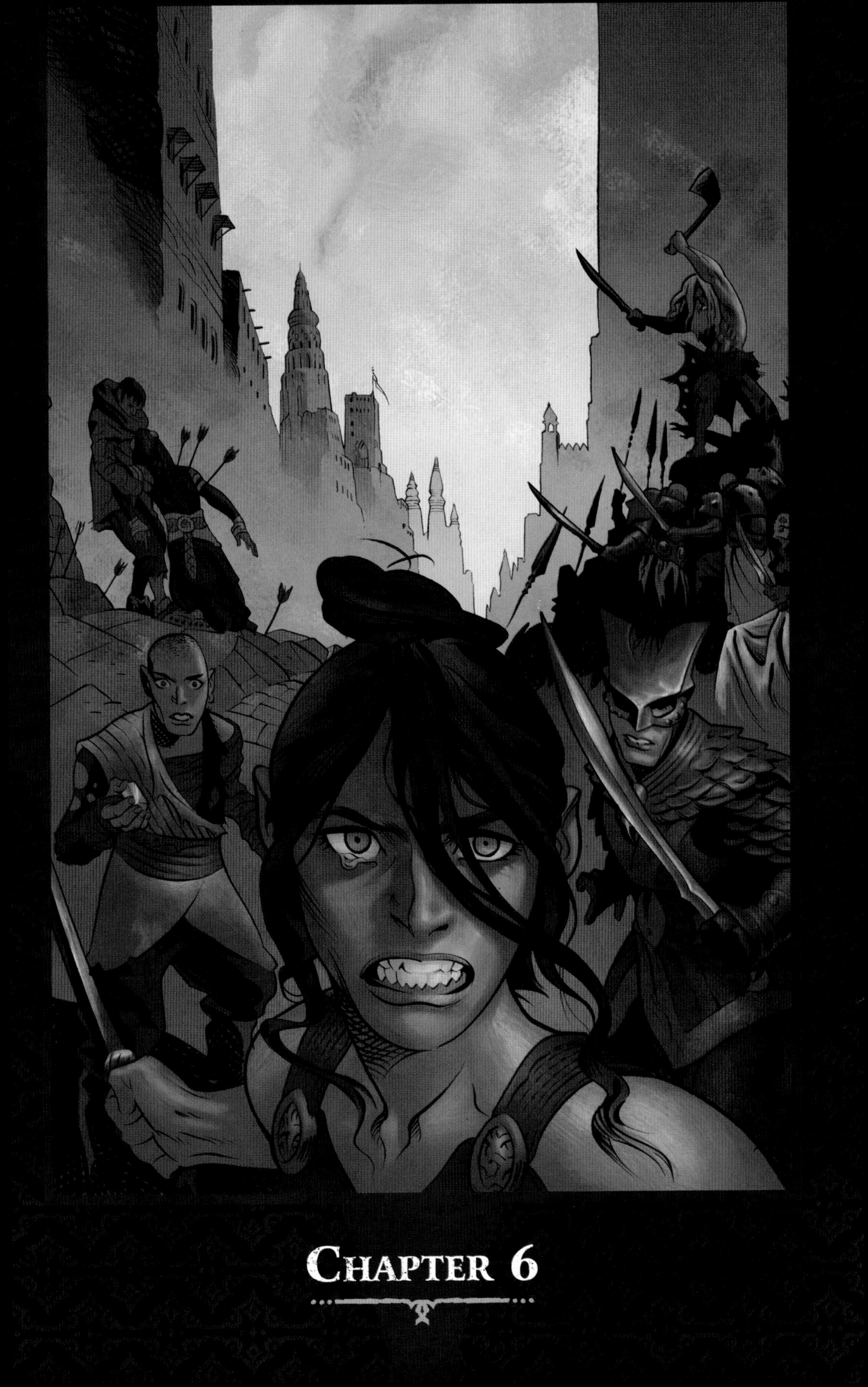

Chapter 6

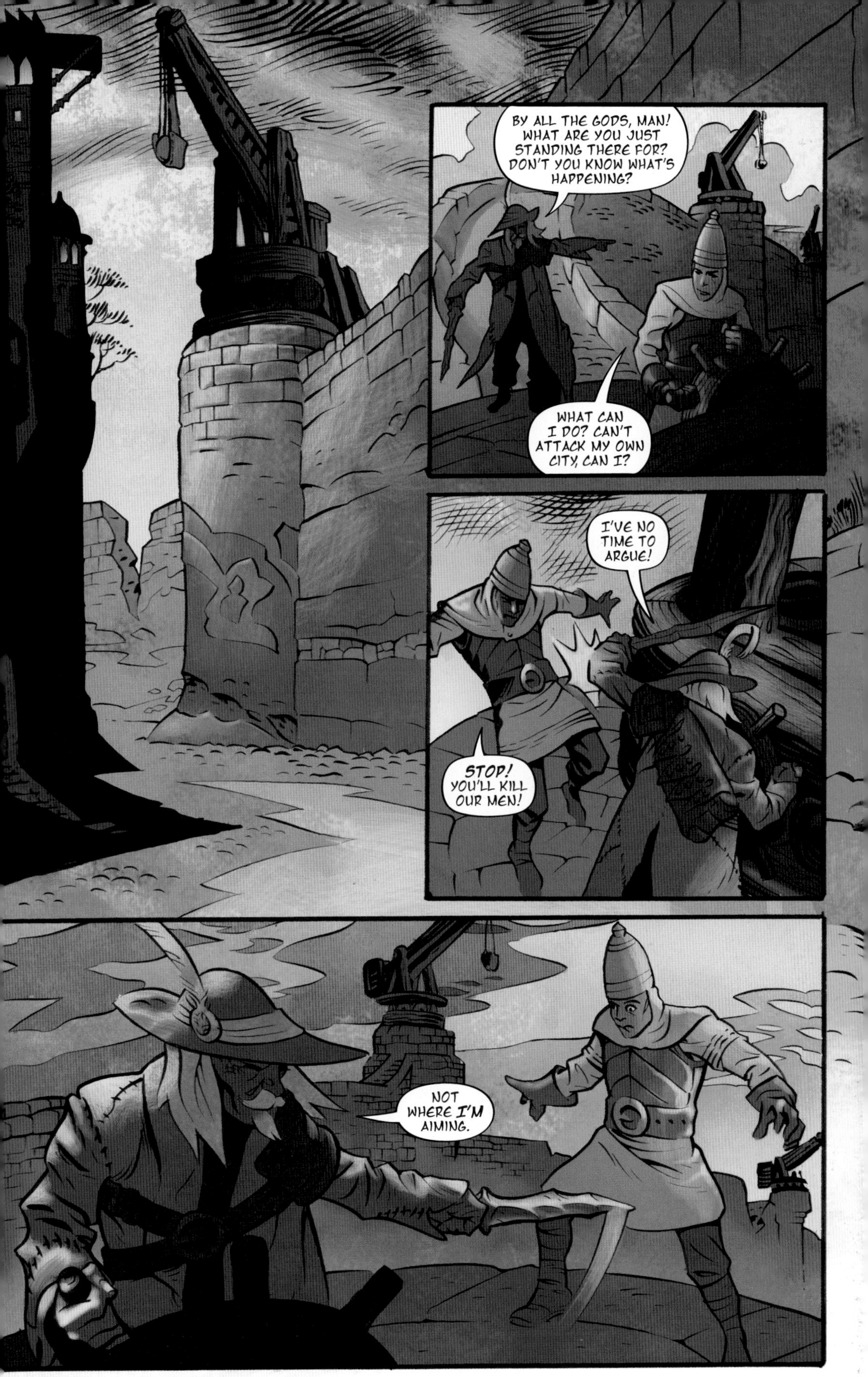
BY ALL THE GODS, MAN! WHAT ARE YOU JUST STANDING THERE FOR? DON'T YOU KNOW WHAT'S HAPPENING?
WHAT CAN I DO? CAN'T ATTACK MY OWN CITY, CAN I?
I'VE NO TIME TO ARGUE!
STOP! YOU'LL KILL OUR MEN!
NOT WHERE I'M AIMING.

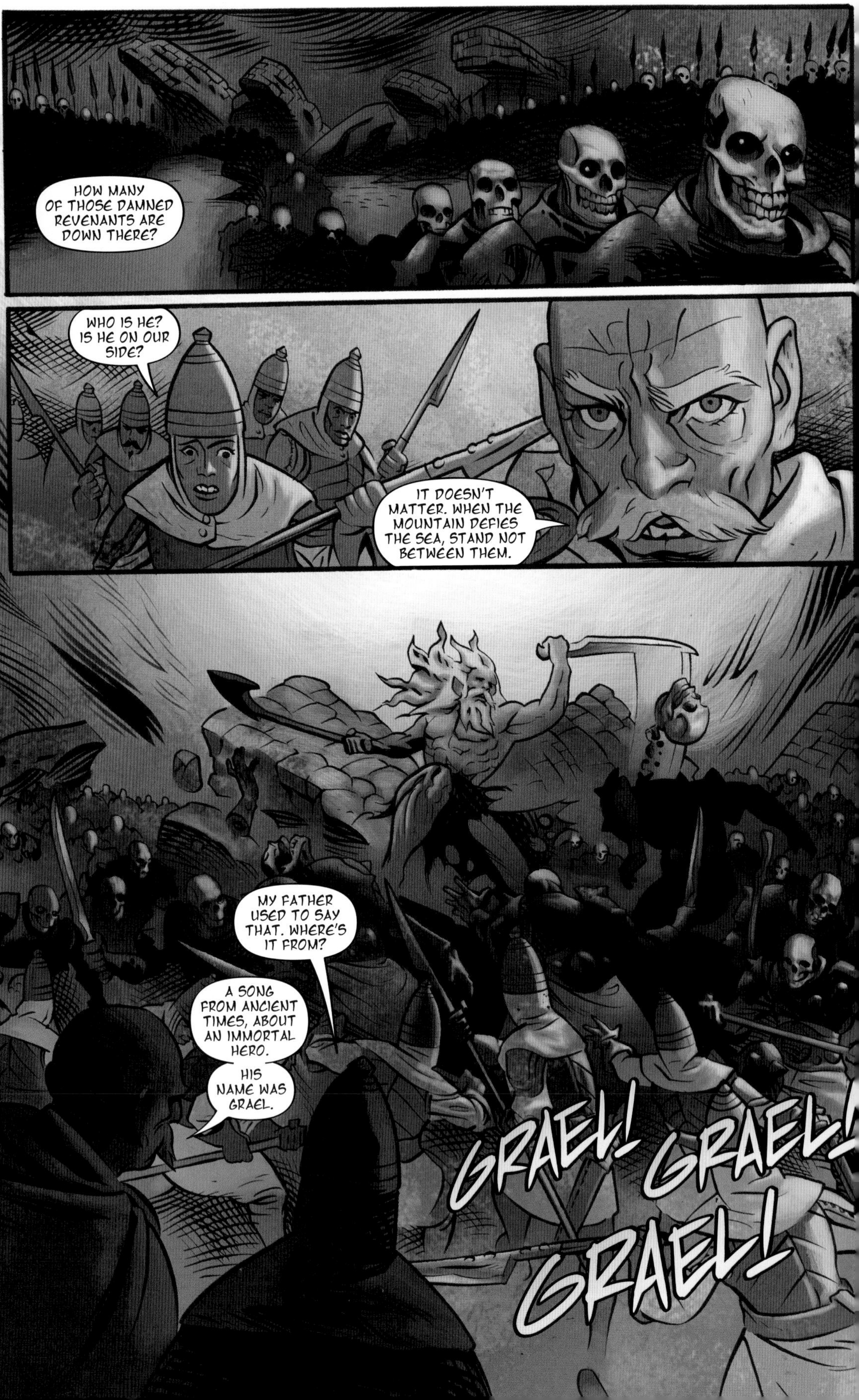
HOW MANY OF THOSE DAMNED REVENANTS ARE DOWN THERE?
WHO IS HE? IS HE ON OUR SIDE?
IT DOESN'T MATTER. WHEN THE MOUNTAIN DEFIES THE SEA, STAND NOT BETWEEN THEM.
MY FATHER USED TO SAY THAT. WHERE'S IT FROM?
A SONG FROM ANCIENT TIMES, ABOUT AN IMMORTAL HERO.
HIS NAME WAS GRAEL.
GRAEL! GRAEL! GRAEL!

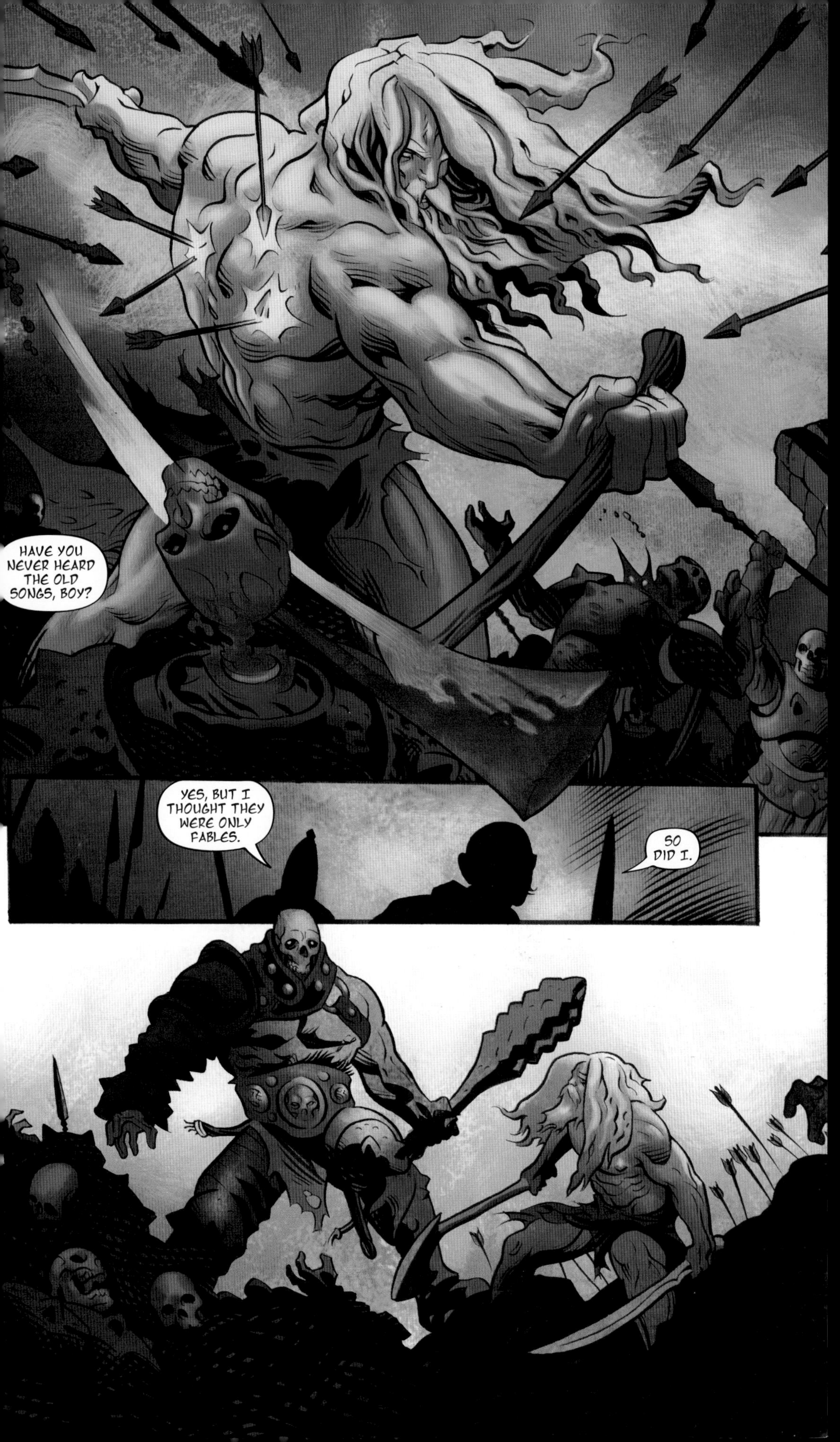
HAVE YOU NEVER HEARD THE OLD SONGS, BOY?
YES, BUT I THOUGHT THEY WERE ONLY FABLES.
SO DID I.

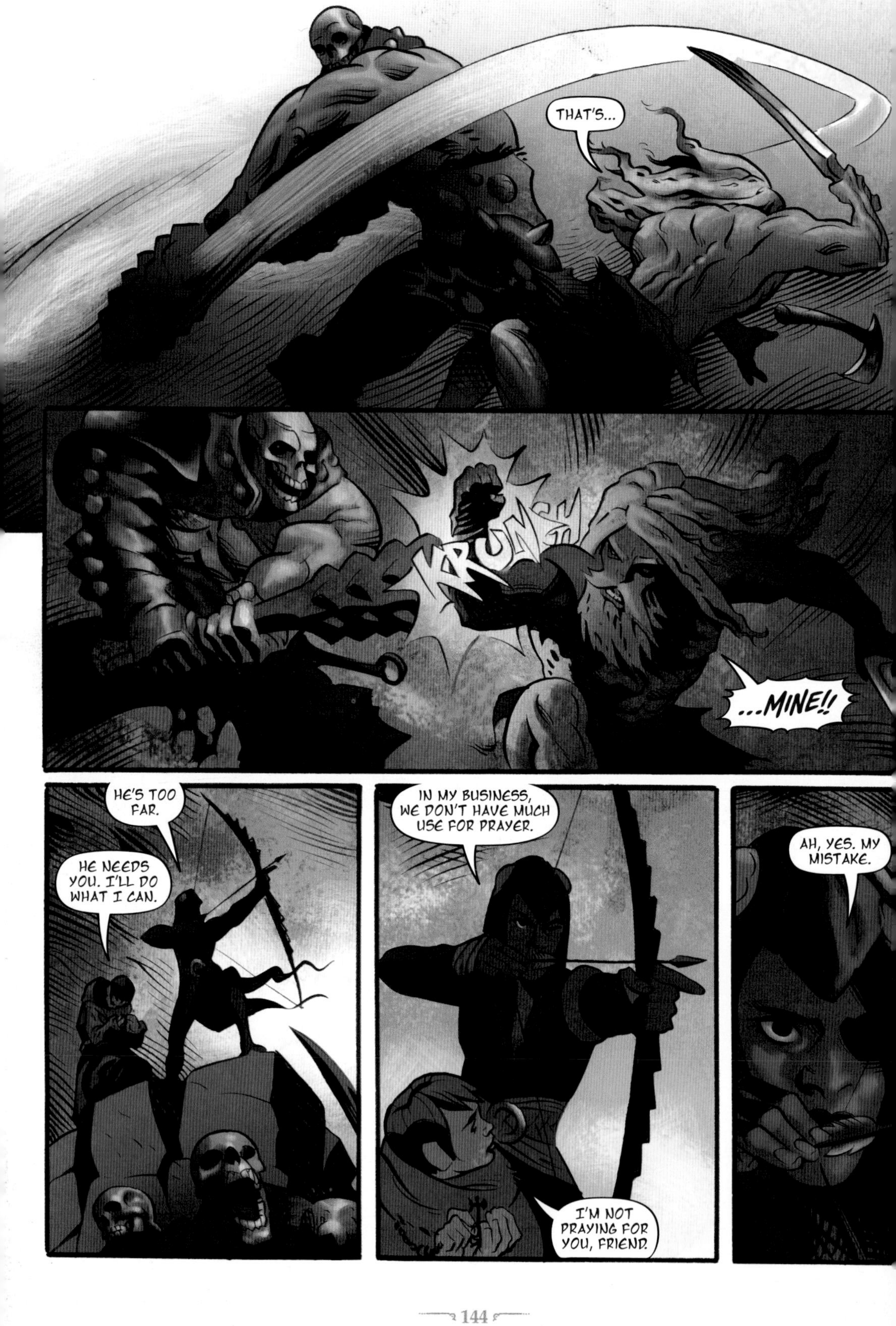
THAT'S...
KRUNCH
...MINE!!
HE'S TOO FAR.
HE NEEDS YOU. I'LL DO WHAT I CAN.
IN MY BUSINESS, WE DON'T HAVE MUCH USE FOR PRAYER.
I'M NOT PRAYING FOR YOU, FRIEND.
AH, YES. MY MISTAKE.

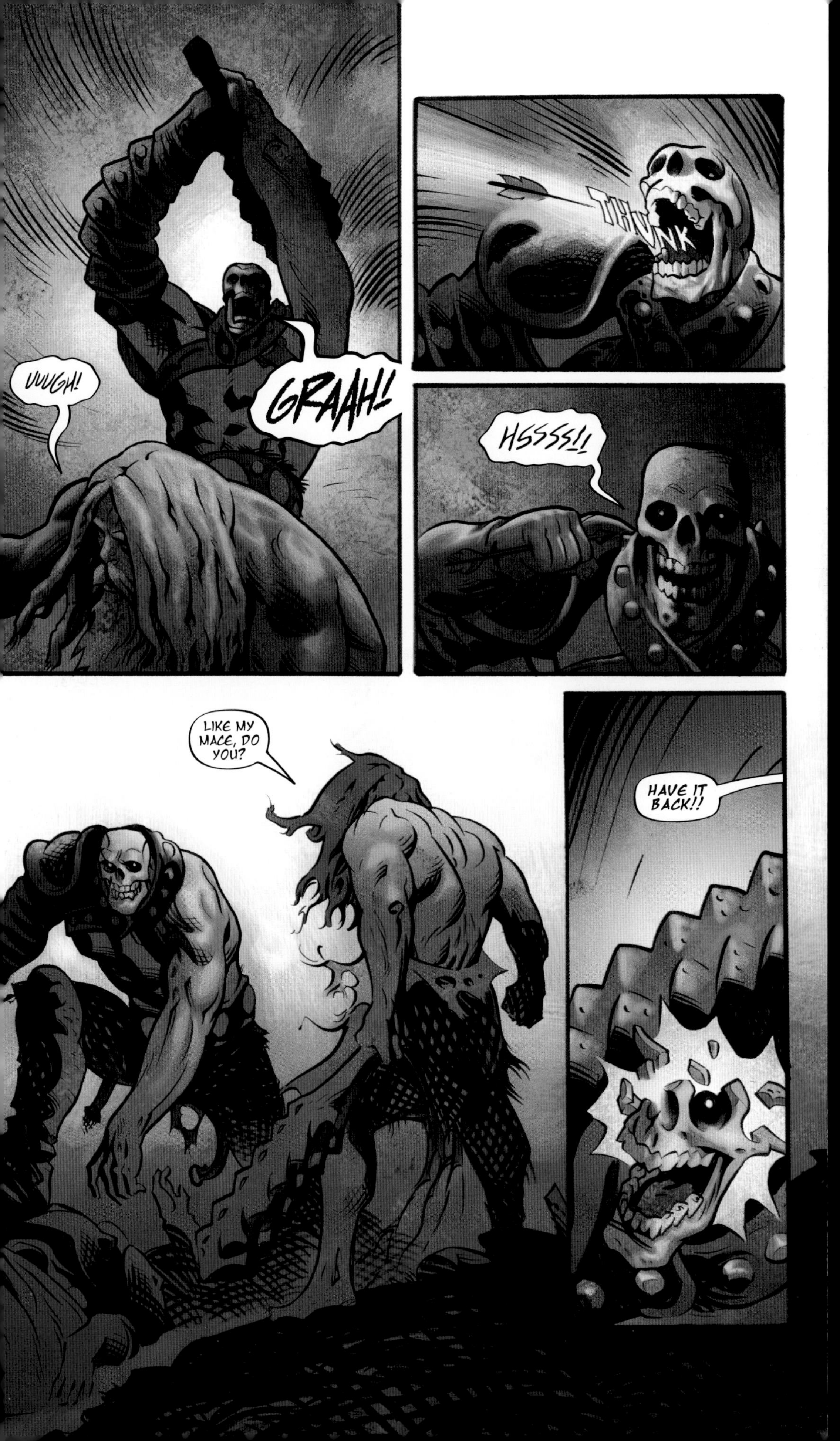
UUUGH!
GRAAH!
THUNK
HSSSS!!
LIKE MY MACE, DO YOU?
HAVE IT BACK!!

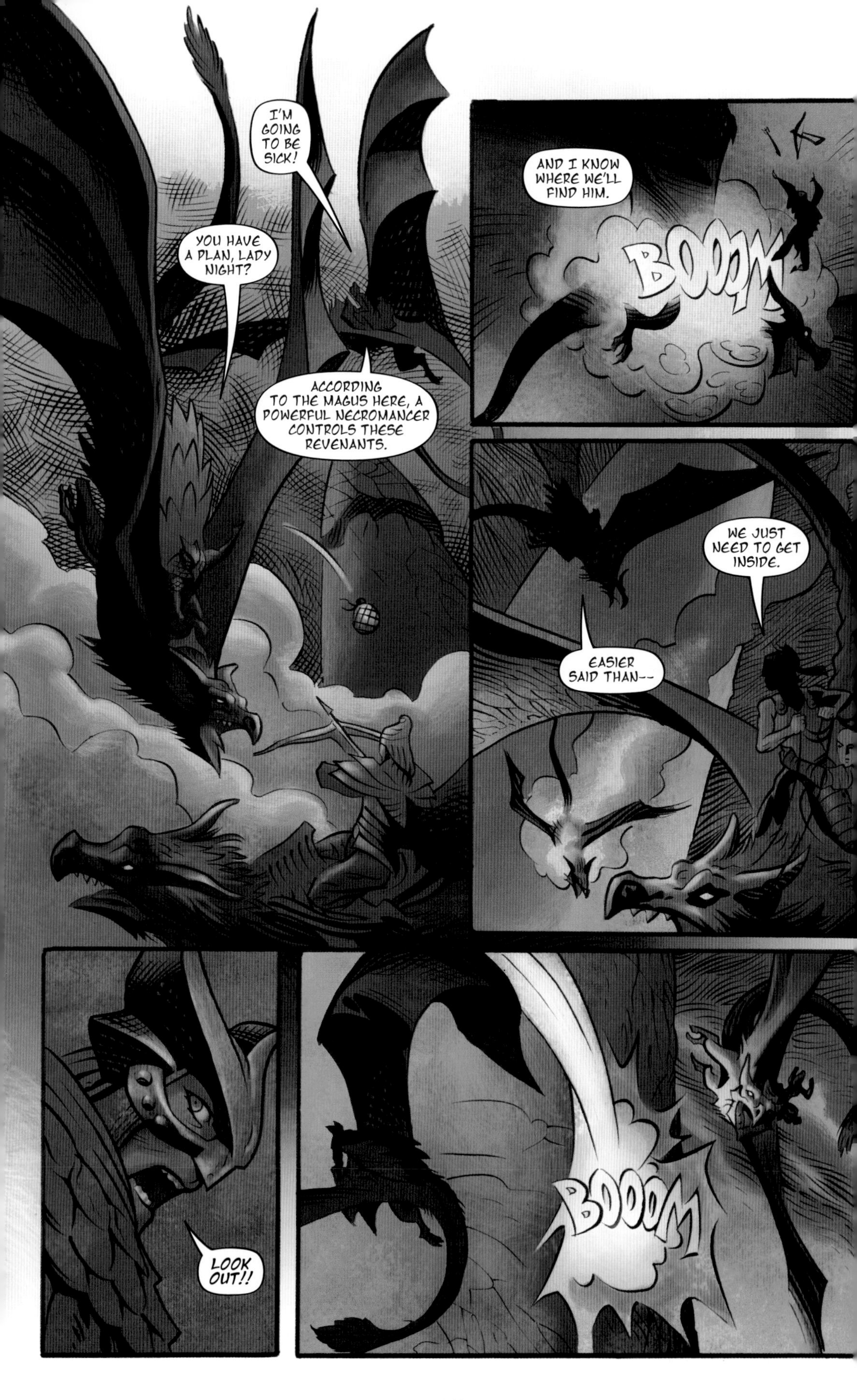
I'M GOING TO BE SICK!
YOU HAVE A PLAN, LADY NIGHT?
ACCORDING TO THE MAGUS HERE, A POWERFUL NECROMANCER CONTROLS THESE REVENANTS.
AND I KNOW WHERE WE'LL FIND HIM.
BOOOM
WE JUST NEED TO GET INSIDE.
EASIER SAID THAN--
LOOK OUT!!
BOOOM

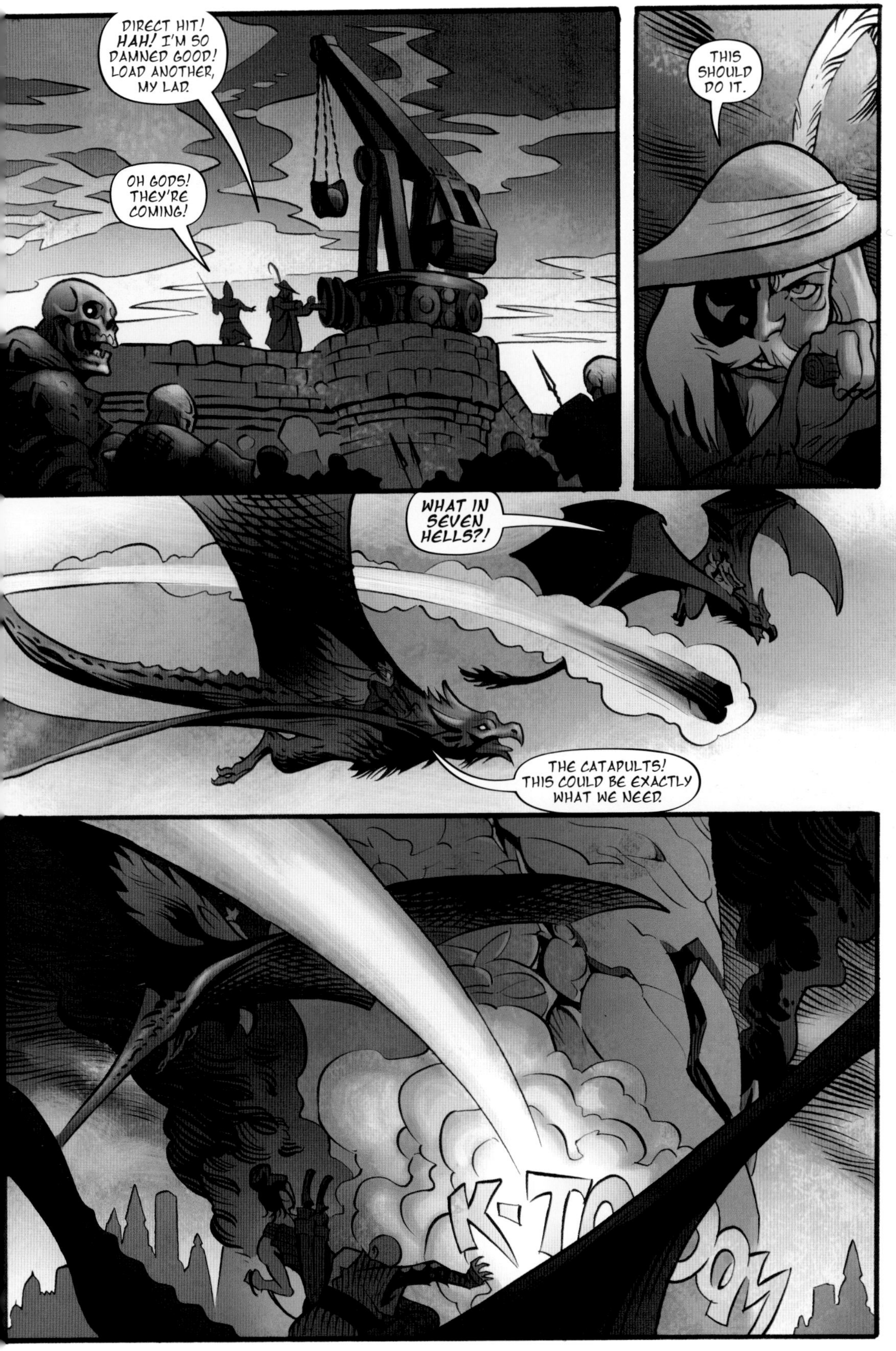
DIRECT HIT! HAH! I'M SO DAMNED GOOD! LOAD ANOTHER, MY LAD.
OH GODS! THEY'RE COMING!
THIS SHOULD DO IT.
WHAT IN SEVEN HELLS?!
THE CATAPULTS! THIS COULD BE EXACTLY WHAT WE NEED.
K-TOOOM

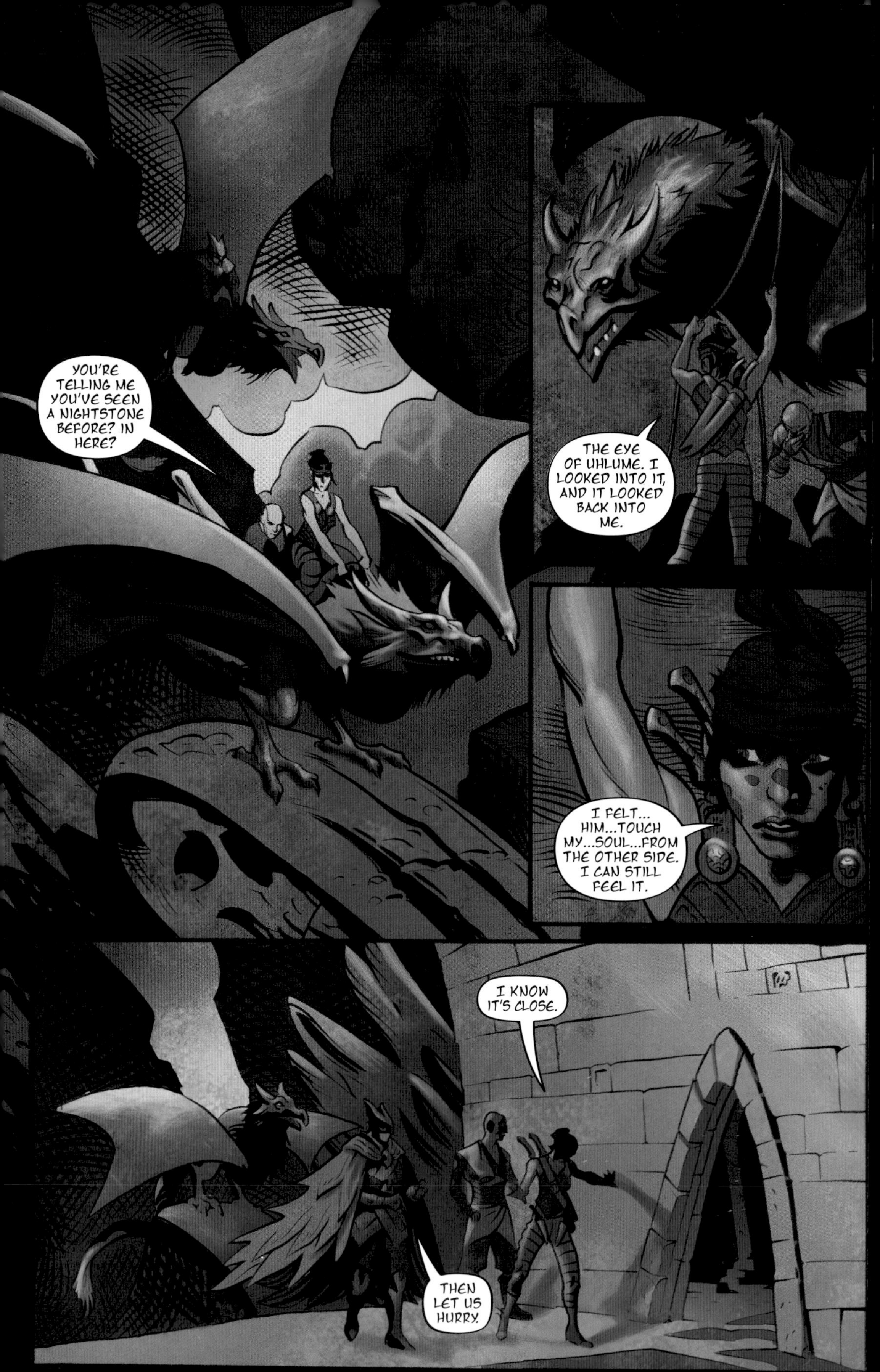

YOU'RE TELLING ME YOU'VE SEEN A NIGHTSTONE BEFORE? IN HERE?
THE EYE OF UHLUME. I LOOKED INTO IT, AND IT LOOKED BACK INTO ME.
I FELT... HIM...TOUCH MY...SOUL...FROM THE OTHER SIDE. I CAN STILL FEEL IT.
I KNOW IT'S CLOSE.
THEN LET US HURRY.

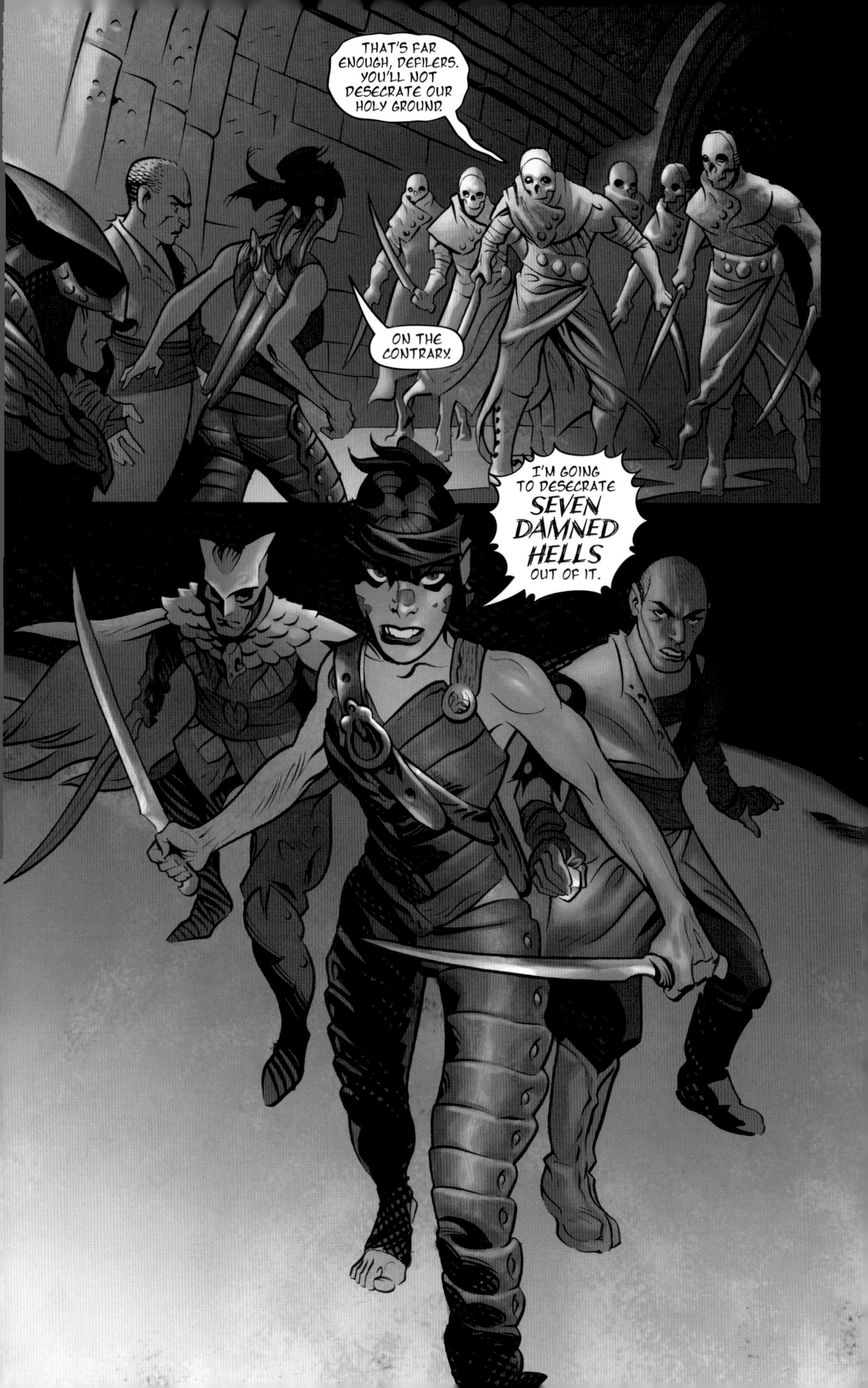
THAT'S FAR ENOUGH, DEFILERS. YOU'LL NOT DESECRATE OUR HOLY GROUND.
ON THE CONTRARY.
I'M GOING TO DESECRATE SEVEN DAMNED HELLS OUT OF IT.

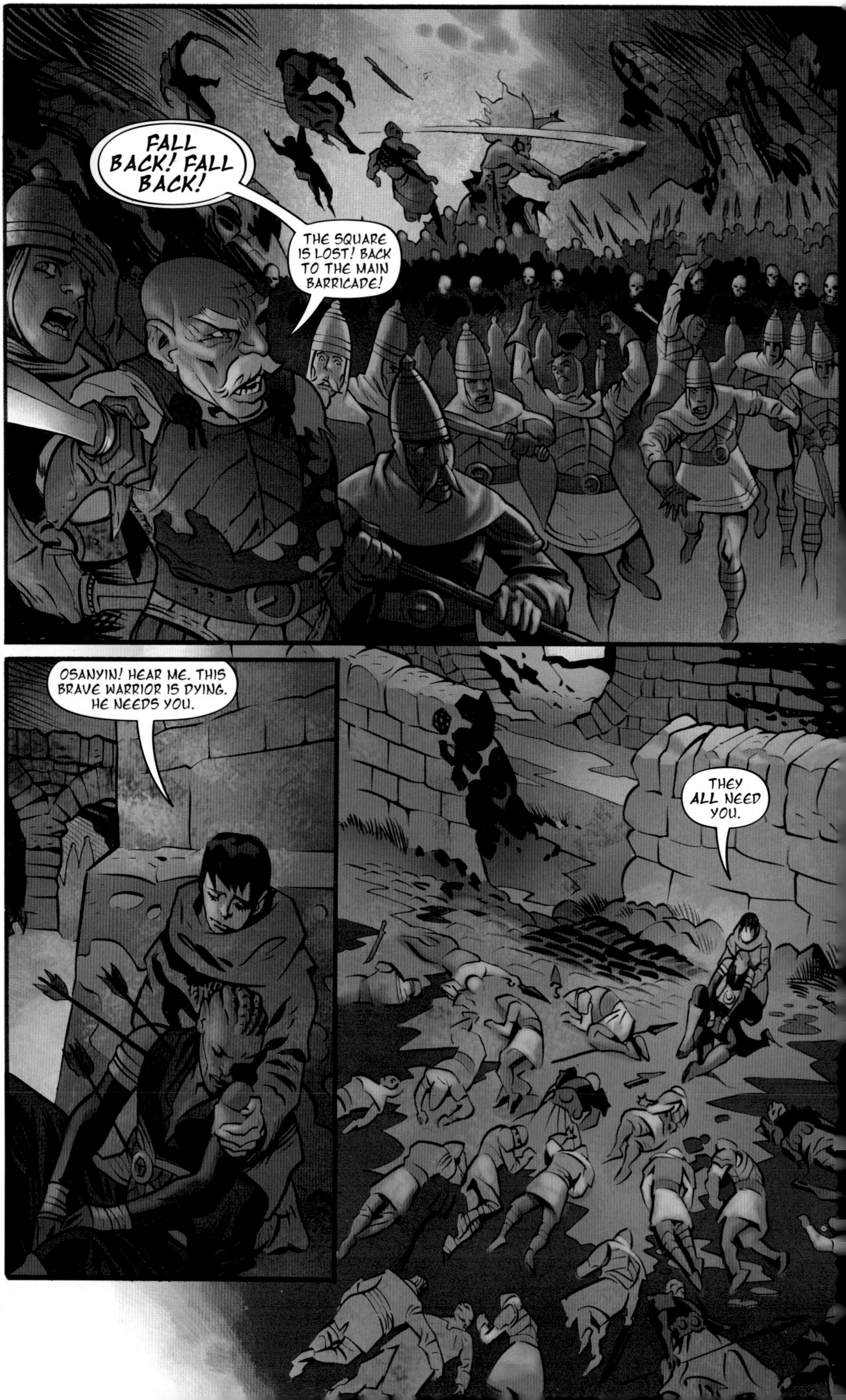
FALL BACK! FALL BACK!
THE SQUARE IS LOST! BACK TO THE MAIN BARRICADE!
OSANYIN! HEAR ME. THIS BRAVE WARRIOR IS DYING. HE NEEDS YOU.
THEY ALL NEED YOU.

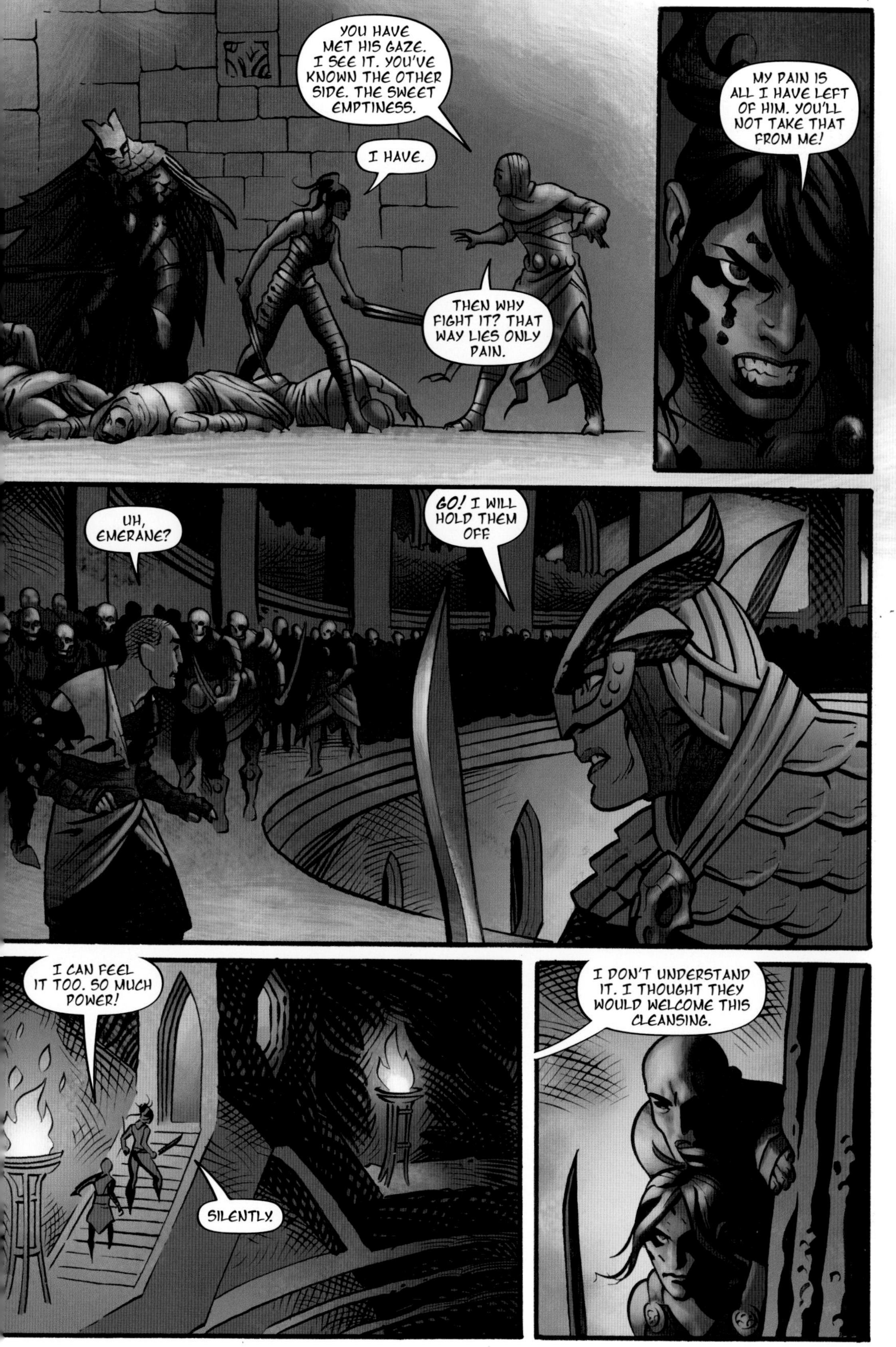

YOU HAVE MET HIS GAZE. I SEE IT. YOU'VE KNOWN THE OTHER SIDE. THE SWEET EMPTINESS.
I HAVE.
THEN WHY FIGHT IT? THAT WAY LIES ONLY PAIN.
MY PAIN IS ALL I HAVE LEFT OF HIM. YOU'LL NOT TAKE THAT FROM ME!
UH, EMERANE?
GO! I WILL HOLD THEM OFF.
I CAN FEEL IT TOO. SO MUCH POWER!
SILENTLY.
I DON'T UNDERSTAND IT. I THOUGHT THEY WOULD WELCOME THIS CLEANSING.

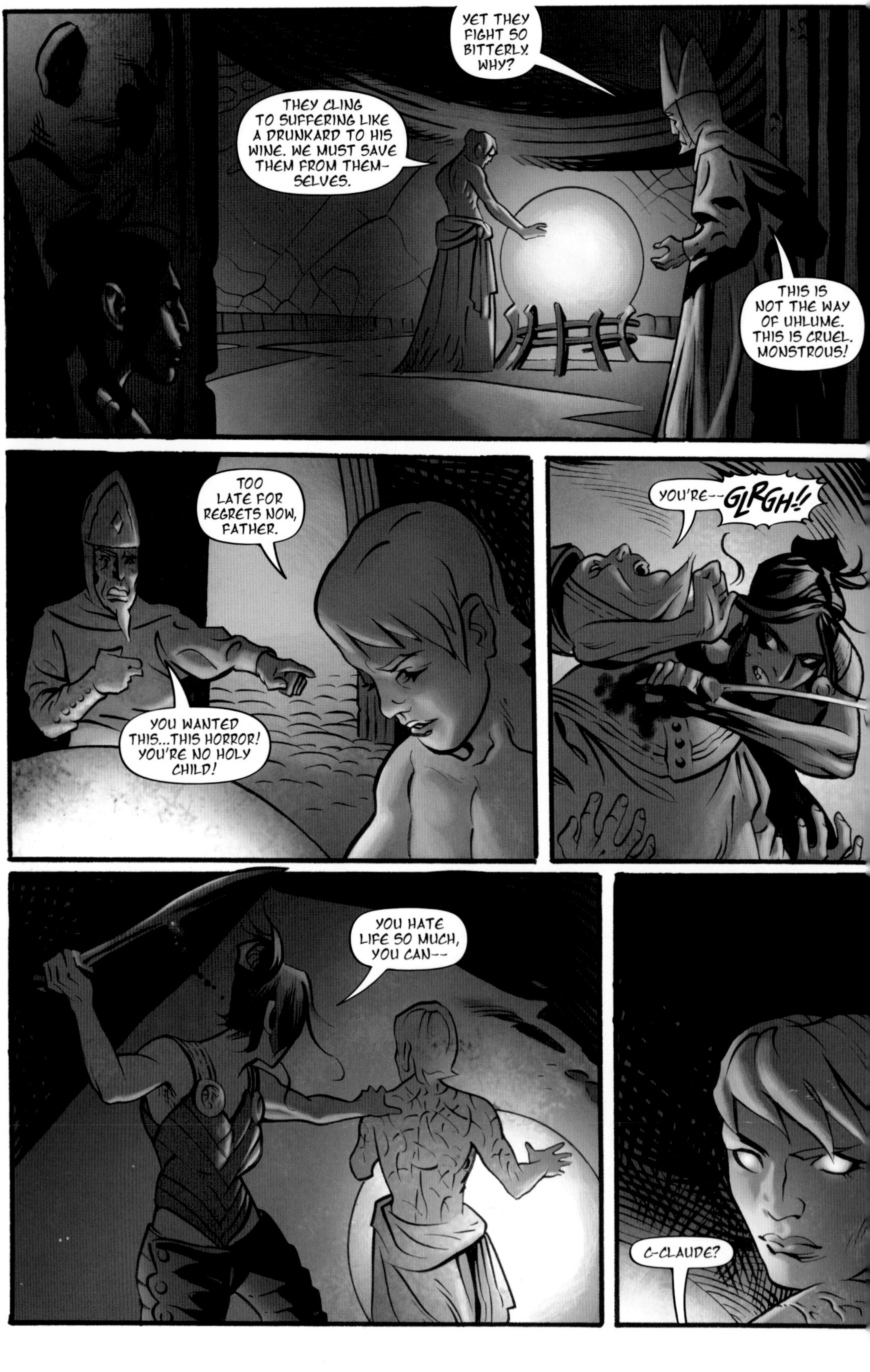
YET THEY FIGHT SO BITTERLY. WHY?
THEY CLING TO SUFFERING LIKE A DRUNKARD TO HIS WINE. WE MUST SAVE THEM FROM THEM-SELVES.
THIS IS NOT THE WAY OF UHLUME. THIS IS CRUEL. MONSTROUS!
TOO LATE FOR REGRETS NOW, FATHER.
YOU WANTED THIS...THIS HORROR! YOU'RE NO HOLY CHILD!
YOU'RE--GLRGH!!
YOU HATE LIFE SO MUCH, YOU CAN--
C-CLAUDE?

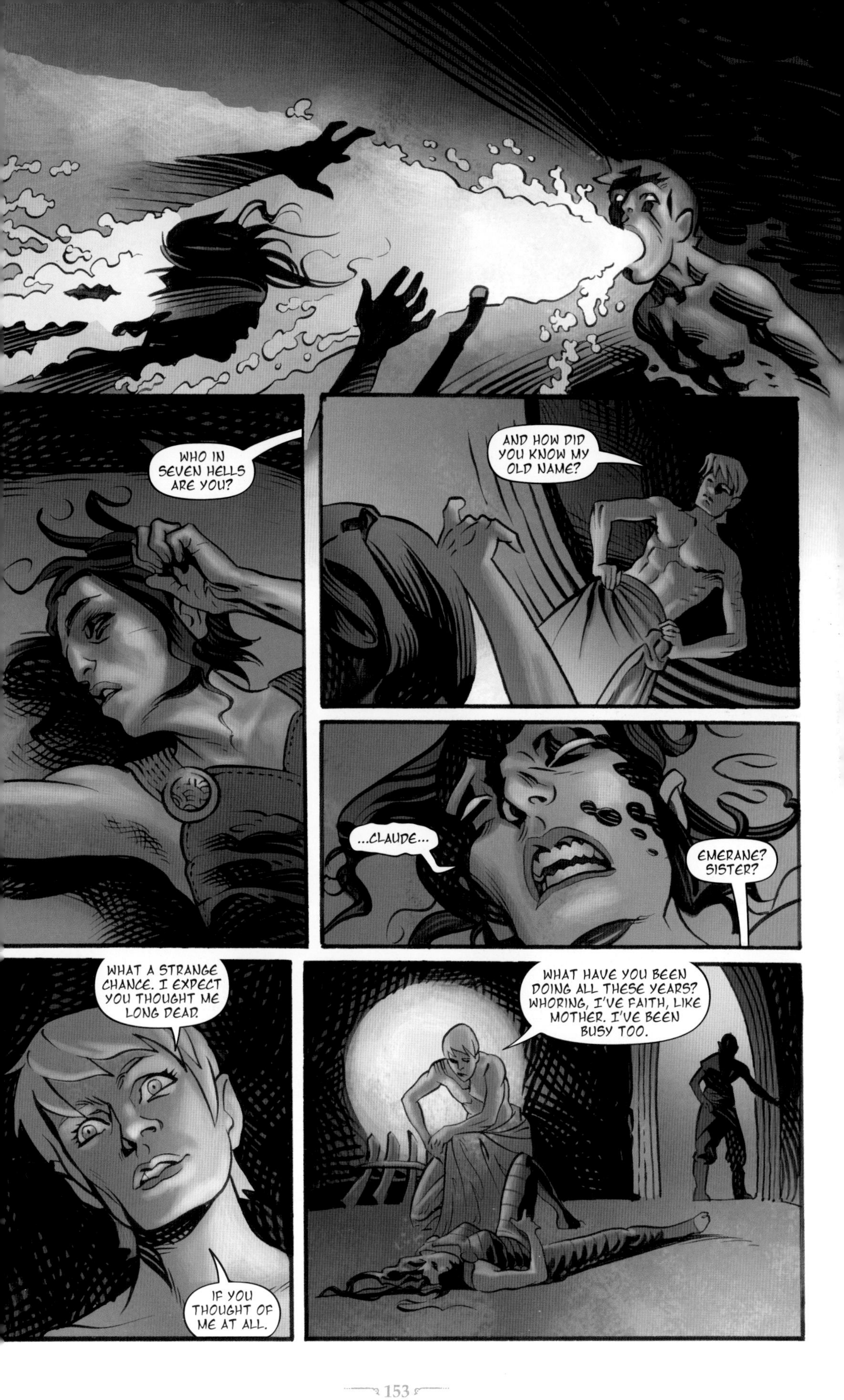
WHO IN SEVEN HELLS ARE YOU?
AND HOW DID YOU KNOW MY OLD NAME?
...CLAUDE...
EMERANE? SISTER?
WHAT A STRANGE CHANCE. I EXPECT YOU THOUGHT ME LONG DEAD.
IF YOU THOUGHT OF ME AT ALL.
WHAT HAVE YOU BEEN DOING ALL THESE YEARS? WHORING, I'VE FAITH, LIKE MOTHER. I'VE BEEN BUSY TOO.

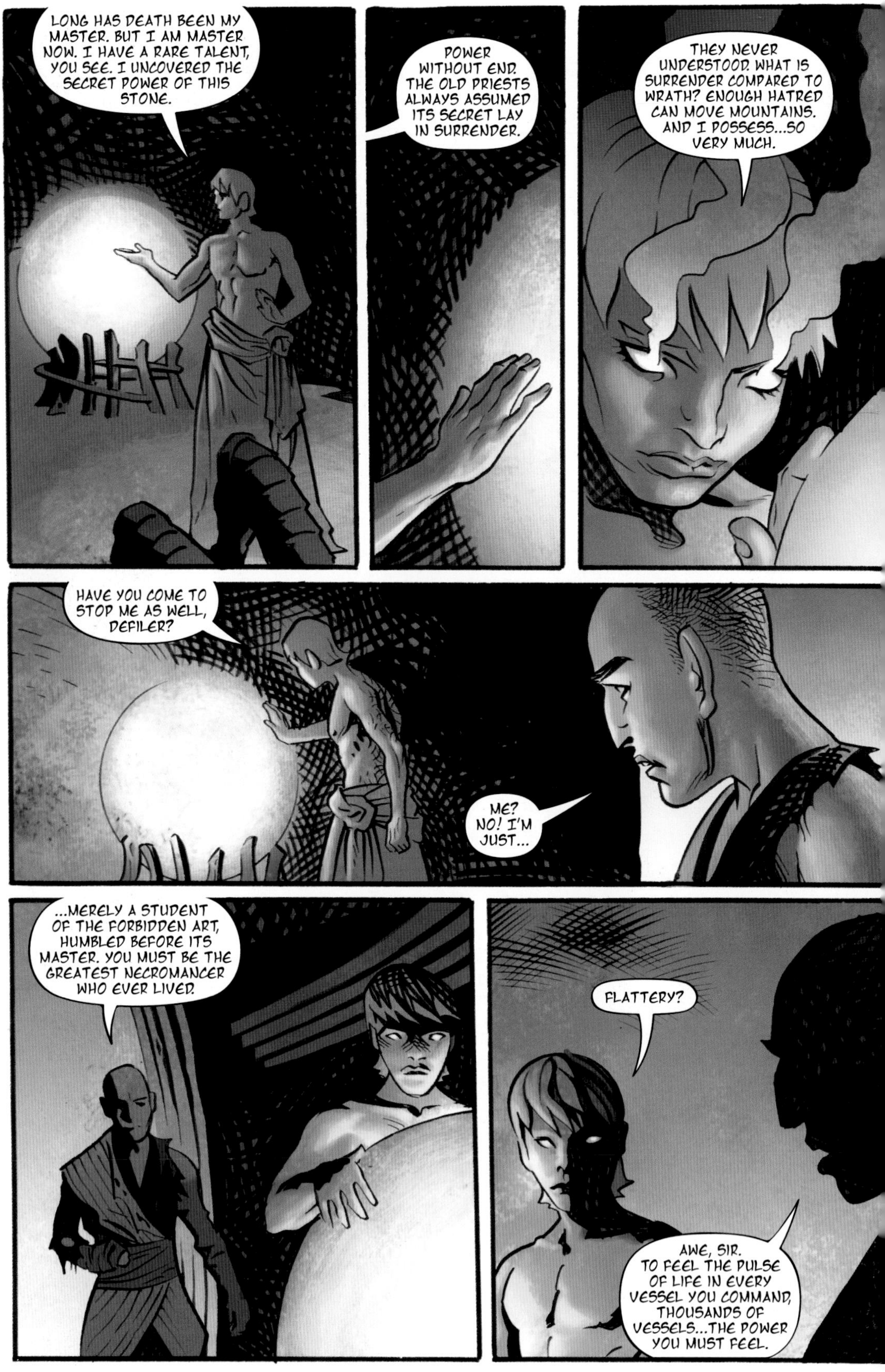
LONG HAS DEATH BEEN MY MASTER. BUT I AM MASTER NOW. I HAVE A RARE TALENT, YOU SEE. I UNCOVERED THE SECRET POWER OF THIS STONE.
POWER WITHOUT END. THE OLD PRIESTS ALWAYS ASSUMED ITS SECRET LAY IN SURRENDER.
THEY NEVER UNDERSTOOD. WHAT IS SURRENDER COMPARED TO WRATH? ENOUGH HATRED CAN MOVE MOUNTAINS. AND I POSSESS...SO VERY MUCH.
HAVE YOU COME TO STOP ME AS WELL, DEFILER?
ME? NO! I'M JUST...
...MERELY A STUDENT OF THE FORBIDDEN ART, HUMBLED BEFORE ITS MASTER. YOU MUST BE THE GREATEST NECROMANCER WHO EVER LIVED.
FLATTERY?
AWE, SIR. TO FEEL THE PULSE OF LIFE IN EVERY VESSEL YOU COMMAND, THOUSANDS OF VESSELS...THE POWER YOU MUST FEEL.

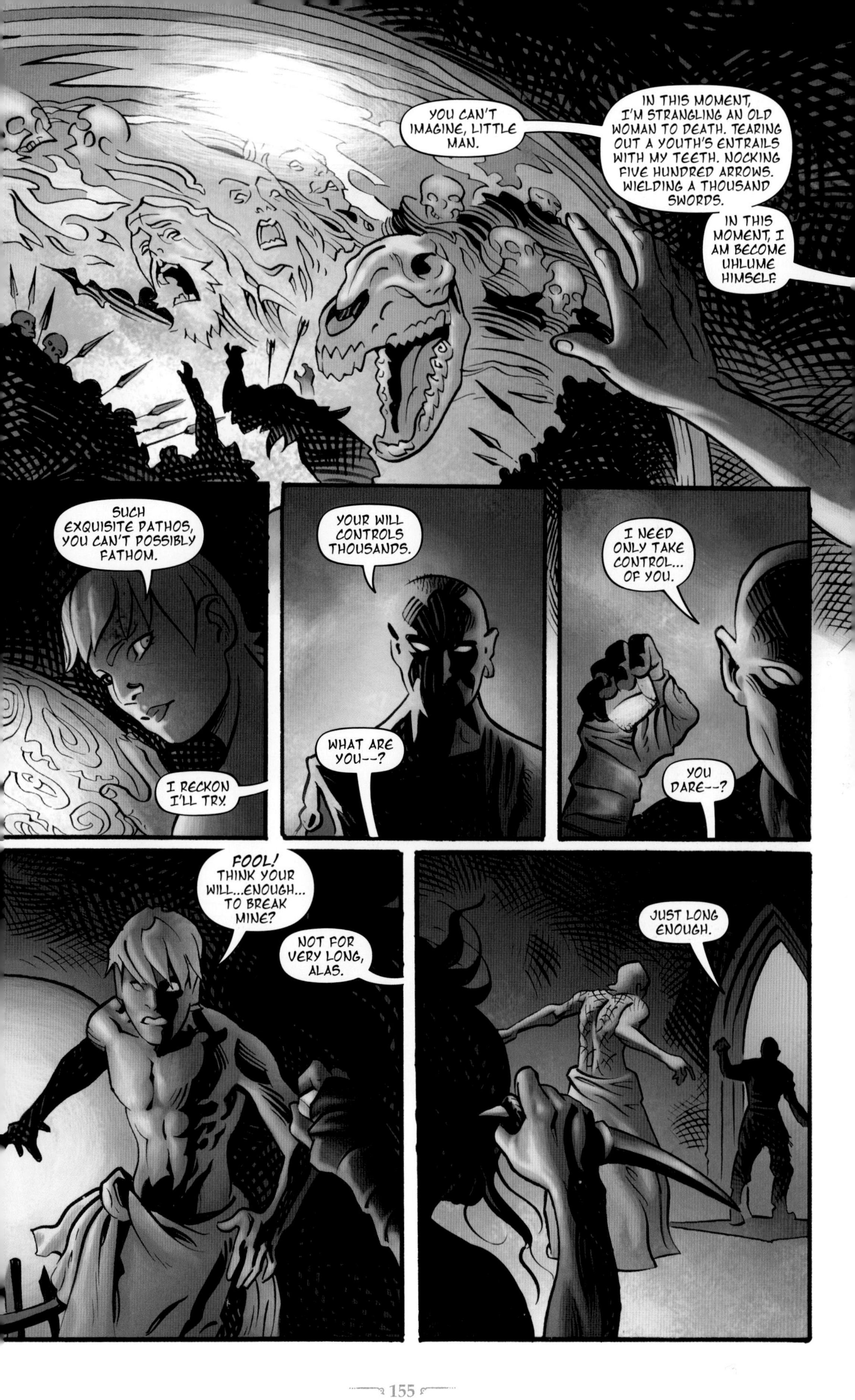
YOU CAN'T IMAGINE, LITTLE MAN.
IN THIS MOMENT, I'M STRANGLING AN OLD WOMAN TO DEATH. TEARING OUT A YOUTH'S ENTRAILS WITH MY TEETH. NOCKING FIVE HUNDRED ARROWS. WIELDING A THOUSAND SWORDS.
IN THIS MOMENT, I AM BECOME UHLUME HIMSELF.
SUCH EXQUISITE PATHOS, YOU CAN'T POSSIBLY FATHOM.
I RECKON I'LL TRY.
YOUR WILL CONTROLS THOUSANDS.
WHAT ARE YOU--?
I NEED ONLY TAKE CONTROL... OF YOU.
YOU DARE--?
FOOL! THINK YOUR WILL...ENOUGH... TO BREAK MINE?
NOT FOR VERY LONG, ALAS.
JUST LONG ENOUGH.

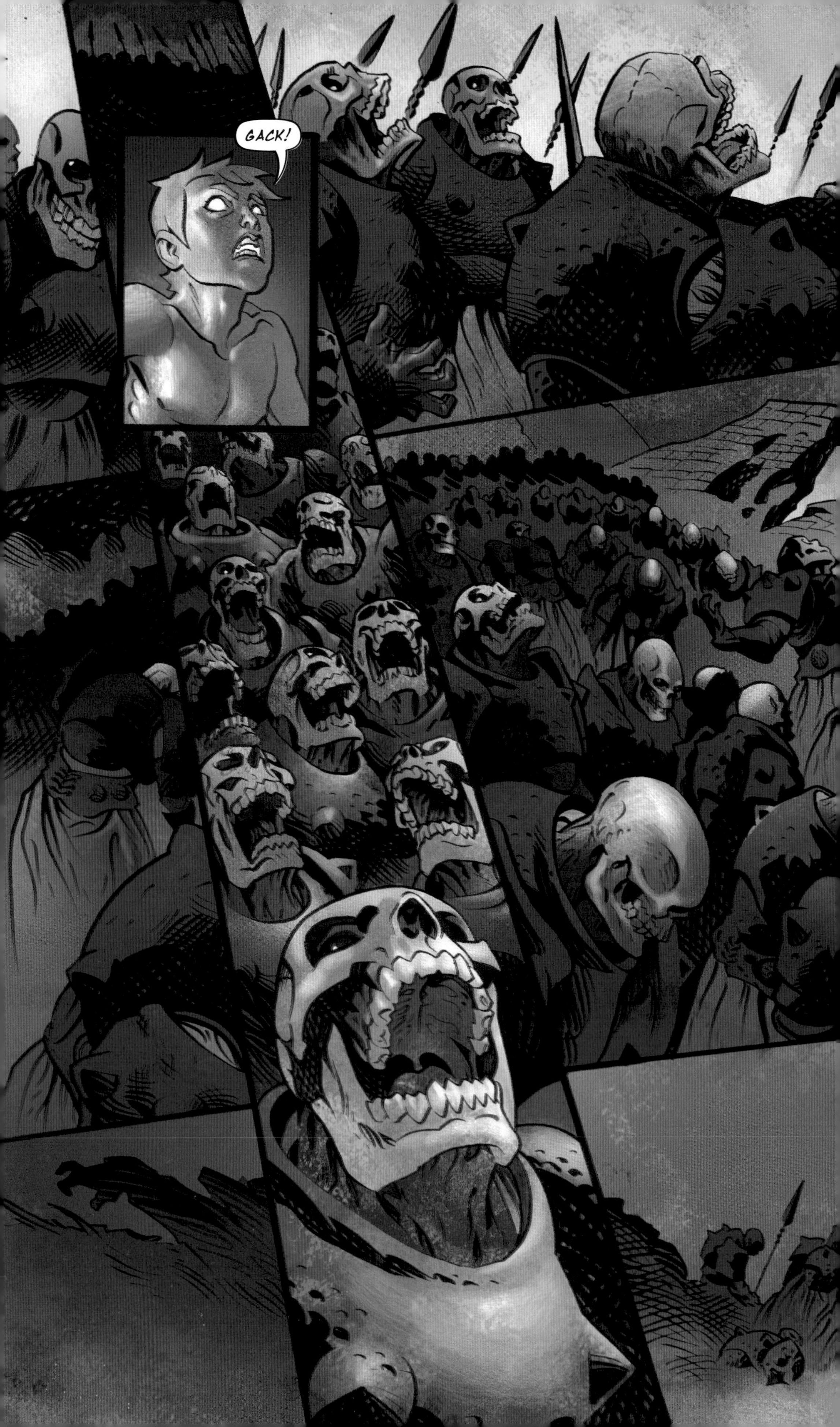
GACK!

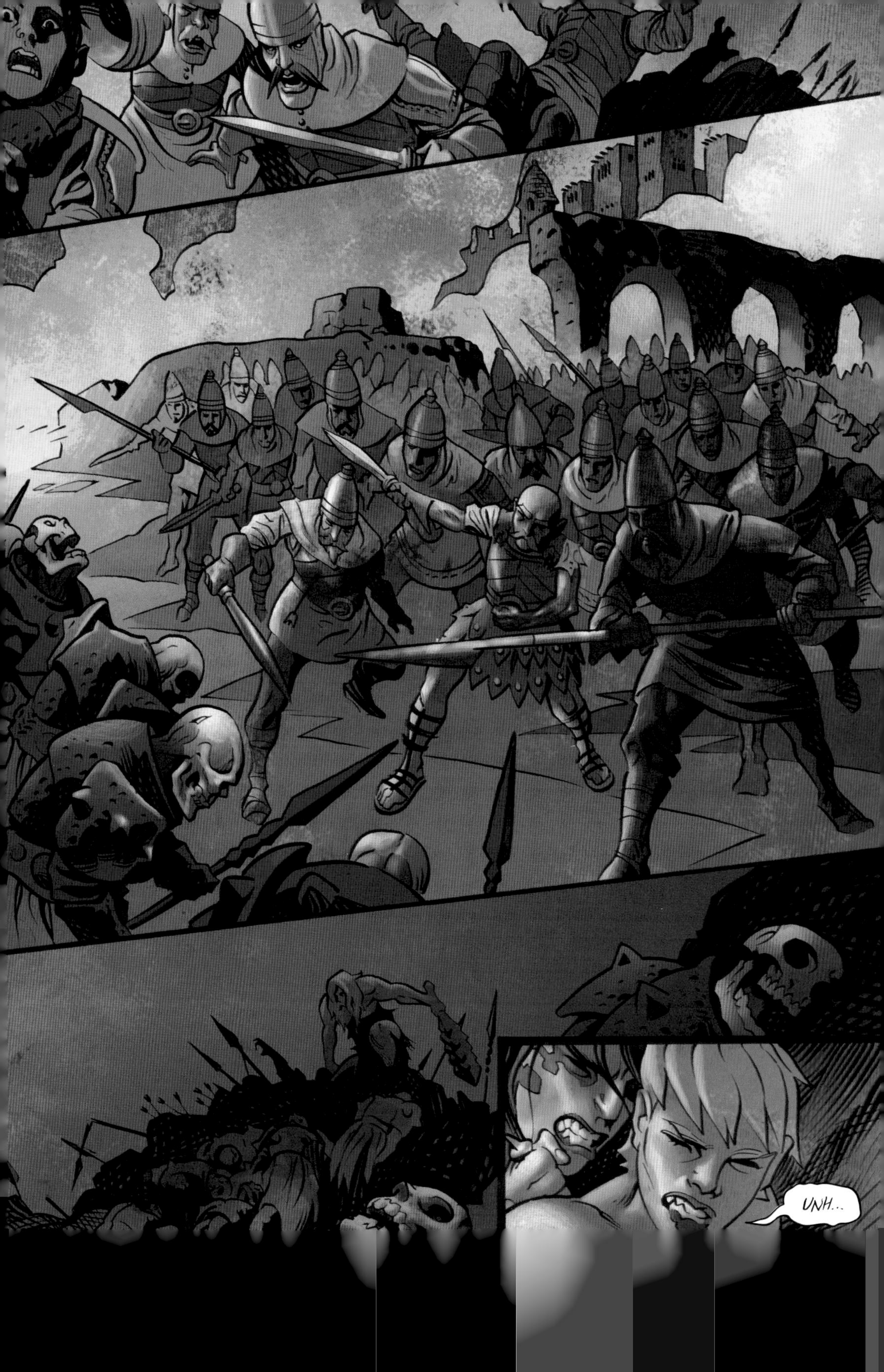
UNH...

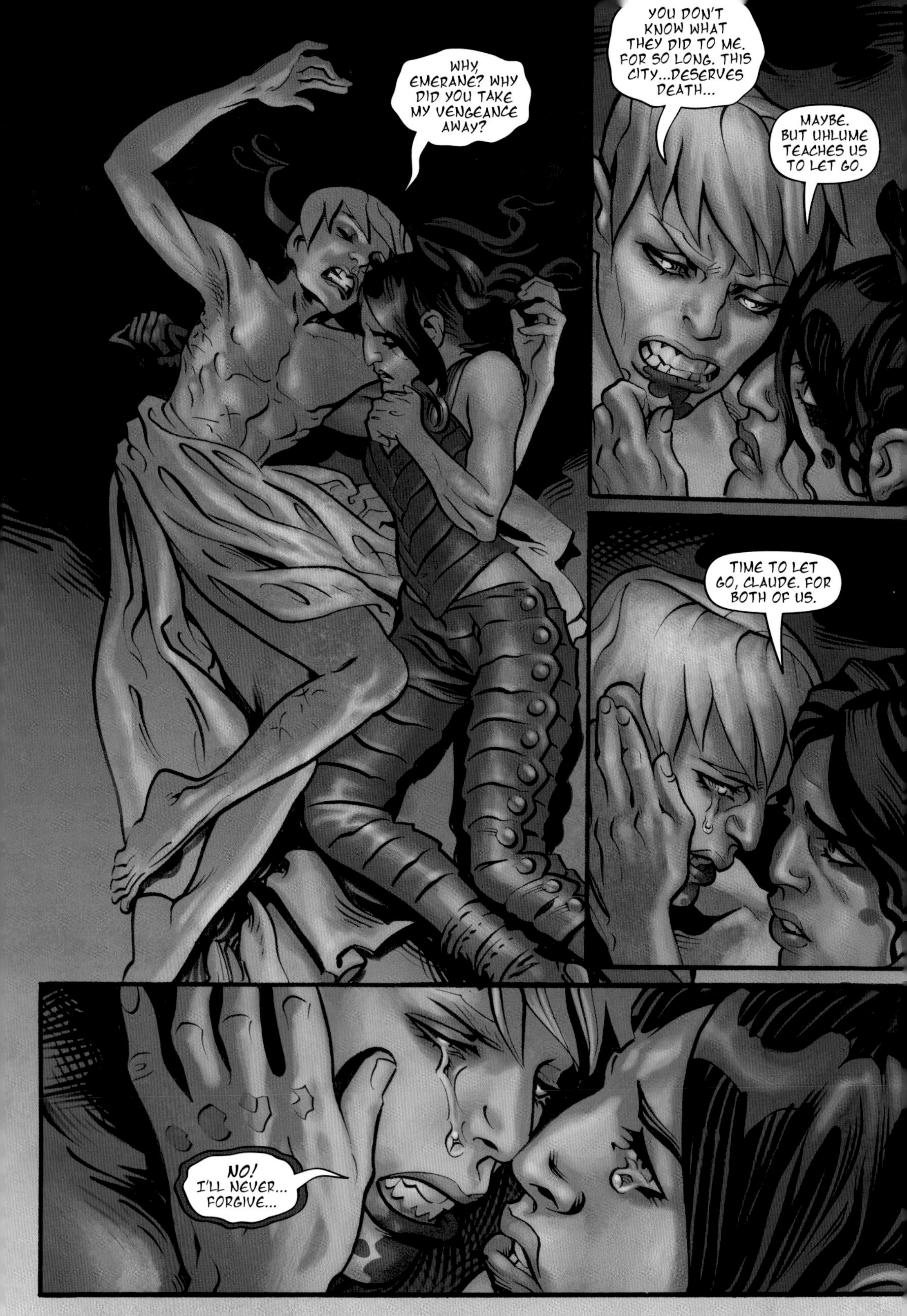
WHY, EMERANE? WHY DID YOU TAKE MY VENGEANCE AWAY?
YOU DON'T KNOW WHAT THEY DID TO ME. FOR SO LONG. THIS CITY...DESERVES DEATH...
MAYBE. BUT UHLUME TEACHES US TO LET GO.
TIME TO LET GO, CLAUDE. FOR BOTH OF US.
NO! I'LL NEVER... FORGIVE...

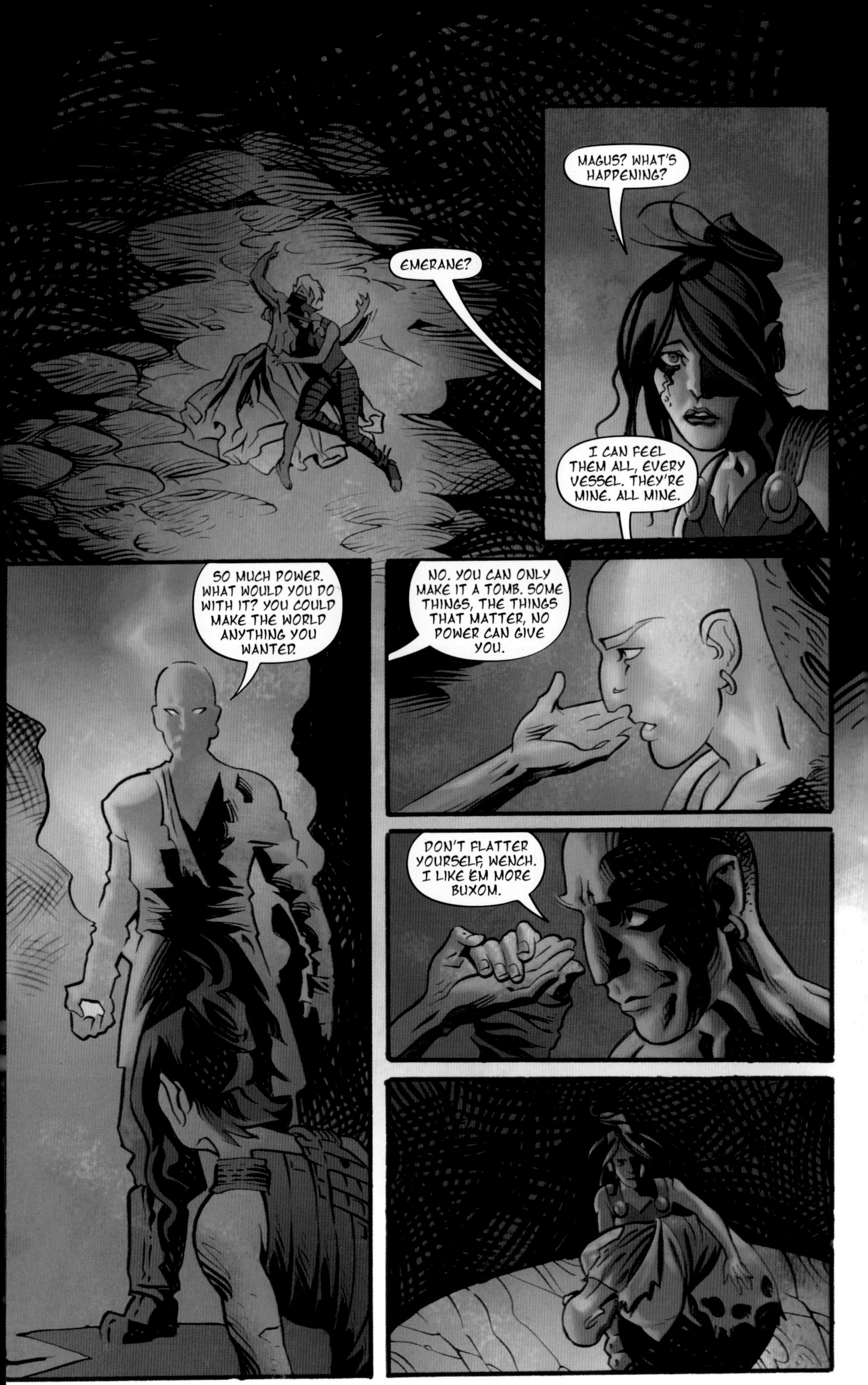
EMERANE?
MAGUS? WHAT'S HAPPENING?
I CAN FEEL THEM ALL, EVERY VESSEL. THEY'RE MINE. ALL MINE.
SO MUCH POWER. WHAT WOULD YOU DO WITH IT? YOU COULD MAKE THE WORLD ANYTHING YOU WANTED.
NO. YOU CAN ONLY MAKE IT A TOMB. SOME THINGS, THE THINGS THAT MATTER, NO POWER CAN GIVE YOU.
DON'T FLATTER YOURSELF, WENCH. I LIKE 'EM MORE BUXOM.

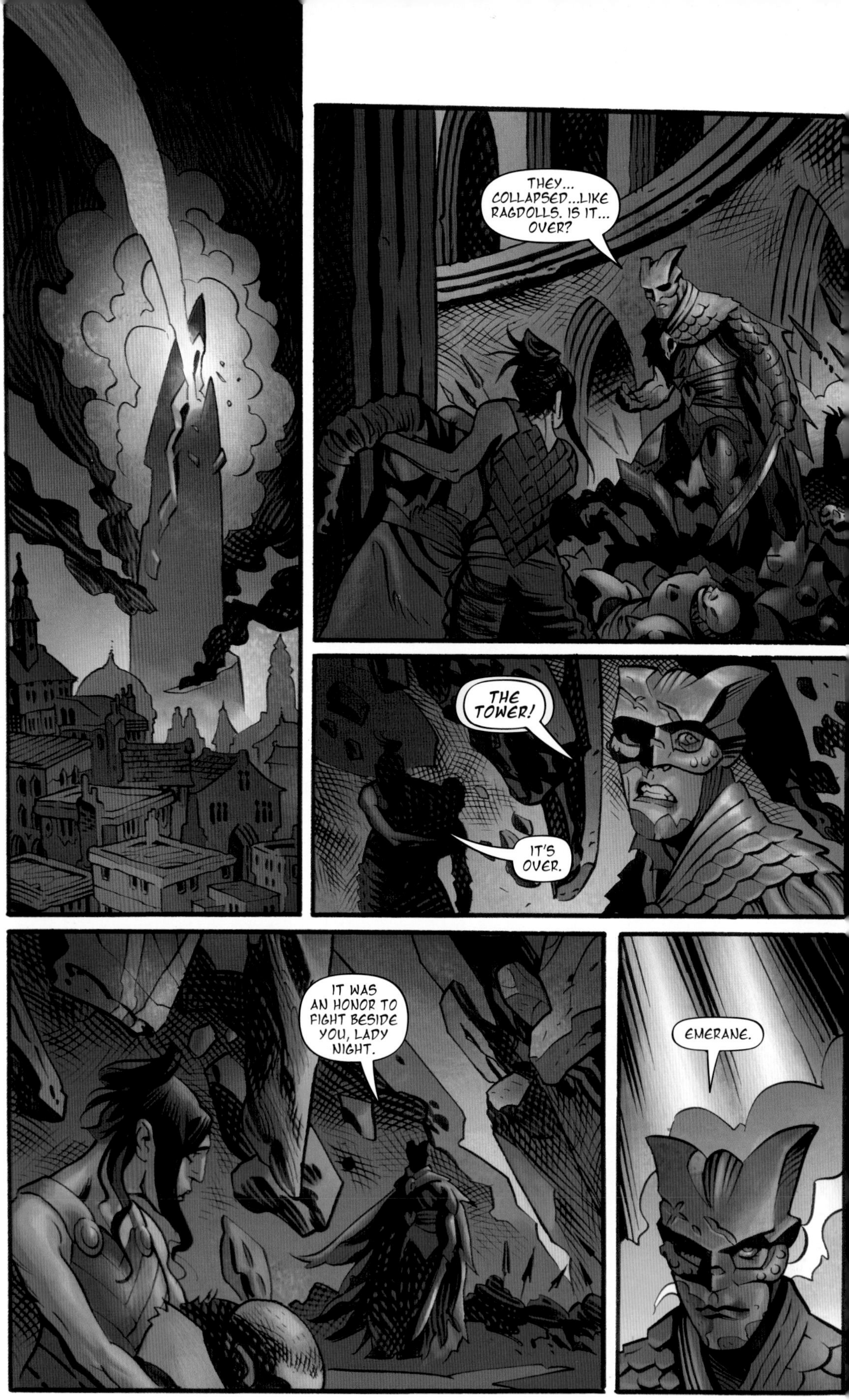

THEY... COLLAPSED...LIKE RAGDOLLS. IS IT... OVER?
THE TOWER!
IT'S OVER.
IT WAS AN HONOR TO FIGHT BESIDE YOU, LADY NIGHT.
EMERANE.

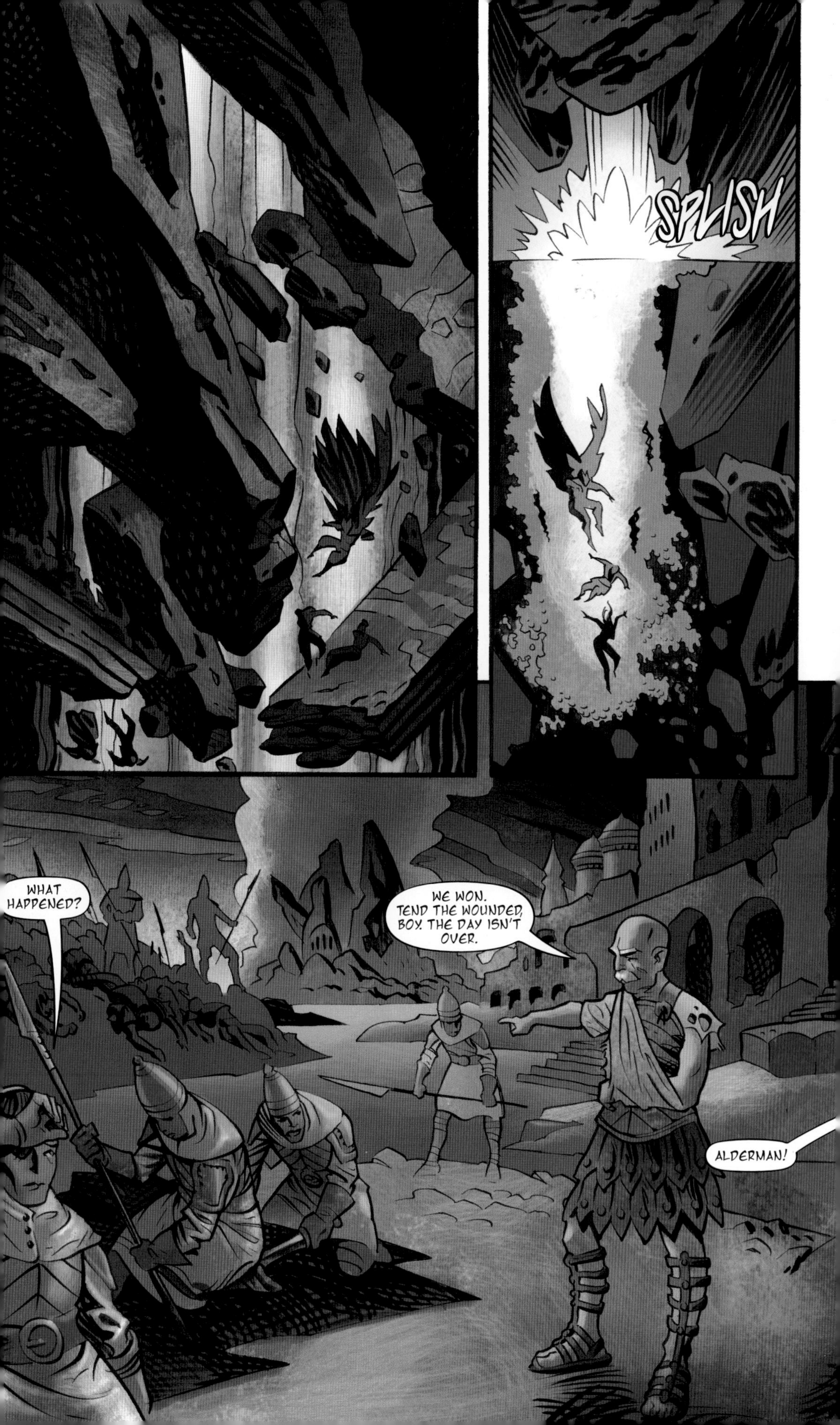
SPLISH
WHAT HAPPENED?
WE WON. TEND THE WOUNDED, BOY. THE DAY ISN'T OVER.
ALDERMAN!

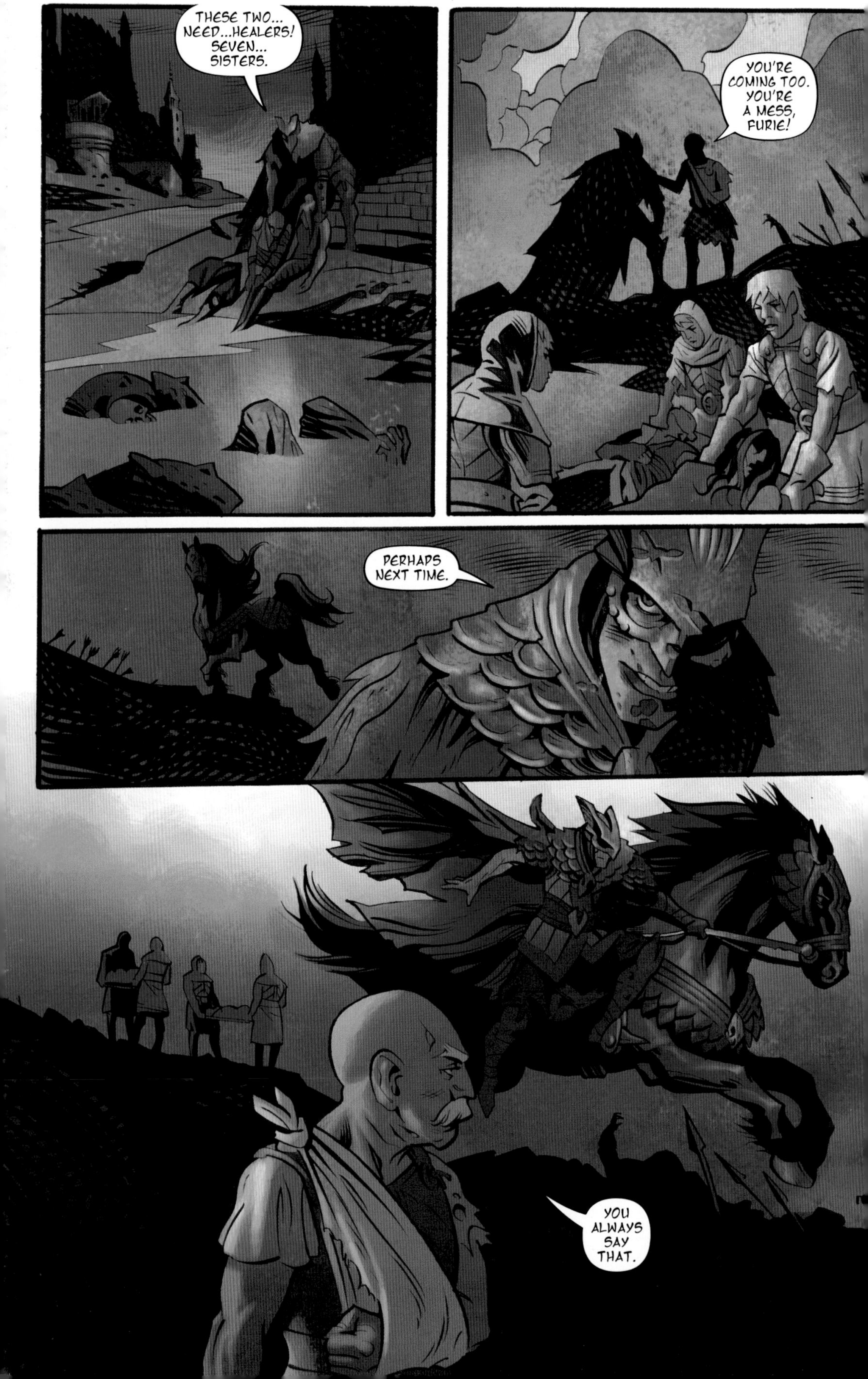
THESE TWO... NEED...HEALERS! SEVEN... SISTERS.
YOU'RE COMING TOO. YOU'RE A MESS, FURIE!
PERHAPS NEXT TIME.
YOU ALWAYS SAY THAT.

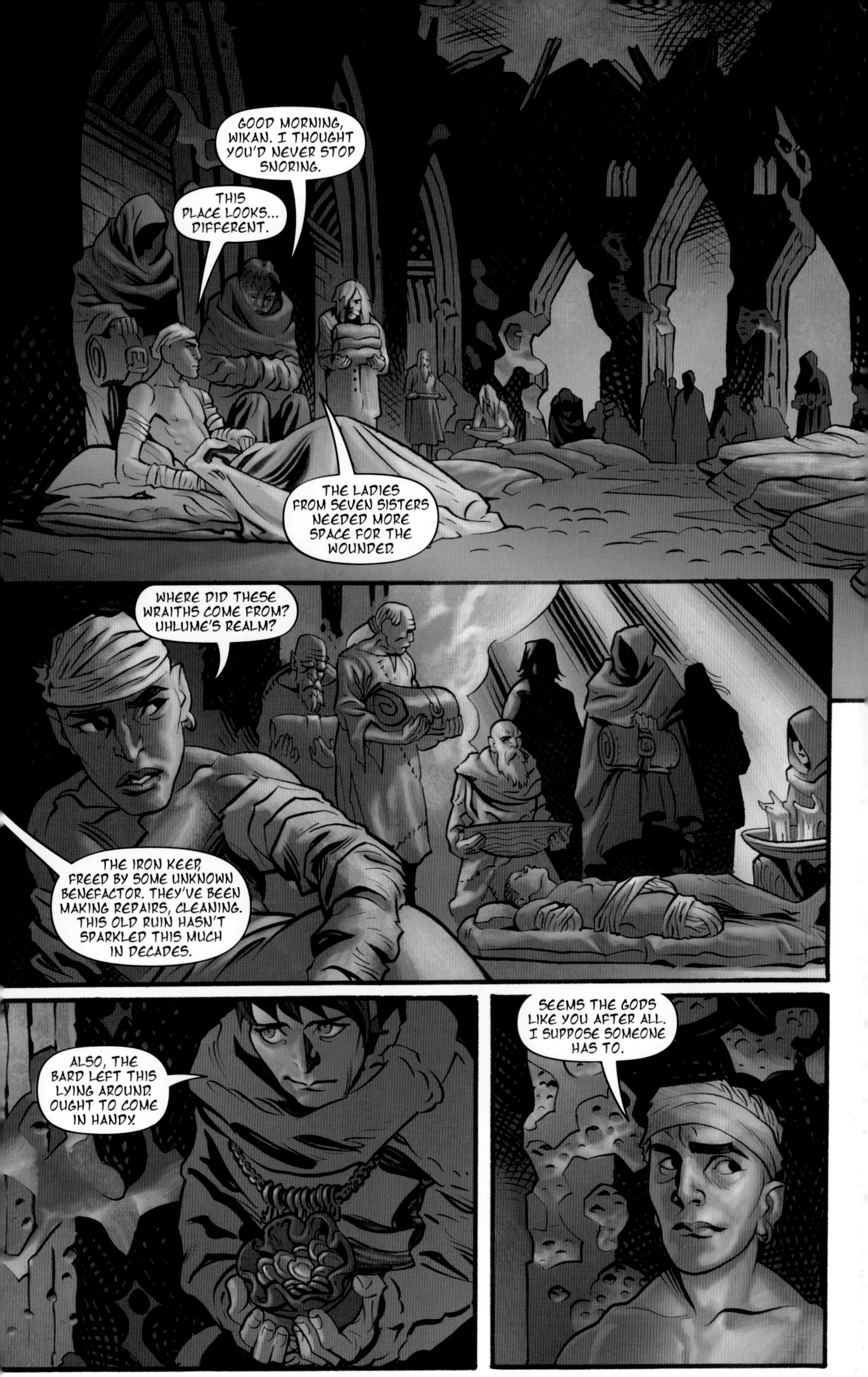
GOOD MORNING, WIKAN. I THOUGHT YOU'D NEVER STOP SNORING.
THIS PLACE LOOKS... DIFFERENT.
THE LADIES FROM SEVEN SISTERS NEEDED MORE SPACE FOR THE WOUNDED.
WHERE DID THESE WRAITHS COME FROM? UHLUME'S REALM?
THE IRON KEEP, FREED BY SOME UNKNOWN BENEFACTOR. THEY'VE BEEN MAKING REPAIRS, CLEANING. THIS OLD RUIN HASN'T SPARKLED THIS MUCH IN DECADES.
ALSO, THE BARD LEFT THIS LYING AROUND. OUGHT TO COME IN HANDY.
SEEMS THE GODS LIKE YOU AFTER ALL. I SUPPOSE SOMEONE HAS TO.

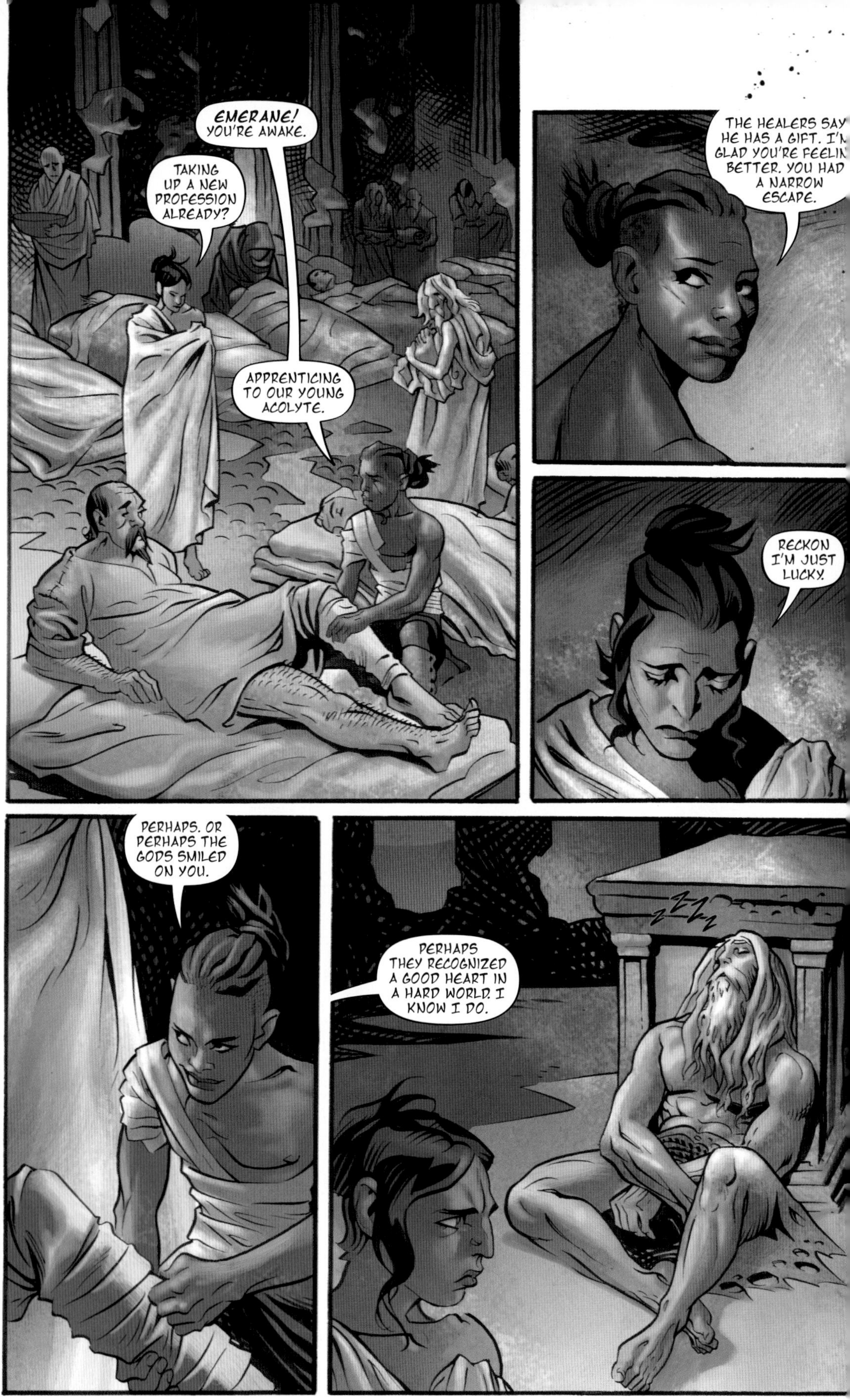
EMERANE! YOU'RE AWAKE.
TAKING UP A NEW PROFESSION ALREADY?
APPRENTICING TO OUR YOUNG ACOLYTE.
THE HEALERS SAY HE HAS A GIFT. I'M GLAD YOU'RE FEELIN BETTER. YOU HAD A NARROW ESCAPE.
RECKON I'M JUST LUCKY.
PERHAPS. OR PERHAPS THE GODS SMILED ON YOU.
ZZZ
PERHAPS THEY RECOGNIZED A GOOD HEART IN A HARD WORLD. I KNOW I DO.

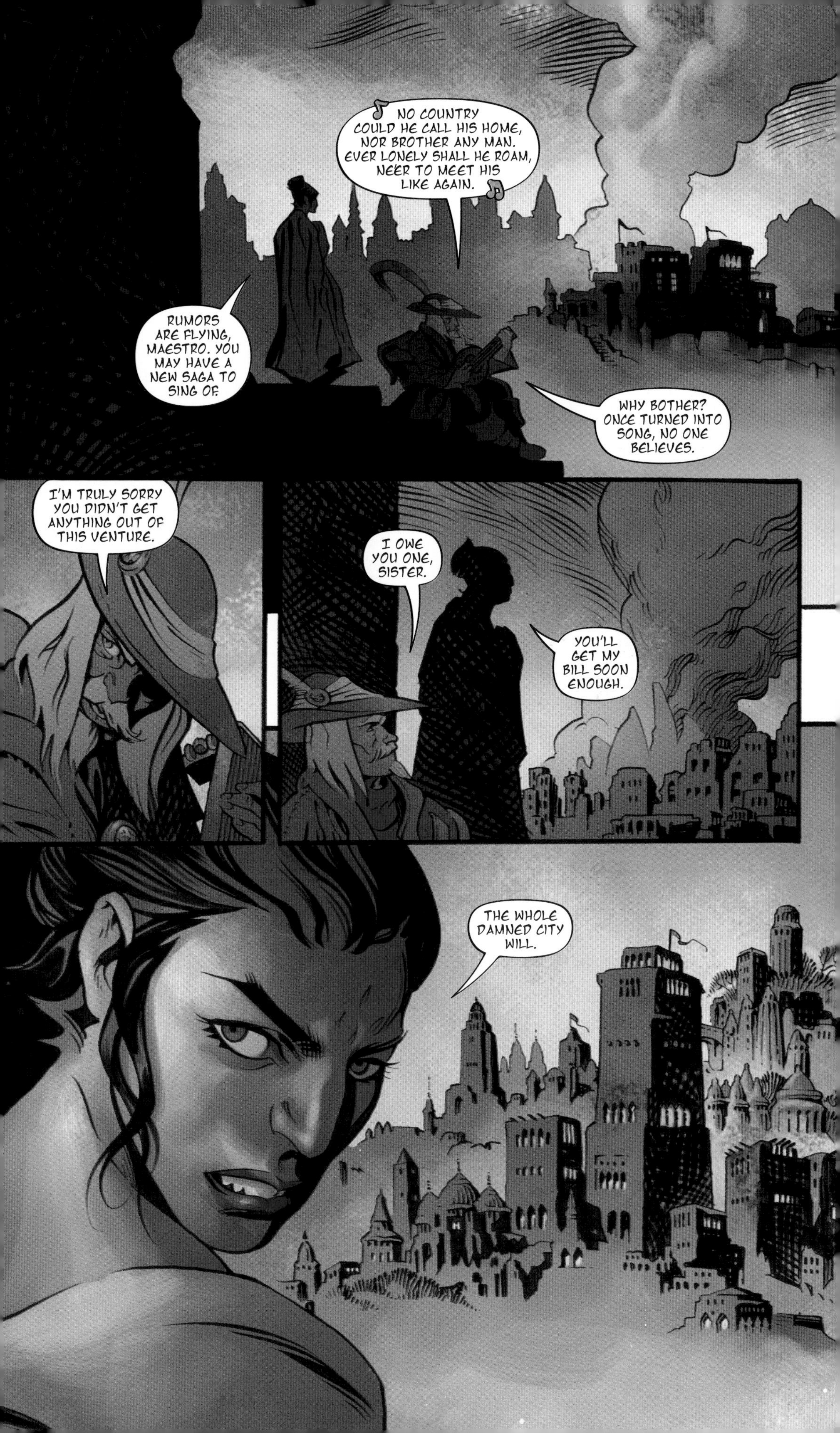
NO COUNTRY COULD HE CALL HIS HOME, NOR BROTHER ANY MAN. EVER LONELY SHALL HE ROAM, NE'ER TO MEET HIS LIKE AGAIN.
RUMORS ARE FLYING, MAESTRO. YOU MAY HAVE A NEW SAGA TO SING OF.
WHY BOTHER? ONCE TURNED INTO SONG, NO ONE BELIEVES.
I'M TRULY SORRY YOU DIDN'T GET ANYTHING OUT OF THIS VENTURE.
I OWE YOU ONE, SISTER.
YOU'LL GET MY BILL SOON ENOUGH.
THE WHOLE DAMNED CITY WILL.

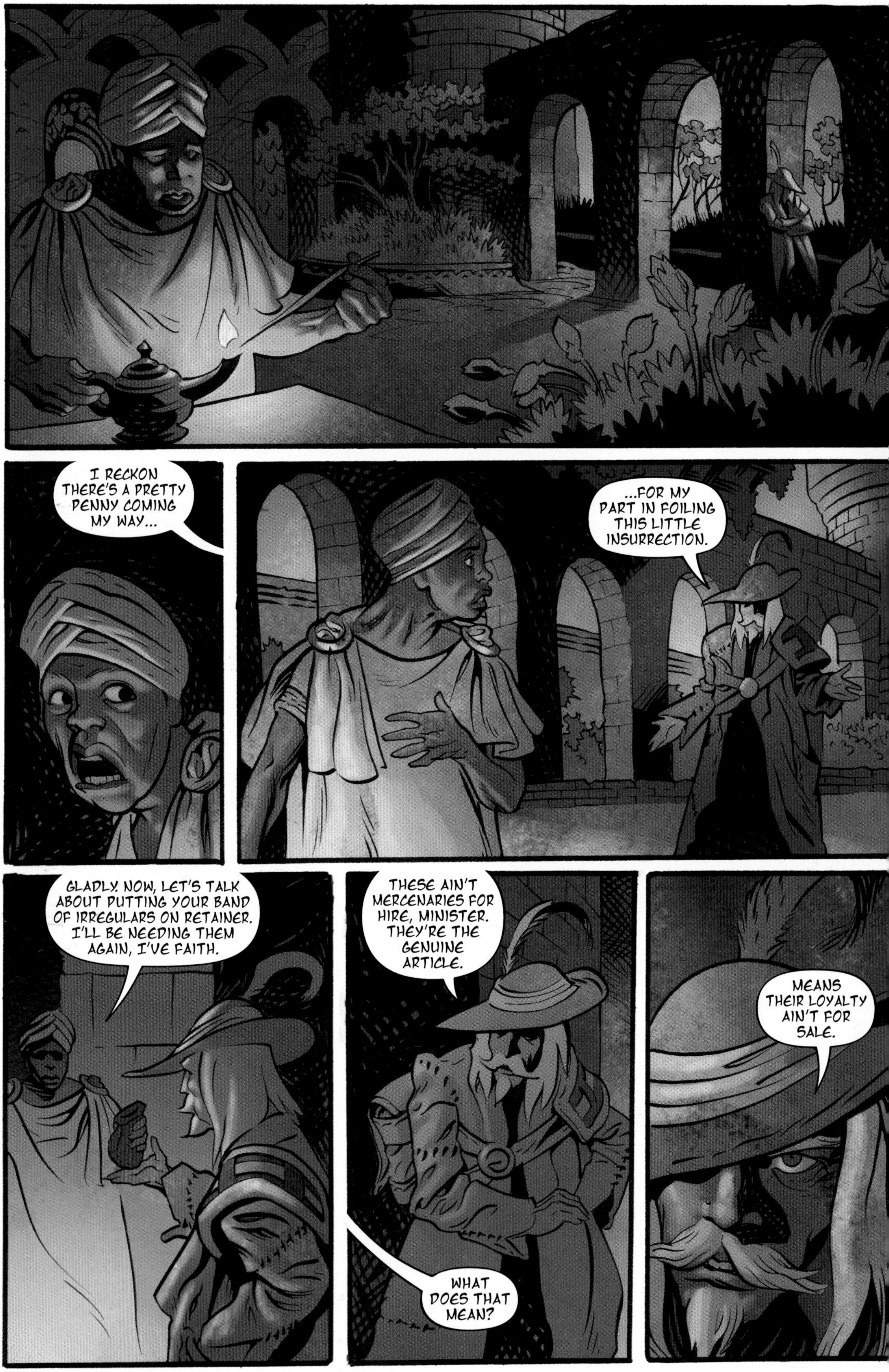
I RECKON THERE'S A PRETTY PENNY COMING MY WAY...
...FOR MY PART IN FOILING THIS LITTLE INSURRECTION.
GLADLY. NOW, LET'S TALK ABOUT PUTTING YOUR BAND OF IRREGULARS ON RETAINER. I'LL BE NEEDING THEM AGAIN, I'VE FAITH.
THESE AIN'T MERCENARIES FOR HIRE, MINISTER. THEY'RE THE GENUINE ARTICLE.
WHAT DOES THAT MEAN?
MEANS THEIR LOYALTY AIN'T FOR SALE.

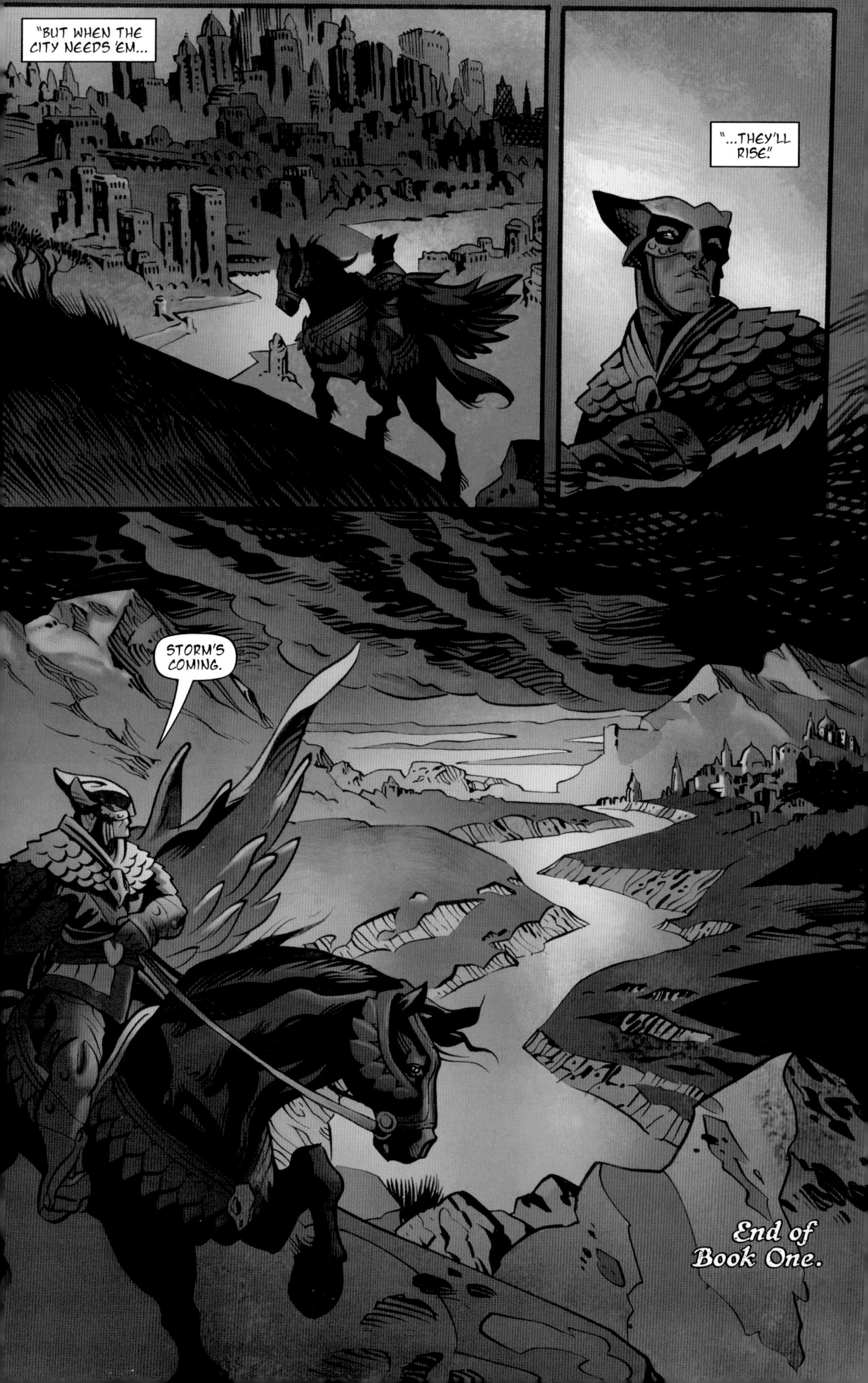
"BUT WHEN THE CITY NEEDS 'EM...
"...THEY'LL RISE."
STORM'S COMING.
End of Book One.

TED NAIFEH

Ted Naifeh has been creating successful independent comics since the late 90s. He co-created *Gloomcookie*, the goth romance comic, with author Serena Valentino, and soon after began writing and drawing *Courtney Crumrin and the Night Things*, a spooky children's fantasy series about a grumpy little girl and her adventures with her warlock uncle.

Nominated for an Eisner Award for best limited series, *Courtney Crumrin*'s success paved the way for *Polly and the Pirates*, this time about a prim and proper girl kidnapped by pirates who believe her to be the daughter of their long-lost queen. *Courtney Crumrin* now has six volumes, plus a spin-off book, and *Polly and the Pirates* has two.

Ted also co-created *How Loathsome* with Tristan Crane, and illustrated two volumes of *Death Junior* with screenwriter Gary Whitta. More recently, he illustrated *The Good Neighbors*, a three-volume graphic novel series written by *New York Times* best-selling author Holly Black, published by Scholastic.

Recently, Ted has contributed work to many major comics companies, including *Batman* comics for DC, and the horror anthology *Creepy* for Dark Horse. His most recent work for Oni Press was *Princess Ugg*, of which there are two volumes.